Rhem

Hearing a Word from the Lord through selected readings from the

Still Small Voice Messages given to Clare duBois

FROM 2014 TO 2016

Published by
Heartdwellers.org
August, 2016

Compiled and Edited by Carol Jennings

Cover Illustration: Elizabeth Wang, T-01088-OL,
'Even in the darkness of our sufferings Jesus is close to us', copyright © Radiant Light 2016
www.radiantlight.org.uk

Copyright © 2016 Clare du Bois
ISBN-10: 0-9980597-0-6
ISBN-13: 978-0-9980597-0-9

Additional Resources
Still Small Voice YouTube Channel
https://www.youtube.com/user/claredubois

SSV Website
Heartdwellers.org

The website contains links to all Teaching Videos, as well as written PDF's of all messages. All PDF's have been compiled by month into a single unit document. Additionally available is a Topical Index and Synopsis Index available for each month. All for free download.

Still Small Voice Triage for Truth Seekers
http://www.stillsmallvoicetriage.org

Much opposition has been launched against these teachings saying that an intimate relationship with God is not possible. But through this Blog we are going to prove, Scripturally, that God has indeed mandated this profound relationship in the last days we live in.

Still Small Voice Search Engine
http://search.stillsmallvoicetriage.org

An essential tool for searching the over 600's messages for specific topics of instruction and explanation.

Heart Dwelling With Jesus Blog
https://heartdwellingwithjesus.wordpress.com

A place to read and post testimonies of breakthroughs in hearing and seeing Jesus.

Other Books/Resources from Still Small Voice
~Chronicles of the Bride
~Love Letters to My Bride vol. 1-3
~The Rapture WAS Real?!
~Tethered (for the left behind)
~The Tethered Thumb Drive –

[a 13.5G drive containing all of the Art, Teachings, Videos, Books and resources that Still Small Voice has produced/accumulated up until Jan. of 2016]

Father Has Shown Us Mercy

Many of the following portions of the messages speak of the very imminent coming of the Lord in the Rapture. This was to be so…until June of 2016. The Lord had been asking us to pray, pray, pray for Mercy for months. We had been praying – Father God had responded by showing Mercy and averting the beginning of WWIII.

Finally, in a series of messages starting in July of 2016 the Lord gave us the wonderful news: our prayers, joined with the prayers of Christians the world over – had moved Father's heart to setting a more distant time for the Rapture:

I was aware that something in the world concerning WWIII - something had shifted. Something had changed. Lord, do you have something to say here?

He began, "The situation is quite convoluted - many, many dynamics and I don't want you involved in-depth, Clare. Please, don't try to figure it out. One thing I do want you to know: I am STILL IN CHARGE What man plans for his evil agenda, I turn to My good agenda. This you can rest in.

"Your prayers have resulted in Satan's plans not moving forward."

And I was very curious at that point, and I said, 'But does that affect the Rapture?'

And Jesus answered me, "It certainly does. You might as well be honest, Clare. That is your trademark, you know.

"My People, you have prayed. The world is waking up and beginning to respond. Those who had power over the world and its peoples because they were ignorant - those people are waking up and opting out. Not only that, they are siding with the opposition - which in many cases is being led by Christians.

"There is still Judgment to come, but just as in Nineveh when men repented, there is a massive grassroots movement of repentance *going* on. It isn't the kind of repentance that happens when a man is convicted of his personal sins. It is more a repentance linked to social sins, and they are asking themselves, 'What can I do to change this?'

"Eventually they are going to come to Me. Justice will come to the surface and it will be seen that evil men have stolen freedoms; evil men have decimated millions - genocides. Evil men must be stopped. There will no longer be the knee-jerk reaction. That is, cooperation with the Elite when they push buttons and set up situations to provoke anarchy.

"Rather, men will reason among themselves and see they are being played. They will choose not to cooperate even against their survival instincts. You see, I have released a Grace to mankind on Earth - the grace of seeing beyond the surface; transparency, seeing what is really intended by those in ruling positions. Not only will the people see, but they will make a conscious choice not to cooperate.

"This is going to impact the entire world, Clare.

"...Do not persecute the prophets among you who have been faithful to warn you. You owe them your lives and the lives of your unsaved loved ones who still have a chance. Do not fall in with the unbelievers and ridicule the Rapture, or WW3 or Revelation - or anything like that. Do not be a naysayer.

"Rather, declare that OUR GOD REIGNS!! And that the prayers of the little ones, the simple ones, the God-loving people of the Earth have broken the flask of their hearts and poured out the ointment of petition on behalf of the inhabitants of the whole Earth. And the

Father, who is Pure Mercy Himself, has relented and chosen to give you all a window of opportunity, another chance for conversions and to get it right."

(from the message Judgment, War and Rapture Delayed)

Later, by August 6th, more clarification was released to us about the delay: *I had begun worship earlier in the evening and He called me to write down a personal message and I started to get sleepy by the end of it...that time of the day, and after dinner. So, He asked me to get a nap.*

When I went to lay down, I saw Him to my right and He said, "Three years."

Repeating Himself two times. I determined to discern that word when I woke up.

As I came in and sat down to be with Him, He began speaking to me, "I am with you and I have been speaking to you. Thank you for trusting Me and listening."

So, we have three years?

"That's correct, provided prayer and repentance and fast offerings continue. I really want to see conversion. Conversion of hearts and attitudes. And this is what's happening."

Are you setting a date for the Rapture, Lord?

"No. I am telling you that if prayer and sacrifice with repentance continue, I will hold off the worst of World War 3, and you will have time to create and do what is on your heart for the Kingdom. I am opening a window no one can shut. But it continues to be dependent on the faithfulness of My People, not just in America, but around the world.

"Let me explain it to you this way. There are those among you who have been biding their time for the Rapture and not serving Me with their whole hearts. I am giving them another chance. They have three years to show their love for Me with deeds… not just words.

"The others among you have already been making plans and I am blessing them and opening doors that have never been opened to them before. This message will give them a measure of peace, that what they've started, they do indeed have time to finish. These are things that I want to do with them, for the Kingdom.

"At the end of three years, we will take another look and see what the climate is. How much repentance has taken place, how many laws have been rescinded - abortion, for example - and how people have turned their hearts back to Me.

"Nevertheless, this IS conditional on continuing prayer. But I will say, there are substantial changes in hearts and attitudes around the world."

(from the message **Jesus Give Us 3 More Years, Conditionally***)*

We continue to pray, fast and give offering for God's Mercy and await the wonders He will unfold in these intervening years. It is our prayer that this book will help to draw you close to His heart and help you hear from Him clearly, as we wait together for Him!

C. Jennings November 10, 2016

Table of Contents

Topics

Getting A Word From the Lord

We'd like to begin this book with a teaching on getting your own word from the Lord. And you know, our channel is not just about intimacy; it's also about learning to hear from God on your own. Just about every other e-mail or private message that comes to us from our different sites is requesting a word from the Lord. But, He has asked us to keep our focus on teaching you to get your own words.

Nothing mysterious about it, **Seek and ye shall find, ask and it shall be given to you. Matt. 7:7** And the Lord is really up for this, guys. He's got His Grace right there ready to give it to you, if only you'll exercise your faith muscle and use it.

When I first became a Christian, the church I was attending was doing a Bible study by Evelyn Christenson, on a book called Lord, Change Me. It was then that I learned to listen to the "message within a message". In this very simple book, you are taught to read a section of Scripture or passage from a holy or anointed book, and listen for the Lord's voice in a personal way, guiding you in everyday circumstance. That is called a Rhema.

There are different levels of training, and as you mature, the Lord will take you into deeper waters with this practice. But for now, let's keep it simple and start with the basics.

What IS a Rhema?

There are two Greek words that describe Scripture which are translated "word" in the New Testament. The first, logos, refers to the inspired Word of God and to Jesus, Who is the living Logos.

In the beginning was the Word [logos], and the Word [logos] was with God, and the Word [logos] was God. John 1:1

For the word [logos] of God is quick, and powerful. Hebrews 4:12

The second Greek word that describes Scripture is "rhema," which refers to a word that is spoken and means "an utterance." A rhema is a verse or portion of Scripture that Holy Spirit brings to our attention to address a need for wisdom and for direction. So, when we are reading our Bible, all of a sudden something on the page catches our attention and is quickened by Holy Spirit for a current life situation. If we are listening very carefully, we hear the Lord's wisdom for us. It's kind of like… reading between the lines. And that wisdom is right for the moment. It just takes a little practice to get the hang of it.

Man shall not live by bread alone, but by every word [rhema] that proceeds out of the mouth of God. (Matthew 4:4).

Jesus said, "The words [rhema] that I speak unto you, they are spirit, and they are life" (John 6:63).

When God gives a rhema for us to act upon, He often confirms it by a second and third one, that **"…in the mouth of two or three witnesses shall every word [rhema] be established" II Corinthians 13:1**

"So, then faith cometh by hearing, and hearing by the word [rhema] of God" Romans 10:17

When the angel told Mary that she would have a child: "Mary said, Behold the handmaid of the Lord; be it unto me according to your word [rhema]" Luke 1:38

Jesus told Peter he would deny Him. **"Peter remembered the word [rhema] of Jesus, which said unto him, 'Before the cock crows, you will deny me three times'" Matthew 26:75**

What is it for?

This is how we get our confirmations from the Lord. Our opinions about things don't matter; it's God's opinion that matters. And when we want an "outside of ourselves" confirmation, we pray and open the Bible and begin to read. But rather than using the entire Bible, we often use a little book called The Bible Promise Book by Barbour Publishers. We have found that the Lord will also use books that He has placed His anointing on in the same way. Others that are often used in this way are such books as writings by Padre Pio or He and I, written by Gabrielle Bossis.

This book, Rhema, has been patterned after the Bible Promises book – but with many additions to personalize it to the teachings and messages given on the Still Small Voice YouTube channel and Heartdwellers.org website. We have compiled it to be used as another source for "getting" a rhema from Him, as all the words and passages contained in it are taken directly from His words to Clare or His teachings through her.

How do I "get" a Rhema?

Once we have opened the book and begin to read, some of the lines will begin to really resonate, deeply in our spirits. At that point, we stop and linger, soaking in the anointed words and allowing them to minister to us. When we're reading, the Lord anoints certain things.

And when you read it slowly, you'll feel it. You'll feel the anointing on those words, just for you in that situation.

So, the way we receive guidance from the Lord is to simply pray for guidance.

If any of you lacks wisdom, let him ask of God, who gives to all liberally and without reproach, and it will be given to him. But let him ask in faith not doubting. James 1:5-6

My sheep hear My voice, and I know them, and they follow Me. John 10:27

And you can really hear the Lord's voice between the lines. It takes a little practice, but it really does work. That Voice has a resonance in our hearts that no other voice can duplicate.

We approach this like an innocent little child:

Truly I tell you, unless you change and become like little children, you will never enter the Kingdom of Heaven. Matt 18:2-4

We really do. We come to the Lord as little children. That's the safest way to approach Him. Not only is there the greatest wisdom in doing that, because it's His wisdom - but the greatest protection, because the Lord protects the little children. It's the "big" people who think they know it all and they can protect themselves who are really in trouble. If you come to Him innocent like a little child, without pride, in humility seeking wisdom, He's going to give it to you.

Very simply, we earnestly pray for an answer and open the Bible, the Bible Promises or other anointed book and start reading. As we read, one of the Scriptures or passages written there will come forth and stand out. And you know, I've seen it where you have to read two or three times before ONE particular portion really caught my attention.

That's Holy Spirit making that "word" come alive in our hearts and minds, or a rhema - a present-time utterance of Holy Spirit directing us according to our needs. We prefer to get three rhemas in a row in order to clarify and establish the Lord's train of thought. So, we take a little more time with it.

A bit of wise caution...

We also have learned that we need to pray over these books before we open them to receive a word from Holy Spirit. The enemy (and don't ask me how, 'cause I don't know how he does it) can also manipulate the pages to bring up a reading counter to what God has for us.

So we simply say, "In the Name of Jesus, I bind all Lying spirits off this book." Believe it or not, we have many times caught the enemy infiltrating our readings! So now, for safety's sake, we always pray that prayer along with, "Holy Spirit, please guide me through this book."

But... isn't this Fortune Telling or Divination??

Some would accuse us of fortune telling, but I'm afraid they just aren't familiar with drawing lots, as it is used by the prophets of old, as well as the Apostles, who drew lots to choose the replacement for Judas in the first chapter of the book of Acts. In that particular prayer, Peter said, **"Lord, you know everyone's heart. Show us which of these two you have chosen to take over this apostolic ministry".... then they cast lots, and the lot fell to Matthias; so he was added to the eleven apostles. Acts 1:24.**

So, when you cast lots, the choosing of that "lot" is totally done by Holy Spirit. And when you open these anointed books – again, they are opened by Holy Spirit. Now, when we use them, we are asking the Lord (who knows everyone's heart) to reveal what is necessary for us to make the right decisions.

Trust in the LORD with all your heart And do not lean on your own understanding. In all your ways acknowledge Him, And He will make your paths straight. Proverbs 3:5

We have walked some VERY crooked paths in our own wisdom, and we've learned that our own wisdom is absolutely a detriment. Always seek the Lord's wisdom before you do anything!

It is SO much easier to do it right the first time, than to plunge headlong into our own wisdom and make a choice not pleasing to God - and in the end, costing everyone a great deal. I would much sooner act like a five-year-old child, throwing myself on the mercy and wisdom of God than to receive a precise report prepared by a human - who at best has limited knowledge.

In the past, coming to God seeking wisdom was called an 'oracle' in the Old Testament. Bible scholars call oracles 'Communications from God.' The term refers both to divine responses to a question asked of God and to pronouncements made by God without His being asked. In one sense, oracles were prophecies since they often referred to the future; but oracles sometimes dealt with decisions to be made in the present. In the Bible, communication was from Yahweh, the God of Israel.

However, in times of idol worship, Israelites sought another word from false gods (Hosea 4:12). Many of Israel's neighbors sought oracles from their gods. THIS you could call fortune telling.

Why was an "oracle" given?

Why were oracles given? To help God's people make the right choices. There were "decision oracles" and "pronouncement oracles." Decision oracles came when people asked God a question or sought His counsel. For example, David needed to know the right time to attack the

Philistines - so he asked God. The answers he received were oracles (2 Samuel 5:19, 2 Samuel 5:23-24).

Saul, the first king of Israel, was chosen through an oracle (1 Samuel 10:20-24). In that case, the communication from God was through the casting of lots. The falling of the lots was considered an oracle from God. So, this is a well-established practice from the holy prophets and patriarchs in Scriptures. This is not some "new age" or fortune telling thing, not at all. This is serious business; this is seeking an oracle from God.

Does God HAVE to answer my question?

When we come to the Lord prayerfully to be instructed through His Word, we must remember that He is God and not a slot machine. He may choose to bring up something totally different than what you asked Him. There may be things in your life that He has been waiting to address for a long time and when you ask about one thing... you may very well get an answer drawing your attention to another thing. I can't tell you how many times that's happened to me! Especially when He's drawing my attention to a fault or a shortcoming. It's like, I want to ask Him something, and He draws my attention to my fault.

And I'll say, "Yes, Lord – I know, I know I have that fault...but can You just tell me what I need to know?" And again He'll draw my attention to the fault.

It's as though He's saying, "I'm not going to tell you what you need to know, until you really, seriously deal with what I'm talking to you about!"

As you can see, it can get kinda conversational, too, with Him!

So, how do I figure out what He's telling me?

There is a learning curve in hearing the Lord's voice through these readings/portions of Scripture. We have to slow down our thoughts and restfully read them. At first, you might say, "What in the world does that have to do with my question?" Like when you get an answer, asking the Lord for wisdom and you open the Bible Promises and it's on a totally different topic – and you're wondering, 'What did this have to do with what I asked?'

Well, I don't know. That's for YOU to meditate on until Holy Spirit illuminates it for you. There are no shortcuts. We all have to suffer through the toddler stage. It is painful – but SO worthwhile!

For instance, if I get seriously ill with something unusual, and it hasn't yielded to anointed prayer, I may ask the Lord, "Why am I feeling so badly? Did I do something wrong? Was Your protection lifted because I strayed out of the corral?" If He gives me the chapter on 'Salvation' or on 'Parent's Duties' or 'Eternal Life' from the Bible Promises and I read those Scriptures, it is safe to assume that, right in this hour, someone's salvation is hanging in the balance and my fast offering is going to tilt the scales. In which case, I will be happy and receive it like Simon 's cross.

However, if He gives me readings under the 'Guilt' chapter, or 'The World' - I'll know immediately the devils have been allowed to sift me for an indiscretion.

As I said, it takes time to interpret what the readings mean. Not everything comes easily. In fact, there are many times when we just don't know what to think and we have to put it on the shelf and pray for better discernment. This is a learning process and Holy Spirit is your teacher. Each day you will learn more and more and more about how God thinks from moment to moment, and in different situations, because you are constantly going to Him for advice.

There are some people who are too 'grown up' for this kind of discernment -they must find their own way. But we've been using it for 35 years and we can testify - it works!

One final caution:

One thing to be aware of, in all discernment situations: if you are attached to a certain outcome, or you want things to go your way, you'll have a very hard time understanding your answers. You have to be willing to completely yield to God's wisdom in everything. Ouch! There are times when you might as well not ask, because you know you're not going to obey Him, anyway. **Let's be real honest here: when we want our own way, we're not willing to yield to God's way.** And rather than pretend that your readings were confusing and you weren't sure what He was saying...well, better to not ask, because you're so attached to the outcome and so set on the outcome, that you can't hear anything else. In that case, a good prayer is, "Lord, I am willing to be MADE willing to be obedient."

So, this is just a primer – something to get you started. I think you'll find that Holy Spirit will be working with you very, very closely, and you'll grow very quickly with this method of what God's heart and mind is about a particular topic.

May the Lord bless and keep you strong.

Clare and Ezekiel duBois

November, 2016

Aliens (demons)

(A mother's words the moment after her one-year-old baby is taken in the Rapture) "I'm so confused, so lost, so terrified! Oh somebody, help me, please! Please! What's going on? Everywhere I turn, parents are holding empty clothes in desperation, weeping bitterly.

"Oh, this can't be happening. I'm in a nightmare. I'm going to wake up.... I'm going to wake up!! "But no...it's real. I'm not dreaming. No one knows what's happened. I can't stop trembling. I'm in shock. Only moments ago she was safe here in my arms. The sun glistened off her golden hair and she laughed at the wind.

"We were so happy, she was so innocent. Now her dress lies limp on my arm, her little sandals on the ground. Is she no more? Oh, somebody help me...what happened? What happened??

"If there is a God and He is Real, tell me what happened to my angel, my little girl, tell me...where is she?

"...No, it can't be, she's been Raptured?? Oh, that's just a myth - a fairy tale, that can't be it. No intelligent person believes that stuff. But...she's gone and everywhere...our children are gone...

"Is it **aliens?** Could it be...all the children...Raptured? But why? Why, God? Why??"

Taken from: **Left Behind in Nuclear War...**

"You are correct, but not all the forces of evil have been harnessed, Clare; there is still much hidden from the world."

But will the Father allow the Rapture as long as the world is turning around?

"That is a good question. I cannot answer that at this time, Beloved. You are getting a little too curious and looking into things far beyond you. However, I have to say your logic is sound; you just don't know about the forces of evil that play into this."

*You mean like the **demon-aliens** and their part?*

"Yes. And more you know nothing of."

Taken from: **God is Hearing the Russian People...**

He has repeatedly called us to account to examine our lives, to make sure we are ready when He comes. He has taught us to discern the truth from lies, and virtue from a lukewarm life.

If I were here for myself, and deliberately trying to deceive you, all I would do is spit out fiery sermons on repentance and sin. With maybe a little love thrown in once in a while. My whole approach would be the Rapture, the Rapture, the Judgments, the earthquakes, the volcanoes, the tsunamis...Over and Over and Over again.

*The **aliens**. That would be my focus and maybe we'd have 50,000 subscribers instead of 9,000. Everyone would be hanging on my next word.*

But, I encourage you to look at the fruit in your own lives. Are you closer to Jesus now than you've ever been? Do you see your faults and sins more clearly than ever? Is your prayer life deeper? Are you getting your own visitations from the Lord?

In short, are you increasing in virtue and cleaning your Bridal gown? Or are you titillated by the next juicy prophecy about Yellowstone taking down America, earthquakes in California, and the US splitting down the middles, etc...

Taken from: **Rapture When?**

Aliens (demons)

We have found that in this day and age that we're also dealing with extraterrestrial oppression.

That is to say that these demon entities that inhabit demon bodies, I call them demon **aliens**, *are sometimes a sign, they are all part of a Spirit of darkness, they are all part of Satan's kingdom. They're just fallen angels that have figured out a way to manifest physically cause they're highly intelligent so they know all the rules of physics, ones that we know and we don't know - and they actually oppress you.*

We discovered that there was a UFO hovering over our house, way up high in the atmosphere, and they were beaming down an oppression into this house that you could cut with a knife, it was so thick.

Taken from: **Experiencing Jesus in Dwelling Prayer**

Can you imagine that? Thousands of body bags suddenly coming to life as Christians who were killed in the holocaust rise from the dead right before the eyes of Homeland Security employees? WOW! That has to be a witness.

They will see that and hear the prepared propaganda that **aliens** *not a 'Rapture' took people from the Earth. But they will be witnesses that no* **aliens** *were present at their resurrection! And as I shared in an earlier video these souls will shoot up to the Throne Room like Fourth of July fireworks!*

Taken from: **What If This Were Your Last Few Weeks…**

"There is also an increase in activity before demon **aliens** make their public entrance on the Earth. Everything is orchestrated to bring forward the last kingdom that will rule the entire world, synchronistically."

"Demon **aliens** will be enlisted by that government to search out and destroy communities of resisters, along with clones that will come forth from every corner of the Earth."

"Even now, small pods of such creatures inhabit even the most remote areas of the world, waiting for the word to come forth to search and destroy resisters. This new government would not be possible were it not for the help of these clones."

"The skies will be so full of demon **aliens** that people will be beside themselves with shock and awe. In the very beginning, they will be led to believe they are benign. Then without warning, the supposed evil ones will 'invade' and a war in the heavens will break out. This is only a staged even to galvanize all the countries into one government."

Taken from: **Jesus Speaks On What is to Come #6**

"Learn of Me, for I am meek and humble of heart. I have left you innumerable love letters - read them, believe them, allow them to take root in your heart. There is no joy that is compared to knowing and loving Me. This knowledge of Me and My love for you, unworthy as you are, will sustain you through every trial."

"No matter what you go through, I will be there on your right, holding your hand, speaking to you, comforting you. Nothing can separate you from My Love."

"NOTHING."

"Not anything on the Earth or above the Earth, not **aliens**, not death, not even when you fall - still I am by your side to pick you back up. Nothing can separate you from My Love."

Taken from: **Jesus Speaks On What Is To Come #5**

Aliens (demons)

But this was a New World Order dream and it was during the Tribulation. The New World Order was in complete control. It seemed to me that everything had fallen into place for them. The people were upwardly mobile, healthy and beautiful. They were engaged in every area of the world, controlling all that went on.

There was no way for me to get food. I didn't have the Mark. I couldn't put gas in my truck and go to the mountain where we had our cabins, our retreat and hermitage. I thought to myself, 'Even if we DID get up there, there's no food. But then, maybe I can hitch a ride up there and find something to eat.'

It was liked we were totally trapped: no food, no gas, no way to get up there. It felt very dismal and desperate.

Well, in this dream I was in town somewhere - and I was visiting a lady, a poor woman who was living in a trailer park. I could see a disc satellite dish out in a vacant field about two streets over. It was on a busy street like a boulevard in an industrial area with high-powered electric lines. I had the understanding that they were tracking devices in the store-bought items in the house, even in the food like the cereal and canned goods.

It made me angry and I knew that satellite dish was tracking us, so I did something - and for the life of me, guys, I don't remember what it was I did. It was probably something in the Name of Jesus. Don't know what it was but the dish fell over and started rolling until it just came to a stop.

There was a young woman who was from the New world Order that came into the trailer. She and I kind of hit loggerheads with each other. And she said, "Do you want me to call for back up?" She called before I could even answer her and a van pulled up outside the trailer with five big guys who got out.

They came into the trailer - and actually they were pretty well mannered, they weren't real bullying. They came into the trailer the way the police would come into a non-threatening situation, kind of to check out what was going on.

One of the men in his 20's sat down with me on the couch and began asking me questions. I could soon tell that something else was on his mind - not sure what. But I began telling him, "You don't really believe these people you are working for are on the up and up with you, do you?" He looked at me with interest.

*I continued, "They're going to use you until you are no longer useful, then they'll do away with you. Probably leave you and your buddies locked out when a neutron bomb hits or lock you out of their underground cities and let you die of the plague. In any case, they are being used by the **aliens**, who are really demons sent to destroy the Earth - and you are being used by them. In the end, they will get what they have sown to others as well."*

Taken from: **NOW & Russian Troupes…**

Who is it that thinks they can destroy what I have created? The prince of demons? His very existence depends on My sustaining energy. His days are numbered and he knows it. What he could not do in his demon kingdom he has enlisted foolish men to accomplish for him. But God shall not be mocked. They may dissemble, but I will reassemble. I will intervene again and again and again. They are wasting their time and Satan is amusing himself with their efforts, hoping that somehow if he keeps feeding them technology, they will hit upon it. But he knows his time is short. And I have all the time in the world to play this game while I am putting the finishing touches on My Brides.

Taken from: **The Love Particle**

Anger

"These recruits have been convinced they are doing a good thing by killing every man woman and child in the name of Allah. They will find a vent for their **anger** at mankind and the hard lives they lived because of the selfishness of many - the inequality, being rejected and looked down upon They will be dazed with blood lust. And there will be no stopping them without lethal force.

"Yet, I will have My pockets of survivors, those who have not bent the knee to Baal. I will protect them, but they will suffer much. They will be tried by fire and when I come - be found worthy. This will be a very small percentage of mankind. Your family will be among those survivors. Much of what you taught them growing up was preparation for this time. There will be much brokenness and repentance among."

Taken from: **Jesus Speaks On: What Is To Come After the Rapture**

"It is of the utmost importance that you put others before yourself. When I came into the world, I did not lord it over others. No, I bent the knee and humbled Myself, washing the feet of My disciples. The lowliest job in the house – left for the lowliest servant. That is what a leader does – he, or she, looks after the interests of others.

"Much, even in your survival and the survival of your loved ones, will depend on your total reliance on Me and My ways. I will always provide a way out for those who have humbled themselves and relied totally on Me.

"Though the mountains shake and the seas roar, I will be with you and never abandon you. You will know them by their love and humility. You will recognize those who are sincere by whether or not they are authentically humble. **Anger**, back biting, strife, insisting on your ways, those are the ticket to defeat. That is NOT humble behavior."

Taken from: **Jesus Speaks On: After the Rapture, part 5**

Jesus continued, "All those years of not being able to lash back at injustices, real or merely perceived. Many times inspired by demonic entities, fueling lies to build the emotions to boiling with nowhere to exit, just getting shoved and shoved and shoved deeper down and bottled up in the soul-ish realm.

"It is very much like the crust of the Earth, if you were to replace each continental mass and assign it a name. Violent, alcoholic parents; brutal child abuse. With another continent: teachers and peers at school. And yet another continent: police inmates and judges. Yet another continent: the public and rejection from jobs.

"All of these plates cause stress at different times and heat up the layers inside a person, forming great magma chambers of **anger**. Sometimes the magma escapes in little streams or blows up and they end up incarcerated. Other times the pressure and the pain becomes so great, the soul is eaten up with evil imaginings on how to retaliate and is constantly picking violent fights and brutalizing others.

"...Nonetheless, I approach every soul with a way out of the loop of violent retaliation. It is their choice to fall in with demons... or fall in with Me. The issue is many times the relief of repressed feelings, rejection, helplessness, hopelessness and injustice. Any escape is relief to their tormented feelings."

Taken from: **Why A Soul Rejects Love**

"... A root of bitterness is a toxic root. It gives off deadly acids, much like the soil beneath the cedar tree. Nothing can grow beneath a cedar, because what is released from the roots is toxic to other plants. That means the soil in the garden of your soul is being poisoned. All that can flourish in this soil is **anger**, resentment, retaliation, jealousy and hatred."

Taken from: **How a Root of Bitterness Can Change...**

Anger

"It's been hounding everyone. These doubts come in waves and sweep over everyone who is waiting for me. You can be sure that what you are experiencing is universal to those who are earnestly waiting for My coming.

"In other words, you are not alone in this. This is why when I give you a post, immediately it soothes the hearts of so many.

"These things are broadcast so to speak. Sent out at large, 'in the air'."

What is their source?

"Need you ask?"

I mean human or demonic.

"Either way, it is what is behind it. But to answer you, demonic. Although mood alterations are also applied by man through electronic devices to sow confusion, **anger** and depression. This is why communing with Me is so important. This is why so much effort was put into developing a technology that would modify the brain in such a way that the person would lose interest in all things spiritual. This has been a benchmark breakthrough.

"My Love, that is the science that developed this evil technology. It is commonly thought to be good for religious fanatics, terrorists, etc. But as usual, man found a more evil and practical application in mind control."

"When I anoint something for you, when you pray for guidance from My Holy Spirit and begin to read, something will catch your attention as being especially relevant to your present situation. You will feel it in your heart. That is a illuminated word for you to apply to current living situations. Once you begin to grasp that, you are coming closer to the tuning that is necessary to hear My Voice from your heart directly.

"When you sit and write or type a letter to Me, I listen and understand very clearly what you are saying. This is entering the foyer of My throne room. As you finish your sentences and expect Me to reply, even asking in faith, "Lord, what do you have to say about this?" I then reply, and you may begin typing as I speak.

"Don't allow fear and scrutiny to get in the way. Just write what you feel I am saying to you. If you are bitter, in a state of **anger** or retaliation, and the words you write that you think I am saying - if they too are **angry** or retaliatory, you are hearing from yourself or a demon. But if the words bring peace and resolution...then, you are most likely hearing from Me."

Taken from: **How to Receive My Anointing for Your Life Everyday**

"When you are under attack you will not feel gentle conviction. When you are under attack from the enemy, you will feel heavy condemnation, as if **anger** is being hurled at you, and it is, if you could see it in the demonic dimension.

"You are being attacked, downgraded, debilitated, robbed of your peace and joy, feeling hopelessness. That is a dead giveaway that what is being fed to you is from the demonic.

"My Brides, be ever so vigilant. The devil comes to kill, steal and destroy. Anytime you are entertaining a thought of that nature you can be sure who the author of it is. Do not be leagued to the devil, do not throw in your lot with the devil whose purpose is to destroy what is good and uplifting."

Taken from: **God's Correction**

Anger

"Do not let the enemy come in and dissuade you into unbelief. He is cruising to steal from you through **anger**, bitterness, resentment and foolish fears. When you feel those things rising in your emotions, it is the enemy stealing from you. He wants to take away your sweetness, your presence with Me, and the overflow I fill you with.

"He loves to incite **anger** to drain you before you can even begin your day or finish a project or your prayers. He loves to lie in your ear, cause you to erupt into **anger** or fear and then drain you of all you had planned for the day and you run off to tend to these decoys. He is very clever and he knows which buttons to push, because his agents, the demons, are forever observing you and taking notes."

Taken from: **Sweet Aroma of Holiness...**

"Well, what I am saying here, there is relief in violence there's a catharsis. All those years of not being able to lash back at injustices, real or merely perceived. Many times inspired by demonic entities, fueling lies to build the emotions to boiling with nowhere to exit, just getting shoved and shoved and shoved deeper down and bottled up in the soul-ish realm.

"It is very much like the crust of the Earth, if you were to replace each continental mass and assign it a name. Violent, alcoholic parents; brutal child abuse. With another continent: teachers and peers at school. And yet another continent: police inmates and judges. Yet another continent: the public and rejection from jobs. All of these plates cause stress at different times and heat up the layers inside a person, forming great magma chambers of **anger**. Sometimes the magma escapes in little streams or blows up and they end up incarcerated. Other times the pressure and the pain becomes so great, the soul is eaten up with evil imaginings on how to retaliate and is constantly picking violent fights and brutalizing others.

"Others who feel the same way begin to come together and form gangs and covens. Their entire life is centered around killing and destroying the lives of others. Jealousies. Getting all the things other people have and getting even. Relieving life's disappointments and wounds."

Taken from: **Why a Soul Rejects Love**

"There most certainly is a root of bitterness in every one of you. It is your job, with My Holy Spirit to identify it, renounce it and pray I will remove it.

"This exercise should not take you long, and it will not hinder your going into eternity. There are many of you that could be detained for unforgiveness. If you have bitterness in your heart, it is the ugliest of stains and will show right on the front of your wedding gown. So, be sure to rid yourself of that. Disarm it. By that I mean, refuse to allow it to pull you into a fury. Renounce this **anger** and unforgiveness in My Name, and refuse to connect with it. If you are faithful to make an honest effort, I will surely be faithful to totally remove it."

Taken from: **Get Ready For Your Journey**

"There are many who wish much evil and death on you and Ezekiel, but they will go unsatisfied. In fact, I am arranging trials for them that will take their attention off of you. But you know, Clare, there are always more haters and nay-sayers. I appreciate your prayers for them; truly they are dark souls in need of Me. I want to give them My love, but they reject it, turn away and prefer **anger**, bitterness, and all things dark. This is where they get their 'high.' From the devils, satanic worship and the pains inflicted on others. They are distorted, twisted souls, Clare. My heart aches for them."

Taken from: **Spiritual Attacks, Prayers for Our Enemies**

Belief, Believe

He continued, "Lack of **belief** in Me, lack of faith in My nearness is one of the most painful things for Me. (that's what the song is about) Can you imagine it? Your daughter is going through a really rough trial and you are there with her, coaxing her, making suggestions, comforting her and she feels something but writes it off and says, 'I wish Mom were here to help me through this.' And you are right beside her all the time. How frustrating can that be?"

~

"May I say to all My children: curiosity is your downfall. There is much I have put on your hearts to do, but you don't have the discipline to stick with them until they are done - or in some cases, like Clare's, even get started. You will look back on your time on Earth and see that you wasted years worth of time doing foolish things.

"The devils know it is not easy to draw you into a sin like adultery or murder, but making you waste time is a cinch, and thereby foils My efforts to use you in your anointing. Part of the issue is deep in your hearts, My Brides. Part of the issue is your lack of **belief** in yourself and I, working together to bring it about. Far too many things are begun and maintained by your own strength, rather than turning them over to Me so we can work together."

~

"The point is not to give up. This is Satan's plan. Again, using the analogy of lions on the hunt, they look for the ones who are separated. Be smarter than the adversary. Cling to and forgive your friends when they wound you.

"I did not give up on Peter. It is written that I '**did not entrust Myself to men, for I knew their hearts**'. (John 2:24) As close as Peter was to Me, I knew his weakness. I knew he was not ready to die for Me. He loved Me but overestimated his strength. Peter did not know himself.

"He overrated his devotion, his love, even though I had appointed him chief of the apostles. In his zeal and self-confidence, he **believed** nothing could turn him away from Me."

Taken from: **How a Root of Bitterness Can Change Your Destiny and DNA**

"You have seen how brutal people can be when they don't approve of your faith: the accusations without cause, without substance, without sense. I do not want to speak here of the punishment of those who repress the faith of others, but know that it is severe.

"Rather, I want to talk about the measures I will take to offset this evil. Dreams and visions, visitations and encounters with Me will replace the approval of men. This is the substance of the faith, Clare. **Belief** in Me, in Who I am - a personal and affectionate relationship without losing respect or the fear of God. I cultivate this in the souls that cry out for Me, whether they be Muslim or Orthodox. I answer the deepest needs of every man, woman and child."

Taken from: **Prayer & Repentance Hold Judgment Back**

"I know it's been a long, arduous wait. I know, My children. My Brides have grown restless, but that is precisely what is fueling revival in Europe with the displaced persons. So great is their confusion that they are more easily dislodged from age-old **beliefs** that have kept them in bondage and created these situations, even in the world. So great is their fatigue with the posturing of nations for supremacy, at the expense of the little ones, truly they are ready for a different life. Yet corruption waxes worldwide and no justice will truly be seen until My Reign. There will always be an element to detract from the progress of nations."

Taken from: **I'm Coming For You & Refugee Crisis**

Belief, Believe

"Most of your problem truly lies in the fact that you do not believe in yourself. But I **believe** in you and I know what can be done when you **believe** in Me. Together we can do this. The hardest part is starting. The next hardest part is overcoming obstacles. Then overcoming boredom or lack of inspiration. All of these problems can be handled in worship and prayer when Holy Spirit refreshes you in His anointing and power.

"It's all about how much do you love Me and how much will you give Me? How much are you willing to invest...even in the little time left to us? Abraham **believed** God and it was counted to him as righteousness. To act on what I have given you is to prove your faith in Me. To let it sit dormant in a dark and dank basement under a pile of waste is almost unforgivable."

Taken from: **Make This Time Count**

"I am ever by your side, continually watching over you, whispering in your ear: 'Don't go there. Do this - it would be good if you did that.' 'Don't answer that, delete it.' Yes, I am advising you continually. But My voice is so familiar to you, you actually ***believe*** it to be your own. But if you listen very carefully, you will realize that thought did not originate with you...it came from a different source.

"My yoke is easy. My burden is light. But getting you into that yoke, Whew! That's a real challenge, for even Me!

"You see, holiness is hard work. It entails much self-denial and refocusing on the needs of others. When you come to serve the Lord, prepare yourself for trials. Yes, many in this world **believe** it is their right to indulge themselves. After all, they worked for it. But all this indulgence leads to blind alleys, wrong turns and bondage. And some of this indulgence is spurred on by the enemy, knowing your weakness.

And knowing that you won't check with Me. He pushes you into things that feed your fancy and meets some need that you're not aware of.

"I would have you free, fluid, mobile and peaceful. Many irons in the fire, many projects, many materials leads to stress, which leads to tension in the home with your spouse and children. Which leads to poor health. Whereas sufficient resource or just a bit under, keeps your life uncluttered and simple."

Taken from: **Freedom Without License**

"I long to speak to you, My people. I am forever trying to find new ways to speak to you: through nature, through events, through friends, even through license plates. There are times when I want to turn you around before it is too late to repair the damage you're going to do. But alas, you just don't hear Me. Part of the deafness is due to self-will, but part is due also to your lack of **belief** that I am so involved in your life that I want to tell you what will make a difference for you. I want to advise you, I want to prevent catastrophes, I want to bless you. You just don't know or *believe* in My goodness. It is more than you can ever fathom."

Taken from: **Are You Wise?**

"Satan sees your like and dislike and attacks that ministry through you, because it doesn't suit you. Whether it be fear or ignorance, something in you doesn't accept it. So you begin to **believe** lies about those who minister that way. ...Once you open your mouth against them, Satan collects two scores: a demon just entered through a door of criticism into your life - and now you will be sifted. And others are provoked into detraction and criticism and the ministry is injured."

Taken from: **Are You With Me or Against Me?**

Charity

When we criticize other people, we are the ones who are suffering. Yes, that other person suffers, but we are the ones who are really suffering, because it causes alienation from the Lord. It's our choice. It's our choice to please Him in our thoughts and our words and to work on these things – or to let it go and don't pay any attention to it, and just do what the world accepts as normal.

And it's NOT normal in Heaven – "let it be on Earth as it is in Heaven." Gossip – it does not exist in Heaven. Judging and Criticizing does not exist in Heaven. What does exist in Heaven, are the saints making excuses for each other – although in Heaven, we tend to be perfect. But what does exist in Heaven is **charity.** *And* **charity** *covers a multitude of sins.*

"As you know the wounded wound," the Lord said. "There is no other solution for the Body than to stop wounding, or the cycle will never be broken. When the soul is intimately bound to Me, and knows Me, not only do I heal them with My love – but they feel the grief I feel when a deprecating word is spoken about another.

"The Body is eating itself alive. This truly must stop if the soul wants to be in Heaven with Me. Rancor, jealousy and bitterness cannot inherit the Kingdom of Heaven.

"One sign of those who are to be Raptured is the refusal to speak negatively about anyone, and their genuine **charity** towards the faults of others, even and especially when they are the victims of that fault. I don't care how many prayer meetings, church services, good works, tithes, or healings and miracles they work – if they are critical and judgmental, they will not be taken."

Oh, Lord – we all have these tendencies in that direction. How then can anyone be saved?

"My daughter, My Bride – what is not possible with man is possible with God if attention is poured into the intimate relationship with Me. You see, when a soul enters this holy of holies, they become One with Me, and through communion, one flesh as well. And this place is so sweet that they learn not to do anything to rob them of this sweetness. They can feel Me recoil in pain when they are critical of another. This hurts them, too."

Taken from: **Prophetic Word Rapture & Conflict in Marriage**

"How I long to gather you to Myself. Press on toward the goal to win the prize for which God has called You Heavenward in Me. For I will bring you to the joy and peace of your eternal home.

"When you arrive, you will see souls going to and fro, all very natural, all very orderly according to My Purpose. You will see, that just as upon the Earth, My People will be serving, praying, praising, and working along with the Salvific Plan for all souls, even until the end of the world.

"Though glorified and perfect, you will yet resemble the human state that you previously lived in - only purified, reflecting Me and My Own Image authentically and genuinely. You will all be perfectly humble, with perfect divine **charity**, wisdom, and grace.

"You will love Me and one another with absolute sweetness. Holiness will abound, and permeate everyone and everything, as with the words to the precious nativity song, "All is calm, all is bright." I will reach you there, instantly, without the slightest delay when you call. I will spread My cloak over you, and draw you again and again to My Heart, that you may drink fully of the consolations of your God."

Taken from: **Your True Home, Chronicles of the Bride in Heaven**

Charity

Clare: That's huge, that is so huge. **Charity** *is so, so important.* **Charity** *and humility are two things that... the Lord, if you're serious about Him and are really committed to Him, He's not going to let you slide in those areas. Because those are the things that He honors the most, that He values the most in a soul, is their humility and their* **charity**. *And if we don't reflect that humility and* **charity** *of Jesus, He will definitely withdraw from us to get our attention.*

There's nothing really worse that I have found, personally, in my walk with the Lord that has grieved Him more than being hard and harsh with some judgment, because we hurt people, whether it's spoken or not spoken. An unspoken word still has the ability to cut a soul. You can feel when people are gossiping about you, saying things about you, and it hurts. It's destructive, and He hates to see someone suffer.

Ezekiel: Or you can feel when you have said or done something, you can feel that conviction. Do we heed that conviction, or do we just go on? Or, are we listening to conversations where we should just say, "Stop, this is wrong. We shouldn't be talking like this".

And if it continues, remove yourself from that company. That will cause Him to pull back, it sure will.

Taken from: **Spiritual Dryness, 2 of 2, Heaven Talk**

"Humility, self-control, honesty, and **charity** are absolutely essential if you want Me to walk with you. If you are used to leading and getting your own way, you won't do very well as a leader. If you are unsure of yourself and know that you need Me more than ever, you will excel as a leader.

"My children, the ways of the world that you have learned are totally inappropriate here. I protect those who humble themselves before Me. If you are prancing around proudly with all the answers, you are bound for destruction.

"I am counting on your breaking when you realize all you've been taught by friends and family has just come to pass before your very eyes. I am counting on you face flat on the floor begging forgiveness for your pride and arrogance. I am laying the groundwork for you to survive the trials that are now at your door, both body and soul.

"If you humble yourself before Me, I will most certainly be with you. Even if you are in a long-standing habit of pride and arrogance, and are aware of your sin and want to be delivered, I will work with you. But if you insist on your own wisdom, I can do little for you."

Taken from: **After the Rapture, part 5   Who I Can Protect...**

"Just as in days gone by, when I supernaturally protected My people, so shall I protect those who must stay behind. There will be one among them who will be designated the leader, and to him or her, I will give supernatural knowledge and wisdom. Protect this one who is critical to your mission. Let not the devils cause division, misunderstand, murmuring and jealousy. Be on your guard against these poisons they will use to divide and scatter you all.

"Together you will survive separated; you will face many dangers without anyone to hold you up. Do not let them divide and conquer. Be smarter than the enemy, walk in **charity** and humility and you will have no problems. Walk in self will, selfishness, suspicion, and rancor, it will be your demise. There will be many testings among the groups, many testings. Painful decisions to make, life or death decisions to make. I will give you peace when the decisions are the hardest. Use lots to help you determine a plan of action."

Taken from: **Provision and Instruction For Those Left Behind**

Charity

"This is what I intended 'church' to be. A coming Home to the safety of My arms. Yes, there are lessons to be learned but when a soul is steeped in My Love, the things they must give up seem inconsequential, so empty. Yet so rarely is such a place found. Once the formality of accepting Me sets in, the rule books come out and I get lost in the translation. Truly, there is not one denomination that is better than another. All have lost the meaning of the family Love, the family of God, the love that expresses everything about My nature. And so that soul ends up living by the rules when I would have them here in My Heart, living by love."

"This is what is missing, has been missing and will no longer be missing as I bring my people back to Me. Love will be the order of the day, the order of every day, every night, every moment of life. So, now I must scrap all these conflicting rules and regulations, statutes, books, jots and tittles created by man. I must sweep the floor clean of all confusion, all contention and start from scratch. Building from a foundation of love, with building blocks of truth, **charity** as the mortar, humility as the roof - for without humility nothing can stand, absolutely nothing.

"So, I want My people to understand: if they are focused on rules and formulas they are doing Me an injustice; they are feeding broken rocks to the lonely and unsaved. Judgment, criticism, scorn and contempt because of their lifestyle is the last thing they should ever have a hint of. Instead, take one by the hand and love them. Be understanding, listen, comfort, lead gently with calm assurance that your God has what they need. The compassion - let them see that in you. Please don't ever present legalities and rote Scriptures! Rather, tenderly draw them in to a safe space, befriend them, lead them by example. Feed them the Word gently. Time is so short, My Bride, people are lonely and broken, sin-sick in this world - handle them with extreme care."

Taken from: **Draw Souls To Me With The Fragrance of My Love**

"There is a purpose for everything, My children. There is a very specific purpose and dynamic for every single thing that takes place in the lives of every single person. You are doing a job that requires intense and careful vigilance.

"But I bring these things to your attention to tell you that you are 'working' when you endure these sacrifices with equanimity and patience. You are doing a job that requires intense and careful vigilance. It's not just an inconvenience; it is a necessary work to alleviate the suffering of another.

"It's not just a sickness; it is a work of **charity** that another may be relieved long enough to get their hope back and rise up out of their particular pit - to life in Me, renewed. So, I am hoping to give you a fresh and heavenly perspective about your crosses, that you might rejoice when others find their way because you cheerfully gave Me your all. This is the true meaning of 'deny yourself, pick up your cross and follow Me.'"

Taken from: **Suffering…**

"Yes, in Heaven it will be safe. But on Earth, knowledge puffs up but **charity** edifies. In other words, you are safer little, unlearned and dependent on Me for understanding. I can impart to you in time so small it cannot be measured by human standards, the deepest understanding of the most complex truths. Whereas you could spend thirty years in studies of Hebrew and Aramaic and still fall short of understanding.

"So, trust in Me, lean not on your own understanding, and I shall direct your paths of understanding."

Taken from: **The Great Revival After the Rapture**

Child, Children

"Nothing is too small. Children who offer prayers are far more powerful than many adults, because of the purity of their souls. So, I am asking you parents to bring your **children** into your prayer circles and explain to them as best you can, exactly what is at stake. Tell them that Satan has been working secretly in this country to destroy it. The forests, lakes, rivers and oceans. He and his minions have been responsible for the earthquakes and weather changes, beached animals and fish. Aborted babies. Use discretion, but make it clear to them that their future depends on this election - whether or not there will be freedom in this country."

Taken from: **The Election: Jesus calls for "War Spiritually"**

He began, "Tonight IS a critical night. There is a stillness in Heaven. Those who have shouldered this burden and prayed - I commend you. You are truly carrying My Cross for the world. Those of you who have longed for the day when righteousness would be established in your country, it will never be so until I come. But steps could be taken to at least move in that direction. The first being to put a total end to abortion.

"Just as the man of sin began his reign in America by allowing babies to be cut into pieces in their mother's wombs, the first act of righteousness would totally ban the practice and begin the steps to ban abortion in America forever. What heavy judgments would be removed from this country were that to take place. What peace could be established at her borders. Can I bless and protect a nation that slaughters innocent **children**? Surely I cannot. But an end to this practice would lift the severe judgment on this land. There is still a hidden monster to be dealt with, it continues to expand under the soil like the infamous Blob monsters of the 60's."

Taken from: **Election Day "The Decisive Hour"**

"Unless you become like a little *child*..."

'Truly I tell you', He said, 'unless you change and become like little *children*, you will never enter the Kingdom of Heaven. Therefore, whoever humbles himself like this little *child* is the greatest in the Kingdom of Heaven....' Matt 18:3-4

"It is humbling to be dependent like a *child*, at least from the world's standpoint. But from where I stand, it is the perfect place to be: totally trusting Me to provide everything, without qualm or question. When you are dependent you have no control, no decision making power, no say in anything - you just take Daddy's hand and walk along the paths of life with Him."

Taken from: **Hand in Hand With Daddy**

"You see, My **children**, it is your many insecurities that motivate you to live a certain life. It is your insecurity about the provision of life's most basic needs that corrals you into a place of subservience, instead of a position of totally fulfilling all I have made you to be. It is also the fear of suffering, the need for comfort, protection and acceptance by society. Once you abandon yourself into My arms, you let go of these concerns and place your life totally in My hands.

"When you are fully released to Me and I am in full control, I can do all that is necessary to guide you into your true mission in life. Yes, there are moments that are scary, painful, confusing. But ultimately, when you trust Me, you cease to worry about these things. Unless you become as a little *child*...Yes, abandonment into the arms of your loving Father, your loving Jesus, your loving Spirit is the key to maintaining peace in the midst of life's contradictions."

Taken from: **Hand in Hand With Daddy**

Child, Children

"You are to be like a little **child** with her hand in Daddy's, walking along the seashore of life, finding ever new joy in the treasures and opportunities I toss up in the tides everyday. Oh, how blessed is the soul that has abandoned all their cares into My capable hands. I will surely commune with them continuously, because their minds are free from earthly encumbrances."

Taken from: **Make Peace With All**

"So many of you, My **children**, are highly pleasing to Me. The sweet aroma of holiness exudes from you."

After He said that, I saw something like that when we were dancing, because it seemed that there was a fragrance emanating from the very top of my head and that's where Jesus was resting His cheek.

"Yes, there is a fragrance about a soul that continually yields to Me. It is sweet and comforting to Me. So many, I can't even get close to. The poison of rancor is so intense I cannot stand to be close. See to it, all My People, that the odor of rancor does not proceed from your thoughts. Yes, the activity of your brain emanates this fragrance. When it is sweet, it is as if I were walking through a well-kept garden. When it is noxious, it is the odor of death and decaying flesh. You can hardly understand how terribly bad it is."

Taken from: **Sweet Aroma of Holiness**

"This is My joy, to see My **children** finally understanding how personal My love really is. I do not sit behind a desk with a Bible between us. I do not hide in elaborate cathedrals. I do not confine myself to My traditional garb. I am not in any way formal or distant from you.

"No, I wear khakis when we explore the cliffs of Heaven, when you draw near to Me, I rush to embrace you. I put nothing between us and forgive you of your sins…because you are so eager to confess and repent, they do not raise themselves up as obstacles to our nearness. There are even times when I approach you as you repent, so that you will know I am hearing your contrite heart and I forgive you."

Taken from: **Who I Really Am To You**

"Oh, how I want My **children** to understand who I AM. Yes, I am the mighty God who spoke creation into being, and then I lowered myself and became subject to the very same limitations you were born into. I did this so we could be truly close and you would come to understand the depth of My love for you as well as My character as a real, true Man.

"…This is the time for a real relationship with Me, though I am your God. This is not the time of posturing and formality. When David was out in the fields with his sheep, then He was closest to Me and we conversed like familiar friends. The same with Moses. We spoke not only in the smoke and fire and lightening, but in the babbling of water, deep into the night. Everything we saw together we shared, even as a husband and wife share their lives with one another."

Taken from: **Who I Really Am To You**

"All of you, My Brides, when you have reached out to souls and touched them with Me, expect trials on the heels of that witnessing. Expect hardship and sacrifice. You are birthing children into the Kingdom. You are with your own life cooperating with Me to bring them into our family. You, too, become the mother of souls. These **children** need prayers, teachings, sacrifice and tending to, so the enemy will not pluck them out of the soil before they take root. They need watering and protection from the harshness of the elements. Agents of the enemy are constantly patrolling sites such as this one to discredit those channels and scare new believers ."

Taken from: **You Are Mothers to Souls**

Child, Children

"Understand that these culminating events will push them over the brink of reluctance and down into My waiting arms. I have prepared a safety net for their souls, so hold fast and confess frequently My promises to you about them. Do not judge by what you see, much is hidden from view in places where they are already scared like little lost **children** and much of their superficial bravado is a cover-up for that nagging feeling that something IS about to change drastically in the world and they will be caught unprepared. But for those who heed My advice and seek Me and not their own devices, those souls shall find rest in these turbulent times unparalleled in history. This is why what I have given you to leave behind is so very important. Your efforts will be crowned with success."

Taken from: **Your Tears Are Stored in Golden Flasks**

"There are many layers to your crosses, My *Children.* Sometimes I call you to carry the weight of your cross only and it is easier for you. But other times, many other times - especially now - you are carrying multiple crosses. You are all intertwined as brothers and sisters and the same Holy Spirit flows through you all."

Taken from: **Suffering – Real Work in the Realm of the Spirit**

The Father continued, "This is what I ask of all, but the greatest burden will fall to My faithful. Pray, beloved **children**, pray! There will be whole days where you may be directed to remain in prayer. My Holy Spirit will direct you in your prayers. The prayers will burgeon and flow through you without effort, as Living Waters, to the parched areas of this Earth that need them. They will rise upward to Me like the sweetest of fragrant incense, and I will hear your prayers. Your prayers will help to determine what will transpire…what punishments will befall those who transgressed My Laws and My Will. Your prayers DO matter!"

Taken from: **Great Suffering is About to Befall the World**

"Just as the man of sin began his reign in America by allowing babies to be cut into pieces in their mother's wombs, the first act of righteousness would totally ban the practice and begin the steps to ban abortion in America forever. What heavy judgments would be removed from this country were that to take place. What peace could be established at her borders. Can I bless and protect a nation that slaughters innocent **children**? Surely I cannot. But an end to this practice would lift the severe judgment on this land."

Taken from: **Election Day - "The Decisive Hour" Jesus said**

"You must cleave to Me, dear **children**! All of you! But especially those of you who choose to stand in the gap and suffer for those who have transgressed. Know, My dear children, that your recent efforts have borne much fruit for the Kingdom of God. Many more of My **children** are returning home. My heart weeps with gladness at your efforts. The fragrance is as sweet as My finest wines. Many of you have suffered in order for these wayward ones to return; and your suffering has been the sweetest of all gifts. How tenderly they touch My Heart. For My Heart has often been battered and My labors scorned, and your efforts come as sweet consolation during a painful time."

Taken from: **Great Suffering is About to Befall the World**

"I am asking you, **Children**: take a long look in the mirror and know yourselves. Ask My Holy Spirit to reveal your true weaknesses. What will this accomplish? Compassion and forgiveness for those who betray you. I want My Body mended, put back together. Satan has spent the last 2,000 years contriving plans that would push the members of My Body apart, further and further."

Taken from: **How a Root of Bitterness Can Change Your Destiny and DNA**

Comfort

"It is not the insecure and unschooled that are in danger; it is those who think that because they are educated they don't need My opinion. They have learned to think on their own and for the most part see consulting Me as a weakness and only for the simpletons. That is precisely the reason why the poor recognized Me when I came and the Pharisees and Scribes, knowing the letter of the law so well, tried to kill Me.

""Yes, there is a fragrance about a soul that continually yields to Me. It is sweet and **comforting** to Me. So many, I can't even get close to. The poison of rancor is so intense I cannot stand to be close. See to it, all My People, that the odor of rancor does not proceed from your thoughts. Yes, the activity of your brain emanates this fragrance. When it is sweet, it is as if I were walking through a well-kept garden. When it is noxious, it is the odor of death and decaying flesh. You can hardly understand how terribly bad it is."

Taken from: **Sweet Aroma of Holiness**

"I believe God's servants and ministers are the most overlooked group of people who work selflessly to help others. They are not the 'hired hands' who run when the wolf attacks the flock. They day after day lay down their lives, their **comforts** and their agendas to protect those who have looked to them for encouragement in the drought, **comfort** in an uncaring and callous world, the truth of Jesus and His teachings in a confused and misinformed world. Their work reaches into the very heart of our lives and helps to keep us connected and healthy to the wellspring of life, Jesus Our Lord."

Taken from: **Grapes From the Vineyard, Wool From The Flock**

He said, "I find **comfort** here. I find caring and focus on what is truly of importance to Me, not the flesh, which matters for nothing, except to sustain the spirit's temple. Oh, Clare, I long to hold all My vessels unto honor close to My heart. I long to hear the pure beating of their hearts. I long for them to be detached from the material things of the world. And I am so glad you are going in that direction. Just be vigilant, you have many enemies. But as you can see, I have not allowed them to do tremendous harm. A little here, a little there."

Taken from: **Your Tomorrow is Not Guaranteed**

"I wish for My faithful ones who are living at ground zero, My Breath will surround and sustain you in those moments and your only awareness will be the freedom from Earth you will suddenly experience, and then My presence, My **comforting** arms, My welcoming smile. Oh, you have waited all so very long for these days to arrive. You have prayed and cried, you have feared and released your fears into My hands. You have watched, waited and prepared, praying for others for so very long."

Taken from: **Tinkling Northern Lights and the Coming Conflagration**

"I want to speak to My Brides about how much **comfort** they bring Me. I see how you recommit your life to Me sometimes hour by hour, day by day, saying over and over again, 'I just want more of You, Jesus. I want to love You with my whole heart.' I hear the times you cry out from the heart, 'Lord, have Mercy on these souls.' I approve the meditations of your hearts and the faithfulness you reach for daily.

"How can I possibly describe to you the indescribable joy you bring Me? You are like a garden filled with luscious roses of all different colors and marvelous fragrance. Jasmine, lavender and lilacs grow in profusion. Hidden between the beds of roses are precious lilies of the valley giving off their own divine fragrance. Yes, your good deeds are manifested to Me and all of Heaven with a supernatural fragrance."

Taken from: **You Are My Bride, My Garden Sealed**

Comfort

I think a lot of folks, including me I'm sure, have gotten it in our heads that, "Oh, THIS is the place to stay!" And there's a **comfort** *level - we know what's happening. Whereas His way, it's a surprise every minute of the day, because you don't really know where He's taking you.*

Taken from: **An Invitation to Come up Higher**

"Yes, there is a fragrance about a soul that continually yields to Me. It is sweet and **comforting** to Me. So many, I can't even get close to. The poison of rancor is so intense I cannot stand to be close. See to it, all My People, that the odor of rancor does not proceed from your thoughts. Yes, the activity of your brain emanates this fragrance. When it is sweet, it is as if I were walking through a well-kept garden. When it is noxious, it is the odor of death and decaying flesh. You can hardly understand how terribly bad it is."

Taken from: **Sweet Aroma of Holiness**

"You see, My children, it is your many insecurities that motivate you to live a certain life. It is your insecurity about the provision of life's most basic needs that corrals you into a place of subservience, instead of a position of totally fulfilling all I have made you to be. It is also the fear of suffering, the need for **comfort**, protection and acceptance by society. Once you abandon yourself into My arms, you let go of these concerns and place your life totally in My hands."

Taken from: **Hand in Hand With Daddy**

"I have proven Myself over and over again to some of you. It is important for you to keep remembrances of the times I have come through for you, when everything looked hopeless. These become altars, just as Jacob built an altar after He wrestled with Me. They are designated places that are proofs and solid evidences of My faithfulness. I will establish you in these altars as you walk with Me and they will become places of ***comfort*** and confidence in the midst of turbulent times."

Taken from: **Hand in Hand With Daddy**

Oh, Jesus, how can I even approach you? I am such a low creature.

He answered me, "I don't know, but I'm glad you do. Maybe because you know how much I love and need you, Clare. I need your affection, your worship, your company. Poor as you are, it is a **comfort** to Me. You may be only a tiny drop in a great ocean, but you're My drop. And I would miss you if you didn't come to Me, though you see yourself so clearly.

"Still, even as the king permitted Esther to approach - I am so in love with you in your poverty, your lack and littleness. I can't stay away and I even long for the time we spend together."

∾

"You have suffered, grown, matured, seasoned, mellowed down to the things that really do matter in life. You are done with youthful pride and competition with those around you. Now is a time when these worldly attitudes have been worked out of your system. In a word, you are much purer.

"Therefore, I can use you to minister. You aren't on an ego trip to prove yourself or excel beyond your brother. Rather, you are on a love trip where you recognize the needs of hurting humanity and want to use your talents to bring them comfort and into the Kingdom."

Taken from: **I Am Serving The Fine Wine Last...**

Comforting The Lord

"And those who are about My business, pressing in? They make Me cry for joy. Why, you say? Because their hearts are one with Mine, and they **comfort** Me with their love for their brother."

Taken from: **What's Delaying the Rapture?**

"I dread this event. Come. Live in My Heart. See what I must see, feel what I feel and understand; while you are looking at a celebration and freedom from this Earth, I am looking at holocaust.

"Do not jump to conclusions here. I did not say I'm changing the timing. Rather, I am asking you to join your heart to Mine and see what I am enduring in these moments. Minute by minute, it is pure torture. Yet at some point, it must go forth.

"All mankind, busy about their daily lives, will suddenly be thrown into an abyss of excruciating pain and loss, confusion. And be in utter shock, stunned, speechless, unable to think. This is what I face minute by minute, until My Father releases it. And then I must deal with the aftermath. Another horror story, horror so great you cannot in your mortal minds understand all the repercussions.

"Oh, stay by My side, My Brides! **Comfort Me** as the angel comforted Me in the Garden before My arrest. Wrap your tender arms around Me and **comfort Me**, for never has there been a time of travail such as is coming upon the earth, and I dread it with all My being. Yet, My Mercy will take over situation after situation at the appropriate time for each poor soul involved.

"This is what I wanted to talk with you about today. I need your **comfort**, your prayers for mankind, those who have been made in My image whether they be good or bad. It is not My heart to see them suffer this way. It is not My Heart.

"Please, I am asking you. Stay by My side, give every spare moment to Me. Truly, I am walking the way of the Cross again and to those of you who have chosen to accompany Me, I tell you it means more to Me than I can ever express. This is the darkest hour for humanity; this is what all flesh has dreaded. It will overtake the whole world and throw it into a chaos which has never been known, and never again will be known, until the end of time."

Taken from: **This is My Darkest Hour, Stay With Me**

"You are My designated assistant."

Wow! What do I do?

"Follow Me around, **comfort Me** and keep Me company." He said very matter-of-factly.

Oh Lord, what an honor.

"No, what a blessing that one of My Creations can't stand to be without me for an instant."

Taken from: **We're Going Home**

I looked across the beach and saw the Lord, the Father and Holy Spirit. The Father and Holy Spirit were comforting the Lord, as He was in so much emotional pain. The Father was directing and helping Him and showing Him what to do. Holy Spirit was standing by, as though He was shielding the Father and Son with love, care and protection. There were several angels around that seemed to be standing in areas assigned specifically for them and each had their instructions as of what they were assigned to do.

Taken from: **Powerful Dream: 660 mph Tsunami Hits San Francisco**

Comforting The Lord

Tonight in prayer the Lord was on the cross, one mass of bloody flesh. I was beside Him like being on the cross on His left. He is always on my right. After a very long time He was standing on the ground and I was in His arms. Both of us were wearing crowns of thorns, and He was sobbing.

"Bitter, bitter, bitter, what I must do, is so bitter. Oh, **comfort Me**, Clare, I really needed you to stay with Me today."

I am so sorry, Lord, please help me be more obedient.

"Well, you are here now, and I am glad - stay with Me."

Taken from: **Attacks Against the Faith Are on the Way...**

"When I see your devotion, your daily struggles, your fresh resolve, your careful examination of conscience and self-correction, I rejoice that such a one as this has given their lives to Me. **I find great solace and joy** in dwelling in your hearts and listening to the meditations of your mind as you continue to draw closer and closer to Me, until we are one. I see your dry spells and watch your grief when you do not feel My presence, though I am with you always.

"I see how you recommit your life to Me sometimes hour by hour, day by day, saying over and over again, 'I just want more of You, Jesus. I want to love You with my whole heart.' I hear the times you cry out from the heart, 'Lord, have Mercy on these souls.' I approve the meditations of your hearts and the faithfulness you reach for daily.

"How can I possibly describe to you the indescribable joy you bring Me?"

Taken from: **You Are My Bride, My Garden Sealed**

"Yes, there is a fragrance about a soul that continually yields to Me. It is sweet and **comforting to Me**. So many, I can't even get close to. The poison of rancor is so intense I cannot stand to be close. See to it, all My

People, that the odor of rancor does not proceed from your thoughts. Yes, the activity of your brain emanates this fragrance. When it is sweet, it is as if I were walking through a well-kept garden. When it is noxious, it is the odor of death and decaying flesh. You can hardly understand how terribly bad it is."

Taken from: **Sweet Aroma of Holiness...**

I felt that I must seek out His presence and **comfort Him**. *I felt Him all day today, but I really especially wanted to really be with Him, with all of my attention focused on Him.*

Ezekiel and I have been feeling snippets of sorrow from His heart and tonight all I cared to do was hold and **comfort Him**. *There are times in our lives and the lives of others when words are not necessary. Just a hug and comfort is all that can be given.*

Taken from: **Mercy! Comet Will Only Graze Earth**

"'Yes, Jesus, I trust in You.' when said from the heart, in total conviction, are the most beautiful words you could ever say to Me. You are saying, 'I know You, Jesus. I know You are faithful, I know You are omnipotent and can do everything, no matter how difficult. That nothing at all is beyond Your ability.

"And I know that You love me and all You ordain for my life springs from that love that drove You to be crucified on the Cross, so my purpose in life could be fulfilled.' Nothing, no Nothing, is more **comforting to My Heart** than to see you believe and act on these words in a world where God is just a nebulous, neutral force playing with peoples lives and the elements."

Taken from: **If You Love Me – Rapture – Sexual Temptations...**

Comforting The Lord

Well I do remember when we first came together tonight, You were all bloody with the crown of thorns and You put a crown of thorns on my head, too. And, then you held me and as I said I was sorry, Your wounds began to heal. Did I cause your wounds to open, Lord?

"What do you think?"

Well, I would say yes, except you gave me a crown of thorns, too. And that just doesn't fit.

"That bears repeating"

'That doesn't fit?'

"Exactly. I want you to resemble Me by doing My will. When you receive My will with humility and cooperation, you resemble and **comfort Me**, the crown fits. But, when you throw it back in My Face, with ingratitude and rebellion, well... I have to wear that crown and those stripes all over again. I know that you know this... did you forget already? It hurts Me, Clare."

Taken from: **The Lord Savors His Time With Us**

"Tell them that I need their sufferings and oppressions for innocent little ones being murdered in cold blood. In this furnace of affliction, you are removing the sufferings of so many little innocents. What is being done is beyond human, it is pure demonic. That is why so many on your channel right now are going through very, very hard times."

And again, an aside on that is, when you're a Bride, truly the Bride of Christ and truly have your heart and mind riveted on the Lord - you pick up on His suffering and on the things that He's having to go through in watching what's going on in the world. You're there to **comfort Him**. *It's a very intimate relationship.*

The Lord continued: "Part of your depression is a suffering in the subconscious for what is happening with others."

Taken from: **Terrors of ISIS, Please Intercede**

If you're called to be a Bride, you're here **to console Him**, *to be close to Him and give Him something that He longs for from all of His creatures. But most of them don't know Him or have the time of day for Him, because they are so busy with the world. So, everyone of us that shows up to comfort Him makes up for thousands who don't even care to know who He really is.*

Taken from: **The Maroon Beret**

"…just the sight of one of My Brides sitting quietly with Me on her mind, though it be interrupted by a thousand and one thoughts… still, it **brings Me much comfort** and pleasure. Here is an analogy you will all understand. When I have been hard at it all the day and night long… though My energy is without limit, My feelings are enormous. And like a pebble thrown into still waters, it vibrates all through My being."

Taken from: **The Lord Savors His Time With Us**

"I'm right beside you. Relishing your discovery of how much I love and honor you. I want to speak to My Brides about how much **comfort they bring Me.**

"My dear ones, stop obsessing over whether or not you will be taken in the Rapture. I have told you before, as long as you have broken with sin and doing your best to stay out of sin, I will take you. When you fall, come running to Me in deep contrition. I will immediately restore you."

Taken from: **You Are My Bride, My Garden Sealed**

Communion

"My daughter, My Bride - what is not possible with man is possible with God if attention is poured into the intimate relationship with Me. You see, when a soul enters this holy of holies, they become One with Me, and through **communion**, one flesh as well. And this place is so sweet that they learn not to do anything to rob them of this sweetness. They can feel Me recoil in pain when they are critical of another. This hurts them, too."

Taken from: **Prophetic Word: Rapture & Conflict in Marriage**

"Begin your morning with Me, Clare. You've fallen for the enemy's ploy to rip you away from Me. You know what a perfectly balanced day looks like. You have some wonderful people on this channel and they understand when you don't have a message up first thing."

"But Lord, I feel badly because I know they look forward to hearing from You."

"If they would say to Me, 'Jesus, Clare did not put a message up yet, would you please give me something to feed on from Your own hand?' I guarantee they will be quite surprised with what they come up with. Sitting quietly before Me, after **communion,** pen or computer in hand, pour your heart out to Me, My Brides. Speak tenderly to Me about your fears, insecurities, hurts and disappointments. And your joys, too! Thanksgiving is the key to My heart. I do so much for My own and yet they forget to thank Me. They take Me for granted like their husband of 30 years."

Taken from: **Nourishment Every Day**

I am going to take a moment here to explain something to you again. Something which bears repeating, again and again, to be sure you really, truly absorb and believe it.

The Lord has broken through my icy barriers and won over my poor, trembling heart. What I want to say is that this is in the truest sense a Monogamous Heavenly marriage, no sex, but **communion** *through receiving His Body and Blood.*

I want you all to understand: I, as a soul bear, very unique attributes endowed into me by God, and I bear that unique pattern just as if it were a fingerprint. In My Lord's heart, He also has that unique combination of attributes He imparted to me at conception even before time and eternity began.

Yes, He conceived me in His Heart, as one who would fulfill His needs for a soul to return worship to her creator in a very unique way. No other individual on this Earth can ever take my place in His Heart. He is totally mine, and I am totally His.

Now, this is what I want you to understand. You, too, are a unique masterpiece and combination of qualities that no one on this Earth can match. You are endowed with a combination of patterns just like a fingerprint, that somewhere finds its total completion and its total perfect match in the Lord.

He created you to be His spouse forever, bringing to Him the unique joys that you were endowed with when He created you. You are the ONLY one who can satisfy that desire in Him.

Because He is GOD, He is quite able to be billions of perfect sets of attributes, or individual finger prints that can only be matched by the one He conceived in His Heart. Therefore, He is totally and uniquely yours and yours alone in that combination of attributes. You are perfect for one another. A perfect fit, a pair conceived in Heaven.

Taken from: **Please, Receive My Love**

Communion

"My Precious - always put Me first. Do not allow the demons to shift your attention off of Me. This is a priceless gift that we share together. It took a long time to cultivate. It can be ruined very quickly. It is the little foxes that ruin the vine.

"This is an age-old strategy of Satan - little by little, line upon line, draw her - the Bride's attention - off. Just a little bit each day. Eventually, she's way off and the gift is gone. No crime scene, just an absence of what used to be a sweet **communion** and relationship, one that nourished and built up the Bride into a fountain of living waters.

"There are so many I long to rest in the arms of, but alas, they are taken up with the world, and have no taste for My companionship. Faithfulness draws the faithful. I will put a longing in hearts for something different, something radically different from the lives they are leading. Just as I did for you.

"First, they must grow weary of all that is around them. There must come a point where it all means nothing to them. When they are at this point, then I can lead them and guide them into that relationship. But mark these words: they must be at the point of weariness with the world and all its allurements."

Taken from: **Longing for a Radical Love for Jesus...**

"That's the exact point: I give the grace, you correspond. When I say I want My Bride's heart emptied, I mean, less attention on every little facet of life apart from Me and My will.

"For instance, vain things...like manicures, and hair, cosmetics, stylish clothing, and matching outfits and accessories. These things, unless they are necessary to your work, occupy space in your hearts and minds that could be dwelling in the abundance of My Spirit.

"You see, when you attach significance to these things, you may not be actively thinking of them, but you are easily snagged by all that relates to them. These are some of the distractions that make prayer more difficult for many. But when you cast off the yoke of your pleasures to make room for My Pleasure, then your **communion** with Me goes deeper, much deeper as matters of the flesh melt away. That's what I'm getting at.

"Not everyone is ready to let go of earthly pleasures to have more of Me, but as they seek Me in their own ways, eventually they head in that direction. I have sublime patience with all those who reach towards Me."

Taken from: **Rapture – We Are Approaching the Point of No Return**

"You see, when you put forth effort and begin to feel like you are slipping, getting tired, restless, bored... immediately you should suspect interference. These are NOT natural feelings. They are generated by demons operating under sloth and laziness to cause you to let go of your attention from Me or what I've given you to do."

But, Lord - what about the times when I feel sleepy? I thought these were ordained by You? Is this opposition, or You?

He answered, "A very good question and here discernment is needed. When I am allowing this to rejuvenate you on deeper levels, I will invite you to lay down and enter into My rest.

"For the most part, when we are together in worship and **communion**, I do not allow interference. But when you are prevented from connecting with Me, then you may suspect opposition. This is the time to pray and bind until we are once more together in sweet fellowship."

Taken from: **How the Enemy Blocks Your Creativity...**

Communion

"But you, My Bride, must be nourished on My Body and My Blood as well. This is our point of physical union: the bread becomes a part of you physically, and because of that, you and I become One. You are fruitful and bear spiritual children, as well as being strengthened for the journey.

"If you are from a liturgical church and receive **communion** from a priest, make sure to reinforce the words -' truly, Jesus - this is Your Body, and truly - this is Your Blood'. In this way, any lack of intention due to the destruction of the church and the faith from the inside out will be accounted for and made up for in your confession. Yes, you will repair for any lack of faith by your deep reverence and the faith proclamation of your heart. I will honor the sincere prayer of faith."

I think what the Lord is alluding to here is that, in this day and age there's so many different kinds of ministers and priests, who then they say, "This is Your Body and Your Blood" - they don't really mean it, they don't really believe it. And what the Lord is saying is that, YOUR confession of faith, that it truly IS His Body and Blood...that it will make up the difference for their lack of faith.

"May I say, I ALWAYS honor the sincere prayer of faith, although I might not always answer it the way you wish. But, in matters of **communion,** I will. It is a Mystery of redemption and salvation, sanctifying you for all eternity.

"I long to be received into the heart of My Bride. I long to share this **communion** with you. I long that we should be One in every possible way. Do not deny Me access to your bodies through **communion**. Do not abstain from receiving Me because you have fallen. It is the sick that need **communion** the most. First, confess to Me what you have done, sincerely from the heart repenting, and then you may receive."

Taken from: **Communion, Jesus teaches on Communion**

There is a God-shaped place inside of you that no demon can fill. There's no demon that can fit into this space and fill it perfectly. And as you get better at prayer, and recognizing the Lord's presence, you'll learn to be able to sense that place inside of you. And when it's full, and when it's empty.

You will above all, feel a deep lingering peace and feel the strength that you need because God is indeed with you. He's there, you can feel it and the words that you're hearing, through your mind when you're in **communion** *with the Lord in this way, are filling that God-shaped place inside of you.*

Taken from: **Experiencing Jesus in Dwelling Prayer**

"There is no force on Earth that can trump communion said with earnest faith and deep remembrance of My Passion. What I have given you, Clare, is far more powerful than even the words that come from your mouth.

"The intension of your heart, covered with the blood of sorrows from My death and resurrection, contains all that is necessary to defeat evil.

"It is so simple, so uncomplicated, yet so very prodigiously powerful. You, My love, must get rid of this ambivalence about its efficacy.

"There's an agony that goes on in Heaven when a communion service is said with great reverence and focus on My Passion. It is like a shiver that passes through everyone as it goes to the throne, touching each like a minuscule bold of lightening. It's a current of remembrance and graces come swiftly pouring out from the Throne Room. Like a shock wave, flipping a switch that opens the doors of grace."

Taken from: **Supernatural Power – The Communion Service**

Contentment

That is when I entered into this amazing bliss, a sense of perfect
contentment *and sweet fulfillment of all my soul has ever longed for.*
Very much like being drenched in the spiritual equivalent of warm honey
beginning at my head and running down over my being to my toes.

"…But if a soul could be penetrated to the marrow of their bones with
the Love I have for them, never would sin reign in their lives again.
The problem arises when the soul will not have Me, when they say 'this
far and no further.' That is their undoing and downfall. …You see, I
should word that slightly differently: 'If only mankind would allow
Me to penetrate their very being with the sublime love I have for him,
never again would sin enter the world. It would not be possible for a
soul saturated with My Love, to sin."

Taken from: **You Are My Heaven On Earth**

The look of **contentment** *and deep joy He had on His face…oh, it was so*
worth it to see that deep, deep **contentment** *from My Jesus.*

"You are going to experience sheer, unadulterated bliss the very
moment I take you up. You will forget about the Earth and be
encapsulated in the joy of My Heart. While I must deal with the Earth,
you will be free from dealing with the Earth and seated at the finest
banqueting table that has ever existed. We will be caught up together
in joy unspeakable. This is a celebration, Clare, a time of ecstatic joy,
for My Bride has been brought home to Me."

Taken from: **The Rapture, What You Will Experience**

"But I am not a legalistic God. I am full of mercy, understanding and
forgiveness. I want your heart. I want you to love Me, to trust Me, to
come to Me and speak with Me about your weaknesses, your sin and
insecurities and fears. I want to help you overcome these things.

"Work on your list and I will help you with each thing you are afraid to face. Use your Bible Promises to verify whether something is right or wrong.

"Watch for things in your environment, a sign from Me: a bird singing, a heart shape in your food or a leaf on the ground. A love song in the store, a sweet wash of **contentment** suddenly flooding over your soul. These are ways I encourage you and show you that I am not only with you but I approve of you and all your efforts are indeed pleasing to Me."

Taken from: **Get Ready for Your Journey**

Settle it forever then, that you are to deal directly with the Holy Spirit, and that He is to have the privilege of tying your tongue, or chaining your hand, or closing your eyes in ways that He does not seem to use with others.

Now, when you are so possessed with the living God that you are, in your secret heart, pleased and delighted over this peculiar, personal, private, jealous guardianship and management of the Holy Spirit over your life - you will have found the entranceway of Heaven.

When you are forgotten or neglected, or purposely set at naught, and you smile inwardly, glorying in the insult or the oversight, because thereby you're counted worthy to suffer with Christ - that is victory.

When your good is evil spoken of, when your wishes are crossed, your taste offended, your advice disregarded, your opinions ridiculed, and you take it all in patient, loving silence - that is victory.

*When you are **content** with any food, any raiment, any climate, any society, any solitude, any interruption by the will of God - that is victory.*

Taken from: **Why Am I Least of All**

Contentment

"In Heaven, it is another kind of dance, a dance of joy, worship and eternal thanksgiving for the living wonders of God through the fabric of your now supernatural life. You have served your term, so to speak. You have sought your higher ground, and now you are graduated into supreme bliss. But what good you have done on Earth goes on and on and on, continuing to bring forth fruit.

"It is all very much of a mystery. Try to **content** yourself in knowing that My ways are not your ways, and in all things you need not know how they work; they just work and you don't question because you trust. Just as you trust that when you turn the light switch, the light comes on. Trust also that when you pray, things happen, grace pours forth, everything proceeds from God and Our divine plan."

Taken from: **Warrior of Lover for Christ**

"Yes, this conformity will be lifted and the true essence of who you are will illuminate all around you bringing joy and worship for how fearfully and wonderfully you have been made by Me. Everywhere you go you will bring your own unique brand of joy and the gifts you have desired on this Earth will be honed to perfection, so you may create to your heart's **content**. Others will seek you out for the inspiration you have to offer them and you will be known even as you have been known."

Taken from: **You Are Unique**

Here is a trustworthy saying: whoever aspires to be an overseer desires a noble task. Now, the overseer is to be above reproach, faithful to his wife, temperate, self-controlled, respectable, hospitable, able to teach, not given to drunkenness, not violent but gentle, not quarrelsome, and not a lover of money. 1 Tim. 1:15

Do you realize what Paul has just said here? Paul has just said that being quarrelsome, being given to drunkenness, being unfaithful to his wife, is being equal with being a lover of money. That's how important this is! I've discussed with you four or five examples of how this corruptions affects the Body of Christ. It prevents people from coming into their full anointings, because they're not of the "right" social status. It cuts off prophetic movements. It cuts off all kinds of things because of appearances; because of social status and money. We'll talk more about social status in our next teaching.

This is really revealing! Paul is saying that being unfaithful to your wife is a major thing. And he is putting a "lover of money" on equal footing with that! He is categorizing that as a serious sin. He is saying that an overseer that loves money should not be an overseer! How stark are the words of Paul, wherein he says,

But Godliness with contentment is great gain. But if we have food and clothing, we will be content with that. I Tim. 6:6

Taken from: **Warrior of Lover for Christ**

"Some of you who have been expecting the Rapture have not been using your gifts, because you have presumed there wasn't time. I am asking you, My people, please do not let Me down. Get busy, there is time - you have been deceived.

"Many have said, 'Well, since the Rapture isn't for three years, I can just take it easy.' You who are thickening on your lees - you will not be taken."

Jeremiah 48:11 says that Moab has "settled on his lees"; that is, they have settled down in contentment with their circumstances."

Taken from: **Faith Without Works is Dead**

Correction, God's

"You mustn't get lax in charity or 'too big for your britches.' I try to pull you down and back in line gently. I can't help it if your pride causes you to overreact to My **corrections**. Sooner or later you will come to the point where you can tolerate it without becoming despondent, or rebellious, as you always do. Besides, what about that little flutter in your conscience that tells you something is not right? Are you listening to that? Yes, you have been listening, but be a little quicker to obey, when you hear that flutter. Keep your conscience clean. Always keep your conscience clean, and you will have very little to worry about in the realm of discernment. It is only when you stubbornly grab the bit in your teeth, and take off in your own direction, despite your husband's warning. But I must let you learn the harder lessons."

"When I chasten and correct, it is for the welfare of not only the one I chasten, but for the whole Body; that all may learn the ways of charity and to avoid evil, because evil hurts and deprives life from others."

Taken from: **Jesus Teaches on Discernment**

Lord, please make me as You say, make me willing to be made willing. Take my heart and make my heart and mind in such a way that I don't want this way that way or the other way.

What's important is what does the Lord have to say about any given subject. And if I need to take **correction**, *I want that. If He coughed, I'd run to hear it. You know? When He* **corrects** *me, I run to hear it! It's not always easy but I love Him and I want to do what's right. And there have been times in the past that we all have to go to the Lord and say, "I don't love You the way I should. I don't think... I guess, maybe I don't want...my motives aren't as pure as they should be. Lord, make me more pure and honest and sincere about what is on Your heart and mind. What's your will."*

Taken from: **My Sheep Hear My Voice**

"I do not **chasten** out of spite, but out of love, in the hopes that the soul will see the effect she has had on others. She stops when she is **chastened** and asks herself, 'Lord why did you allow this to happen?' And I am quick to reply, if she remains truly open. Her **chastening** produces in her the result that her sin produced in others, so she can taste and feel the harm she has done. In this way I give her new grace to overcome this sin and she can rise above her own selfish motives and conquer the evil that is offered to her at every moment."

Taken from: **God's Correction**

"And to those of you who feel it is your job to reveal error in My servants, be ever so careful. For I alone am qualified to judge, lest you step into My place and usurp My authority. There is still much you don't understand; there is still much quarreling and division among you. As Scripture has it, I wish to feed you on solid food, but you are not mature enough yet because you are saying 'I am with this one.' and 'I am with that one.' and 'I was baptized by this one.'

"Is this not the immaturity of a child yet in diapers? Yes I say to you it is. This is why you are lacking for sound teaching that could prepare you for My coming, because you are busying yourselves with foolish ideas. Please, please, take heed. Do not go on recklessly injuring others, there is a price to pay. I prefer to love you with blessings rather than to **correct** you with chastisements."

Taken from: **God's Correction**

The reason it took me a few days to get this out is, I was under **correction** *for something - living situations and what have you. I've got my faults, just like everyone else, and He tends not to talk to me when I'm doing something that isn't pleasing to Him, to get my attention.*

Taken from: **President Putin Takes Aim...**

Correction, God's

Ezekiel and I've seen it many times before in our marriage. I'll get a critical and impatient attitude towards him and the Lord will allow a fall or a failure to get my attention. Oh, how hard those **corrections** *can be: a twisted ankle, a fender bender, a cat gone from home for three days. Uh! They are always painful! So, the last thing in the world I want to do is give the enemy permission to sift me by abandoning charity and giving place to a critical spiritual.*

Taken from: **Refining Fires are Coming**

Many of you don't need this lesson. Many of you've got it right. But I needed this lesson.

It all began when Ezekiel was under attacked again, with yet another, strange malady that we couldn't diagnose. We had no idea what it was! We just knew that the Lord was allowing it as a **correction**, *because we got* **God's Correction** *in the Bible Promise Book. And He's always faithful to show us that.*

Anyway, the subject of pride came up. And I realized that somehow, we had opened the doors to Pride, and I soon found out that pride was the culprit for both of us. Ezekiel recognized his sin, but I couldn't see mine. Oh, I knew it was there, alright. I know I've got a lot of pride, and it surfaces when I lose my temper or get angry. I realize that that's complaining against God, because He allows these circumstances. And I know I've got lots of pride. I didn't know what manifestation of my pride the Lord was trying to draw my attention to.

"Create in me a clean heart, oh Lord. Let me be like you in all my ways."

I kept singing that over and over again, really feeling conviction, but not being able to identify its source. I came into prayer asking Him: Lord, I just don't understand what you mean by 'pride'? I'm blind to it just doesn't make sense. Please reveal it to me. I realized it must be serious, because I don't see it and I think whenever pride is the worst it's invisible to us. I was a little confused and hurt, and I didn't understand.

Taken from: **How We Miss Our Breakthroughs**

I have always believed that our trials contain two components: graces released for sufferings endured, as in Simon's Cross, and God's correction for things that should not be a part of our nature, and must be removed. We have been assailed by many supernatural attacks, which are bringing us closer and closer to the Holy Mountain. Even though they are painful, the fruit is amazing.

Taken from: **How We Miss Our Breakthroughs**

You see He wants us to live very, very simply, more simply than most poor in this country, as a testimony to others that He is our all. We do have a staff to support, so that's where our donations go. Satan knows how we think...'Oh, It's little, it's not a big deal.' Oh, yes, little IS a big deal. If we are not faithful in the little things, how can we be entrusted with the bigger ones?

And this last **correction** *was the capstone on all the others, and in all honesty I don't see how even the God of endless patience could allow any more presumption, because He's gone way out of His way to warn me. I have to shape up, dear friends, because you are watching, and I am now accountable to the Body for my behavior. It just has to stop.*

I suppose if you weren't watching... and just God and Heaven were watching, I would be more tempted to give in. But you ARE watching, and because I love you all and want to be a better example of God's grace at work, I just can't let my vice go any further.

Taken from: **The Precipice of Presumption**

Courage

"Please, make your choices wisely. I am forever at your side calling you upward. But the climb is painful! Once you make up your mind to forsake your pride and defensiveness, I lift you up into My arms and carry you all the way to the top. This is My Heart's desire.

"Will you come with Me? Or abandon Me, like so many others have done. Do you have **courage**, character and relentless honesty with yourself?"

Taken from: **How a Root of Bitterness Can Change Your Destiny and DNA**

"As you grow in virtue, I will begin to release to you the secret dreams of your heart. The pure ones, not the concocted ones that feed the ego, the bank account, or your popularity. No, the ones from Me, planted there to someday be activated and grow into a tree that bears sweet fruit and shade for the birds of the field.

"Some of you have had glimpses of this place but not the *courage* to pursue it. The **courage** will come from Me. I will anoint you, open doors and bring you along by a way you've never thought possible. I will lead you down crooked paths that result in a straight line to the destiny I planned for you before you were sent into this world."

Taken from: **Your Very Special Destiny**

And I had a thought here I wanted to share with you. I know that when I was younger and single and raising four children, wow - I had a lot of temptations. Not only was I needy for affection, but my hormones were also very strong. When I found myself at a point where I could compromise, one of the things that gave me **courage** *to pass that temptation by was comparing the object of my affections to the beauty of Jesus.*

Taken from: **Temptations Against Purity**

"This is the heritage of the children of God. Freedom from oppression and the constraints of the enemy. There are many, many times when I am testing your **courage** and your charity, and so it is essential that you remain close to Me so that you know the season you are in. Is this a time to be conciliatory or a time to stand your ground?"

Taken from: **How Prayer Fails**

"Yes. Binding and loosing prayers are very effective for stopping demon traffic in your home. As a believer, living in your house, you have rights over evil and you can pray against it and receive angelic assistance. But you are somewhat limited by the workings of evil spirits that are there by consent of the others who live in the house. Still, your prayers are powerful and very often whoever you are praying for, removing their demons and their company, they don't know what hit them. Just all of a sudden, the oppression and impulse to do evil leaves - with no explanation.

"This is the heritage of the children of God. Freedom from oppression and the constraints of the enemy. There are many, many times when I am testing your **courage** and your charity, and so it is essential that you remain close to Me so that you know the season you are in. Is this a time to be conciliatory or a time to stand your ground?"

Taken from: **How Prayer Fails**

"It truly is well spoken that '**Courage** is not the absence of fear, but rather the judgment that something else is more important than fear.' That 'something else' is the substance of your dreams, and within that is contained the DNA code for you to attain impossibilities with My Grace."

Taken from: **God's Will for You Involves Your Heart Dreams**

Courage

"You have been chosen to lead, to guide and to fight against evil. You are not among the left behind because you did not give yourselves to Him. No. You are among the called and chosen Remnant.

"Some of you are warriors and have been created for such a time as this. For those of you who have been called to engage in the battle to restore our nation, the Lord wants you to know He is with you. You are not fighting alone. His arm is mighty and powerful, not only to make you invisible but to confuse and defeat the enemy.

"Begin all your battles with prayer and end them with thanksgiving. Through you He is going to raise this nation from the ashes and restore her to righteousness.

"Don't let anyone belittle you. You were not negligent, you were chosen by Him to be warriors for righteousness and even to give witness to Jesus through martyrdom. Be **courageous**. Let no one demean you. Don't believe the enemy's lies, for he surely will torment you with lies to try and discourage you. Stand tall in the Lord; He is with you."

Taken from: **Remember These Things & Remnant Church**

"Some of you have anointings. You can feel them rising up in you. Things to do you've never had the **courage** to do before. You will be opposed, but ignore the opposition and hold to the inspiration. Protect it like a newborn babe, for surely it is just that full of life and vulnerable to the scorn and contempt of those who prefer to stay where they are and not tackle anything that could result in failure.

"But the wisdom you have garnered about the operation of the enemy against you is something you need to set in concrete and not allow the enemy to steal from your memory."

Taken from: **How Does a Fall Happen?**

Now, that (part of the binding) prayer is important, because the longer you're a Christian, the longer you're a human, the more times you're hurt. And when we're hurt we tend to withdraw, and our charity begins to cool down.

So, the first item on that list is to restore Love for Others, because that's the most important thing that we need. We can be sick, but love others and it's still powerful. We can be weak and love others and it's still powerful. We can have **courage***, but if we don't love others, it's useless. We can have focus and faith, but without love - it's not effective.*

Purity. We can have a pure heart, but no love. And we can be fractured and damaged, rather than whole.

We can have peace and joy, but no love for others - and some people might dispute that and I might agree with you - but the point is: without love, we're USELESS. We're like clanging gongs.

So, there you go. Restore love for others is a number one item on that list. Then health, strength, vigor, **courage***, focus, faith, purity of heart, wholeness, peace and joy to the places the enemy, the world and our own flesh have defiled.*

Taken from: **Binding Demons Teaching**

"I am proud of you, My Brides. I see rising up before Me a glorious Church, without spot, wrinkle or blemish. I see rising up before Me the Love of My life, bedecked with jewels.

"Go forth in **courage** and commitment and know that your love for your brothers and sisters is the Fuller's bleach that will remove every last stain from your garments."

Taken from: **Glorious Bride Arising w/Her Torch...**

Courage

"Many of You are scared to death to introduce Me to others. But nothing could be more simple, if You go about it as My friend and theirs."

Then He began to offer a suggestion on how to approach them: 'Let me introduce you to My friend, Jesus. He is with you everywhere you go, He listens to every cry and shares in all your laughter. He rejoices with you in the springtime...when new life is budding out of the Earth. He rejoices with you as you lie in piles of golden leaves and with the wild lavender asters that dot the fields in the Fall.

'He laughs with you at the antics of the new puppy, and cries with you when you must say good-bye to your beloved pet. Oh, He is so present to you, my friend, so familiar to you, you don't even notice Him - but He is here. When someone passes away, He upholds you with infusions of peace, allowing you to go through the steps of saying good-bye to your loved one. He slowly releases the sorrow in you, so you are not overwhelmed. When He brings a new life into your womb, He provides all that is needed to raise that child.

'Oh, everything He does is underpinning Your life, and He is so close... and so much a part of you, you don't recognize Him, until it is His time to reveal His presence to you.

"Then the joy of discovery is there. 'You WERE there when my mother passed! You WERE there when I made that career decision that changed my life! You WERE there when I went to the pound to get a kitten. You have ALWAYS been there, and I never knew it. You were there in the ER when I thought I was dying, and You held me securely so that fear did not overwhelm me. You were there when I was all alone after that abusive relationship. You were even there during that, waiting for me to say 'enough!'

'You gave me the **courage** to begin a new life! You encouraged me that I COULD do it. You were there when I walked into the thrift store needing new clothes with only a few dollars and You filled my bag with everything I needed and then some! In fact, You were the one who inspired the wealthy lady to get rid of those beautiful clothes she never wears. You even measured the timing, so I would walk in just as they were putting her clothes on the rack.'"

Taken from: **Introduce Me, Not Religion…**

"Well, My Love, I am coming now to take My Bride. The one who harkened to the whispers of her heart, the one who longs for Me, the one who weeps at My Feet for what I must suffer.

"Lift up your eyes My Beloved ones. Soon, we will embrace and soar to the Celestial City, where your reward awaits you. And, for those who must stay behind, I say, **Courage**. I will be with you. Great will your exploits be before man, and great shall be the harvest you reap. I will never leave you or forsake you. Rather, I will equip you for this Battle and you shall take plunder from the mighty.

"And, when I return - you shall receive your everlasting reward."

Taken from: **You Have Rejected My Rule**

"Your adversary has thousands of years of practice corrupting human nature. Stay in obedience to Me and you will be protected. Yield up your will, 'Lord, please reveal to me that this is not pleasing to You and I will stop.' And expect Me to do it. Expect Me to reveal My will. There is little as pleasing to Me than a soul who values obedience above their own desires.

"I bless you now to see through My eyes the things that you are giving your time to and the **courage** to let go of them if need be."

Taken from: **Jesus Speaks on The God Dimension…**

Dancing with Jesus

I want to take a moment here, guys, to mention something, because there's been some terrible lying and slandering against the relationship that we have with Holy Spirit and with Jesus.

So, I'm going to take a moment to establish something again, something that somehow my critics don't seem to be able to hear, though I've said it so many times before. While the relationship with Jesus and Holy Spirit is very, very romantic, it is even more pure and never is there a hint of impropriety or sexual innuendos.

Jesus is a virgin and so is Holy Spirit, and anyone who cannot see or receive that needs a grace to deliver them from unclean obsessions with sex. God is pure, love for God is pure, and if you ever have any hints of sexual behavior, understand you are dealing with either a demon or your own mind that needs deliverance. People who take these messages and twist them to be sexual have serious psychological problems and need help. Please pray for them.

There is no sex in Heaven, just to reiterate what I've told you so many times before - there's no sex in Heaven. There is no sexual relationship with any vision of Heaven, God or the angels, or saints. If you are seeing something like that, you are looking at a demonic manifestation. Rebuke it and renounce it in the Name above all names, in the Name of Jesus. And if you must, call upon the Holy Angels to remove those filthy unclean creatures.

So - that said, I can continue on with this message, knowing that you're not going to take it the wrong way.

Holy Spirit is a wonderful man. Very clean cut, blond hair, blue eyes, tall and slightly Nordic looking. He is a total gentleman, totally focused love and totally ours, in a very unique way. Both yours and mine individually.

As I have explained before, there is an imprint from God - this is what I've been instructed in. An imprint from God, a combination of unique attributes that each of us possesses, and none of us is identical.

For that reason, God finds consolation in each of our unique personalities and you satisfy His longing for Love and Worship in a way no other soul can. He longs for you to see Him as the God He is, in the form of a man, and for you to cultivate your own relationship with Him. The Comforter.

It has taken me a long, long time to finally accept His Person in the image of a man. For years I kept Him at arms length, but He continued to try and break through all my silly fears. Tonight, I finally relaxed with Him as we danced and just fell head over heels in love with Him! Oh, how gentle He is! He gave me lots of time to adjust to His person, rather than **dancing with Jesus.**

Taken from: **Holy Spirit's Desire for You…**

I see I've gotten nowhere with You, Lord.

"On the contrary, you have made Me very, very happy because now there are Brides who truly believe and want to **dance with Me.** I was beginning to feel like a wallflower." He made a sad face, and I laughed.

Oh, that's too funny.

"Yes, but it is true! The music plays, I sway - but My Bride…runs away!"

Oh, no. You are making rhymes.

"That's right, and some will not forget those words and press in. OK?"

Taken from: **Persevere in Intimacy With the Lord…**

Dancing with Jesus

Okay, so this is a beautiful concept that I want to share with you, about perceiving flowing thoughts drifting through our minds. We can tell the source of those thoughts by their character. If they stir up fear and anxiety, then they're from the evil ones. But, if they stir up peace and wisdom and good fruits, then they're from the Lord.

In the same way - we have streaming visions. We'll see flowing pictures and they will be flowing pictures that are good and holy and bring us into the presence of the Lord. For instance, one night I was praying and I saw clouds and angels holding a dance floor in the heavens. And, then I saw myself **dancing with Jesus** *on that dance floor in the heavens. Now, that's something I never would have thought of!*

So, it's more likely, when you think of things that are that outrageous, that it's really coming from God, and not yourself. Because, it's not something in the ordinary course of things that you'd be thinking about. So, we're going to see flowing pictures, and those flowing pictures are an invitation to us to enter into the vision with the Lord. Just as the flowing thoughts are an invitation to enter into a conversation with the Lord, and listen to Him.

Taken from: **Clare Shares her Insights on Mark Virkler...**

Oh, the Lord Himself was so immersed in my love for Him! It was a sight to behold, I could feel His warm presence wrapped around me, in of course such a pure and holy way. But when I caught a glimpse of His Holy Face, I was just amazed. **We were dancing** *to Terry MacAlmon's songs, especially "Praise Him." And Jesus' eyes were closed as He rested His head on mine and was the perfect picture of someone totally transfixed in Love.*

Oh, there is one verse of a song we listened to that says, "Let me pour my love on you, the fragrance of my heart." And that always makes me ashamed, and I flinch when I hear that line, because I don't see my heart as being fragrant at all. I see it riddled with faults that make me recoil at the thought of pouring those on My Jesus. But when I saw how He was enjoying the contents of my heart, all that began to change. He must have some kind of filter!

As I gazed upon His sweet face, totally absorbed in me, I began to reckon that there must be something fragrant there or He wouldn't be so absorbed. As I was thinking these things, I saw tears rolling down His cheeks and I heard Him say, "If only you knew how much consolation you bring Me. This is My Heaven on Earth."

Taken from: **You Are My Heaven on Earth..**

I let the song just run over and over again, and **we were slow dancing**, *just kind of swaying gently back and forth to the music. I drifted off into a sweet reverie with the Lord, my forehead was nuzzled under His beard. Every once and a while, I'd draw back and our eyes would meet and He was becoming peaceful and calm. As the song repeated itself, I began to see that His suffering was alleviated and the pain surrounding His Head was beginning to dissipate and I even spotted a twinkle of joy in His eyes.*

I told Ezekiel what was going on and he said, "I don't think we know how much the Lord suffers with us, how many times He cries with us." *And right after he said that, the Lord began to speak to me.*

"Never underestimate the power behind consoling your God. Do you know the heartbreaks I must suffer everyday, and when I come into the throne room of your heart and find you waiting there for Me, just longing to be with Me. Oh, you cannot imagine how you brighten My Heart."

Taken from: **Oh, How You Comfort My Heart!**

Dancing with Jesus

I saw myself **dancing with Jesus** *on that dance floor in the heavens. Now, that's something I never would have thought of! So, it's more likely, when you think of things that are that outrageous, that it's really coming from God, and not yourself.*

Taken from: **Clare's insights on Mark Virkler's, 4 Keys to Hearing God Part 2**

Because the devil will try to find all kinds of ways to turn us off. And I thought for a minute, 'This worshipful presence of the Bride must be highly threatening to the kingdom of darkness, or he wouldn't try so hard to kick me out of it.' The enemy has tried to lie to me again and again that I am shallow and pleasure seeking for wanting to **dance with Jesus**, *hold Him and comfort Him.*

I wanted to take a moment and clarify a few of the forms of worship that I've witnessed and experienced - there are so many. These are just three that I can really verify.

There are times when we enter joyously into worship and find ourselves in His arms, or before the Throne, and the Glory is so thick you could cut off a piece and wrap it in foil. There are other times when travail and holy grief take us over and all we can do is cry.

And then, there are other times when we experience something like a glance into His holy face, and we really, really, really connect with Him on a deeper level and we become so love-sick, our heart just drops out of us, and we're left an empty shell - so great is our longing for Him.

Taken from: **Your Very Own Gift of Worship**

Today, as I came into worship, (and actually, that was yesterday) I felt strongly the need to be present to the Lord as His Bride. I was soon feeling and seeing myself in His arms, moving to the music and really getting ministry from the songs as I sang them to Him in my heart. I knew He was singing some of them back to me as well, and all my fears and false guilts just melted away.

I began, "Thank you, Lord, for the extra strength and wonderful **dance** *time."*

Jesus answered me, "I was hoping you'd like it. I sing to you from My heart, you know. I pick those songs because they truly mean something to Me. They convey how I feel about you."

Taken from: **Lord, What Are You Doing With Us in this Hour?**

"Tell them I am coming for them and they will never know the kind of love I have for them until they are on this dance floor in Heaven with Me. In the meantime, I would like them to make practice runs. Simply go to the holy place of your imagination and visualize a grand ballroom with Me standing there in full, formal, military attire, saying, **'May I have this dance?'**

"Bowing before you, I take your hand in Mine, and gently hold you as we begin to gracefully waltz around the floor. No matter that on Earth you could not dance, here in My arms it is second nature to you as we glide along. No matter that you are a man on Earth - for these moments in Heaven, you are My Bride.

"As you settle into this gentle place with Me, our eyes meet and you begin to feel a fleeting wave of admiration coming from My eyes. Being shy, you dare not look into My eyes for very long... yet. But, as the evening wears on, our eyes meet, more and more until we are both gazing into one another's eyes, drinking from the deep pools of pure celestial love for one another."

Taken from: ***Jesus said,*** **"May I Have This Dance?"**

Death

"Obedience in the little things leads to obedience in the big things, and for those left behind, obedience may mean life or **death**. So, now is the time to seek My will, to be sure you are moving forward in obedience and not in self-will."

Taken from: **Are You Wise?**

He began: "The **death** of America, spiritually and physically."

"You know well what is being played on the surface, saber rattling, exercises near the North Pole, all of that is just for show.

"The man people call your president, the man of stealth and intrigue who gains office by deceit is merely playing to the masses, so that when destruction comes, it will look authentic - when in reality it is no more than a superficial show to cover for the destruction of all sovereignties, that only one may dominate the world.

"He has done a stellar job of destroying you, America. This I have allowed - you have played the harlot and slept with every passerby - while I, your Husband, stood by as each had their turn in our bed."

Taken from: **The Death of America Revisited...**

"My rules are not crippling. Sin is crippling. My rules foster and protect life, not only in the next world but right now, here in this dimension. Choose life or choose **death**, but understand: any way that contradicts My way will result in **death**, despair and failure."

Taken from: **Overcoming the Deceptions of This Age...**

"I have spoken with you all about this dynamic, where a soul makes a choice before birth and must live with that and die a premature **death**. These are things that will only be understood in Heaven, looking back. But I share them with you now in hopes that you will not grow despondent over the suffering of others you cannot bring comfort to.

"There is a purpose for everything, My children. There is a very specific purpose and dynamic for every single thing that takes place in the lives of every single person."

Taken from: **Suffering – Real Work in the Realm of the Spirit**

"Clare, the saddest part of all of this is that there are so many who never took the time to know Me. I knocked and knocked, but no one came to the door. Now **death** is at the door. Very much unknown to them, it is at their door. And really, for most, it is too late. They have rejected My attempts so many times that now their hearts are hardened and impenetrable.

"There will be so many that will not even be awake; they will go in their sleep. This is going to be the greatest tragedy Earth has ever known. Never were there so many souls on the Earth, never was there My provision on Earth for their salvation. The tragedy is that the opportunities to live in Heaven with Me forever have been lost to these souls and they will look back and see what they pushed away time and time again.

"There will be no excuses. 'Bible fundamentalists were too harsh. Others were not intellectual enough. Others were not loving enough. Pentecostals were too intense.' None of these will fly, for I sent them Mother Theresa's, missionaries, bishops and priests - highly trained and still in love with Me. Evangelists and miracles of healing. They have seen in this world the entire gamut of My servants and heard their miraculous, self-sacrificing stories and still pushed Me away. So indeed, there will not be one excuse."

Taken from: **The Day of the Lord is Upon Us**

Death

"So, when you live your life by the world's standards you are walking in darkness, snuffing out your light and reflecting that which is deteriorating and bound for **death**. Oh, highly precious souls, imprints of the God Who created you, your worth is immeasurable! And nothing short of My **death** on the Cross can atone for your wayward ways and bring you back into the Light of eternity.

"What is needed from you is to walk in nakedness before man and God, that your light might shine. When you discover My love for you and realize who you truly are in My presence, your value system changes immediately. What was once highly prized is seen for what it is: unclean rags hanging from your body. Like a leper, the contamination of the world smothers the light given you at conception.

"Open yourself to My Love. I am not like any man you have ever known; all are corrupt and lacking in authentic love. When I love you I do not mix My love with earthly values. I look at the beauty and uniqueness of My Father, whose substance formed you. And I long to redeem you from among this decaying world and have you in Heaven with Me for eternity."

Taken from: **Choose God & Sanctity...**

"Yes, there is a fragrance about a soul that continually yields to Me. It is sweet and comforting to Me. So many, I can't even get close to. The poison of rancor is so intense I cannot stand to be close. See to it, all My People, that the odor of rancor does not proceed from your thoughts. Yes, the activity of your brain emanates this fragrance. When it is sweet, it is as if I were walking through a well-kept garden. When it is noxious, it is the odor of **death** and decaying flesh. You can hardly understand how terribly bad it is."

Taken from: **Sweet Aroma of Holiness...**

"I know what you're thinking," He said, "I can hear your ruminating. I also hear the enemy whispering and insinuating. There are many who wish much evil and **death** on you both, but they will go unsatisfied.

"In fact, I am arranging trials for them that will take their attention off of you. But you know, Clare, there are always more haters and nay-sayers. I appreciate your prayers for them; truly they are dark souls in need of Me."

Taken from: **Restoration Will Come**

"Then there is the additional influence of chemistry in the substances carried in forced inoculations. There is a huge amount of damage done by these 'vaccines' and in some cases electronic devices. As these children mature and vaccines produce the intended result, pharmaceutical companies benefit from all the drugs made to control this engineered madness, which they began in the first place.

"These are done en masse so that an entire generation comes forward that is hell bent on **death** and destruction. This is the generation of the young people now, in this age. It takes every moral fibre to resist finding a violent or drug related outlet for repressed feelings. That is why so many children are committing suicide, whether intended or accidental, from drug overdoses. I have much mercy and compassion on them.

"Oh Clare, it is truly tragic what has been done by the elites. The end result in these days is a culture of **death** and destruction and when the appropriate time comes, mankind will be set aflame with dark matter and demonic manifestations such as have never have been seen. Even now it is on the increase."

Taken from: **Why a Soul Rejects Love...**

Death

I was sick many days in the spirit during the preparation of this report. If you read in Daniel, he also got sick when God began to reveal certain things to him. There are things of darkness that are too horrible to write down. Horrible forces of **death** and the smell of decaying flesh, flash fires of hell and deep pits with no bottoms. Evil laughter of demonic forces everywhere and when you die, my friend, if you're a sinner you go to a living hell.

People, repent of the work of darkness before it's too late! For we all shall stand before the judgment seat of God some day. I feel right now to pray, by the power of the Holy Spirit, and to pray for you out there. I pray in the mighty Name of Jesus, if you're a sinner, if you're in the occult that you'll repent right now and give your heart unto the Lord Jesus Christ and be saved from these sins and these abominations unto God. Amen. (Mary K Baxter)

*Oh, Lord. Tonight, I felt such sick pain in Your heart. And it occurred to me: You have said about the timing of the Rapture, You are extending the time in tiny increments and then You explained to me that that means by minutes. That being the case, at every moment You must re-evaluate and make a decision. Every moment of every soul on the face of the Earth, and make a decision in that moment, whether to go forward to the eventual **death** of millions - or whether to wait. Oh, how painful!*

Jesus began, "It is still My Father who makes the choice, Clare. He is the one Who must re-evaluate moment by moment, as I stand in the gap. But My heart is heavy with sorrow.

"What you have seen glimpses of, in Pam's dream, by the ocean in California is the devastation of My heart when it finally all comes down."

He's talking about the beach scene, where His heart was so crushed by all the deaths and the Father is comforting Him, there by His side. Oh, how shall we EVER understand these things? The Trinity is so immense, and yet SO personal!

Taken from: **Mercy! Comet Will Only Graze Earth**

"...Did I not create creation just to bring you joy?

"I did, and neither did **death** or suffering enter in until your ancestors fell. That was not My plan. Yes, what I created for you was a perfect world. One where the animals ate from your hand, the fish rushed to greet you in the water, the flowers turned their petals and followed you. Everything was full of Divine Life, because that is what held it together, uncorrupted. My Love held it together and My Love still holds it together, though it is monumentally corrupted by Satan."

"Yes, what must come to pass is a terrible thing - a terrible thing. But this is the refining fire I must prepare My people with. Every one must pass through this fire, even as the Earth passes through it.

"Yet, I will never abandon them. Never. I walk beside each one, even those who do not call on My name. I walk with them in hopes that they will finally confess their sin and come to Me fully repentant, ready to start a new life. Even if it begins with the body's physical death - yes, even that."

Taken from: **Mercy! Comet Will Only Graze Earth**

"I know you have no confidence in yourself. But I am here to help you. I know you've heard that before and still gone your own way, that is why the lessons are getting stronger, clearer, with more dire consequences. Clare, ask Sister **Death**."

Taken from: **The Precipice of Presumption**

Demons

When you live with someone, there's familiarity - like leaving your towel crumpled up on the floor, (which he doesn't do by the way) or leaving your shoes out in the middle of the room - which I DO do, by the way! There's a point where we lose patience with our partner and not even saying the demeaning words in an out-loud conversation but play out your dialogue on the inside. That is depreciating him.

*The **demons** are working on that little job, the little foxes that spoil the vine. We're a vine together, the two are one. The little foxes are coming along and biting the grapes and spoiling them on the vine. These interior dialogues are going on inside of you and don't kid yourself: the **devils** are working just as hard as you as they are him. He might be thinking, "Why doesn't she have dinner on time? For Pete's sake, she knows I don't like to eat that - why is that on the table?" There are a million different ways we could show disrespect or downgrade our spouses that are just secret, quiet things going on inside the heart.*

Taken from: **Honoring Your Husband**

*But the Lord will allow and does allow deception. The **demons** have been around way longer than us. These are created beings with high intelligence, they watch every move of every eyelash and they've been able to do that for over 6, 7, 8 thousand years now. So, they know the Scriptures inside out.*

Taken from: **My Sheep Hear My Voice**

*Another medicine against fear is singing praises to the Lord. That accomplishes two things: it helps us to worship the Lord and be in His presence and also helps us to recall His faithfulness... and it infuriates the **demons**. I love to infuriate the **demons**! I think they deserve to be infuriated as much as we can do it. Just by singing praises to the Lord with thanks, it infuriates them. A lot of times that will break it. The*

demons *can't stand to be around all of that so they'll leave. Whatever you're battling against will just vaporize.*

Taken from: **Have No Fear of the Future...**

"Don't despair over your past mistakes. The past is in the past. Leave it there, for your good, for My good, and for the good of all. Forge ahead into your calling. Be fearless. Do not be swayed by what you imagine anyone has to say about you or your work. For I am with you. Scrupulosity kills the anointing. It pitches the soul back into the mire of their sins and shortcomings. Let not this evil scourge enter your heart or commandeer your thoughts at any time. These things strictly originate from the **demon** world. They do not come from Me.

"My conviction is gentle, wise and easily received. Theirs pits you against yourself. How foolish to reminisce over past failures, or should I say, even just perceived failures, because they will use anything with a hook on it. They fish for creepy crawly things to dredge up and hook you into deep self-condemnation. Even as an alligator grabs its victim and rolls with it over and over and over, then pulling it down into the deep and leaving it there to rot - so do these despicable creatures torment My children's souls, leaving them under some miry ledge to decay until the time is ripe for these leviathan creatures to come back and feed on them again.

"Yes, they gain power and momentum each time they succeed. They feed on suffering just as surely as you are strengthened by righteousness and joy. So, do not allow yourself to be drawn into this combat with the evil ones. Recognize it and see it coming. Bind it. Bind them and put them in their place. May they be tormented even as they wish to torment you."

Taken from: **Condemnation is the Food of Demons**

Demons

*But, our insidious enemy, the **vicious ones**, the **accusers of the brethren** are constantly using this against us in our walk. We know when we offend God with some thought, action or thought action. This is His gift to us, to keep us spiritually healthy. But what do we do once we've recognized our fault? Well, I can tell you for years, I would go run and hide. I've been walking with the Lord 25-30 years and I can't tell you how I spent many, many years running and hiding after I blew it.*

*Generally speaking, we tend to cower and avoid Him, just as Adam and Eve did in the garden. The **evil ones** are standing there encouraging us to do what we somehow suspect or know is wrong. They're saying, "Oh, it's okay, really. You can do this. God won't be offended. Or, "He'll forgive you, really. It's just a little thing."*

*And once we've committed the fault, the **devils** come back and say, "See? You're good for nothing, you can't be faithful for one hour. Now God is angry with you - He won't hear YOUR prayers! You aren't worthy of Him. And forget ministering to others!"*

At this point, we run for cover instead of running into His waiting arms. All the while, HE'S looking on with mercy and compassion. This fall, which He most likely allowed to humble us, is our opportunity to grow in humility and faith. He's waiting with open arms and kisses, to receive us back into fellowship, wanting to strengthen us and assure us of His love, which is impossible to earn. He loves us because He is God. And Love is His nature -He can't help Himself. He IS Love! He created us for fellowship with Him, He enjoys our company. He's not like an earthly father, waiting for us to prove how good we are before He showers His love and approval on us. So, what are we do to? The sooner we forget ourselves and turn to Him, knowing that He will forgive and restore our peace, the sooner we'll be happy again.

Taken from: **Tag-Along Monsters...**

*There was a 6-year-old boy I saw in an interview. The interviewer asked if he had seen the devil and the boy said, "Yes". Then he asked, "What do **demons** do?" The boy answered, "They mostly sit on people's shoulders and tell them lies." These **demons** are professional murmurers.*

Taken from: **Rapture Delayed, Dealing with Disappointment**

*I just want to say that the most threatening thing in the world to the **devils,** the **demons**, to the kingdom of darkness is a discerning Christian in intimate communion with the Lord. That is a VERY, VERY threatening person. So, they do everything they can to keep you from becoming intimate with the Lord and learning how to discern the truth from falsehood.*

Be encouraged, press in and know that the Lord is mercifully waiting to pick you up every time you fall.

Taken from: **Tag-Along Monsters...**

Well please, Lord - give me some names. Like the handles of the demons with which I can grab hold of them, which I can use to clear the air. "

I was taught early in my Christian walk that it was important to have the name of the demon that was oppressing you. And so I asked Him to give me some handles.

I heard "**Lying spirits, Beguiling spirits. These are your major enemies. Fog, Brain Fog. Curtains. Voices. Vehicles of Disturbance. Hindering, Obstacles and all Vehicles of Demonic Oppression.**"

Taken from: **Demonic Obstacles against Hearing and Seeing Jesus**

Demons

"Don't engage in 'I've gotta fix this, I've gotta fix that.' These are the **devil's** ploys to draw you into projects that will tire you and deplete you of your spiritual peace. They very often require trips to the store or shopping on the net. This is very, very, very detrimental to a spiritual person and alas, they don't pick up on it; they think it is just innocent work that has to be done. But Satan knows better so he commands his **demons** to work on guilt over projects that should be done…"

Taken from: **Jesus is Coming, Draw the Line…**

"Guilt and condemnation are the number one tools used by the enemy to disable a Christian. This is what the **demons** are taught, 'If you want to bring a Christian down and make them stop, bring up their sins.' And sadly, it works! But forewarned is forearmed. If you know this is the area of attack, you can come before Me repentant and go into battle fully equipped. What better way to demoralize a man that to make him feel badly about himself? Do you see? You are victims of psychological warfare if you give into the lie that your sins are not forgiven.

"… It should be clear to you by now: condemnation belongs to **demons**, conviction belongs to My Spirit. When I convict you, there is a sweet, sweet sense of being sorry for having offended Me, and with it comes a real desire not to repeat the act, and I am with you in that moment, encouraging you to call on Me for strength in the future.

"When the enemy condemns you, it is to convince you how bad and worthless you are, that you are doomed and can never be used by God, you are utterly lost and useless. Along with that comes overwhelming shame and a desire to run from Me instead of to Me. Once you are convinced to run from Me, the spiral goes down swiftly into hopelessness."

Taken from: **Do You Feel Condemned? …**

"These times you are living in are thick with deception, and you can be sure the rule books are open wide, as the **demons** gather round to choose their arrows. They are tipped with the poison of pride and legalism, the ways of the Pharisees and Sadducees. And when they penetrate, they release a 'flesh rotting' disease targeted for your very hearts, that the tender life I live inside of you be utterly destroyed and replaced with pride and stone---cold knowledge.

"Those who have been afflicted with this poison will be wrestling with scruples, doubts, fears and find that they no longer have any peace. This should be a sign to them that poison is afoot in their spirits; no peace is a preeminent sign of **demonic** influence. You have been taught this for months now, so do not fail to recognize when your peace is stolen, you have taken in a *demonic* poison."

Taken from: **These Times Are Thick With Deception**

For though we live in the world, we do not wage war as the world does. The weapons we fight with are not the weapons of the world. On the contrary, they have divine power to demolish strongholds. We demolish arguments and every pretension that sets itself up against the knowledge of God, and we take captive every thought to make it obedient to Christ.

II Corinthians 10:3-5

Jesus continue, "When you speak My words, you are speaking as one who is creating or bringing into being, even as I spoke the world into existence. Therefore, your mighty weapon penetrates weapons of the air and dismantles what has been constructed by the demons and renders it powerless against you."

Taken from: **Spiritual Warfare: 10 – The Armor of God**

Depression, Discouragement

"The enemy is plotting waves of **discouragement** and distraction. **Discouragement** comes first, leading you into seeking distractions. Do not fall for his ploys, rather stay secure in what I've given you - not only your prayer times but the messages also. Keep your focus like the captain of a great ship on the ocean. One degree off can result in the wrong destination."

Taken from: **Resist Gossip & Judgment...**

"I want to talk to you about dissatisfaction and how it ruins a soul and turns them bitter. In life there are many ups and downs, and when a soul can weather these in equanimity she is way far ahead. So many things arise from dissatisfaction, bitterness, complaining, negativity, **discouragement**, fatigue; it spawns multiple symptoms that slacken a souls resolve and pulls them backwards."

Taken from: **Follow Your Dreams...**

The Lord continued: "Part of your **depression** is a suffering in the subconscious for what is happening with others."

*Yeah, I've been hit with some nasty **depression**, and Ezekiel as well. So, part of it's a suffering for what's happening with others around the world.*

"You are all united by My Spirit and the Spirit is strong on little children - you are intercepting some of their cries and pleas. Many of them are too little to understand what is going on. I cannot tell you how much comfort you bring by your intercession and the cross you are carrying right now."

Taken from: **Terrors of ISIS, Pleas Intercede**

"Nevertheless, don't stress over what you cannot complete. Do what you can and rest in My presence, and I will make up the remainder in grace. One of the most serious preparations you can make, any of you can make, is to prepare your hearts for Heaven. In Heaven there is no slander, no backbiting, no jealousy, no fear, no gossip, no hopelessness, and no **depression**. In Heaven there is supreme bliss. And as you choose to dwell in Me, you will have a taste of this bliss."

Taken from: **Maintain Your Purity and Light, My Bride**

"I am telling you this now so you will not grow weary in well doing. What are your crosses? Surly people who mock you, inconveniences like flat tires, frustrations when things aren't working for you, mental and spiritual pain, when you are travailing for others and they simply show no signs of conversion. You mothers and fathers are suffering greatly, because the world is so enticing to your children you just can't compete with it or their peers. Mental health, **depression**, anxiety. Some of you are carrying almost unbearable crosses. Cry out to Me and I will strengthen you."

Taken from: **Carry the Cross, Don't Judge…**

"This will be the day your life is transformed from something singular and special to something eternal and glorious. It will be the culmination of all the plans and dreams you never even knew you had. It will be the day you take on the mantle of Glory given to those who have left themselves and the world totally behind. It is the day I look forward to, because you shall know even as you are known. This will be the day you leave pain, suffering, darkness, doubt and **depression** totally behind you as you walk into the life I've always longed for you to have. I know every particle of your DNA, I know what makes you exceedingly happy and fulfilled. I know your very purpose and on this day it will be your all-in-all. The angels will rejoice as we walk down the aisle, our life-long goal together met."

Taken from: **The Deeper Meaning of Our Wedding Day…**

Depression, Discouragement

"I want to speak to you about Grace and it's all sufficient significance in your lives. Many, if not all of you, My Precious Brides, find fault with yourselves and fall into the trap of comparing yourself to someone who has an outstanding attribute, but in fact you know nothing of their lives. This comparison leads to **discouragement** over who I have fashioned you to be and leaves you open to the sin of envy, as well as emulating them so you distort who you truly are.

"Firstly, I want you to know that no one is as they seem on the outside. No, not one. There is a hidden side to each of you, the side you have either conquered or are still hiding, hoping that it will some day die. While you are traveling this road of life I have given you graces for the moment, they are unlike the graces I have given anyone else, because you are My own unique creation."

Taken from: **My Graces Accomplish All Things, Even Prayer**

"They (demons) cause us to drift apart, they cause you to judge others, and they represent Me as a cruel taskmaster. Do not buy into these lies about My character, do not walk around gloomy and condemned. This is the fruit from listening to the evil ones.

"And unfortunately, the evil ones find many willing vessels who have also lived under condemnation. So, you will hear these things from those closest to you; mother, father, brother, sister, pastor, church workers. But if your relationship is solid with Me, you will immediately recognize the enemy's signature: condemnation and accusation.

"So, now I have taught you well; you are warned, armed and ready to take on the opposition who is afoot in great numbers at this hour. They are seeking to demoralize you, looking for your hot spots, places that still carry infection from injuries borne in the past. Oh Yes! They love to shoot their poisoned tipped arrows and make a direct hit into that still inflamed area of tenderness. Be on your guard --- they are coming to you in legion, filled with condemnation and **discouragement**. Do not listen, do not take it in --- be on guard, recognize and repel them. Take every thought captive. If it does not align with My loving, encouraging nature, you can be sure it is demonic masquerading as holiness.

"Now I have warned you. RISE UP, repel and take captive."

Taken from: **Discouragement & Condemnation are Afoot...**

"As long as you allow the devils to put you under condemnation, you will look at others through the same lenses through which you see yourselves. This is the reason for the main assault against your characters. Don't you know that, as they succeed in turning you towards yourself and faultfinding, you will withdraw more and more from Me and from one another? When you are focused on your faults, you more readily see the faults of your brother. When you are focused on My Love, you more readily see the goodness in others and in yourself. I reflect back to you the goodness I see coming forth as you travel this road with Me, as you allow Me to carry you.

"I will even show you the perfection I have planned for you, which in truth has been completed in Heaven and has yet to be manifested here on Earth in its time.

"So, keep your eyes on Me. Have nothing but scorn and contempt for the ugliness of the world and your own failings. Declare that you are under My Blood and I have already perfected you. Short circuit their strategies to keep you in a downward spiral of **discouragement.**

"Yes, rise above. Rise through resting in Me as I bring forth all the beauty of your souls I have envisioned from the very foundations."

Taken from: **Minister to Me, My Tender Bride**

Depression, Discouragement

"My beautiful ones, you are full of grace and beauty, and so highly desired and valued by Me. What you have shines from within, whereas what the world has shines from the outside... yet is dead within. You mustn't ever compare yourselves to the celebrities of this world who are fair and skilled in conveying outward beauty, but inside may very well be spiritually dead. What I see when I look upon a man or a woman is the interior light - whether it be shining brightly, barely flickering, or even non-existent.

"When you are weighed down from this false sense of ugliness, you tend to withdraw and not allow that light to shine on others. Rather, you run and hide, are easily persuaded to give up, and are weak in your resolve to touch others. This is being used against you right now.

"Part of the fatigue you have been feeling is **discouragement** from unhealthy self-abasement. The enemy uses this as a two pronged attack. When you feel ugly on the outside, it cripples you from approaching others, and the worst part is that it returns the focus on yourself instead of on Me or the souls I send to you. It is very effective in curbing your outreach to others.

"When you feel beautiful and inspired, you are outgoing, confident, and ready to give. This is how I wish for you to see yourselves, not as expired, old wineskins ready to be discarded."

Taken from: **The Uglies**

"The devils will use every little thing to cause disillusionment, **discouragement**, especially in yourself. Condemnation, to cause you to be less effective. For instance, when you come under condemnation, and you take the bait, the enemy will tell you, 'No use to pray now - you just blew it and God won't hear your prayer'. Like... He would have, if you'd persevered in fasting?

"Lies and half-truths. I appreciate your fast offerings, but I also know your limits better than you do. And when the enemy inspires you to go further into a fast offering than you can handle with My grace, he will wait for you to fall and then slap you down with condemnation, making you want to abandon prayer - because, after all... you failed and they've become worthless.

"May I say, your prayers are NEVER worthless in these situations? Well, they are not. So, don't allow the enemy to lie to you."

Taken from: **Baptize Them in My Love...**

The second (voice you hear) is the demon's voice, which sounds affectionate, reasonable, persuasive, and very compatible with our own thoughts and desires. It tells us what we want to hear or what makes sense. At other times it accuses us or other people, drawing us into judgment, which the devils know is a way to open the door for them to come in and sift us. If they can't get away with lying to us about good things to set us off course, it will switch to the **discouragement** *mode.*

Taken from: **Discerning Between the Three Voices You Hear in Prayer**

And we know that God works all things together for the good of those who love Him, who are called according to His purpose. Romans 8:28

"You see, if you embrace this with all your hearts and KNOW beyond a shadow of a doubt that I am bringing good out of everything that happens, even the very worst things, if you have true faith in Me, you will not fall prey to **discouragement**, sadness and despair."

Taken from: **Lost in the Woods, Seeds of Bitterness**

Discernment

"My children, there is nothing worse than Pride. Not murder, not divorce, not adultery, not failure in business, not sickness. Pride is the number one most dangerous thing in your life. And if you think you are without it, you are in fact worse off than most. You have nothing to lose by handing your opinions over to Me for confirmations and everything to gain.

"Nevertheless, if you fail, I will still be with you - it will just be much more difficult for you. Humiliation, sorrow, hurting others - all these things you will have to face because you sought not the counsels of your God. How I wish some of you would listen to Me. How I have tried to reach inside of you and coaxed you to use the childish ways of **discernment** before doing something! In essence, I have asked you to hand over your free-will decisions and let Me advise you."

Taken from: **Are You Wise?**

"We've been talking a lot about **discernment** lately. There are so many different facets to discernment, to correctly discerning. It's really difficult to pin them all down, but I'm going to share a message I had from the Lord with you tonight.

"This year - it's part of the whole process of purifying your soul to be able to see and hear the Lord. It's written in the Beatitudes, "Blessed are the Pure in Heart, for they shall see God." He comes to the pure in heart for consolation, so if you purify your heart more and more - cooperate with Him.

"This isn't something you can do. With the cooperation and help of the Holy Spirit, your heart can be purified and that prepares you for being able to communicate clearly with Him. None of us are perfect, we're always going to make mistakes in discernment. I made one this morning, and the Voice (of the Lord) seemed to change places with a familiar spirit. I bound a Lying spirit and that was the end of it. I deleted everything that he said to me, but the beginning of the communication WAS from the Lord."

Taken from: **Discernment: Fingerprints of the Enemy**

I'll tell you guys, I do this every day. You can laugh, and you can accuse me of 'Bible Roulette;' I don't care. It works! The Lying Spirits get shown up for what they are when I use The Bible Promise Book. There are times the Lord allows me to be tested one step further, and I have to bind Lying spirits off The Bible Promises, but He does reveal the truth. He uses the Rhema Box, and He uses The Bible Promises, and readings from Scripture.

"You mustn't get lax in charity or 'too big for your britches.' I try to pull you down and back in line gently. I can't help it if your pride causes you to overreact to My corrections. Sooner or later you will come to the point where you can tolerate it without becoming despondent, or rebellious, as you always do. Besides, what about that little flutter in your conscience that tells you something is not right? Are you listening to that? Yes, you have been listening, but be a little quicker to obey, when you hear that flutter. Keep your conscience clean. Always keep your conscience clean, and you will have very little to worry about in the realm of **discernment**. It is only when you stubbornly grab the bit in your teeth, and take off in your own direction, despite your husband's warning. But I must let you learn the harder lessons.

"This is an ongoing lesson, My Beloved. This is the fine art of **discernment,** and the more you abandon the purse of your own opinion, and renounce your own self-will, the easier it will become."

Taken from: **Jesus Teaches on Discernment**

Discernment

*But, the other thing is, guys, our channel is all about teaching you
discernment and hearing from the Lord. So, I don't want you to get
addicted to ME. I'm just a vessel bringing something. I want all YOU
guys to be vessels. I want you to cultivate your gift of hearing from the
Lord. We've gone to great pains to put playlists together on Intimacy and
Discernment for a specific reason: because we want YOU guys to grow
up into **discernment** and hearing from the Lord the same way that He
has brought US up. So, please don't get addicted to me! (chuckle)*

Taken from: **You, Too, Are Vessels Unto Honor**

"Listen carefully to the instructions I am imparting to you. Prayer will
be your greatest weapon and I will teach you how to pray - it will flow
from within you without any effort so strong will My grace be among
you. Prayer will well up from inside and overtake you in moments of
fear and danger, and you will be kept safely hidden as well as have My
Peace.

"Many will betray each other and only **discernment** by My Holy Spirit
will alert you to who cannot be trusted. If you judge by outward
standards, what is said, what they look like, how they act, if you judge
by normal human standards you will be fooled. You must rely on Me
to detect weak souls or those sent to find you out. Again I want to say,
this is for the left behind ones."

Taken from: **Provision and Protection For Those Left Behind**

*But what was different last night is that I wasn't comfortable with the
message. The content began to bother me, but every time I would protest
this content - that I didn't like it, this 'Jesus' would tell me to be obedient,
that He had His reasons. And thinking back, that may have been the
Lord, actually. Well, when I read through the message it seemed to flow
and it seemed to have the weight of truth, but I wasn't at all comfortable*

with the content. Because it brought up something I thought we had closure to. So, I was iffy.

*I am so blessed to have a mature and **discerning** man of God to cover me and help me stay in His will. Ezekiel was seeking the Lord on my behalf during this whole time, because he also had qualms about the content and finally he shared that with me. When Ezekiel shared with me that he wasn't comfortable with the content, we put it down. I said, "That's it. We're not going to use this. We're just going sleep on it." When we woke up, the answer from the Lord through our different channels of **discernment** was the same - that this message was NOT from Him.*

Taken from: **Rescued From a Familiar Spirit**

*So, this is why I teach **discernment**, because many men have many things to say and a lot of what they say contradicts one another. But if you know Jesus, and you know what God says, then you have the answers that you need.*

Taken from: **The Calm Before the Storm**

Lord - what about the times when I feel sleepy? I thought these were ordained by You? Is this opposition, or You?

He answered, "A very good question and here **discernment** is needed. When I am allowing this to rejuvenate you on deeper levels, I will invite you to lay down and enter into My rest. For the most part, when we are together in worship and communion, I do not allow interference. But when you are prevented from connecting with Me, then you may suspect opposition. This is the time to pray and bind until we are once more together in sweet fellowship."

Taken from: **How the Enemy Blocks Your Creativity w/Demonic Intervention**

Discernment

"This is why I tell you continually, opinion is no substitute for **discernment**. When you discern My times, My seasons, My choices, you will go against the current being generated by the ruling elite. When you think for yourselves, basing everything on your personal preference and the opinions of others, you will find yourself endorsing evil. **Discernment** takes time. Opinion is the lazy man's way. This nation is in this fix right now because you were lazy. Don't make the same mistake. **Discern** My times, My seasons and My choices. Stand with Me, not with popular opinion."

Taken from: **Why Your Failures Qualify You For Success...**

"I'm sure you've noticed how you get interrupted the minute you try to do something holy or go into prayer, and the more important the task, the stronger the resistance. The number one threat to the kingdom of darkness is a spiritual Christian who hears from God. A person's intimate relationship with God is the most threatening thing to the kingdom of darkness. That's why so many of the really spiritual moves of God have come under so much opposition and fire.

"In the course of events, Holy Spirit brings on a new movement of holiness and the devils respond by sending a counterfeit to confuse and scandalize anyone drawn to that movement. The enemy uses people short on **discernment**, who label it "from the Devil" and thereby try to put a stop to it. So, anytime you go deeper with the Lord, you will get demonic resistance: whether it be a child getting a fever just before you walk out the door to go to church, or telephone calls during prayer time that never seem to end if you haven't been smart enough to unplug your phone... The more important the Godly activity, the more opportunity there is for you to be blessed and grow in the Lord - the more the demons are going to oppose you."

Taken from: **Sexual Temptations in Prayer**

My husband is a very cautious man and has many times uncovered hidden and spiritual things, keeping us from falling into error. After I was given the part 6 message, the one preceding this one, he was very concerned because he knows from experience how much the Lord hates to talk about aliens and things that seem out of this world to most people. So he had a serious check about the veracity of this message.

Given that, he went into serious prayer. Well, during the making of that message, a Scripture verse from a site that gives out random Rhemas just happened to pop up...you know, just "happened to"!

*And it said, **He who believes in Me, as the Scripture has said, from his innermost being will flow rivers of living water." It's John 7:38***

So, I knew when I was finalizing the message, that it truly was the Lord. Because I had some doubts, too, since the nature of the material's pretty far out.

*Even though I had that confirmation, and I had an inner sense that truly it was from the Lord, I still would not publish a message that my husband was not comfortable with. Because I totally honor and believe in his **discernment** and it could very well be that I was making a mistake - so I was willing to put it on hold here.*

Taken from: **Prophetic Dream: Aliens Disguised**

"You, My Beloveds, are under a tremendous cloud of uncleanness which causes not only your **discernment** and thinking-spirit-soul connection to be tattered and worn thin, but it affects your body and aging as well. Just as in My Being I have three parts: Father, Son and Holy Spirit - you, too, have three parts: spirit, soul and body. These must be in agreement, in alignment, in unity."

Taken from: **How To Receive My Anointing For Your Life Everyday**

Enemies

He began: "Oh, My precious, you mean so much to me. Don't ever allow yourself to be duped into thinking otherwise.

"Your **enemies** are very clever and no matter how much you know or think you know, or I've shown you - it is still a matter of cooperation and casting down everything that lifts itself up against the knowledge of God. Your **enemies** are clever and relentless.

"They wait for you and spring on you like a lion. They wait and slowly stalk you when you're not exactly consciously aware until you feel the very thing they are forcing on you. You become hoodwinked, netted like a butterfly. They lie and wait for My little butterfly and then suddenly swoop their evil net over her, to be captured so they can tear her wings off.

"Oh, My Beloved, don't ever allow them to take your wings, your freedom in Me. The beauty of your wings, painted by Me, supremely beautiful and free. Oh, so free! Oh, so calm and at liberty to fly and create with Me. Fly into the heavenlies. Oh, how they hate and even envy her freedom! It reminds them of all they forfeited when they rebelled against Me.

"And now they will never get it back - so they can't stand to see you happy, creating, praising, resting and loving Me. It reminds them of their bondage and what they gave up. Bitterly, they look back on their past, but even then their hatred for Me burns, and you are their target. All of My Brides, who I adore, targets for their malice - because they figure if they can't hurt Me directly at least they can do harm to My Brides and hurt them.

"Oh, My Beloved, don't let them steal what you and I have together. Be vigilant, Clare! Be oh, so vigilant. When you feel even the slightest agitation in your soul, know that they are present and intending to hurt you.

But you have all the weapons to fight them. Fight valiantly, My Bride."

Taken from: **Jesus Teaches on Restoring our Peace, Journal**

"I have some wonderful things planned for this horrendous time. Many a wall will come crashing down upon the **enemy** because of prayer. I will supernaturally and literally move Heaven and Earth to protect the holy ones. Some will be martyred, some will survive but all will be provided for, I will not abandon them to the will of their enemies. Yes, unsurpassed suffering will be witnessed but also unsurpassed glory and the triumph of faith. There will be many sent from Heaven as visitations to encourage and provide. My angels will be most solicitous for the welfare of the remnant I am shielding from the full force of My wrath.

"Listen carefully to the instructions I am imparting to you. Prayer will be your greatest weapon and I will teach you how to pray - it will flow from within you without any effort so strong will My grace be among you. Prayer will well up from inside and overtake you in moments of fear and danger, and you will be kept safely hidden as well as have My Peace."

Taken from: **Provision & Protection for Those Left Behind**

He said, "I find comfort here. I find caring and focus on what is truly of importance to Me, not the flesh, which matters for nothing, except to sustain the spirit's temple.

"Oh, Clare, I long to hold all My vessels unto honor close to My heart. I long to hear the pure beating of their hearts. I long for them to be detached from the material things of the world. And I am so glad you are going in that direction. Just be vigilant, you have many **enemies**. But as you can see, I have not allowed them to do tremendous harm. A little here, a little there. Just to keep you on your toes."

Taken from: **Your Tomorrow is Not Guaranteed**

Enemies

"When a soul puts all their confidence in Me, I am free to provide everything they need. Rather than providing and surviving, be about My business and all these things will be added unto you. Your insecurity and panic do nothing but give the devils permission to sift you, wear you out and cause you to move prematurely right into the **enemies'** waiting arms. But with your focus on bringing souls to Me, I am free to provide all you need. My faithfulness is your rear guard and covering."

Taken from: **Jesus Instructs the Left Behind: Put No Confidence in the Flesh**

"There is so much more to the refining fire of **enemies** than anyone is truly aware of. They are My refining fire, a force to be reckoned with when loosed, a force to be pitied when bound. And I have total control at all times."

"You see, the demons are My policemen. They wait in line all day to sift a believer, sometimes they line up around the block, so to speak, just to get one shot at a soul. Once a believer has crossed a line and disobeyed, however, permission is given – but only so far. In other words, what they are allowed to do or not do is controlled by My permission.

"In other situations I allow the demons permission because I'm perfecting a soul in virtue and patience - forgiveness and virtue needs to be cultivated. At the very same time, when I allow an attack from the demon, I know how it will affect a soul and that they will, in turn, pray for those who are being used to attack. Very often those souls have no one to pray for them and the one whom they attack are My very last resort to find intercessors."

Taken from: **Jesus Speaks: Why Our Enemies are Important**

"I have told you before, Dear One, Pres. Putin is not a free agent. If he were, things would be different. The overthrow of the Elite is the next thing on

My agenda. As the peoples of the world wake up to the manipulation, slaughter and total disregard for the lives of the common man; as they wake up, they can and will overthrow this evil force.

"More and more from higher levels are falling out of agreement with the plans to annihilate the populations of the world. More and more in very high levels are beginning to see: what they have planned to end others, will in fact be their own demise. This is the effect of your prayers.

"As we stay on the edge of our seats, interceding, massive movements are beginning to emerge. Those who were with the agenda are turning away and joining others in a counter-movement."

I asked Him: Does this mean the whole world will convert?

"I wish..." He said wistfully. "There are still plenty with controlling, greedy agendas completely in league with the devil. It will be a battle, a big battle. But I am with those who are with Me. Though they be outnumbered, I am on their side, doing things that will give them an advantage over their **enemies.**"

Taken from: **Higher Realms of Prayer …**

I knew that God was merciful and when He asks us to pray to avert something, so far that I know of... it never happens. I know that. It is a rock-solid belief in my heart. He wants to stop something, so He asks for prayer - and then it stops.

So, I knew in advance I would be open to ridicule, from not only my **enemies** *but from the skeptics and weaker listeners on our channel. But I also knew I could not let My God down; I had to speak what I knew to be the truth - ridicule or not.*

Taken from: **My Personal Struggle With Unbelief**

Enemies

"When a soul puts all their confidence in Me, I am free to provide everything they need. Rather than providing and surviving, be about My business and all these things will be added unto you. Your insecurity and panic do nothing but give the devils permission to sift you, wear you out and cause you to move prematurely right into the ***enemies***' waiting arms. But with your focus on bringing souls to Me, I am free to provide all you need. My faithfulness is your rear guard and covering.

"It is a lack of knowledge of Me that causes others to dive in and apply themselves to providing for their own needs. When you know Me, you know I have already provided a way out, complete with food, medicine and cover that will make you invisible to the **enemy**.

"This is for the benefit of those left behind, Clare."

Taken from: **God Will Provide For Those Left Behind**

My mind began to drift on the outrageous and evil things being said abou me lately on the Internet. And though I did not say anything to Him, He addressed it. Sometimes I think He puts those distractions in my head so He can answer them!

He continued, "Were your **enemies** to walk all over you with your faults - they would be justified. But unfortunately, they are way off base and even laughable to those who know you. But you enduring in patience, without hostility, is witness enough that I am truly living in you, Clare. No one could endure these things without supernatural love and come away still praying from the heart for their **enemies**."

Taken from: **Why You Are Hated…**

"You are formed in My Image. 'Male and female He made them.' You also have an unseen and sometimes unheard **enemy** translating words into subtle messages, that subliminally penetrate into your mind and before you know it you are dealing with unbelief. Your *enemies* are many."

And I asked Him at that point, 'cause I was thinking of human **enemies***, and I said, "Please Lord, bless my* **enemies** *with a knowledge of Your Love for them."*

"This is a continuing effort for Me, however I do not bless the demons. But back to the point, I know what you are struggling with. I am not without compassion Dear One, and I forgive you. As I said, your **enemies** are many. Some things they accomplish subliminally and that makes it most difficult to detect until it is strongly implanted in your consciousness."

Taken from: **Enemy Tactics…**

"What is the cure? It is too simple for the 'intelligent' to grasp. Keep your eyes on Me, focus on Me, know that I am protecting you. As you focus on Me, you become more and more like Me. You learn that I 'have your back' so to speak.

"You learn that it doesn't matter who your **enemies** are, all that matters is that you love them. The fear drops away, because you are looking at Me and trusting in Me. Fear is the engine that drives this kind of judgment. Once the fear is gone, the need to judge in order to survive is also gone.

"That is why people who teach focus on Me, intimacy in prayer, knowing and hearing My voice, are so targeted for persecution. When you listen to Me, I navigate you around the reefs of judgment and now their door-opener will no longer be effective."

Taken from: **Spiritual Warfare: 8 How One Demonic Strategy …**

Envy, Jealousy

"Many, if not all of you, My Precious Brides, find fault with yourselves and fall into the trap of comparing yourself to someone who has an outstanding attribute, but in fact you know nothing of their lives. This comparison leads to discouragement over who I have fashioned you to be and leaves you open to the sin of **envy**, as well as emulating them so you distort who you truly are.

"Firstly, I want you to know that no one is as they seem on the outside. No, not one. There is a hidden side to each of you, the side you have either conquered or are still hiding, hoping that it will some day die."

Taken from: **My Grace Accomplishes All Things, Even Prayer**

"To them, I was but a phantom, a deception who never existed. My overtures of love have been scorned now and replaced with bitterness, **envy** and pride.

"Oh, how I lament for these who have slipped through My fingers. Pray for them, dear ones, pray for their salvation. For the judgment they passed on this channel has become their own before the courts of Heaven. Yet, never will I abandon them.

"But do you understand? I offered them the choice fruits of My Kingdom: My love, My fellowship, My very heart. And now all of that has been swept away and concealed under a carpet of bitterness woven with beguiling threads of self-righteousness, **envy**, pride and arrogance."

Taken from: How Does a Fall Happen?

"Oh, how they (*demons*) hate and even *envy* her (*believers*) freedom! It reminds them of all they forfeited when they rebelled against Me. And now they will never get it back - so they can't stand to see you happy, creating, praising, resting and loving Me. It reminds them of their bondage and what they gave up. Bitterly, they look back on their past, but even then their hatred for Me burns, and you are their target. All of My Brides, who I adore, targets for their malice - because they figure if they can't hurt Me directly at least they can do harm to My Brides and hurt them.

"Sometimes that's all we can do. We can pray, 'Lord, I'm willing to be made willing to forgive so and so.' We have an invisible enemy who is constantly trying to cause us to fall and to lose grace. He's a reminding us of things and trying to make us **jealous**, get angry, and to make misunderstandings.

"We had a week where I would say something, and you would hear something else, and then I would hear it differently. We finally figured out that it was a demon trying to twist our words. We started binding it. The Lord told me that the demon in our communication was trying to cause division. We both slowed down to take a look at that."

Taken from: **Rapture Delayed, Dealing with Disappointment**

"Oh, how I love each and every one that is seeking Me. That is why I am here to explain the direction they need to take. You know the things that offend Me.

"Sin offends Me very much. Sin in clothing, or lack of it, sin in violence, crime, hatred, gossip, backbiting, **jealousy**, adulteries. Soap operas are the epitome of sin and extremely noxious to Me. Like your-nose-in-fresh-dog-excrement noxious. I mean very, very bad.

"These things not only offend Me but also the Heavenly court, the angels and the saints. Yet in your world they are matter-of-fact, part of everyday life."

Taken from: **Jesus Answers His Bride on How to See Him**

Envy, Jealousy

"Don't think for one moment that I love you any less for it. In fact, it endears Me to you, and all My Brides who see their littleness. This is the robe of humility Rick Joyner talks about. And Paul as well when he talks about boasting in his weaknesses. It is a mark of predestination to be so empty, poor and frail that in order to succeed you must have My Grace. In Heaven it is a great distinction. I wish that all My Brides would see things that way.

"It would close a major door of attack against you. You see, the enemy is always downgrading and lying, 'You are so stupid, what do you know, who do you think you are? God speak to you -LOL you've got to be kidding. You're a failure, you'll never amount to anything.' Then he loves to stir you to sin through **jealousy**, 'Look at so and so over there. Now they are something, they are brilliant and qualified, but you? LOL You'll never amount to anything. Everything you believe is a lie."

Taken from: **Attacks Against Faith Are on the Way**

"Many are so sure they are ready to stand before Me, but they're not taking a good look inside themselves or in My mirror. This concerns me, Clare. It concerns Me that they are so ready, and yet they still quarrel and bite at one another. They still gossip and tell lies about one another. They still accuse with impunity, thinking they are so right, and the other is so wrong.

"Yet, I tell you, they are not ready to stand before Me. They are blinded by self-righteousness. They are on a crusade to set the world straight, but they are unfit for the Bridal gown. I cannot put a clean, white garment on those who are still **jealous** and destructive with their tongue. I cannot put that gown on anyone who does not love their brother as they love Me."

Taken from: **Without Love You Will Not Be Taken in the Rapture**

I'm really glad you said that, Lord - that You would have many followers. I don't want followers. Besides I'm not leading, You are!

"This is very true, but nonetheless you will be misunderstood by those who have hidden agendas, **jealousies**, and just refuse to open their hearts. They will suffer the most. It is good for you to continue to teach how destructive judgment is to each soul. It is good for all of you to take these words to heart and not allow an entrance for pride and judgment.

"My children, I have warned you again and again about judging, but when you judge My prophets you incur serious repercussions in your life, immediately. You will find that the results will be immediate, because I am trying to break you of this wicked habit.

"Do you understand, when you judge others and especially My vessels unto honor, that you invite in a host of demons to sift you and your family?

"Do you understand that when you spread false reports about the innocent and slander their character that you have brought a curse down upon yourself? I have to tell you, you will see more and more division and strife among your friends for such behavior, because beneath it all there is spiritual **jealousy**, the most destructive force in My Body.

"When you engage patterns of **jealousy** you actually oppose Me and the operation of My gifts and I will hold you accountable for the souls I could not reach because you spread lies about a vessel.

By their fruits you will know them.' And I encourage you to look at the fruits of those whom I have chosen to minister, there you will find their accreditation."

Taken from: **Carry the Cross, Don't Judge, Preparation for War...**

Envy, Jealousy

"My Children, when you are taken up with the faults and shortcomings of others, you are inviting a serious fall. You are also causing Me to withdraw a distance from you and oppose you even in your 'holy' undertakings. For truly, how holy is an undertaking when underneath the surface you are seething with **jealousy** and fault-finding and even spreading it to others?"

Taken from: **The Last Stains on Your Wedding Gown**

"I love the sweet little flock I have sent you, soul by soul. I love them dearly and it is My great desire to speak with them everyday. Oh, how I love them. And what I will leave behind for others will be invaluable in building their faith. There will be a great harvest from these messages and I will have many followers who will be strengthened.

"This is very true, but nonetheless you will be misunderstood by those who have hidden agendas, **jealousies**, and just refuse to open their hearts. They will suffer the most. It is good for you to continue to teach how destructive judgment is to each soul. It is good for all of you to take these words to heart and not allow an entrance for pride and judgment.

"My children, I have warned you again and again about judging, but when you judge My prophets you incur serious repercussions in your life, immediately. You will find that the results will be immediate, because I am trying to break you of this wicked habit. Do you understand, when you judge others and especially My vessels unto honor, that you invite in a host of demons to sift you and your family?

"Do you understand that when you spread false reports about the innocent and slander their character that you have brought a curse down upon yourself? I have to tell you, you will see more and more division and strife among your friends for such behavior, because beneath it all there is spiritual **jealousy**, the most destructive force in My Body. When you engage patterns of **jealousy** you actually oppose

Me and the operation of My gifts and I will hold you accountable for the souls I could not reach because you spread lies about a vessel."

Taken from: **Carry the Cross, Don't Judge, Prep. for War...**

"See, these demons and these lying spirits, they work in tandem. So, a group like that? You probably have Lying spirits, Lying Symptoms that mimic sickness, spirits of **Jealousy** and Strife, spirits of Fear, spirits of Unbelief. And they love to work together in a nest and in tandem - and I tell, you when I pray against these things, there are so many of them, they have backup. They have those who sent them. So, "in the name of Jesus, I bind you lying spirits, I bind your backup, and I bind those who have sent you." And just get the whole slew of them bound. Send them to the abyss. Some people might argue with me on that but, you know what? It works."

Taken from: **Do Not Fear or Reject Intimacy w/God...**

"No, I had planned a paradise for My people, My children a literal Paradise. I had to give reign to free will, because free will carries consequences and all must learn through consequences to call upon Me and choose Me above and beyond the learning institutions and the pop culture of their generation."

"They must go deeper. I have called to them deeper and deeper. Deeply I have planted My Word to them. Deep in their consciousness, I left have My calling card of love and warning. They've gone unheeded supplanted by the glitter of your culture. The living will **envy** the dead but the (RFID) chip will not allow them to die. There is the technology to keep people alive through the chip. They will search for death, but it will elude them."

Taken from: **Hell on Earth, Prophetic Word**

Eternal Life

"If you are not working for Me in this hour, you are standing before Me blind and naked. Rise up and take on your Master's business. Bring forth fruit worthy of My Bride, and while you are doing this I will see to it that you grow into the fullness of who I've called you to be as My Spouse. My promise to you is **life eternal** and the choicest lands of Heaven, the sweetest intimacy possible to a created soul. Don't let Me down in this hour; rise up, harness yourself to My carriage, for My yoke is easy, My burden is light, and I will make joyful for you the act of going out and gathering to Me My Bride."

Taken from: **Blood Moon Rapture, Prophetic Word**

"So, now I tell you there is but a short way to go, but it's going to get stormy. Stay onboard, don't fall into despair and jump overboard. You have all come so far, the devils are filled with wrath for you who have grown deeply intimate with Me. He will attack this channel, but you stand on the truth you have experienced in your own hearts and do not give way to illusions and clever arguments. Follow your heart and protect what I have sown in it.

"This is why I say things will get stormy. There is only One whom you have to please... Me. So, stand in courage and strength and turn a deaf ear to detractors lest you lose what you have gained for **eternal life**."

Taken from: **The Frustration and Anger of Waiting for Jesus**

"Some of you listening to this will come before the Judgment Seat, where all your works, good and bad, will be exposed and your fate for eternity will be determined. To you I say, you are facing choices in this very moment that will determine the rest of your journey, your life path - whether you will live a life of virtue or a life of sin, whether you will serve Me or serve the Devil, whether you will die in virtue or die in sin.

"I am coming back. This is no time to play with fire. This is no time to compromise. Rather this is the time to renounce and repent of your sins and compromises. This is a time to embrace brotherly love, extend a hand of help, live for the good of others, not for your own advantage. This is a critical season. Many of you listening will be facing physical death this year. If you are not right with Me, come, come to My loving arms and though your sins be as scarlet I will wash them white as snow.

"You are not guaranteed life tomorrow. Yet Heaven and Hell lie directly before you. Choose this day who you will serve, and if it is Me, you have only to ask for the strength to break from your sinful past, and I will enfold you in My arms with great compassion and forgiveness. However, if you choose to continue on in your sinful ways, I have warned you, death is at the door and your tomorrow is not guaranteed. Do not sell your souls for a trifle.

"Repent, break with sin, come to Me. I will restore you and rebirth you into **life eternal**, fully equipped to live a holy life, from the inside out.

"I am here for you. Come."

Taken from: **Your Tomorrow is Not Guaranteed**

"Now that we have established your new life in Me, I wish for you to rest. Yes, rest. Your life is hidden in Me now. No more striving. Striving to become holy, striving to accomplish, striving to produce, striving to impress... No, that is over now. All shall be done by Me, through you. Wait for Me to move. Catch the wind of My Spirit. Flow with My leadings... I am at the helm, My Spirit powers the sails, together we will live this new life, together we will finally arrive at Our final destination - the very shores of **Eternal Life**."

Taken from: **Rope of Grace**

Eternal Life

"My people, even if they should bring you before the executioner for your faith in Me, be not afraid. In seconds, I will embrace you for eternity. Mercy will surround and anesthetize you in those last moments. Supernatural peace will also engulf you as you are led forth to execution. I know it is hard for you to accept now, and even some of you tremble in fear, but I tell you the truth: it will be much harder for those who must live hidden lives, than for those who come to Me early for their faith.

"In any case, I will be at your right hand and waiting for you to join Me in **Eternity**, where I have **Joy Eternal** planned for you, and you will forever be joined to Me."

Taken from: **Evading Capture, Jesus Instructs Us**

"That day, you will at long last discover your indescribable beauty, hidden from you during your earthly sojourn. That day, you will put on the incorruptible, untarnishable crown of **eternal life** and step up to the throne I have created for you since before time began. No, this surely will not be a time of correction and purification, it shall be a time of transformation and freedom from the past."

Taken from: **The Rapture, What You Will Experience**

"You may not see it now, but in **eternity** all will be crystal clear and all those things you never understood will be thoroughly revealed to you. Oh, what a joy it will be to go back in time and understand how I was present to you and leading you even though you didn't perceive it.

"Beneath every event on this Earth, there is mercy. I could not sustain creation without it. My heart would break if I did not bring Good forth, from disaster. Many of you look upon the approaching great Tribulation with fear and trembling. And well you should, it will be a time unparalleled in grief."

"But it must happen to clear the way for My Kingdom to manifest on this Earth. Evil must be harnessed and held in abeyance that you may grow into the spotless creature I made you to be.

"The Earth must be cleansed from the foulness of greed, the destructive chemicals, the diseases brought forth by evil men, the desolation of the lands I made beautiful, the trash and off---scouring of industry that has so defiled the pristine Creation I made for your enjoyment. The way must be cleared, My children, and it is not going to be pretty.

"The institution of My Government, will cause all to come forth, grow, expand, create, joyfully bringing forth the fullness of the gifts I have bestowed on man. What a wonder it will be to see farming, industry, education, proceed without destroying the Earth or the pristine beauty I will restore to it.

"All will be given tasks to complete, artisans, politicians, farmers, educators. All that you have now will come forth without corruption and the greatest focus of all will be on worshiping Me. It won't be knowledge, wealth, beauty or talent; it will be the love of your brother and Me. Oh, how this will change every thing. It will turn bitter, bitter, things to sweet and nourishing."

Taken from: **My Mercy and the Millennium**

Well, getting back to this soaking prayer. Which we've termed Dwelling Prayer now, because what we try to teach is that the Lord dwells in us and we are entering into the place where He dwells. Which is also the door to Heaven - He is the door to the sheepfold, He is the door to **eternal life***.*

Taken from: **Dwelling Prayer 2**

Eternal Life

"Though it is My love for you that brings you to repentance, and the rejection of sin and evil. (Romans 2:4) It is well that you should hate these things. But, how can you hate what I love? I love YOU. So, how can you hate you? You can't. You shouldn't! It's NOT what I intended. If I wanted you to hate yourself, I wouldn't have come into the world to bring you **eternal life.** Rather, I'd bring eternal condemnation.

"But is it not written, '**For God so loved the world that He gave His only begotten Son. That whoever believes in Him shall not perish, but have eternal life. For God did not send His Son into the world to judge the world, but that the world might be saved through Him.'** John 3:16

Taken from: **You Must Love Yourself Before You Can Love Your Brother**

"Even now, in worship, you can access the River of Life, the creative, cleansing power of the Father, through worship. That is why it is so important for it to dominate your lives. To the degree that you partake of the degradation of Earth, to that degree you need cleansing from that influence. It is very rare soul that gets a thorough and complete cleansing from the contamination they have accumulated...very rare. Baptism can be one of those times. Being born again can also be.

"But, there is nothing quite like worship. Lift up your eyes to the hills from whence comes your redemption. Lift up your hearts to heaven and drink from the rivers of living waters flowing from the throne of the Father; dancing, alive and yearning to wash over each and every one of you restoring to you virginal purity and **eternal life** in the wholeness never before experienced on this Earth since Adam and Eve.

"Yes, hope is great indeed. I will make all things new. I will liberate this Earth from its endless cycles of death. And you, too, My Brides, will meet with your **eternal** purpose in Me, excelling in excellence, creativity, love and service. And, you will return to rule and reign with Me, that justice may be restored and evil defeated."

Taken from: **Hope & Defeat Fatigue...**

"Human nature is an inexplicable and inexhaustible well of conflicting emotions and thoughts competing for dominance in your life. Yet, when I take over, I sort these out and make them work to the soul's advantage. I have imparted so many dormant gifts to the soul at the beginning of their journey, they have no idea the wonder of what lies hidden inside of them. Yet, it is My part to reveal to them and motivate them to pick up the tools.

"It's a tempering process and requires many trips through fire and ice. Yet the souls that say 'yes' at every juncture of the journey, at the end, shine like diamonds illuminating a murky, grey world; bringing hope, inspiration and a vision of Heaven because they are a likeness of Me.

"It is a vastly immense concept. Only those who have graduated truly understand the journey. When you are in the midst of it you can't see more than a few feet ahead of you. But at the end, you see from My perspective and the brilliant light you've shed from your earthly light.

"And that light never goes out. It serves as a beacon to all who are searching for the Truth. That is truly what I am calling you to be. Your accomplishments working with Me are secondary.

"What is truly important was the character of your life. Not what you did, but who you became when you died to yourself. So, My dear ones, I know this is difficult for you to grasp. All I can promise you is supreme happiness and fulfillment at the end of the journey. You have My word on it. If you die in Me, you will be raised to **eternal life** with Me."

Taken from: **The Journey of Holiness**

Faith

"Waiting is not easy. Waiting implies solid hope; hope is in direct proportion to **faith**, that what you are hoping for will become an eventuality. That is the realm you are all operating in. And the stronger your **faith**, the more productive and peaceful you will be.

"That is why Satan tries so hard to undermine your **faith**; so much depends upon it. When a soul becomes impatient, they choose many wrong turns and I must go ahead of them to steer them back on the right track. As your **faith** increases, so does your hope increase, until you are so full you are spilling over onto others. You are radiant with hope, because you know Who you have put your trust in. This is the point at which you can touch others in the deepest way.

"As My Bride is waiting in **faith**, she is hoping and increasing in glory, which will flow out on to others. Without waiting, there can be no hope. And without **faith**, waiting is fruitless. What I am saying is that you are all growing in **faith**, hope and trust. Each day you are stronger. "

Taken from: **Lord, What Are You Doing With Us in This Hour?**

"I will provide for My remnant in the wilderness, as it is written. Not only those of Jerusalem, but those grafted into the vine, (He's speaking of Christians there) in places of refuge around the world. My people, do not fear those who kill the body, but He who has power over your souls.

"The **faith** of all shall be shaken in the coming war, but I shall faithfully abide with them and remove My Bride in a timely fashion. All of you, My faithful Ones, all that you have or will suffer is to bring the lost. Be steadfast and practice the art of waiting on Me in a state of perfect rest, knowing that soon all will be fulfilled. But until that very moment, My grace is shining in and through you and touching all souls of this world with the supernatural expression of your faith in action."

Taken from: **Rest in Me Until I Carry You Over the Threshold of Eternity**

"All that is left for you is to have **faith** in My Mercy.

"What is coming is horrendous in scope and there will be unavoidable isolations. That is when you are to CLEAVE TO ME with all your heart and soul. Until then, pray with one another. But when it all happens, pray for each other and stay tightly holding Me as I hold you. The wind will be ferocious, but in My arms it will be a gentle breeze. That is why you mustn't, for a moment, lose your focus and look outside of Me. I will keep you in My Peace if only you will rely on Me alone."

"I told you these things ahead of time, My Brides, because I could see what was coming. It is so important for you to take these kinds of warnings seriously and remember them in the fray of the battle, so you don't grow discouraged. I have seen all of you fighting to keep your **faith**. I have seen all of you growing weary in the battle. But I'm here to tell you there is an end coming. Dare I say soon? No, I don't think I will. I will just promise you, there is an end coming.

"What Clare and Ezekiel have suffered is but a fraction of suffering for those who have been displaced and lost everything: children, husbands, wives. Please, put this into perspective. You are going to be reunited with your families in Heaven, but for now, at least you are still able to stay warm and fed and receive treatment when you are sick. Although I truly want to be your first recourse in illness.

"But I want to commend you that you are STANDING, you are not caving in. You are not shaking your fist at Me, although the devils have tempted that response. You are holding on to the gift of **faith** and shouldering your crosses, custom-made crosses that I have designed specifically just for you, knowing your strengths, weaknesses and how much you would rely on Me."

Taken from: **These Lite and Momentary Sufferings**

Faith

"The warring angels search out child-like souls to stand beside, and you have artfully corresponded to this call of being child-like. When they see you, they jump to attention and immediately seek to assist you. So, be of good cheer! Your entire demeanor calls out to Heaven for backup and assistance. It is those who think they are mighty and have it all together that My angels respond less eagerly to. Continue in your littleness and child-like **faith**, it is glorious to Heaven."

Taken from: **Prayer Alert: June 9, 2016**

"When I said that Satan goes for the jugular, I mean his minions know where to place the sucker punch. And you all suffer grief over your children, asking if you did the right thing, grieving over your mistakes, wondering if there is still hope for them. May I say, the accusers stand beside you, thrusting your hearts through with all manner of lies about them? And I am here to remove the lance and restore the wounds with the balm of **faith** with My goodness and mercy. Even now your suffering is backing up the harvest of souls and their turn is coming.

"Many of you have labored for Me tirelessly: praying, fasting, serving and doing your very best as a parent, while you watched your children walk off into the world. Even those of you who had the best resources and intentions have witnessed this tragedy. But you see, I am with you and your children in a way you will never understand until Heaven. Indeed, when you see how I am accompanying them you will exclaim, 'Oh Lord, why did I worry and fret so???!' And I will answer you gently, 'Because you didn't see what I see. But now you know, I had My hand on them the whole time and never let them go.'"

Taken from: **Trust Me With Your Children**

"I don't want to go on and on about this. I just want you to cultivate togetherness with Me and be mindfully aware that I am working through you; I am with you, I am for you. Do not listen to those condemning liars! They are the ones condemned, not you. I bless you now, My Beloved ones, with a keen awareness that I am by your side, advising you every minute of the day. Awaken this awareness by inviting Me. 'Jesus, help me do this, put the right words in my mouth, show me the right actions. Do this in **faith** and see if I do not increase your joy in all that I help you with."

Taken from: **Togetherness**

"The world is beginning to see that politics without God are more entrapping than politics with God. Pres. Putin has been better to his people than Pres. Obama. Waking up from communism and embracing the moral standards of the **Faith**, protecting the concept of family and nurturing her people. Giving the poor opportunities, building bunkers for her population...preventing Sharia law. While Obama is counting on the decimation of the masses without protection from nuclear war, and allowing America's laws to be changed by Muslims."

Lord, I don't understand. You have said this was scripted, yet Putin's spoken agendas are far different than Obama's. I don't get it.

"I have told you before, Dear One, Pres. Putin is not a free agent. If he were, things would be different. The overthrow of the Elite is the next thing on My agenda. As the peoples of the world wake up to the manipulation, slaughter and total disregard for the lives of the common man; as they wake up, they can and will overthrow this evil force.

"More and more from higher levels are falling out of agreement with the plans to annihilate the populations of the world. More and more in very high levels are beginning to see: what they have planned to end others, will in fact be their own demise. This is the effect of your prayers."

Taken from: **Higher Realms of Prayer...**

Faith

He chuckled, "Daughter, I live and breathe and have My being in you, with you and through you. We are so coordinated, you would be hard pressed to tell us apart. Although your sins will always reveal who has the upper hand at the moment.

"The **faith** I speak of is the **faith** of a little child who does not worry about entering a university when she is three or four. She doesn't question the future - unless it's the immediate future, such as obtaining a treat when she is at the store with her mother.

"She cares not about the stock market, qualifying for a loan, obtaining a vehicle, and which insurance policy is best. No, she puts her little hand in Daddy's and walks along the sandy shores of life taking in the pretty shells and foamy water. She doesn't worry about what grades she is going to get or how to qualify for college. She only thinks about the present moment, because her Father is always supplying all she needs.

"This is **faith** in action."

Taken from: **Hand in Hand With Daddy**

"As souls continue to be gathered into the Kingdom, I continue to hold back the wrath from moment to moment. Do not grow bitter like those of the world who say, 'Where is the hope of His coming?' These thoughts are of Satan and meant to undermine your **faith**. If you give them airplay and go into agreement with them, your **faith** will be compromised. Rather stand strong and tall with Me as I gather in those that remain and remember the parable of the virgins.

"They all fell asleep, but only the wise virgins had flasks of oil with them. Do you see the wisdom and warning of this?"

Taken from: **Stand Up, America & The Wise Virgins**

"By the way, when I talk about obedience, you are never required to do anything against your conscience or your **faith**, to be obedient. There are times when you cannot obey those in your lives who you normally would. For instance, normally you would obey the custom's rules when you are entering a country, but if Bibles are illegal, you are not required to obey the laws of men. You are fully in your rights to smuggle them in, for this is your obedience to Me. If your spouse tries to interfere with your **faith** and you've done everything in your power to appease them, but they are still striking at the heart of your **faith**, you are not required to obey."

Taken from: **They Will All Be Taught By God**

"You see, there is no such thing as just a little of Me. The tiniest bit contains the entire Trinity and all that comes with the power of God. You do not receive all I can impart to you because you do not expect it, and you are not asking for it, so I am limited by your lack of **faith** in what I can impart to you, that will be active in your soul."

Taken from: **The Power of Communion Well Received**

"You who are blessed with the cross of sickness, which you carry knowingly, are among the most powerful of My intercessors, because you have offered your own bodies as a living holocaust to bring Heaven to Earth. I am with you and will multiply graces released on your behalf. Those of you who are suffering morally: wrongfully accused, unjustly incarcerated, discriminated against, beaten and imprisoned for your **faith**, experiencing persecution from relatives for your faith, losses of homes and goods through unusual weather conditions. All these sufferings, every one can be offered to My Father for this election."

Taken from: **The Power of Communion Well Received**

Faithfulness, God's

"I have proven Myself over and over again to some of you. Others are new to this concept and are proceeding with caution, one step at a time. It is important for you to keep remembrances of the times I have come through for you, when everything looked hopeless. These become altars, just as Jacob built an altar after He wrestled with Me. They are designated places that are proofs and solid evidences of My faithfulness. It could be a rock with an image on it. It could be a drawing, a song, an entry in your journal. Anything that points to **My faithfulness** in this 3-dimensional reality we live in together."

Taken from: **Hand in Hand With Daddy**

"When a soul puts all their confidence in Me, I am free to provide everything they need. Rather than providing and surviving, be about My business and all these things will be added unto you. Your insecurity and panic do nothing but give the devils permission to sift you, wear you out and cause you to move prematurely right into the enemies' waiting arms. But with your focus on bringing souls to Me, I am free to provide all you need. **My faithfulness** is your rear guard and covering."

Taken from: **God Will Provide For Those Left Behind**

"Soon my whole Christian community will be sifted and tested. This will cause them to leave the wilderness of their own worldly devices and into the freedom of My eternal Kingdom and sure provision for them. My children will have to let go of the foolish things of the past – things that I will not provide them with all the time, because they are not necessary to life - and indeed, in their super-fluidity, are harmful to the spirit.

"They are to receive their sustenance from My words to them, from My love for them and from **My faithfulness** as a husband. What I did not provide is surely of no use to them. Rather it is a hindrance that I am pruning away, so they may bear more fruit. This is why you question the necessity of some things. And rather then tell you what they are, I wish for you discover them and offer them to Me. I will replace them with what is good and right for you. I am needing you to let go of more of your comforts, Clare."

Taken from: **Dancing on the Waters of Adversity**

"It is SO SIMPLE. But your insecurities have you habituated to the latest news. I would have you habituated to Me in worship, and totally abandon yourselves to My divine providence. Be as little children. They play in the sandbox to their hearts content, without ever giving a thought to their own needs, because they know their parents have already provided for them. They simply don't question.

"Oh, come on, My Bride! When will you ever cast your cares on Me, because I care for you! You are trying to do My job and your job by constantly focusing on what's going to happen and what your needs will be. If you will just constantly focus on ME and **My faithfulness**, worshiping Me, the Heavens would open upon you."

Taken from: **Build With Fire-Tried Gold**

"Your love for Me. The triumph of your love for Me and how you have weathered all scorn and contempt and loved Me beyond all reasoning. How you have put men in their place, under your feet and kept your focus on the higher things, on Me and **My Faithfulness**.

"You could never fully comprehend the immense treasure that kind of love is to Me. When you refuse to reason with doubts, when you come running to Me because you have felt threatened and tuck into the shadow of My wings - what a thrill touches My being, because My little creation has defended Me to man."

Taken from: **The Triumph of Your Faith Brings Me Joy**

Faithfulness, God's

"Any disturbance of peace and joy is the work of a demon. When you feel fear, stop. Use My word and destroy that lie. Fear, anxiety, insecurity, doubt, panic, all of these are weapons of warfare used to disable and destroy you. Doubt, Fear and Confusion, are signs of demonic intervention. Take up your sword and destroy them, before they get a stronger foothold.

"They will try, but when they come at you from one direction, I will help you fight them off in seven directions, I will scatter them and put them on the run, but I need your cooperation.

…"This message is so important to preserve peace, you can already see how the enemy has been at work trying to undo the good that we have done together. Trying to steal joy, plant rumors, denigrate you and all the prophets I have given wisdom of these hours to. You mustn't let them succeed, defend Me defend and My honor. **My faithfulness**, My commitment to My Bride to bring her joyfully, whole and happy into My Kingdom."

Taken from: **Attacks Against Faith Are On the Way**

"It is not a sin to be weak. Merely declare, 'Lord, I am willing to be made willing'. It is a sin to say, 'Lord, I am not willing to be made willing.' In that case, I leave you in the desert for a determined amount of time, to experience the folly of your choices. Then, when you are weary of yourself, I come and deliver you into a new life. So, do not fear change. Do not fear the consequences of the changes I lead you into. Fear nothing but sin, and Trust Me.

"The more painful and insecure the change is, the greater benefits to your soul. You see, there are many things you cling to out of worldly wisdom. The very thought of letting them go is scary, but remember: I have put a net of grace beneath you and nothing I ask you to abandon will be of any benefit to you in the future - and more likely than not, it will be in the way and prevent the blessings I have in store for you. When this fear grips you, reflect on all the life events and situations you called out to Me to help you with. Reflect on **My faithfulness** and how well I resolved them for you and the many blessings that followed that time of crisis."

Taken from: **I Am Leading You Into Your Dreams; Trust Me**

"There is a HUGE door of the NEW before you, but to enter it requires your complete 'YES' of trust. In this NEW door before you, in this place of 'letting go' and 'relinquishing control' He is going to show you again, His faithfulness, His extravagant provision, His strength, His alignment, His promotion, His favor, His healing and His goodness and never-ending, mind-blowing kindness.

"You are going to be IN OVER YOUR HEAD at the GOODNESS and KINDNESS OF JESUS!"

"Many of you have been looking at the feeling of being 'out of control' and not knowing what's going on as a bad thing. The Lord is shifting your focus. In your LETTING GO, your place of DEEP TRUST you are moving into a level of freedom you have NEVER known, a place of JOY you have never known, and in that 'in over your head place' you will receive exactly what you need..."   by Lana Vawser

Taken from: **In Over My Head**

"Now I bless you, My dear ones, and commend you for your efforts and prayers. Together, we have truly made the difference in this nation and the world. You have done well and even greater graces shall be given you for your **faithfulness**."

Taken from: **Trump Wins - The Battle Begins**

Fear

"Do you know how many times a day **fear** interrupts us?" (He means the ability to communicate together.) "You were bound by **fears: fear** of displeasure, **fear** of dying, **fear** of disease, **fear** of losing your husband or your children, **fear** of Me... Even as kind as I am and as gentle with you, you're still afraid. **Fear** of uselessness, **fear** of failure... Don't you see how controlled you are by **fear**? This is universal to man."

*I confess I struggle with **fear** a lot. I feel like a dartboard that the enemy throws a dart at and it sticks. I have to work it out using God's Word as the forceps and my history with Him as a clamp. I can look back upon my history and that holds me in place, and I can hold that wound while I use His Word to pull out that poisonous dart. It makes total sense to me that this would be the final teaching after intimacy, because without intimacy with the Lord you're really susceptible to **fear**. When we don't meet **fear** head on, it can become an underlying, motivating force that colors all of our actions and relationships and we don't even know sometimes how that's happening.*

*We just respond certain ways, because there's a memory back in there that causes **fear**. It hasn't been confronted and it hasn't been dealt with. It becomes a button, really. We end up doing things automatically without even understanding "Why did I do that, why did I say that, or react that way?" This is universal to all men and women. It's **fear** of being ridiculed, **fear** of loss, **fear** of sickness, **fear** of rejection, **fear** of failure, **fear** of helplessness, and **fear** of poverty.*

*Let's get back to the Lord's remedy for **fear**, which is the Word. I have to say the Word won't do you a great deal of good if you don't know the Lord. People who don't have a relationship with the Lord and quote the Word is just empty religious jargon. It's just history of the Jewish nation. But the Word to a Believer is a vital, living force that transforms and translates us from darkness into light on a daily basis. It's so powerful.*

*Falling into **fear** can change the whole course of your life. If you're* *dedicated to serving the Lord, the last thing the enemy wants you to do is serve the Lord. He wants to put you back out into the secular world and make you too exhausted to serve the Lord. There are people who are called to make tents and to teach. That's up to God. He makes the choices with His servants what He wants them to do.***

*In my very first YouTube video called "Overcoming **Fear**" I shared that most of the time the enemy is not allowed to touch us, but he is allowed to threaten us with a smoke screen filled with **fear** and fearful possibilities. He's allowed to do that, but they're not allowed to touch us. People spend their entire lives being influenced by these smoke screens. He allows them to threaten, to cause **fear**, just like the movie Monsters, Inc. I've heard it said that demons feed on **fear** just like fire feeds on fuel. I don't claim to know the answer to that for sure, but I know that they generate a lot of **fear** about things that will never happen or may happen... b*

*There's also another thing that can get us into trouble. There's no end to **fear** that can be generated unless you deliberately observe a 'no negatives' rule, forbidding talking about things that threaten, destroy, and discourage. We make a point to keep those things out of our lives and refuse to engage with other people over them.*

*In our mission, we have people who come here and they are **fearful** about the future. And I have to say, "Not today, let's not talk about that". I'm not saying ignore everything. There are some things you should take care of. But this mindless gossip and going over and over again about how bad the environment is, how bad the financial crisis is - it doesn't serve any purpose at all. It takes our hearts and minds totally away from the Lord Jesus Christ. We're the temple of the Holy Spirit and He doesn't want to see it or hear it. That's what He told me.* He has said, "I live in your heart, I don't want to hear that and I don't want to see it. This is My temple - you need to protect it."

Taken from: **Have No Fear of The Future**

Fear

"Because this is so dark, (talking about demon aliens) I do not want you looking into it. For many it can become frightening, even terrorizing. But you have My Scriptures and promises to sustain you. 'No evil will befall you, nor will any plague come near your tent.' These are not idle words; they are promises for those who belong to Me and obey Me.

"The whole world will be terrorized by the discovery and disclosure of these creatures, but My people have nothing to *fear*. Whether visible or invisible, every knee will bow, every tongue confess that I am Lord. In other words, they are subject to Me. My Name, when used by My Believer, is a strong tower, a mighty fortress and an offensive force that is mightier than any weapon they have."

Taken from: **Overcoming the Deceptions of This Age...**

So, I'm going to say something that might kind of shock you but, I believe the number one problem that we have with intimacy and why we don't have enough intimacy with the Lord; it's not our work, not our children, not our spouse, not entertainments, not sickness and not homelessness, not poverty, not wealth and not possessions. The number one problem we have is **fear***. Now, why should we be afraid of the Lord? Well, Satan's done a pretty good job of slandering His character. We're going to go into that. So, there is a lot of* **fear** *there, I think. Don't squirm and deny this, okay? No one is listening in on this but the Holy Spirit - so I want you to, if you don't think this is true of you, I need you to maybe turn the video off for a minute and think about it. Think about if there is some kind of secret, hidden* **fear** *or outright* **fear** *that you have when you come to be in the presence of the Lord.*

Taken from: **Do Not Fear of Reject Intimacy with God**

"I see the heartbreaking struggles you go through. I see your tears and resolve to stay away from sin. I see and I honor, so do not *fear* to come to Me when you fall. I wait for you with open arms. Understand that I do see everything about your life and I know where you are sincerely trying and where you are not. I am a God of forgiveness and restoration. When you have done your best, your very best and still fail, humility is worked deeply into your soul. Did I not say tax collectors and prostitutes will enter Heaven before the self-righteous? Indeed, I did. And whether you are aware of it or not, your weakness has kept you from joining ranks with those who congratulate themselves that they are not like other men."

Taken from: **You Are My Bride, My Garden Sealed**

"Stand on My Words. Watch them unfold. Know that I am in total control and I will keep you in the palm of My Hand and bring you into eternal glory. Do not *fear* any man, any weapon, any demise. Cleave only to Me and I shall make Myself clearly known to you in that hour, and you shall have Peace."

Taken from: **The Day of the Lord is Upon Us**

"He (the enemy) is cruising to steal from you through anger, bitterness, resentment and foolish *fears*. When you feel those things rising in your emotions, it is the enemy stealing from you. He wants to take away your sweetness, your presence with Me, and the overflow I fill you with."

He continued, "He loves to incite anger to drain you before you can even begin your day or finish a project or your prayers. He loves to lie in your ear, cause you to erupt into anger or **fear** and then drain you of all you had planned for the day and you run off to tend to these decoys. He is very clever and he knows which buttons to push. His agents, the demons, are forever observing you and taking notes."

Taken from: **You Are My Bride, My Garden Sealed**

Fear

"That is what this is all about. Relationship. There is nothing that pleases Me more than to be recognized for who I am and trusted that My love for you does not stop Me from being approachable. When you learn of My true nature and cultivate this friendship, you begin to reflect Me to others and they, too, begin to hunger for an intimate relationship with Me. They feel peace and comfort in My presence, rather than **fear** causing them to shake and cower. This is the lot of My Beloved ones, those who from the heart want to live a holy life.

"The wicked tremble, as well they should, because their hearts conceive only of evil and destruction of all that is good. But for you, who are My precious ones, wherever you are in your journey, I am all loving, receiving, and nurturing."

Taken from: **Who I Really Am To You**

"This is why our trysting time is so key and central to our relationship. Love will triumph when discipline fails. Love will triumph when temptations assail you. Love will triumph when exhaustion would take you down. Do you understand? You are hated because of this. The devils hate the sweet and pure intimacy you have with Me. They hate you teaching that to others. Because the **fear** of Hell and punishment will keep a soul out of sin, but just barely. And those who avoid sin because of punishment eventually become lukewarm and are of little threat to the enemy and the kingdom of darkness."

Taken from: **Your Greatest Strength**

"My Love, I am not distant from you as your heart has allowed you to imagine. I am still here, faithful as always, ready to instruct, reassure and love My children and My Bride. **Fear** is useless - what is needed is faith. Faith that I am in control, faith that nothing can trespass the limits I have ordained for each and every soul.

"Faith that no matter how bad it looks, there is still a silver lining to that dark cloud. I may be hiding behind that cloud at the moment, but I will burst through again and bring the warmth of My presence to inundate your heart."

Taken from: **You Are Mothers of Souls**

"Really, what are you willing to suffer for Me? Are you willing to fall from favor in the eyes of man? Call to Me in these moments and I will instruct you and lead you out into an open place where you can find peace in My presence without the entanglements of men.

"Never **fear** to call evil what is evil, never **fear** to stand when you know what is right. It will sooner or later bring you into confrontation, so the sooner you master your **fears**, the more freedom you will have in the long run. Remember: I am always with you, beside you, in you, and I will come to you and give you comfort for the wrath you incur on My behalf. (Communion) is a great gift that He's given us and is definitely a weapon that the enemy fears, and that's why he puts it down and minimalizes it."

Taken from: **How Prayer Fails**

"It is one thing to know all about holiness; quite another to live it because you value the smile on My face more than all the laurels and accomplishments of the world - even the religious world.

"Your knowledge of Me must be intimate, your love for Me authentic. Not born of **fear**, but born of head-over-heels love. If you do not have this love ask Me for it and I will not deny you."

Taken from: **Election Day - "The Decisive Hour" Jesus said**

Food and Clothing

"Many of you have very solid hearts for Me but you haven't quite been able to bail out of your security zone to do My will. You are thinking as the world thinks, and as such your time is taken up by the world. You are working for the securities of a roof over your head, a car, **food and clothing**, and whether you admit it or not, approval from others, even in some cases, your parents."

Taken from: **What's Your Price?**

"Do not allow yourself to be alarmed by things changing around you. I am speaking to all My Brides right now. This is most often the tactic of the enemy to cause insecurity: the tangible things in your life undergoing change.

"When your heart is centered on Me, and not your family, your housing, your **food and clothing**, no matter what goes on around you, your heart will not be moved. In order to have this disposition of heart one must put their absolute, first priority in their relationship with Me, because I never change.

"When you begin to set your heart on other things, you are slowly being drawn off into a trap."

Taken from: **When a Sigh IS a Prayer**

How many people in our culture would be content with **food and clothing**? *That's not even mentioning a roof over your head or a hot shower. I'm not saying that we should be that primitive, but I am saying that all these other entanglements that we get ourselves into to conform and to look good are very destructive and not pleasing to the Lord at all. And they prevent you from growing spiritually.*

Taken from: **The Bride Will Not Yield Her Holiness to Money**

I guess my advice to you, to pass it on is: keep watching, but work really hard at what He's given you to do, especially works of charity. **Feeding the poor. Clothing the poor.** *Visiting at the hospital or the prison. Taking people somewhere.*

There are just so many things that you can do. Ask the Holy Spirit to help you be aware of the needs of the people around you. Just stay busy knowing that any minute, He could look in on you and say **"Okay it's time and you were working and that's wonderful. Now enter into your master's joy." (Matthew 25:21, 23)**

Taken from: **Work as If There Were No Tomorrow**

"So, there is a point to being exercised in self-control and self-denial. By My grace, you ascend on high to the throne I have prepared for you in Heaven. You say, 'But Lord, I don't care about a throne.' Ah yes, I understand. But do you care about justice and righteousness, healing the sick, **feeding and clothing the poor**, teaching the uninformed?

"Yes, of course you do. Do you wish to give wedding presents to Me? Do you wish to make Me ecstatically happy? Do you see My point? These offerings will bring you into a greater degree of authority and with that comes the privilege of doing more good for the Kingdom. Don't you know the Bride looks after the Groom's welfare and happiness?

"So, make Me happy. Throw off this harness of guilt and condemnation. Let these little self-indulgences - which the enemy makes light of before you commit them - but afterwards hammers you as with a maul... Let them fall away. Walk away from them. Leave those demons hanging in mid-air, with no results."

Taken from: **Guilt Dams Your Living Waters**

Food and Clothing

"This is the way My Bride acts: she doesn't pull the tares up with the wheat, rather she continues to cultivate that field. She binds up the wounded, lives a life of love before the community that all might embrace this way. While others are wagging their fingers at this or that Christian teacher, she is welcoming in the lame, the deaf, the blind, **feeding and clothing the poor,** and teaching them about My love by her actions."

Taken from: **Lord, Why Are Things Falling Apart?**

"As you look around you at those who do not know what is about to happen, do not allow pride to enter in... do not look down on anyone. Rather, if that thought enters your mind, immediately crush it by recounting all the virtue that person has that you don't have. And if you have a difficult time assigning virtue to them, imagine if you were brought up in a heavy drug and violence environment, where your mother was prostituting herself for drugs and where different men abused and hated you, where you were poor and never had **decent food to eat or warm clothing.** Imagine 15 years of that and what sort of person you would not be.

"Each soul I bring into the world has graces that accompany them. Some who are born into holy, ministering families came with 60 graces. Others who were born to prostitutes and drug addicts came into this world with only 6 graces.

"It is not what I gave you to begin with, but what you did with them that counts. How does that translate? That woman you know who is manipulative and sneaky is that way for a reason. She began life with inadequate means, and to survive she had to be sneaky. Some would be full blown criminals robbing, raping and destroying everything they could get their hands on. That she is just a little sneaky... well, that's nothing compared to what the demons wanted her to become and how they tempted and taunted her. But she used those 6 graces, she made the decision to be 'mostly' honest and good to others. Whereas another, raised in a well provided for household, with a university education, might be self-centered, proud and harbor resentment towards the poor and have failed to use the 30 graces they were given. Because without love, you have nothing."

Taken from: **I Am Clothing You in My Lowliness**

"My Darling Bride, I am calling you to enter into My Passion with Me, for very specific purposes. All of you, My Brides, have cordoned off your heart from My torments. And how do you expect to know My Love for humankind if you do not accompany Me in My sacrifice? These are deep things. Not all will follow.

"But you who are My Beloved ones, cleaving to Me with all your hearts, you must open those chambers and drink from that cup with Me. Of all the delights and consolations I could give you, nothing approaches what you will experience in My Heart of Hearts. That said, for those who cannot accompany Me, I love you all the same and there is no condemnation for those who do not have the stomach to follow Me.

"Lest you misunderstand, it is not about the blood and gore. It is about the absolute desolation of My Heart - that those I have created and provided this beautiful planet for and breathed life into them. Those I have blessed with children, **food and clothing**. Even those I healed of leprosy abandoned Me in the hour of My agony. They sided with Satan's agents and spat upon the ground at the foot of My Cross. Can you imagine that? Taunting, ridicule, contempt, all heaped upon Me during My unbelievable torments as I suffered for them and they knew it not. Yes, you are beginning to get the picture now. 'Forgive them Father, for they know not what they do.'"

Taken from: **Drink of the Deep Things of God**

Food and Clothing

Ezekiel: Being Jesus, being His hands and feet to a hurting and confused world. And the one that you reach out to, Paul says, that you could be entertaining angels, unaware. But, I guarantee you, many times that's Jesus at the door.

Clare: Absolutely. As Mother Theresa used to say, "in the distressing disguise of the poor." And that's why she was so wonderful with the poor, because she really saw the suffering Christ under the appearance of it, distressing disguise of the poor.

Ezekiel: …Compared to the rest of the people around this globe, most of us have more **food and clothing** *and shelter than what we need. We have SO much and so give us a heart of gratitude, Lord.*

Taken from: **The Bride's Joys and Sorrows Intensify…**

"Many of these have been abused and rejected from childhood and their only interaction with the world was to get what they needed through every deceptive means. They do not understand family or love and protection; they've had to fend for themselves - fighting off hunger, loneliness, the cold and hostility of those around them.

"It is truly sad and breaks My Heart to see how children are treated - but the issues go back through many generations of drinking, crime and drugs. These who are so looked down upon have been rejected from birth and do not have the normal social skills of you who have been raised by good parents.

"Were I to show you what their childhood was like, you would be horrified. Many of these children were tended only by My angels. They went from dumpster to dumpster looking for **clothing and food** while their parents locked them out of the house or were constantly gone, either under the influence or walking the streets looking for their next fix. I have put these poor ones before you as an exercise in mercy.

Many, but not all, who came from middle class and functional lower class families do not understand the principles of mercy and reaching out on a personal level to the unfortunate."

Taken from: **From Jesus with Love**

So, I went to the Bible Promises and opened to the heading, **Food and Clothing.** *My first reaction was, "Yeah!! The Lord's acknowledging that I need clothing!" Oh, boy... But then common sense settled in and I said to myself... Clare... what else could this mean?? Better look at both sides. Better look at both sides - better safe than sorry...*

You see, one of the biggest impediments to clear discernment is an attachment to getting things your own way. You want to be justified in your desire for something, and in an effort to be justified you even twist the Scriptures that you get, even just a little, to accommodate your self will. That's deadly in discernment! You have to be willing to get a big NO from the Lord without pitching a pout. Easier said than done.

The "roughness of that" calling and "the primitive church" calling and I got quite involved in that and cultivated a much deeper relationship with the Lord - and really did give up my social idols, you know: clothing and food and impressing people, society and all of that.

Taken from: **Conversion to Christ testimony (pt.2)**

Lord, we simply come before You, thanking You that You Love us more profoundly than we can imagine. We might not always sense and feel it, but it's by Faith. You tell us that over and over again, but we are so fortunate. Compared to the rest of the people around this globe, most of us have more **food and clothing** *and shelter than what we need. We have SO much and so give us a heart of gratitude, Lord.*

Taken from: **The Bride's Joys and Sorrows Intensify**

Forgiveness

These little tag-along uglies (the demons) know this – so they work energetically to cause toxic guilt that paralyzes our relationship with God. We have to learn to outsmart the little monsters, and go directly to the Lord when we've fallen short. Confess our weakness, our sin, and ask **forgiveness** *in all humility. This needs to be done without delay. The longer we delay, the more monsters accumulate on our backs, shouting how worthless and bad we are.*

Taken from: **Tag-a-long Monsters**

When we are critical of others, and attack people, we injure, hurt, make them weaker. That's not the spirit of the Lord, that's the spirit of the Pharisee. That's legalism. I don't think any of us wants to have a religious spirit because a religious spirit is sent by the devil to cause division in the Body. And when we insist on having our own way, when we defend things or attack things, then we do damage. That's not the spirit of the Lord, that's the spirit of the Pharisee, a religious spirit. That's something we need to repent of, and ask the Lord's **forgiveness**. *And if we have offended our brother or our sister, go to them and make amends, tell them we're sorry.*

Taken from: **Spirit of the Lord or Spirit of Pharisee**

"My children, the ways of the world that you have learned are totally inappropriate here. I protect those who humble themselves before Me. If you are prancing around proudly with all the answers, you are bound for destruction.

"I am counting on your breaking when you realize all you've been taught by friends and family has just come to pass before your very eyes. I am counting on you face flat on the floor begging **forgiveness** for your pride and arrogance. I am laying the groundwork for you to survive the trials that are now at your door, both body and soul."

Taken from: **Jesus Speaks On What Is To Come #5**

"In other situations I allow the demons permission because I'm perfecting a soul in virtue and patience - **forgiveness** and virtue needs to be cultivated. At the very same time, when I allow an attack from the demon, I know how it will affect a soul and that they will, in turn, pray for those who are being used to attack. Very often those souls have no one to pray for them and the one whom they attack are My very last resort to find intercessors."

Taken from: **Jesus Speaks on Why Our Enemies Are Important**

"But this generation is the most magnificent in faith because the opposition is more advanced and powerful than it has ever been. This is the critical generation, the one to witness My coming and the one to witness the most ferocious attacks of the enemy in all dimensions. From beheadings to powerful nightmares to doubts about your sanity, these are all the tactics of the enemy on My People and a force to be reckoned with. And those of you who have run to Me seeking the shelter of truth, I have bathed in My **forgiveness** and strengthened in authority to proclaim the truth boldly."

Taken from: **The Triumph of Your Faith Brings Me Joy**

Not that you are perfect every moment of the day, but that you're constantly, continually focused on pleasing Him, on being obedient and on doing the right thing. And that when you do fall, you don't beat yourself up. That's pride! When you beat yourself up, it's pride, because you're saying you should have been perfect. And nobody's perfect but God. But when you do fall, coming to Him and being truly sorrowful for falling, and asking forgiveness - repenting and turning around 180 degrees and going the right way direction. That's SO pleasing to Him! That's what He's looking for in each of us in our hearts.

Taken from: **Ezekiel's Rapture Dreams: We Can't Make it Happen**

Forgiveness

"The bitterness of her losses was so overwhelming, she chose to hide away and waste her life. Some do that. Some never learn. Some find out at the last moment and they are ripe for the picking. Yes, that is what I am biding My time for. Yes, that is My strategy. At that fateful moment, I will reveal the poor choices they made to the soul and give them one last chance to repent and accept My **forgiveness**. They, in that moment, are totally broken down and have no more fight in them. That is when I visit them with My Love. They have no more resistance...pray that in that moment, she will embrace Me, the lover of her soul."

Taken from: **Talents: What Did You Do With What You've Been Given**

"Be peacemakers. Be the one to take up for the absent when cruel things are said. Be the one who puts a stop to gossip and calumny. ... Oh, how beautiful you are when you defend righteousness and sow peace among brothers and sisters. You most resemble Me when you bring order out of confusion, understanding out of conflict, turning bitterness to **forgiveness** and kindness. There is no price worthy of such a soul as the one who goes around bringing brotherly love and concord. The fruits of such a one as this will testify to her virtue throughout eternity."

Taken from: **Blessed are the Peacemakers**

"I am asking you, Children: take a long look in the mirror and know yourselves. Ask My Holy Spirit to reveal your true weaknesses. What will this accomplish? Compassion and **forgiveness** for those who betray you. I want My Body mended, put back together. Satan has spent the last 2,000 years contriving plans that would push the members of My Body apart, further and further.

"If you are dividing My Body, you are working for Satan. You are being used by the demons if you are separating brethren. If you are taking the failings of others as a final door slammed shut, you are creating pockets of bitterness for the demons to create strongholds in YOUR life, not the lives of those who hurt you. They will walk on, but you will stumble because of what you are holding onto.

"That is why **forgiving** is a work of charity, a work of mercy. It makes up for judgment, calumny, and lying. What sin has severed, you can restore by your charity. Just as surely as wounds heal, forgiveness cleanses those pockets of corruption and allows tender flesh to grow back.

"When you refuse to **forgive**, you are only demonstrating your lack of knowledge of self. This calls Me to your side. Now, I must reveal to you your weakness and how you fail others. I do it again and again and again until you finally understand and learn to forgive and go on."

Taken from: **How a Root of Bitterness Can Change Your Destiny & DNA**

"I see the heartbreaking struggles you go through. I see your tears and resolve to stay away from sin. I see and I honor, so do not fear to come to Me when you fall. I wait for you with open arms. Understand that I do see everything about your life and I know where you are sincerely trying and where you are not. I am a God of **forgiveness** and restoration.

"When you have done your best, your very best and still fail, humility is worked deeply into your soul. Did I not say tax collectors and prostitutes will enter Heaven before the self-righteous?

"Indeed, I did. And whether you are aware of it or not, your weakness has kept you from joining ranks with those who congratulate themselves that they are not like other men."

Taken from: **You Are My Bride, My Garden Sealed**

Forgiveness

"Getting ready. Getting ready to meet Me. Preparing their hearts before My mirror and asking **forgiveness** for what they see that is not right. All these years My people have gone one of two ways: being constantly guilty or constantly OK - like, 'nothing wrong here.' But now I am asking for a deeper look. A more candid look, not glossing anything over. It is incomprehensible to you, My children, the demands of personal holiness. Because of My mercy, much is overlooked. But rather than be shocked, as that young boy Nathan was when he stood before his audience and his sins were revealed. I want you to spend time with My Holy Spirit and ask Him to reveal the darkness still inside of you.

"When you discover it, I don't want you going over the deep end. I already knew it was there. All I want for you to do is confess it, ask *forgiveness* and make a resolution in your heart to avoid those sins and pray for the grace not to repeat them. You see, though you fall and are not perfect, because you confess and work on it I will forgive you and continue to pour out the graces you need to finally overcome your faults. You do not have to be perfect but you do need to be perfectly repentant."

Taken from: **Get Ready For Your Journey**

"You are not guaranteed life tomorrow. Yet Heaven and Hell lie directly before you. Choose this day who you will serve, and if it is Me, you have only to ask for the strength to break from your sinful past, and I will enfold you in My arms with great compassion and **forgiveness.** However, if you choose to continue on in your sinful ways, I have warned you, death is at the door and your tomorrow is not guaranteed. Do not sell your souls for a trifle.

"Repent, break with sin, come to Me. I will restore you and rebirth you into life eternal, fully equipped to live a holy life, from the inside out."

Taken from: **Your Tomorrow is Not Guaranteed**

"That is why so many who visit Heaven are amazed at the simple people that have been exalted to positions of great authority. I have been watching the hearts of My Brides, transformed into hearts very much like My own. I have seen their wounds, the scorn and contempt, the rejection, the acts of **forgiveness** - and their hearts look so very much like Mine. Many look for a Queen, but I look for a servant. I am a King, but I came as a servant. This is why the Bride must resemble the Groom."

Taken from: **Your Lives Have Not Been Wasted**

"Precious ones, I want you to consider the fruits of your accusations and how you have divided My Body. What was meant to be a blessing has instead become a curse to you. So, I am asking you all to repent and beg **forgiveness** from one another, get back on the right track, let your sanctity remain intact and moving forward."

Taken from: **Division in the Body is Grieving the Lord**

"What the enemy has meant for evil, I intend to use to teach you all how to handle opposition more effectively. The first thing to remember is that where charity and **forgiveness** abound, there is healing. Where contentiousness and self-will, self-assertiveness abound - there is injury.

"My Brides, it is by your behavior that you open or close doors. When you are docile, kindly and humble you leave little wood to put on the fire. Where there is contentiousness, Pride is stimulated and every evil springing from Pride - especially having to be right and downgrading others. This only leads to injury. It takes two to fight or disagree."

Taken from: **Spiritual Warfare: 1 - Enemy Tactics**

Fruitfulness

A lot of times people use judgment and social norms, and what have you, rather than using discernment, spiritual discernment. That's' not easy to come by. That's a **fruit** *of a deep relationship with the Lord, with knowing the mind of Christ. Feeling the Holy Spirit quickening you. That's not gained by a superficial prayer life.*

The Lord once told me, "Some people swim in the shallows, romp and play. Other people swim and play in the water in deeper levels. Some go boating in the water. But the ones that dives for pearls – that's what I want you to be. I want you to be a pearl diver. Not someone who sits on the beach and wiggles their toes in the water. Not someone who plays in the shallows or swims on the surface. But someone who goes DEEP to find the Pearl of Great Price."

Taken from: **The Straight-Jacket of Poverty**

"You have pleased Me. That is all that counts. You have taken quite a bit of calumny from those closest to you, but others see the pearls in My Kingdom that you are. But even if you were fortunate enough that no one could see, still, you have born much **fruit** by your simple detached (from worldly rewards) obedience. And without self-seeking; rather at all times, seeking Me and My approval alone. This is what I have meant, this I will reward and still you will stay small and safe. Tucked away in My Heart, abounding in love and grace, much to My glory."

Taken from: **My Bride is Not Responding**

"If you are not working for Me in this hour, you are standing before Me blind and naked. Rise up and take on your Master's business. Bring forth **fruit** worthy of My Bride, and while you are doing this I will see to it that you grow into the fullness of who I've called you to be as My Spouse. My promise to you is life eternal and the choicest lands of Heaven, the sweetest intimacy possible to a created soul. Don't let Me down in this hour; rise up, harness yourself to My carriage, for My yoke is easy, My burden is light, and I will make joyful for you the act of going out and gathering to Me My Bride."

Taken from: **Blood Moon Rapture: Prophetic Word**

"I'm asking you, in a way, to please examine your life. Are you wasting your time on empty things? On beauty that can never satisfy? Feathering your nest or impressing people? There's nothing wrong with being simple and looking nice, but when you make an occupation and a lifestyle out of it, it eats you alive. It eats your time alive. What beautiful gifts for the Kingdom of God has the Lord placed inside of you that are not coming into **fruition,** because your time is tied in knots around all of this?"

Taken from: **Black Panther Prophetic Dream**

"Soon my whole Christian community will be sifted and tested. This will cause them to leave the wilderness of their own worldly devices and into the freedom of My eternal Kingdom and sure provision for them. My children will have to let go of the foolish things of the past – things that I will not provide them with all the time, because they are not necessary to life - and indeed, in their super-fluidity, are harmful to the spirit. They are to receive their sustenance from My words to them, from My love for them and from My faithfulness as a husband. What I did not provide is surely of no use to them. Rather it is a hindrance that I am pruning away, so they may bear more **fruit**. This is why you question the necessity of some things. And rather then tell you what they are, I wish for you discover them and offer them to Me. I will replace them with what is good and right for you. I am needing you to let go of more of your comforts, Clare."

Taken from: **Dancing on the Waters of Adversity, Prophetic Admonition**

Fruitfulness

*Each of us has comparable gifts and even those who love and pray for us are a gift. We want to give a return on His investment, but we do have an enemy who is very clever and knows our weak spots. I'd venture to say that every one of us has a lazy bone somewhere. Reasoning, "Aw, that's too much work! We're going to be raptured soon, there's no time for that!" Well, even if that's true, still we have given Him our ALL every day of our life. And some of those things will yield **fruit** before we're raptured, so there are no excuses to put off using our gifts.*

Taken from: **Do It Anyway**

"To see it in the spirit is hard enough, even the mention of Orlando and its implications. It's only the beginning...even that is taking a toll right now and I must say, bringing forth **fruit** as well, though you are totally unaware of it by My design. All of you have been told about these things for months.

"Now that you see them happening, you can at least have confidence that I am in control and not even a sparrow drops to the ground without My awareness. You only see the tip of the iceberg. But someday in Heaven you will know completely and no longer have any questions as to why this happened here and why that happened."

Taken from: **Permission to Burn and Travailing Prayer**

"Removing this elaborate interior structure and replacing it with your infinite value to Me takes many years of maturing and coming to know Me. Your safest posture, My precious loves, is that of a very little child about to cross a rush hour freeway. Your only recourse, "Daddy, help me." Do you know how pleasing that posture is before Me?

"The snow-capped peaks are magnificent to behold, but as the snow melts, water flows downwards until it comes to rest in the lowliest places, producing much fruit. And so the lofty heights are barren, but the lowly valleys are fruitful. And so the more lowly you are, the more **fruitful** you will become.

"I say this to you, because many of you have reservations about how I can use you. What I am saying to you now is that the more worthless you are in your own eyes, and truly believing you are the least of all, the more precious the gift of yourself is to Me. No one will assign you as the author of your deeds, but they will clearly see it is Me.

"So, My beloved ones, do not be dismayed at your lack of talent, intellect, experience, status before men - for all those things are useless to Me. So, even the most astute prognosticators and scientists may see what is, but they do not see Who I AM. They do not see WHAT I DO. They only see the hard evidence...not the One who created it and what He will allow and what He will not allow.

"Wake up, My people, produce fruits of repentance, worthy of being saved on that day. You're chasing your tails people. You are wasting precious moments of time that has been granted to you for other souls. You will look back on what you did in your life and be distraught when you see the opportunities you passed for ministry, to the hurting and lost souls all around you, because you were so busy seeking the latest news on the latest comet.

"What else can I say to you, My Children? Please, stop this behavior and get busy with the lost. I am not fooling with you. I am dead serious. You are putting yourselves in harm's way by ignoring the real needs of My Kingdom. Ones that I send you daily. When the time comes for the worst humanity has ever seen I, Myself, will deliver you if you yourself are relying on Me and Me alone, and have put your attention on the souls I send you. I, Myself, will guard you."

Taken from: **Whisperings and Forebodings of Disaster**

Gossip

"A root of bitterness is a toxic root. It gives off deadly acids, much like the soil beneath the cedar tree. Nothing can grow beneath a cedar, because what is released from the roots is toxic to other plants. That means the soil in the garden of your soul is being poisoned. All that can flourish in this toxic soil is anger, resentment, retaliation, jealousy and hatred. Then you must work to disguise these evils under a smile and fair words. This will eventually wear you out and open the door for disease in your body.

"Hatred, unforgiveness, retaliation and bitterness create energy waves that poison your body. These feelings can be measured electronically. They actually weaken and change your DNA, allowing cancer cells to proliferate. This is the environment the demons plant their seeds in. Discontent opens the door to sin, retaliation, **gossip**, stealing, plotting evil and cheating. Your lives become a tangled web for unclean things, and soon the fragrant garden you once had is turned into a wretched tangle of darkness, where demons defecate to fertilize roots of bitterness growing all around you - until all your good intention is snuffed out and you are controlled by self-defense, bitterness and fear.

"You have a choice to make, My Children. You can either play into the enemy's hands or resist him, crying out 'Lord, deliver me from evil!'"

Taken from: **How a Root of Bitterness Can Change Your Destiny and DNA**

"My children, never, ever, throw off prayer and discernment for the opinion of men or demons. Never respond to rancor and throw your lot in with evil-doers. Never trade the mansion in Heaven for a place in the furnace prepared for the devils. Never be lazy in prayer and discernment. Understand: your very salvation can be put at risk by coming under the yoke of calumny and **gossip**."

Taken from: **How Does a Fall Happen?**

"One of the most serious preparations you can make, any of you can make, is to prepare your hearts for Heaven. In Heaven there is no slander, no backbiting, no jealousy, no fear, no **gossip**, no hopelessness, and no depression. In Heaven there is supreme bliss. And as you choose to dwell in Me, you will have a taste of this bliss. Each day you will be tempted to enter into gossip, tale bearing, lust and all the other sins that have plagued your whole life."

Taken from: **Maintain Your Purity and Light**

"I have prepared an army of men and women to recover this country from the enemy. They will swing into action and have an active part in taking ground away from the Order. Never since the history of man has there been a time such as what is coming, and never since the history of man has My protection been as strong as it will be.

"But there are certain rules you must live by. Honesty is first and foremost. Vigilance over your own sins and bad example. The devils are clever and they know how to provoke a soul to cause a breach in their covering. Charity, humility and patience also score high on the list of things targeted and necessary to maintain My Protection.

"Come to Me immediately when you fall. Don't waste a moment. Make a sincere confession and renounce that sin. I will then restore your covering and add to it protection, and the grace to not repeat those sins. I have already taught you about judging others. The quickest way to lose your covering is to slander, calumniate, or **gossip** about another. Not only will the enemy use this to divide and conquer, he will use it to make you vulnerable to attack. The more key your position is, the more careful you will have to be about your heart attitude. Never disparage anyone who is sick or weak. Their prayers are essential and extremely important."

Taken from: **Surviving the Coming Tribulation**

Gossip

"Spiritual warfare will be needed just to get through the day. This will not be a time of ease but a time of fighting to maintain ground, and pressing in to take more ground. Those who do not have an authentically intimate relationship with Me will be grossly led astray into counterfeits which are about to spring up everywhere. Bashing and gossip will reach an unprecedented level and those who do not live by My Ways will fall. The enemy will use **gossip** to create a breach in their armor and on the heels of that, demons will enter and wreak havoc."

Taken from: **Refining Fires Are Coming**

"For some of you Satan is counting on your past weaknesses to bring you all the way down, even into his pit - were it possible. Now is the time to grow up, see others as fragile and needing much grace, and see yourself in My mirror. Yes, when I withdraw My protection and allow you to fall, My mirror will be there so you will see your faults are much greater than your brother or sisters. This is My gift of grace to you, I will show you who you are and who you aren't, and if you are wise you will never again lift your head to condemn another.

"Oh, how I love each of you so tenderly, even those of you with the blood of **gossip** on your hands. I still love you."

Taken from: **Refining Fires Are Coming**

"Many are so sure they are ready to stand before Me, but they're not taking a good look inside themselves or in My mirror. This concerns me, Clare. It concerns Me that they are so ready, and yet they still quarrel and bite at one another. They still **gossip** and tell lies about one another. They still accuse with impunity, thinking they are so right, and the other is so wrong.

"Yet, I tell you, they are not ready to stand before Me. They are blinded by self-righteousness. They are on a crusade to set the world straight, but they are unfit for the Bridal gown. I cannot put a clean, white garment on those who are still jealous and destructive with their tongue. I cannot put that gown on anyone who does not love their brother as they love Me."

Oh, Jesus, in this moment, I don't live up to that standard.

"With you, I count your will; as with others, I will do the same. If you willfully put down your dislike, hatred, resentment, jealousy, or distaste for others, I will help you and fill in the rest. It's all in the will. If you willfully engage in jealousy, *gossip*, hatred, pride, and self-righteousness, you're in serious trouble.

All I am asking of you – so you will fit into your pristine bridal gown – is an honest self-appraisal. If you're holding scorn and contempt for anyone voluntarily, willfully… you will not stand before Me on that day."

Taken from: **Without Love You Will Not Be Taken in the Rapture…**

"Yes, I humble the proud, I allow them to fail in many, many different ways because pride was and is the original sin by Satan. Pride is the grandfather of sin and more than any other sin, I hate pride. It breeds judgment and **gossip** which destroys the life of My Body and deprives it of My gifts. It destroys marriages and leaves children without guidance from both parents. It degrades the simple and takes the meaning of their lives from them. There is nothing more destructive than pride - it can be found behind all the other sins, greed, lust, and too many things to mention."

Taken from: **Blessed Are the Pure**

Gossip

And I have to tell you, in my experience, there is NOTHING more vile to the Lord and the Great Cloud of Witnesses than **Gossip**, *Slander and Detraction. It's like a filthy, dirty baby diaper – I mean a BAD one. We have an expression around here, "Dirty Diaper!" Which is kinda like, "Be careful! This is not God – this is a dirty diaper. We don't play with dirty diapers, we put them in the trash and leave them there!!"*

Taken from: **Discernment: Fingerprints of the Enemy**

In our mission, we have people who come here and they are fearful about the future. And I have to say, "Not today, let's not talk about that". I'm not saying ignore everything. There are some things you should take care of. But this mindless **gossip** *and going over and over again about how bad the environment is, how bad the financial crisis is - it doesn't serve any purpose at all. It takes our hearts and minds totally away from the Lord Jesus Christ. We're the temple of the Holy Spirit and He doesn't want to see it or hear it. That's what He told me. He has said,* "I live in your heart, I don't want to hear that and I don't want to see it. This is My temple - you need to protect it."

Taken from: **Have No Fear of the Future, The Bride Knows Her God**

Ezekiel: *Those little Holy Spirit nudges that says, "Mmmm, it might be better if you don't say this" or "Maybe don't go there." Here's another example, "I normally wouldn't say this but we need to pray with so and so about this situation." It's* **gossip** *- just leave it. Many things don't need to be said.*

Taken from: **Rapture Delayed, Dealing with Disappointment**

But this mindless **gossip** *and going over and over again about how bad the environment is, how bad the financial crisis is - it doesn't serve any purpose at all. It takes our hearts and minds totally away from the Lord*

Jesus Christ. We're the temple of the Holy Spirit and He doesn't want to see it or hear it. That's what He told me. He has said, "I live in your heart, I don't want to hear that and I don't want to see it. This is My temple - you need to protect it."

Taken from: **Have No Fear/Future…**

Holy Spirit said, "The only reservation you should have concerning Me is not to ever grieve Me. Yes, truly I am a gentleman and **gossip**, impure conversation, bearing false witness, stealing and sexual sins I can not bear to be around and so I withdraw from those who practice these things. I am ever so sensitive to the wounding of other souls, when they are not present to defend themselves or even at all. I hate to see anyone hurt. I am so easily grieved by talk about My vessels unto honor and when you begin that kind of detraction, I have no other recourse than to withdraw from you."

Taken from: **Holy Spirit's Desire for Your Company**

"Those of you who have been the victims of **gossip**, slander and evil men, yet have prayed for them with sincere intention from the Heart – you very much resemble Me in My Crown of Thorns.

"Those of you who refuse to lie to the government, refuse to bear false witness – well done. I say to you. It may have cost you some great earthly good, but what does it profit you to gain the whole world and lose your very own soul? You may be poorer for it, but you have chosen what was right. Those of you who have kept yourselves clean from defilements in the world – well done, I say to you. You have followed the delicate leadings I've placed in your conscience. I am happy in your heart, and find great solace there."

Taken from: **Are You Ready for Rapture**

Grace, Graces

Now, I think it's important here to take a look at how hard we try on our own to be holy. This is a big mistake, because the harder you try the more you're going to fail. This is a job for God, this is not a job for us, guys. Consider that, if you began today, by the end of your life...do you think you could be perfect? Well, if you said "yes" to that - let me know how you're doing a year from now!

*On the other hand, for the rest of us who answered "no", this is the good news: we can't change anything about our character. Not one thing without **grace** from God. And if we think we can, He'll let us in for a little surprise because:* **"The Lord opposes the proud, but gives grace to the humble." James 4:6**

*So if you come to Him wanting His **grace**, He's going to give it to you, knowing that you're weak. But if you try to do it on your own, you're going to be in for a few... hard knocks. Let's put it that way. And, you know, we're partners in this endeavor and He didn't come to call the healthy. He came to call the sick. I don't know about you, but I've got some sickness in my soul! There are things I'm not – that are not holy. And I have things that I need to be redeemed from; need to be changed – habit patterns. But He didn't come to call the healthy, but the sick.*

Taken from: **Wounding Waters Part 4: Fear of Intimacy With God**

"No, I say to you work while there is still time. Do not waste what has been given to you. Cease from your self-centered activities and go out of yourself to reach others. That indeed is what My Bride is doing right now. Consider, she's flesh of My flesh, bone of My bone.

"And she longs as I do for souls to be brought into the Kingdom. She is doing everything in her power to accomplish this in the last hour. I have spread the **grace** far and wide to motivate My people into ascending into the Bridal Chamber with Me, where they will be fully equipped through intimacy to go out and bring the lost into My banquet.

"If you are not working for Me in this hour, you are standing before Me blind and naked. Rise up and take on your Master's business. Bring forth fruit worthy of My Bride, and while you are doing this I will see to it that you grow into the fullness of who I've called you to be as My Spouse. My promise to you is life eternal and the choicest lands of Heaven, the sweetest intimacy possible to a created soul. Don't let Me down in this hour; rise up, harness yourself to My carriage, for My yoke is easy, My burden is light, and I will make joyful for you the act of going out and gathering to Me My Bride."

Taken from: **Blood Moon Rapture**

"In the meantime, there are suffering souls that need the light to shine on their darkness so they may be lifted up to Me. Many are the sufferings of the lost and My heart is to bring them salvation from their enemies, and from themselves.

"Deep and dark is the pit they have dug for themselves. As the saying goes, 'If you want to get out of the pit, stop digging'. I say stop sinning and take hold of the rope of **Grace**. I am lowering it now into your life. Come forth out of this pit, this deep darkness and let the sun shine all around you. I have a new life in Me to give you.

"This life will be full of gifts and challenges, but it will not be fruitless as your former lives have been. No, this life will bring you the peace you have never had, a sense of purpose, a sense of destiny that speaks to the very core of your being. Yes, I have waited for you. I have waited, holding all these gifts for that special day when you will forsake yourself, and come to Me."

Taken from: **Rope of Grace**

Grace, Graces

"Please don't grow weary in well doing. Please don't allow your faith to backslide. You see, you must exercise these gifts for them to grow. Don't allow the weeds of unbelief spring up around them. You know the parable about the seed: some seed fell among the thorns and the cares of this world grew up around the seed and choked it out. (Luke 8) This is something for you to be aware of right now. This is the approaching season when the demons incite avarice, greed and busy work, luring you away from spiritual things into carnal things.

"To survive this and see your faith seeds grow, you will have to use them more often. Invest more time in using them, step forward in faith at every opportunity. Don't be shy. The fact that you were obedient, even though you didn't really feel the anointing, draws down My Mercy and **Grace**."

Taken from: **Water Your Gifts, Teaching from Jesus on Persevering**

"...this man - I only gave him one **grace**, but he used that to the maximum! This man saved the life of another man. He gave his life to keep a man who was drunk on the street, alive; to keep him warm. He laid on top of this man through the night to keep him warm - but, in the process of doing that he, himself, died."

Taken from: **Wounding Waters Part 2: Social Status**

"It is not a little thing to be entrusted with the knowledge of God, and be chosen by God to serve. No, it is a very high calling and requires the utmost amount of dependence on My counsels. The utmost amount of humility and understanding that you don't have all the answers. It is not the educated that will survive; it is the meek and devout who move neither to the left nor the right until they have sought My will. How many times in Scripture have I inferred or outright said, 'I have chosen the foolish things of this world to confound the wise?' Read the

Beatitudes. My blessings are poured over the very ones this world scorns: the poor, the meek, the grieving, the persecuted. These are the ones no one wants to be, but they are the very ones chosen for My **graces.** If you would be among them, throw out the purse of your own opinion and seek Me until you find Me, until you hear Me, until you read between the lines of Scripture and hear Me loud and clear."

Taken from: **Are You Wise**

"This is what I require of My Bride - she be steadfast, enduring and persistent. This is what I require and will reward with fresh *graces* from Heaven. I do not wish to make it difficult for you, but your mettle must be purified to carry the **graces** I wish to give you."

Taken from: **Persevere in Prayer...**

"The focus must be on charity and virtue, trust and faith in My ability to provide. Without these pivotal attitudes, they will not succeed. My protection can make you invisible. My protection can turn wild beasts away. My protection can save you from the ground giving way beneath you. My protection can provide water and food when there is none. I can do all things, and I will, for those whose agenda is to gather in souls to the Kingdom. Those who give and lead unselfishly, those who are honest and caring for others, these are the ones I will supernaturally protect and provide. Many I will add to your numbers that need salvation. Their eternity is hanging in the balance and if you make their eternity your priority, I will cover you. Souls are going to be racked with confusion and fear, not knowing up from down, so severe will the trials be on the Earth. They will be so thoroughly disoriented that nothing can calm them down but a supernatural **grace**. A healing **grace**, laying hands on them and praying for My Peace to descend upon them."

Taken from: **God Will Provide For Those Left Behind**

Grace, Graces

"It is not a little thing to be entrusted with the knowledge of God, and be chosen by God to serve. No, it is a very high calling and requires the utmost amount of dependence on My counsels. The utmost amount of humility. So in your situation, it was the suffering entailed in getting the barest necessities of life, water, for the animals.

"For someone else it may have been an old injury that flares up with arthritis. For someone else it may be a change in plans that delays the completion of a project. While on the other side of the world are children who are barely skeletons; they may have had a meal that day for the first time in weeks. Another family could be on the run from ISIS and your delay over cherished plans could be the **graces** needed for their escape from being murdered.

"Oh, don't you see, My Children? It may be a little thing to you that means life to another. I am telling you this because I want you to be cheerful givers and trust that every inconvenience in your life has a specific purpose.

"Every cross given has major significance in the salvation of souls. You will most likely not know about it until the day when all works are revealed, but you can trust that I allowed it for a very, very good reason. and understanding that you don't have all the answers. It is not the educated that will survive; it is the meek and devout who move neither to the left nor the right until they have sought My will."

Taken from: **Are You Wise**

"There are times of infusion. An infusion of **grace** and wisdom, love and healing. Yes, as you enter My gates with thanksgiving and praise, My heart is stirred into flame again and again for you and I impart whatever is most needed to your soul.

"Some of you who are new to this channel have not heard or understood how I long for your company. I have spoken on this many, many times. But it bears repeating even in the presence of those who have heard it before.

"I long for you. I ache for you. I know the hurdles you must conquer in the days ahead and I want to be there for you every inch of the way. I want you to know that there is nothing ahead in your life that we cannot accomplish together. There is no dream I have put in the deepest places of your heart, that I will not grant you the **graces** to accomplish."

Taken from: **From Glory to Glory**

"So, this is about having the faith to believe that the Lord is going to **guide** you. He's going to *guide* your fingers and He's going to pick the reading that YOU need.

"So really, what I am asking you to do here, if you want to have continual **guidance** directly from the Lord, is pick a handful of books you've been led to for inspiration, keep them in your prayer place or even in the bathroom, and when you are praying you will find that Holy Spirit will draw your attention to one of these books. You know, you'll be glancing at the books and one will just catch your attention.

"So, pick it up, pray over it binding a lying spirit and open. Then sit and read and consider. God has just spoken to you in this book. Now, write down what He has said on a file card. Keep it visible for a few days and then put it in your Rhema file box. In no time you will have at least 100 cards in that box, which gives Holy Spirit a wonderful selection of readings to choose from."

Taken from: **How to Build a Rhema Box**

Guidance

"I want to talk with you about obedience. My Children, My Bride, what good does it do you to hear My words, knowing My intentions for you and then not obeying? It is not of any benefit to you but is most surely a detriment. It is damaging to know the will of God which in itself is one GREAT grace and then not follow through with it.

"This channel is like a classroom. A great classroom. Each day I bring you a fresh lesson for you are in the school of holiness. The whole curriculum is tailored to prepare you for the day I take you to Myself. All the angels in your life are working in cooperation with My Spirit and arranging your lessons for the day. That is why you so often find yourselves getting the answer you asked Me for on this channel. You are in a great classroom, and I am your teacher.

"I created that space inside of you that has been covered over with the rubble of sin. I created that space so I could fill it someday with My love, My caring, My gifts and My *guidance*. You've not experienced love, so you have no idea how that satisfies that secret place in you. Well, I am here to tell you, there is a place in My Heart for you. You are a masterpiece of My Creation, living in a sewer - and I am coming to get you and restore to you your dignity and the love you crave. You needn't live this way anymore. Come to Me and I will bathe you in My Blood and make your blackened soul as white and pure as snow."

Taken from: **To Satan's Servants, An Invitation From Jesus**

We can't rely on other people for discernment, because they're not walking in our shoes. They don't know what God is doing in our lives, they don't understand the gifts that we've been given from birth and the graces that the Lord wants to give us. So we can't go to other people for discernment for ourselves, at least I can't. I've tried all my life to find someone who could help me discern, and I've never really found anyone, other than my husband. He's really helped me with discernment, the Lord created that relationship dynamic for **guidance** *and especially for* *preparing us for Heaven - we prepare each other for Heaven by being obedient to the Lord. So, it's IMPERATIVE that we can discern God's will for us, that we don't have to go to someone else.*

Taken from: **How to Use the Bible for an Anointed Word, part 1**

"Oh, pray for the repentance of your children, America. For those caught in disobedience and sin. Pray that they will repent and not join the ranks of those who are bitter and shaking their fists in My face, cursing Me. Pray that a wave of repentance will be sent to bring them to their senses and that they will come to Me repenting and seeking **guidance**. Many heroes will be born in that hour. And many that you thought were heroes will crumble in the dust, revealing their true interior emptiness."

Taken from: **Invasion, Underground Cities, Prayer Defeats the Enemy**

"You see, My children, it is your many insecurities that motivate you to live a certain life. It is your insecurity about the provision of life's most basic needs that corrals you into a place of subservience, instead of a position of totally fulfilling all I have made you to be. It is also the fear of suffering, the need for comfort, protection and acceptance by society. Once you abandon yourself into My arms, you let go of these concerns and place your life totally in My hands.

"When you are fully released to Me and I am in full control, I can do all that is necessary to **guide** you into your true mission in life. Yes, there are moments that are scary, painful, confusing. But ultimately, when you trust Me, you cease to worry about these things. Unless you become as a little child...Yes, abandonment into the arms of your loving Father, your loving Jesus, your loving Spirit is the key to maintaining peace in the midst of life's contradictions."

Taken from: **Hand in Hand With Daddy**

Guidance

"Do not be dismayed as you see things falling apart in your life. I allow these things to teach you and **guide** you into right paths so I may truly bless you and you may truly become who I created you to be - Clean Vessels unto honor, dedicated to Me."

Taken from: **Lord, Why Are Things Falling Apart?**

"So, I'm asking you to put down your university degrees and pick up a pacifier. It will do you a world of good to get closer to your childhood. I want to be your Father, your Counselor, your Prince of Peace, but you are still too worldly. The intellectuals are your father, the scholarly are your counselors and you have no peace.

"For those of you who will listen and act in faith, I have some wonderful **guidance** for you. And, for the others who are still questioning Me, I'm sorry --- you'll have to continue to live in the confusion of your own minds until you figure out that your way is NOT My way. When you figure that out, I will have answers for you.

"My children do not be stubborn. I will instruct you and teach you in the way you should go; I will counsel you with My eye upon you. Don't be like a horse or mule, that has no understanding, that must be held in check by a bit and bridle. I am, in this moment, blessing you with a teachable spirit and Godly wisdom, if you will have it. "My sheep hear My voice. Press in, I am longing to speak with you."

Taken from: **The Sucker Punch Revisited**

The devils are opportunists and tag-along monsters. God has given us a tender place in our souls, a place where He speaks without words. A gut-level place where He **guides**. *"You will hear a voice, 'This is the way, walk in it. Whenever you turn to the right or the left"* **Isaiah 30:21.**

Taken from: **Tag Along Monsters, When You Fall...**

Oh Lord, I feel so wonderful. These two days have been SO wonderful. It's been a long time since I've been able to relax totally in Your sweet presence and allow You to take me where You will. Thank You for this sublime gift. Please, please help me to **guide** *others to this sweet place.*

"That's the idea," He answered with a hint of excitement and a twinkle in His eye. "The world is totally ignorant of Who I am and what Heaven is all about. Man has painted so many distorted pictures of Me that I don't even recognize Myself in them all.

"Yes, some have successfully portrayed Me, but they are few and far between. And to tell the truth, they haven't even begun to touch on My humanness, My playfulness, My love of beauty and the very real joy I feel in sharing it with them in Heaven.

"Oh, do tell them, My Beloved. Tell them over and over again. I have gone to prepare a distinctly different place for each and every one of you. No dwelling I have created resembles another; just as My beautiful Bride is varied in her individuality and taste, so are the delightful places I have prepared for Her."

Oh, Lord, my heart is bubbling over with joy - but who will ever believe me?

"Don't worry, there will be confirming signs. Just tell her - I am madly in Love with you, who have given your lives to Me and I'm going to fully convince you of that the very Day you come to Me. But, for those who will have Me now, you have only to close your eyes and enter into My rest, and I will carry you tenderly to the delights I have prepared for you.

"Only just Believe."

Taken from: **Singing River Chronicle...**

Guidance

"My Precious - always put Me first. Do not allow the demons to shift your attention off of Me. This is a priceless gift that we share together. It took a long time to cultivate. It can be ruined very quickly. It is the little foxes that ruin the vine. This is an age-old strategy of Satan - little by little, line upon line, draw her - the Bride's attention - off. Just a little bit each day. Eventually, she's way off and the gift is gone. No crime scene, just an absence of what used to be a sweet communion and relationship, that nourished and built up the Bride into a fountain of living waters.

"There are so many I long to rest in the arms of, but alas, they are taken up with the world, and have no taste for My companionship. Faithfulness draws the faithful. I will put a longing in hearts for something different, something radically different from the lives they are leading. Just as I did for you. First, they must grow weary of all that is around them. There must come a point where it all means nothing to them. When they are at this point, then I can lead them and **guide** them into that relationship. But mark these words: they must be at the point of weariness with the world and all its allurements."

Taken from: **Longing for a Radical Love for Jesus...**

"(In Heaven) You will see into the future and know whatever is necessary to you. You will never guess at anything again. You will never fail to understand Me again, or anyone else for that matter. You will have perfect vision into hearts, that you may help them escape death and decay."

"You will have perfect discretion, timely and sensitive. You will understand the ways of men without effort and easily be able to **guide** them back to center. You will appear glorious, because you will be like Me. Like Me in so many ways. You are going to love how I transform you. You are going to be unspeakably happy and satisfied."

Taken from: **Heaven & the Millennium...**

"But for now, America has another chance to drop her compulsions with materialism and begin to take responsibility for the policies in this nation. People have been led around by a golden ring in their noses, enjoying the fat of the land. This in turn produced a blind generation, all taken up with material comforts and education, thoughtless about the true nature of those she elected.

"Nonetheless, I am with this man, and I will reorder things through him. This nation has made a wise choice and now I can work with it."

And I asked Him at that point, "But Lord, how will he escape assassination? That seems impossible to me."

The Lord replied, "With God...."

And I finished the sentence, "....Nothing is impossible." Lord, how will this happen?

"Clare, I have given My angels watch over him, nothing escapes their notice. Your job is to lift him up over the altar every day, Mine is to protect him and his family. I have chosen him, I will not abandon him to the will of his enemies, as long as you continue to pray for him. There will be new hurtles, but together we will overcome them, one by one.

"Whatever your thoughts about this man, those who call yourselves by My Name, he is now your president and has authority over your country. Pray for him, he will do well. Grow lax, and he will be replaced with a dictator. Do not grow lax, strengthen him with your prayers and fast offerings when called for.

"This is a new day for America. Be faithful to pray, I will be faithful to **guide** and protect him and his family."

Taken from: **President Elect Trump**

Guilt

"So, when you start to feel that peace going, you need to suspect right away that you've got some kind of demonic toxic streaming thoughts into your head that are damaging to your peace and damaging to your faith. Also, you'll have doubts about the faith. All of a sudden, out of nowhere, issues that you have resolved in your heart and mind all of a sudden start pounding you again that these things are not really true. You might be feeling **guilty** or condemned and not have any reason to feel condemned. You might feel depressed or hopelessness."

Taken from: **Do Not Fear or Reject intimacy With God**

These little tag-along uglies know this - so they work energetically to cause toxic **guilt** *that paralyzes our relationship with God. We have to learn to outsmart the little monsters, and go directly to the Lord when we've fallen short. Confess our weakness, our sin, and ask forgiveness in all humility. This needs to be done without delay. The longer we delay, the more monsters accumulate on our backs, shouting how worthless and bad we are.*

They take a certain delight in seeing a Christian cowering in **guilt**, *while they invisibly go on beating us with self-hatred and condemnation. And it sticks, unless we deal a decisive blow to these crippling lies.*

Taken from: **Tag-a-long Monsters**

I had been busying myself with many things and finding excuses not to get into prayer. I believe this was a result of false **guilt**. *Many times I have felt* **guilt** *for doing things that were God's will but I was unsure of that at the time, so I just did the best I could to discern what would please Him the most. But the enemy sends in lying spirits that accuse when we are innocent, so that we will avoid the presence of God.*

Taken from: **Demonic Obstacles against Hearing and Seeing Jesus**

"I've created souls to love Me. The ones who do are a priceless treasure to Me. That's you! You are My priceless treasure. I long for the comfort of your worship, your praise, and holding Me tenderly in your arms. I long for this. How many ways do I have to tell you before you believe Me? So, I'm asking you once again: put on some good praise music, something deep and tender. Embrace Me without **guilt** or shame and just comfort My heart that is so bruised and bleeding right now."

Taken from: **I'm Calling You Closer, Our World is Coming to a Head**

I think one way that Satan creeps into our lives is by accusing us and making us feel **guilty** *and condemned. He wants to separate us from the Source of Love and forgiveness and grace and faith. He wants us to believe we could never be good enough, that we could never deserve it. Well, he's right - we can't be good enough and we cannot earn or deserve it. All these things were given freely on the Cross of Calvary. We only need to accept this free gift and it is ours.*

Taken from: **Your Pets Will Be Taken in the Rapture**

"And for those of you who have already fallen into uncleanness or fornication, I say, repent and make a resolution not to do it again. Call on Me in that hour to strengthen you. Those who willingly give their eyes over to that are far more *guilty* than those of you who are weak and refuse every opportunity to look, but still find yourselves overpowered.

"I do not condemn you, but the demons do. They bring on the temptation and give you to think, 'God will forgive me'. Then when you fall, they pour on the condemnation and claim you as their own, bound for Hell."

Taken from: **Blessed Are the Pure, For They Shall See Me**

Guilt

"For the sake of survival in the past you have hidden certain things from yourself because it was too painful to look at. But you needn't hide anything from Me. I already know about your sins, dearest. I want to work with you and lift the burden of **guilt** deep down inside where you have hidden things too painful and disturbing to bring up.

"There is nothing that can keep Me from loving you, absolutely nothing. But our relationship must be built on honesty. I cannot perfect that which you refuse to see. In order to bring you to perfection, you must be willing to admit the truth about yourself. You are beautiful beyond imagining and there is nothing that will change My mind about that. But these deep dark secrets and unconfessed sins let off a scent of **guilt** and shame.

"This, too, is responsible for you distancing yourself from Me. You know there are things too dark to confront but that in My presence all things are seen. May I say I have seen all these things even before they happened? No one wants to see themselves as evil and so they hide their evil thoughts and deeds even from themselves and make excuses to cover them up, or invent stories."

Taken from: **Honesty, Looking at Yourself in God's Mirror**

"Many of you have labored for Me tirelessly: praying, fasting, serving and doing your very best as a parent, while you watched your children walk off into the world. Even those of you who had the best resources and intentions have witnessed this tragedy. But you see, I am with you and your children in a way you will never understand until Heaven.

"Indeed, when you see how I am accompanying them you will exclaim, 'Oh Lord, why did I worry and fret so???!' And I will answer you gently, 'Because you didn't see what I see. But now you know, I had My hand on them the whole time and never let them go.'

"So, don't allow the devils to come and torment you over their destiny. It is with Me. I want you to reflect that trust in your dealings with them. Do not add to their burdens of **guilt** which you can be sure the devils taunt them with in an effort to alienate them from you. Rather, show them My unconditional love, let them see Me through you. This will remove any obstacles of mistrust and fear they may be struggling with and foster good relations with them. You do not have to approve of their sin, neither do you need to attack them for it. They already know the difference between right and wrong, what you approve and what you do not approve. This is enough to convict them. But by your quiet unconditional love you show them the way to the Kingdom."

Taken from: **Trust Me with Your Children…**

"Oh, My People, so few understand just how tenderly I love them and just how fully engaged I am in their every day affairs. The enemy spends much time heaping all kinds of condemnations on you. He will choose one thing and pound on you with it. And even if you were to do that one thing, he would turn around and tell you, you should have been doing what you were doing when he falsely accused you!"

*You can't win for losing with the enemy. All he's about is confusion and condemnation. So, even if you were to stop what you were doing in present time and go off and do the thing that he's trying to make you feel **guilty** about - it's going to be a ruse, just to get you off track.*

He continued here, "You see, manipulation of this sort is an art form they have mastered. But they will never master Me. And if you rely on Me mindfully, you will see right through their tactics and bring them down on the spot. They want you to be confused. Well, if they enjoy confusion so much, why don't you confuse them!"

Taken from: **Togetherness**

Guilt

"Oh, My People, so few understand just how tenderly I love them and just how fully engaged I am in their every day affairs. The enemy spends much time heaping all kinds of condemnations on you. He will choose one thing and pound on you with it. And even if you were to do that one thing, he would turn around and tell you, you should have been doing what you were doing when he falsely accused you!"

"You can't win for losing with the enemy. All he's about is confusion and condemnation. So, even if you were to stop what you were doing in present time and go off and do the thing that he's trying to make you feel **guilty** about - it's going to be a ruse, just to get you off track."

He continued here, "You see, manipulation of this sort is an art form they have mastered. But they will never master Me. And if you rely on Me mindfully, you will see right through their tactics and bring them down on the spot. They want you to be confused. Well, if they enjoy confusion so much, why don't you confuse them!"

Taken from: **Make Peace With All**

"And I declare to you all: My power is perfected in your weakness. No weapon formed against you will prosper. Even if you should lose your body, you will not lose your soul. But I am telling you these things because many of you walk around in blinding *guilt*, that you failed as a parent. You are with all kinds of sicknesses, brought about by corrupt governments. You are so far down into condemnation that you view your life as a total waste."

"Others of you are saddled with all kinds of sicknesses brought about by corrupt governments. Others of you are hopelessly addicted to drugs, or so you think. There is a good reason for this all. I want you to dispense with the **guilt** and get to the bottom of this."

Taken from: **Why a Soul Rejects Love**

"Most of you have been ruined by **guilt**; you aren't good enough, you dare not approach Me. But look at the men I chose to be My apostles. None of them were well-educated, except the one who betrayed Me. They were simple men, lowly, hard working laborers, not educated, rich or of the ruling class."

"These choices were deliberate on My part. I wanted you to see that you qualify for being My friend."

Taken from: **Nourishment Every Day**

"In Heaven, you will have much fruit because you once again shouldered your cross and followed Me all the way to Calvary. If you live to please your flesh, what have you in Heaven to look forward to? But if you die to yourself and follow Me, surely your resurrection will be glorious.

"In the meantime, I will take you from glory to glory as you learn the ways of darkness and respond by growing in virtue."

"Yes, I have told you many times about your sins. Some of you have even been **guilt-ridden** when you should have abandoned yourselves to My Mercy and forgiveness.

"There will be no excuses. 'Bible fundamentalists were too harsh. Others were not intellectual enough. Others were not loving enough. Pentecostals were too intense.' None of these will fly, for I sent them Mother Theresa's, missionaries, bishops and priests - highly trained and still in love with Me. Evangelists and miracles of healing. They have seen in this world the entire gamut of My servants and heard their miraculous, self-sacrificing stories and still pushed Me away. So indeed, there will not be one excuse."

Taken from: **The Day of the Lord is Upon US**

Healing

"I know, but I am forewarning you who will listen here. I am telling what is planned for those who find themselves left behind. The only way to escape at this point is to rely totally on Me for healing and food. One good rule of thumb: eat what the wildlife eat, watch where the birds and bees (if you can find any) go for water. Many will lose a great deal of weight living on a foraging diet. But there will be times when I will miraculously intervene and provide food when there is no hope.

"Remember always, only two things are needed for a **healing**: a sick patient and a believing Christian. When that Christian calls upon Me to **heal**, whether it be out loud or quietly from the heart, I will reach through them and **heal** those who are sick. Nothing more is needed.

"**Healing** has become some sort of Miracle Cult, where people with the 'gift' are worshiped rather than what it truly is: the natural consequence of Me living inside of you and every other believer who has opened the door of their hearts to Me."

Taken from: **Evading Capture, Jesus Instructs US**

"And for you who are called to heal, I live inside of you. Place your hand on the injured or suffering and imagine My hand moving from your heart, out through your hand and onto the soul. I will do the rest. All you have to believe is that I AM and I LIVE IN YOU. This is all that is required for a complete **healing** of even the most dramatic sicknesses."

Taken from: **God Will Provide for Those Left Behind**

"Some of you, who have presented yourselves as shepherds, delight yourselves in criticism of those who are feeding My sheep and in no way are you providing for My flock. You are not strengthening the weak, but strengthening rancor and division in My Body. You are *not* **healing** the sick, but provoking them to sickness of soul and isolation.

"You are not binding up the injured, rather you are teaching them to injure and divide. You have not brought the strays to Me, rather you have picked them off from Me. You have not sought the lost, you have separated and divided until they are without a shepherd and vulnerable to wild animals."

Taken from: **I Wanted To Go Fishing, But the Nets Were Torn 2**

"And all you can do is pray for those pitiable souls that find fault with what I am teaching. Pray, pray, pray. They are indeed a sorry lot, many blinded by jealousy and others by fear. If only they knew. I called them here so they could grow and come forth out of their insecurities, out of their fears and into My arms, where I administer **healing** and profound peace and acceptance of how beautiful they truly are to Me. But now they will have to wait for another time, another opportunity, to embrace Me without fear."

Taken from: **Events Before the Rapture…**

"You have many such subscribers who understand what it's like to receive the blows of the world. They are seasoned with many injuries I have **healed**. They have learned the ways of My love because they spend so much time with Me, seeking My Heart and My Mind and putting it to practice. In this regard, you are truly blessed.

"So, when you encounter the harshness of the world you have a whole company of intercessors who will lift you up to Me so you can keep going. All of you are seriously damaged soldiers. The difference between those who deeply know Me, is that they have had tremendous measures of **healing** and the bitterness and fear that mark those still wounded in battle, isn't there anymore. They also know themselves very, very well."

Taken from: **Support One Another in Your Weakness**

Healing

"Remember little Audrey?"

Yes, the girl who was totally incapacitated, but when people came to visit her and her mother read her prayer requests, some marvelous miracles happened. I even remember that a group of ladies undergoing chemotherapy came and left with the burning pain from the treatment totally gone, and soon after little Audrey manifested chemo burns.

The Lord replied, "Here is the heart of a pure child. I came to her that day she drowned in the pool and she chose to be My instrument of **healing**. I showed to her all the people she would touch by just praying in her heart, and she humbly received that assignment, Clare. And now she is in Heaven with Me."

Taken from: **Powerful is the Prayer of the Heart**

"My dear and holy ones, clothe yourselves in love, as I clothe you in Love. Each day as you spend substantial time with Me I give you rest and restore your souls. When you feel that jealousy and bitterness are rising up in you, come to Me immediately, confess it and beg forgiveness as well as **healing**. My heart is to make you whole, so the Body can be whole. But I need your cooperation. I need you to recognize that this self-righteous spirit is poison and not from Me. You are not defending My honor when you attack others and find fault - you are sowing division, breaking the nets, chasing away MY catch .

"Oh, how I weep for those who are scandalized through bad example. I see their hopes dashed to pieces when they see what Christians do to one another. Some are blessed, they know Me, and know that is not My Heart, not My Way. But others don't recognize that is not My Heart and they turn to witchcraft and divination and the New Age to fill their spiritual void."

Taken from: **A Bruised Reed He Will Not Break**

"Long have I waited for such an army of souls that would look out for one another with not a thought of their own reward. And on this channel I have found such as these. All of you have been drawn together by the Love flowing from My fountains of grace in Heaven. All of you have brought your own tributaries into the mix, adding grace upon grace upon grace. And that is as it should be. The experience of My Love is heightened on this channel because of your self-sacrifice and focus on Me and those I entrust to you. How beautiful to see this symphony of love playing on the sweet strings of Heaven and drawing all men to Me.

"You have weathered many storms: many barrages of arrows, many attempts to corrupt your pure and loving sacrifices, many attempts to turn you against one another. You have shown great patience and virtue, you are My trusted servants and having been faithful with the littler things, I can increase now the gifts of grace to My proven souls. Yes, I am going to increase your gifts of wisdom, love, patience and effectiveness in prayer...you are also going to see more **healings** and more hearts melting in your arms as they give their lives to Me."

Taken from: **You Are My Heaven on Earth...**

"I will catch your tears in My crystal vase where the other tears from your life are stored. I will apply those tears to the suffering ones, especially those who do not know Me and have never conceived of having a pure, loving relationship with Me.

"Each tear you shed for Me and for the suffering ones, each tear is the product of deep graces granted to you, and therefore carries with it healing properties in the spirit. When you weep with the gift of tears, I cherish each and every drop and I know exactly where I will apply it."

Taken from: **The Fragrance of Longing For Me is Upon the World**

Healing

"In order for justice to prevail, hearts must be clean before Me. Make your peace with all men, My people. Always strive for honesty and integrity. Where you have failed, confess and ask forgiveness. Sometimes it takes only a word to calm troubled waters. Recognition and confession of sin clears the way for **healing**. Now I can move forward with My plans and all will follow as I lead.

"My Children, never underestimate the cleansing power of confession of wrong doing on your part. Many grudges can or could have been completely avoided if fault and mistakes were clearly admitted. The tendency today is to cover up weakness and proceed as if nothing were wrong. That doesn't wash in the hearts of men, it leaves a sting and resentment. Bitterness sets in and life takes a turn for the worse. In My Heart and Mind, brotherly love, reconciliation, are of the utmost importance. When people hold onto their pains, it twists their lives and sends them in a wrong direction."

Taken from: **Power In Reconciliation**

"And My Brides you will be opposed by spirits of unbelief that will try to get you to back down before you obtain results in prayer and in ministry. I am asking one simple thing of you: believe that I live inside of you and believe that when you reach out, I will reach out through you and accomplish the task at hand, either **healing** or a vision to share, wisdom for their situation or deliverance from an evil spirit. Listen very carefully for Me and I will do it."

"I am making it easy for you. Believe that I will "do" the doing, be it a **healing**, a word of knowledge through a vision and wisdom that they might be delivered of whatever is being held in bondage. Yes, more and more will I respond as you bind things in belief and command them to leave. How do you know what to rebuke? What is that person feeling? Sickness - a spirit of infirmity. Fear - a spirit of fear. Confusion - a spirit of confusion. What are they feeling? Ask them to describe it, then use that as the name to bind and rebuke it."

*Taken from: **Stand in Resolve, The Gift of Healing...***

"The gift of **healing** is always active within Me, there is never a time I cannot heal, and the cry of your sincere heart is the key to activation.'

"You don't expect enough from Me, My Children. You don't realize I languish over the suffering souls and with a burning love you cannot comprehend, I long to touch them and make them whole. Where you feel a mere nudge, I feel deep passion and you have the authority to bridge that gap and bring Me to that person. When you respond in faith, obeying that still small voice, I am enabled to penetrate that soul with feelings they can barely understand, but feelings and sensations that are uniquely My way of touching the hurting, the languishing, the confused and lost."

Taken from: **Touch Others Tenderly For Me...**

So, should He live inside of us like a phantom that has no emotions and doesn't react to our sorrows and joys? Should He never hold and comfort us? Should He never dance and rejoice with us?

*Don't you see??? We live on a dark, sin-swept planet and Jesus comes to regenerate new life in us. During worship, holding us to His heart, kissing our foreheads and **healing** our fears. How can we survive without this interaction with Him??*

Personally, I was a very lame Christian until I had this kind of interaction with Him. I needed...MORE.

Taken from: **Is SSV a Study in Blasphemy?**

Hearing and Seeing Jesus

And the Lord addressed this confusion of mine, my fears about myself and **hearing Jesus** *and Jesus only, clearly, and He did it through the Bible Promises. When I asked Him about Israeli News Live and if I should share one of their videos, I opened to Marriage, and this line stood out,* **"Drink waters from your own cistern. Flowing waters from your own well." Proverbs 5:15**

This has always meant 'Don't drink from other sources.' That's the history of that Scripture verse.

I truly got it in that moment. Jesus has assembled a group here, a group of Heartdwellers who love to rest in His heart. He is forming us in a very specific way, unique to us. And the way in which He is leading us is not just prophetic, but intensely focused on preparing us with the virtues He loves in His Bride.

Taken from: **Higher Realms of Prayer and Sacrifice Changing the World**

"Do not waste time, My Love. Make the best of what you have before you. I know your physical limitations, I know you can only do so much. But I can do so much more if you will rely on Me and not your own devices. For instance, in this moment you came to Me in poverty of spirit and now you are **seeing and hearing Me** clearly.

"Always come to Me this way, even when you haven't indulged yourself. Always come to Me blind and naked and I will always reach over that barrier and touch you. Do you understand? Your poverty and littleness cry out to Me and I cannot resist you. It is the proud and self-satisfied I resist, but the little and weak I shed mercy upon."

Taken from: **Your Prayers Are Working**

"Oh Clare, you have much to learn about the ways of these (evil) spirits. They never give up, Child. They are like opportunists...jackals on the prowl. Whatever they can accomplish before they are found out, they will do. They will try to trick you into **seeing them instead of Me**. Or trick you into **hearing them instead of Me**.

"I never allow that unless it is for a specific lesson. And you know from experience it is always pride and arrogance in serious situations that I correct you in this way, allowing them to replace Me, either in vision or speech."

Taken from: **How the Enemy Blocks Your Creativity with Demonic Intervention**

Clare: Well, yeah - there's quite a few...I have some things to share with you on that point, as far as, there's been some frustration for some folks, who say **they're just are not hearing from the Lord,** *and no matter how many hours in prayer they put in. And, we're gonna talk about that in a moment. But, one of our emails today, from one of our listeners...*she writes:

"I'm still having great difficulty establishing a closer relationship to the Lord. I've listened to all your videos, and have been using your musical selection plus mine, and I dedicated an entire day to make certain that no one could interrupt me. And....nothing. Nothing happened."

But she said, when she went to the Bible Promises the Lord gave her Patience."

"....and so, I'm trying to be patient. But truth be told, at times I feel as if my heart is breaking. I did tell Jesus that I would bear some of the Cross, so that those feeling the wrath of ISIS in some way could have respite. It could be that." - above two quotes, are not from Clare.

"Uh, huh... it really could!"

Hearing and Seeing Jesus

"Seek Me and I will answer your questions. All of you who have been following Me closely through this vessel, are so close to breakthroughs in **hearing and seeing Me**. Persevere, don't grow weary and don't give in to unbelief or discouragement. Those are your worst enemies. May I say laziness is part of the problem? You must press in, those who seek Me with their whole hearts, they shall find Me. Seek Me and live the life that I promised you - the abundant life of communion with Me, righteousness, peace and joy, the fruits of fellowship with Me. Confidence, courage, growth in charity, humility - these are the sweet flavors of the grapes that abide in the vine."

Taken from: **Jesus' Perceptible & Manifest Presence is With You**

"There are many who wish to have this relationship with Me. I exclude no one - let that be made clear. My arms are wide open to all who seek Me...until they find Me. I am not an easy catch. I need to know how much I am wanted, I need to see a relentless Bride searching high and low for Me. Then, I shall surprise her with My presence. Most people give up way too easily; this is the majority of the problem.

"Most people give in to the lies of the enemy, 'you're not worthy.' Nothing could be further from the truth. Unless you want to say, 'Unless you are willing to seek Me until you find Me, you are not worthy.' Now that would be correct.

"The other issue of Purity is also major. Two facets: one is that the more stimuli you glean from the world, the less sensitive you are to My presence, My still small voice, My gentle breeze and embrace.

"The other facet is uncleanliness. Feeding on the filth of the world makes a heart very soiled and unfit as a habitation. The house must be clean or at least committed to cleanliness. Oh, how I love each and every one that is seeking Me. That is why I am here to explain the direction they need to take. You know the things that offend Me. Sin offends Me very much. Sin in clothing, or lack of it, sin in violence, crime, hatred, gossip, backbiting, jealousy, adulteries. Soap operas are the epitome of sin and extremely noxious to Me. Like your-nose-in-fresh-dog-excrement noxious. I mean very, very bad. These things not only offend Me but also the Heavenly court, the angels and the saints. Yet in your world they are matter-of-fact, part of everyday life.

"If My Bride wants to find Me, she must lay aside these things and purify her heart and mind from all forms of entertainment that portray sin. This means music, clothing, behavior, speech, murder mysteries, wars, things that portray sin in any form. I don't have a problem with biographies that show the progress of a soul coming to Me, that doesn't make entertainment out of their sin, but simply portray where they were and where they are coming to. It is the scintillating entertainments that spoil the perception of the delicate and clean things, dulling the senses and offending Me greatly.

"Understand that I, too, must endure what you are watching and thinking about. I, too, am in that bedroom watching unspeakable filth. I, too, am at that murder scene with all its suffering. I, too, am present at that intrigue that will steal and ruin the lives of hundreds caused by greedy men. These things HURT Me. Please My Brides, do not watch these things in movies or TV - they are SO hurtful to Me. Do not listen to music or look at magazines, billboards, pictures that depict suffering or sin."

"Well, My Brides, I am not saying this to condemn you. Do you understand that? I am answering your prayers, this is what I require of you, this is why you have such a **hard time seeing and hearing Me**. Work on this and I will bless you with visitations and consolations. I promise you."

Taken from: **Jesus Answers His Bride, How to Hear & See Me...**

Hearing and Seeing Jesus

Lord, I am having struggles **hearing and seeing You** *really clearly. My heart is beginning to ache because I miss you SO much.*

"And the tragedy of it is that I am right here beside you, living in you, guiding and planning your day. Sending the right person at the right time to diffuse situations...."

Yeah, there was a situation today, and I said, "Yes, that had Your fingerprints all over it. She is an obedient vessel."

"My dear ones, don't you know that it is your attitude towards My instructions and corrections that determines your spiritual growth, not your ability? I ask for supple hearts that are eager to obey out of Love for Me. With this kind of heart, I can do anything. It is the disposition of your hearts that makes the difference."

Taken from: **There are No Losers in My Kingdom**

There's no set formula. But we have found a formula that most often works for us. And we begin by playing worship music and entering into the song. Worshiping the Lord through the lyrics of the song and, many times we'll begin to see Him very clearly while we're worshiping. And then we just connect with Him and continue to worship Him.

Let me read to you what else I've written down here.

As we worship, images may come to mind, like Jesus standing nearby. These are not usually just imaginations that you make up. They aren't! They're sanctified images that God puts before you in your imagination. Don't brush them off, take them for the real thing.

Take them seriously because you have just reached out to the Lord now He's reaching out to you through some kind of image of Him being present to you.

Continue to worship, continue to enter into that vision that you have, but paying attention to what you see in the 'spirit' or in your sanctified imagination. Continue to Love the Lord and adore Him.

The Lord may invite you to dance, or He may walk with you on a beach or sit with you in a garden. Be sensitive to the imagery around you in the spirit, He's a master at creating beautiful environments for you to be in with Him. Go with Him. Stay focused on adoring the Lord. His love will draw you into Himself - and you'll feel His affection for you, you will sense that He is happy to see you. Stay with that. 99% of the obstacles in **seeing and hearing the Lord** *is our own unbelief or false guilt about ourselves. Our own self hatred.*

Taken from: **Experiencing Jesus in Dwelling Prayer**

"That is why people who teach focus on Me, intimacy in prayer, knowing and hearing My voice, are so targeted for persecution. When you listen to Me, I navigate you around the reefs of judgment and now their door-opener will no longer be effective.

"This is why it is so effective. A fear demon lays the groundwork, then coupled with a sense of self-preservation, you set up a screening device looking for certain characteristics in people.

"Whether real, imagined or deliberately distorted by the enemy, this screen will capture many who might have the outward appearance of the enemy, so that you will accuse them falsely and open the doors for the demons to oppress you with many maladies.

"Knowing this, if you act in accordance with what I have told you, and make Me the center of your reality, this will never happen..."

Taken from: **Spiritual Warfare: 8 – How One Demonic Strategy ...**

Heaven

"I am saying that I have a plan of escape for all. It is up to them whether or not they take it. But, believe Me, I leave no one without recourse. I found you, didn't I? I had to wait until you were ready, but I found you and delivered you out of the hands of darkness and into My marvelous Light, did I not?

"Then, trust Me. I have plans for each and every soul. Plan A, Plan B, Plan C, and even Plan D. Oh, Clare I am relentless in following up on souls until they flat out reject Me or accept Me. Relentless. You needn't worry, there will be so many surprises in **Heaven**. Children of My Mercy."

Taken from: **Talents, What Did You Do With What I Gave You?**

"Clare, I want you to love the unlovable. Go out of your way for those who have rejected Me. Be My hands, My feet, My mouth and My ears. At least in that final moment, I can reason with them. I can remind them of your kindness, even when they didn't deserve it. This, many times, is the very last straw on their resistance and they break...a flood of tears, a deep knowledge of their sins and an even greater knowledge of how enormously special they are to Me...so special, that I endured torture to bring them to **Heaven** with Me forever. I treasure them, I love them and I embrace them, never to part.

"These are the days when many souls will be rescued in this way. That is why I am constantly admonishing you to love the unlovable. They are the most destitute of all, especially those who have known wealth."

Taken from: **Come to Me, My Lost & Lonely Ones**

"When you see Me tenderly reach out for those who don't know Me, back Me up! In **Heaven** you'll be trained further to reach souls. This IS the work I have for you. This IS My daily preoccupation, that NONE should be lost. Back Me up, My Bride. Pray for those who visit this channel, that they will invite Me into their hearts and give Me their very lives. Oh, how I so desire they would come to Me. My heart burns with longing to comfort and console them. To heal their lethal wounds, and shed light on the suffocating darkness they walk in.

"Let them see that your heart is for them, too, by the generosity of your remarks and prayers. Let them know, that you care not for just yourself, but for them, too. That is a major problem with My Church - enough people don't really care. They don't care to go out of their way, for those who have yet to find their way."

Taken from: **Minister My Love on This Channel**

"My Precious Brides, this is what it boils down to. If you Love Me, REALLY Love Me, you will deny yourself, pick up your cross and follow Me. In short, you will obey Me, even My every, little wish. And I wish for nothing but your good and the salvation of souls. When I correct you, it is a pruning. I am cutting back the dead wood to increase the yield of grapes. As I said, it is for your good and for the good of souls for **Heaven**.

"Although at the time it isn't pleasant, still it will bring forth an abundance of sweet fruit. You prove your love for Me through your obedience and faithfulness to Me. I see what is around the next bend, you do not. I am ahead of you and fully aware of Satan's next move with you. I prepare and protect you, even though at times, it is unpleasant.

"What joy it brings Me to see you bend your will to Mine. There is nothing quite like it in **Heaven** or on Earth: a soul who has free will, free agency to do whatever they please, but they are only pleased with what pleases Me."

Taken from: **Obsessive Compulsiveness...**

Heaven

"When flaws are out in the open they have to be worked on. They won't be tolerated by others, in the sense that they can continue to do damage. I address them openly and ask you to do the same. Without solidarity between people, you become islands impenetrable, hidden, dark, shameful, obtuse and closed. This is the state of society now, but not in **Heaven**. In **Heaven**, all thoughts are open and visible to everyone because compassion abounds and charity rushes to comfort those who are lacking."

But, Lord, I thought that in **Heaven** *we didn't have any faults?*

"Oh no. In **Heaven** you will continue to have areas where you need to grow in depth and understanding. What you won't have is sin."

I have always heard that in Heaven we are perfect, whole, entire, lacking nothing. But, I remembered the River of Life for the healing of the nations... so there will be shortcomings, and healing will have to take place.

"My Love, in **Heaven** all knowledge will be available to you even as you question it. But, wisdom is an acquired quality. It takes time and experience to cultivate and wisdom is greatly lacking on this Earth.

"Each soul is capable of infinitely more understanding and love, but these areas have to be opened up in layers, by inquiry. Inquiry happens when the soul develops a hunger for something. And in **Heaven**, it always has to do with love and healing. Everything in **Heaven** is done from the motive of LOVE."

Taken from: **Sincerity, Prophetic Word…**

"Over and over again, I have used them (animals) to minister to you. A look in their eye, a touch, a nudge. Such joy they have experienced in your sweet embrace. They love you - and I shall not abandon them.

"Your grandchildren, as well. Some of you have suffered such alienation from your children that they've deprived you of your right to see your grand-children. This will be the time of restoration for you as these little ones are removed and taken to **Heaven**. Many of My ministers have no knowledge of the extent of My Mercy to creatures. They do not understand the true role that animals on this Earth have played. Adam had fellowship with the creatures as well. But, despite his closeness to the animals, none proved to be a suitable companion until I created Woman.

"Nonetheless, do not underestimate your relationship with animals and pets. I love them dearly. Not one sparrow falls to the ground that I do not embrace it and bring it back to **Heaven**.

"In **Heaven**, you will communicate freely with them, and most of your interactions will be times of love and play. You will swim with dolphins, tumble with lions, glide with otters, float with polar bears and tuck into the giant paws of grizzlies. They will welcome you with Love. All things in **Heaven** are saturated with Love. Even the bees will express their appreciation of you."

Taken from: **Your Pets Will Be Taken in the Rapture**

"In your dealings with others, bend over backwards to show mercy, clemency and charity. These are the attributes of My dear ones. Some of you have the resources to alleviate the sufferings of those whose paths you come across. When I send you someone, or arrange a situation where you are passing them by, stop and give aid as your resources allow. Then you will be like My Father in **Heaven** who rains upon the land of the just and unjust alike, but Who especially looks after those who cannot look after themselves. Kindness preaches volumes to the unsaved and lifts the spirits of those without hope."

Taken from: **Your Pets Will Be Taken in the Rapture**

Heaven

"And that was merely a whiff of joy from your honeymoon. And I say to you, all My Brides, I have a wonderful escape to Paradise planned for you all. Oh, you have no idea. Eye has not seen and ear has not heard the wonders I have prepared for all of you in **Heaven**!

"After the wedding supper, we will disappear into Paradise, and spend our days joyfully exploring the oceans, mountains, forests and streams of living water in **Heaven**. Each of you has a very particular place that is in your dreams, a wonderful place to be that you've always dreamt of. Understand, I know all about that place. I have been there and seen the things you love, as well as reading your minds as to what else you would love to see there. And I have, down to the last detail, prepared many places for you that we will frequent during our honeymoon.

"You will even meet people there who are longing to see you, as well as your favorite animals and My wedding presents to you. Everything on Earth you ever dreamt of doing, we shall do together in Heaven and these places shall be ours to return to, time and time again. They each are tailored exactly to your tastes.

"There are longings in each of your hearts to visit places you have seen in passing. In **Heaven**, those places are real, just for you. What joy will be yours as I answer all the questions you could ever have about Creation and you are able to observe its beauty microscopically just by desire. You will even be able to walk into tiny worlds and explore their patterns and composition from inside. Nothing, absolutely nothing will be impossible to you.

"Our Honeymoon will be a whole year long, as you and I experience one another together in an innocent and pure relationship. There will not be a care in the world for the entire time. It shall be nothing but a Paradise and seemingly unending vacation. All this is necessary to adjust you to **Heaven** and its joys. You will never exhaust all of them, but you certainly will have an entirely new reality and outlook on life.

"No more pain, no more fatigue, no more bills. Oh yes, you are going to love it. Everything necessary will be provided free of charge. Every discipline you have ever wanted to master will be given into your hands with barely an effort. Inner scars will be healed and you will be released into a new freedom unlike anything you've ever known.

"…Could there possibly been anything more wonderful? I say to you, 'No.' Heaven is beyond wonderful. **Heaven** is all you've ever dreamt of or wanted in your short life on Earth."

Taken from: **The Honeymoon**

"Yet I am not saying to isolate yourselves from love. On the contrary, I am calling you to live love and bring My love to all. If you are detached from the results of your endeavors, you will even find more freedom from suffering. I suffer when My children suffer, so never am I isolated from others.

"Rather I am totally immersed in their affairs and their sufferings. I feel their disappointments and losses keenly. Did I not cry when Lazarus died? Yes, indeed, My heart was rent in two for this precious soul whom I loved dearly and for the whole family who were the heart of My heart.

"So, there is no way to avoid suffering. Even when you came from **Heaven** and could return there at any time, even if you have a glorified body, your connection with humanity is so ingrained that you cannot help feeling their joys and sorrows most keenly. That is also why I promised you that I would wipe away every tear from your eyes. Every last tear would someday be gone. Oh, I do hope you hold onto this My Love. Grasp this firmly and never let it go, it is your hope."

Taken from: **The Will of My Enemies**

Help in Troubles

'There are angels that protect you. Your mindful pursuit of the goals set before you will help to get your attention and ask for **My help.** Too often you assume you can do it on your own, just because it is such a simple thing. Yet, there are a hundred different ways you could get thrown off course and distracted, ending in frustration, as you march off on your own to do it.

"And everyday you both get distracted. Seriously distracted. Wouldn't you like to be more productive, Clare, and feel more on target?

"Well, I am answering your prayer and the prayers of many on the Channel. The dark forces, the demons, have your number. They have a file a mile high on you and know precisely what action will most likely cause you to move in the direction they want you to move in. Which is ALWAYS off course.

"But when I am by your side and you are mindfully aware of **My presence and help**, I protect you from going the wrong way."

Taken from: **Togetherness**

"Beloved, this is about failures leading to the greatest success and seeing yourself in My mirror as the little kitten in need of protection and *help*. When you finally see yourself this way, that is when the lion will rise up to do it all through you.

"May you be confident in My Love. So confident that you allow yourself to see clearly in My Mirror who you are and who you are not. May you trust no longer in your own devices, but come to Me on your knees. 'Lord, I am too little, I cannot do this.' In your hearing ears, I offer you these graces. Take them, cherish them, and become who I have always created you to be."

Taken from: **Why Your Failures Qualify You For Success**

"The spirit realm is more real than the natural realm. And we fail to see that. In whatever is not covered with Jesus Christ is an easy target to bring down. Atheist - they are easy to kill. The Jehovah Witness was easy to destroy. The Mormon was easy to destroy. The people that walk around and say, "We don't believe in the devil." they were easy to destroy, because they didn't know how to seek any spiritual help.

Taken from: **Message to Ex-Satan Worshiper, John Ramirez Testimony**

"Whenever I instruct you, there is a very specific reason. I am warning you of the enemy's next move. I can see the traps as they are preparing for you. I can also see your weaknesses. I pinpoint a dynamic everyday to warn you of what is coming. If you don't obey, you open yourself to a fall. You cannot outsmart the enemy if you do not follow Me in obedience. You are no match for them without Me. And when you go out from the sheep pen without Me leading you, you are indeed without Me, in the sense that I cannot protect you from what you openly pursue against My will.

"So, I gave some very serious warnings beginning in February, that evil had increased and would continue to increase as we approached the day and the hour. I told you it would get harder and harder but **I would be with you to help** you overcome your trials. I never left you, but some of you left Me."

Taken from: **The Enemy's Next Move Against You**

Well, when all was said and done, I wondered how would we have handled this if the intercessors had not been present? And the Lord answered very simply, "**Call on Me in the day of trouble** and I will deliver you. You are mine. Just say, 'Jesus save me!' and I'll do the rest, whether you say it out loud or in the spirit...'Jesus, save me!'

Taken from: **Ezekiel Snatched from the Jaws of Death**

Help in Troubles

"Yes, there are times for worship when you lift your hearts to Me. It seems more formal as you worship Me as your God. But other times, I want to be as approachable and easy to be with as a real companion on Earth. I promise you, that if you begin to presume or act in pride, **I will swiftly correct you and help** you restore your footing. I care enough to correct and sometimes be distant that you don't grow complacent. But this only done when it is necessary. The rest of the time, I am Jesus. Your Jesus. Your friend and lover. The one who knows all your ways, when you sit and when you stand. And I long to take an active part in sharing your life with you."

Taken from: **Who I Really Am To You**

"So, I am asking you - speak to Me, I am listening. Tell Me, 'Jesus, I know I have sinned. I know I have avoided facing what I've done and indeed I know there is little time left. Forgive me, have mercy on me and receive me into Your Kingdom. I know You died for my sins. From this day forth, I turn my back on my sinful ways and with **Your help**, I will live my life for You. Amen.'

He continued, "What is necessary here is that you say this with all your heart, you truly repent for the evil you have done, you truly want to change and give your life to Me, the Son of the Living God who died for you and rose again. Without true repentance, there is little hope for you. Reach out to Me but one step forward and I will draw you into My everlasting and loving arms and you will find peace for your soul. My children, do this now. There is little time left and for many of you, there will be no time when calamity hits the Earth."

Taken from: **War, Comet, Rapture, Treaty – Order of Events**

"I do not want to shame you. I see you are truly sorry and afraid to buy anything at this point. You are familiar with this medium, and you can work your pastels into it. This can be done, quite easily I might add. You can have a peace about this, Clare, this is Me. Work with what you have a few other things, and we'll be able to do this together. I will not let you down. I know how frustrated and disappointed you are. **Let Me help** you, we CAN turn this around."

He continued, "You are in a good place now. A really good place. Contrition is always the very best place to be. Oh, if only My children could stay in this place, how humble they would be. Contrition and humility go hand in hand."

Taken from: **Why Your Failures Qualify You For Success**

"Make your gifts and your time count. Every second you live, every second given you in this life will be accounted for, whether you used it wisely or wasted it. Everything you undertake to gather in souls, to bring Me to them, to instruct them when you are gone, all of these endeavors will be richly rewarded because My words do not return to Me void.

"There are those who are confused, lost and alienated and are in need of being touched, either now or in the time to come. If you are bored, you are not pressing into Me and seeking My will. Your eyes are on yourself, and not on the work that needs to be done for My Kingdom. You are falling asleep and running out of oil. Wake up! Wake up and listen to the cries of the lost that I hear from every corner of the world. **What are you doing to help them?**

"Your prayers and fast offerings are so very powerful. Knowing the plight of those who are suffering will bring you into the throne room in intercession. That's your greatest gift."

Taken from: **Stand Up, America & The Wise Virgins**

Help in Troubles

The Father continued, "This is what I ask of all, but the greatest burden will fall to My faithful. Pray, beloved children, pray! There will be whole days where you may be directed to remain in prayer. My Holy Spirit will direct you in your prayers.

"The prayers will burgeon and flow through you without effort, as Living Waters, to the parched areas of this Earth that need them. They will rise upward to Me like the sweetest of fragrant incense, and I will hear your prayers.

"**Your prayers will help** to determine what will transpire...what punishments will befall those who transgressed My Laws and My Will. Your prayers DO matter!"

Taken from: **Great Suffering is About to Befall the World**

"No matter, keep on walking. Part of your problem is an upset schedule and a sense of suspension."

And guys, by that I think He means, what happens to me every time I complete an intense project, before I begin the next project there's that lull in between where I just feel a little bit disoriented.

He said, "You'll have to fight your way through this, Clare. Your efforts will bring results but the lack of ease with which things happen is a challenge to your perseverance. I know how you feel and I know the remedy.

"Press into Me, My Love. Press in. Don't allow the enemy's smoke screens to **trouble you,** just keep on walking, **calling for My help**. 'Lord, help me get a handle on this and keep moving.' Ignore that opposition and keep on walking. There is an end in sight."

Taken from: **War, Comet, Rapture, Treaty – Order of Events**

"People of the Earth, you who have not received Me into your hearts, do you know there will come an hour when you stand before the Judge of Heaven and Earth? Do you know that your conscience has been warning you throughout your lives that something is seriously amiss inside of you? Do you know that there are consequences to ignoring Me?

"I have knocked and knocked at your door, but you refuse to open to Me. Now you are in the anteroom of horrors that are to come upon the Earth, and many of you have obstinately locked the door and ignored Me.

"If you die in this state, you will never see your relatives that accepted Me, again. You will never see your beloved pets that I sent on loan to you to comfort you in your sorrows. You will never see your grand-babies again and you will live in the Lake of Fire with the Devil and his evil angels for eternity. Not an hour, a day, a week or a lifetime, but forever. The choice is yours. You know you are not right with Me. Your spouses and children and parents have told you about My love over and over again, but you have scorned and rejected Me.

"**I cannot help you in the day of trouble.** It will be too late. You will be petrified at what is coming upon the Earth, heading your way within hours, if you even have that warning. There will be no escape for you.

"It will be so sudden that your mind will be jammed in overload. You will not repent or receive Me then. Rather you will be dragged by demons down to Hell where you will be assigned a place of torment, where worms eat your flesh and it grows back, only to be eaten again. Where fire burns with excruciating pain, only to heal again and be burned again. Over and over and over again throughout eternity."

Taken from: **War, Comet, Rapture, Treaty – Order of Events**

Holy Spirit

And He replied, "There are many layers to your crosses, My Children. Sometimes I call you to carry the weight of your cross only and it is easier for you. But other times, many other times - especially now - you are carrying multiple crosses. You are all intertwined as brothers and sisters and the same **Holy Spirit** flows through you all."

Taken from: **Suffering: Real Work in the Realm of the Spirit**

The Father continued, "This is what I ask of all, but the greatest burden will fall to My faithful. Pray, beloved children, pray! There will be whole days where you may be directed to remain in prayer. My **Holy Spirit** will direct you in your prayers. The prayers will burgeon and flow through you without effort, as Living Waters, to the parched areas of this Earth that need them. They will rise upward to Me like the sweetest of fragrant incense, and I will hear your prayers. Your prayers will help to determine what will transpire...what punishments will befall those who transgressed My Laws and My Will. Your prayers DO matter!"

Taken from: **Great Suffering is About to Befall the World, Prophetic Word**

"Many of you have had ideas from My **Holy Spirit** at the most awkward times: taking a shower, putting dishes away, walking the dog, driving to work (that is, when you don't fill your ears with the radio) walking across the parking lot, taking a break with your feet up. These are opportunities to hear from Me. Times to share with Me as you would share with a spouse sitting at your side. Confide in Me your emotions and ask Me to moderate them.

"Oh, My People, you rely on Me far too little; far, far too little. Your awareness of My presence is almost zero compared to how present I am to you."

Taken from: **Togetherness**

"I am asking you, Children: take a long look in the mirror and know yourselves. Ask My **Holy Spirit** to reveal your true weaknesses. What will this accomplish? Compassion and forgiveness for those who betray you. I want My Body mended, put back together. Satan has spent the last 2,000 years contriving plans that would push the members of My Body apart, further and further."

Taken from: **How a Root of Bitterness Can Change Your Destiny and DNA**

"I wish for you all to stick together and be supportive of one another. This is the mark of My end times army: Brotherly Love. For however long you are here, I want you to advance in holiness, My Brides.

"There will be ample opportunity. Remember: it's not about prosperity, popularity, and power, but righteousness, peace and joy in My **Holy Spirit** in the midst of a corrupt and challenging world.

"Moments of triumph will be gratifying and I will reward each richly with the sweetness of My presence. The number of those who leave will decline, no one can argue against brotherly love and unity of purpose."

Taken from: **These Lite and Momentary Sufferings**

"Most of your problem truly lies in the fact that you do not believe in yourself. But I believe in you and I know what can be done when you believe in Me. Together we can do this. The hardest part is starting. The next hardest part is overcoming obstacles. Then overcoming boredom or lack of inspiration. All of these problems can be handled in worship and prayer when **Holy Spirit** refreshes you in His anointing and power."

Taken from: **Make This Time Count**

Holy Spirit

"My people, if you want to draw closer to Heaven, you must learn to deny yourself and walk in self-denial. You cannot continue to feed the flesh and expect eternal rewards, for the flesh is in opposition to the **Spirit** and one cancels out the power of the other. So, if you want closer encounters with Me and with Heaven, deny yourselves some choice morsel and come into My presence stronger in resolve than ever.

"I am not an easy catch. My royal dignity does not allow for Me to be an easy catch. Rather, you must reach up and out of yourselves as you seek My fellowship and the sweetness of My presence."

Taken from: **The Way to His Heart and Intimacy in Prayer**

"All these years My people have gone one of two ways: being constantly guilty or constantly OK - like, 'nothing wrong here.' But now I am asking for a deeper look. A more candid look, not glossing anything over. It is incomprehensible to you, My children, the demands of personal holiness. Because of My mercy, much is overlooked. But rather than be shocked, as that young boy Nathan was when he stood before his audience and his sins were revealed. I want you to spend time with My **Holy Spirit** and ask Him to reveal the darkness still inside of you."

Taken from: **Get Ready For Your Journey**

"The heart of this exercise is preparation and readiness to face Me. So much will be forgiven and removed on the way up to Heaven, but I do insist that you forgive everyone that ever offended you. I don't want this experience marred by unforgiveness.

"What may help you in that area is that whoever was a challenge and injured you, had My permission. I am not the author of evil, but I did allow it as a challenge in loving others and dying to yourself. So, ultimately you can only blame Me for allowing it. Therefore be sure that you forgive the person, that you forgive yourself, and that you forgive Me. Cover all three bases. Ask Me to remove the root of bitterness you allowed to grow in your heart and defile it. There most certainly is a root of bitterness in every one of you. It is your job, with My **Holy Spirit** to identify it, renounce it and pray I will remove it."

Taken from: **Get Ready For Your Journey**

"Do be baptized in the **Holy Spirit**. Do pray in tongues. Do sing over people in tongues - you are speaking MY language and I am praying through you, the perfect prayer. Do not allow anyone to discourage you from speaking in tongues - the devils will use self-conscious, insecure and poorly informed souls to try and stop you from using this powerful gift. Don't let them.

"Now more than ever you need to pray in tongues. I will for some of you give the interpretation while you are praying which will inform you of what your true opposition is, be it man, beast - or even your own self. There will be a great need for supernatural wisdom, so many different opponents will be coming against you.

"I will warn you of them if you make prayer your absolute priority."

Taken from: **God Will Provide For Those Left Behind**

"It is good that you've been calling upon My angels more, particularly your guardian angel. I HAVE given them charge over you. And one very important thing that they do for you is to remind you. They work very closely with My **Holy Spirit**, of whom it is written: 'He will guide you into all truth concerning me.'"

Taken from: **The Vine of Our Love**

Holy Spirit

"We are working on this together, Dear One, it is a joint venture in cooperation with **My Spirit**. What is good is the attitude of your heart.

"My dear ones, don't you know that it is your attitude towards My instructions and corrections that determines your spiritual growth, not your ability? I ask for supple hearts that are eager to obey out of Love for Me. With this kind of heart, I can do anything. It is the disposition of your hearts that makes the difference.

"You worry so much about your mistakes and failures, but I am using them all. And in some instances, I deliberately allow them to humble you. I cannot pour My finest wine into cracked vessels: vessels cracked by judgment of others, harshness, un-teachable-ness, stubbornness, pride and self-will. First the vessel must be made whole and docile, then I can pour My finest wine through it."

Taken from: **There Are No Losers in My Kingdom**

*Such a deep and undisturbed peace set in and ever since then my heart has been able to rejoice in the accomplishments of that soul and others, who seemingly have much greater gifts. This place of peace is a warm, fuzzy place of affirmation that is supportive of all **Holy Spirit** wants to do through His Brides and leaves absolutely no room for feeling threatened by their accomplishments. If all of us look at the good in one another and refuse to enter into jealousy, we are supporting **Holy Spirit** in His wonderful works and cheering on those who are highly gifted.*

For every gift there is a price, and for every price the soul must die to itself and give their all. How wonderful to see that example in others... it spurns us on to give up more for our sweet Jesus. For every ministry there are challenges and all the glory goes to God for those He enabled to cooperate with them. As the Scripture says, if you see good imitate it.

Taken from: **Spiritual Jealousy**

One other short point I need to make is that the Baptism of the **Holy Spirit**, with the evidence of speaking in tongues, is THE weapon of choice for prayer. When you pray in the Spirit, you speak the language of the Spirit of God and the very exact prayer that is needed in the situations you find yourself in. Do not allow the enemy to lie about this gift anymore; it is powerful and that's why he hates it and slanders it. **Holy Spirit** is praying the perfect prayer through you.

If you have not yet received the Baptism of the **Holy Spirit**, all you need to do is ask. A good way to begin is to sing and allow Him to take over your speech while you are in worship. Many, many gifts come with this grace: discerning of spirits, healing, miracles, words of knowledge, prophecy - so many wonderful gifts accompany this sign. I would ask you not to disdain it, and not to allow anyone to prevent you from using your heavenly language.

Taken from: **Remember These Things & Remnant Church**

"This channel is like a classroom. A great classroom. Each day I bring you a fresh lesson for you are in the school of holiness. The whole curriculum is tailored to prepare you for the day I take you to Myself. All the angels in your life are working in cooperation with **My Spirit** and arranging your lessons for the day. That is why you so often find yourselves getting the answer you asked Me for on this channel. You are in a great classroom, and I am your teacher.

"So in a classroom, you come to be taught and you do your assignments so you can pass your tests and get an A, as well as graduating with honors. Yes, this is an honor class for those who have chosen to give Me their all. If you do your homework, you will pass in flying colors."

Taken from: **They Will All Be Taught By God**

Honesty

"Please, make your choices wisely. I am forever at your side calling you upward. But the climb is painful! Once you make up your mind to forsake your pride and defensiveness, I lift you up into My arms and carry you all the way to the top. This is My Heart's desire. Will you come with Me? Or abandon Me, like so many others have done. Do you have courage, character and relentless **honesty** with yourself? Or are you just getting by..."

Taken from: **How a Root of Bitterness Can Change Your Destiny and DNA**

"But some of My children have been Christians for years and are still toying with their walk. They have an inkling they are on the edge, but consider My Mercy will cover for their laxness. No, My Children. My mercy is not for those who have held Me off. It is for the lost who have never known Me and the weak that falter with every other step. For those sheep who are big and strong but still have no time for Me, they will stay behind until they are perfected in charity, **honesty** and devotion to Me.

"For them, there is a choice to make. Many of them have been given very great graces but used them selfishly, even in the faith, to accumulate wealth, popularity and influence. Or instead, they have used the grace for the world to live like kings."

Taken from: **Who Will I Rapture?**

"So, a major part of your job in restoring souls to Me is opening those watergates of unbelief, convincing them of their great worth in My eyes. Convincing them that their lives have a very unique and important purpose. That I use everyone to the degree they are willing to be used.

"If they are mothers, I use them to love their husbands and children and raise them up in the way they should go. If they are businessmen, I present opportunities in their lives to witness to their associates. And as they mature, I also bring before them the challenge of **honesty** and faithfulness to Me, which very often costs them much.

"But in each of these little scenarios, the faith is spread and grows. The place that is still most often stunted is their own deep-down opinion of themselves and a false notion that they are not worthy of Me - this keeps them from intimacy with Me."

Taken from: **Open The Watergates of Unbelief, Jesus teaching on reaching souls**

"And for you, this death on a cross is death to your egos, vanities, protective masks and devices, and approaching others in **honesty,** *lowly before God and man. I mean, let's face it. When you stand before the Lord, there's nothing hidden. And we need to stand before men that way, too, so they can relate to the grace of God - they can see that if God can use us, He can use them. This is SO important."*

Taken from: **Glorious Bride Arising w/Her Torch**

"I have prepared an army of men and women to recover this country from the enemy. They will swing into action and have an active part in taking ground away from the Order. Never since the history of man has there been a time such as what is coming, and never since the history of man has My protection been as strong as it will be.

"But there are certain rules you must live by. **Honesty** is first and foremost. Vigilance over your own sins and bad example. The devils are clever and they know how to provoke a soul to cause a breach in their covering. Charity, humility and patience also score high on the list of things targeted and necessary to maintain My Protection."

Taken from: **Surviving The Coming Tribulation**

Honesty

"Now, many of My generals and lieutenants are captive in ritual Christian culture. Mind you, I did not say simply 'culture'. I love the cultures and the varieties of the whole Earth. I gave to each their own unique flavor and purpose on this earth and all are dear to Me. I want only to infuse them with My Spirit.

"Not with social correctness and cover-ups but with transparency and **honesty**, that they too have fallen short of the Glory of God. Not with rules and gates, but with Love, seeping from every pore of their being.

"I wish to reach the pastors of the churches that are dying. I want them to see why I have withdrawn My miraculous presence. Why people are leaving. Why they are luke-warm and worn out. I want a whole new and fresh breeze of My Spirit to permeate the churches and I want to say it will not be dependent on your fasting and sacrifices, so stop torquing over this!"

Taken from: **Come Out of Religion, Come Dwell in My Heart**

"Humility, self-control, **honesty**, and charity are absolutely essential if you want Me to walk with you. If you are used to leading and getting your own way, you won't do very well as a leader. If you are unsure of yourself and know that you need Me more than ever, you will excel as a leader."

Taken from: **Jesus Speaks on What is To Come #5**

Yep, it was my black panther again. It had been bothering me for weeks that we might not have enough really healthy food, and I began thinking about what we would need before the Lord took us in the Rapture, if we were here for a week or two. I reasoned in my mind that whatever was left would be given to others anyway in our little food bank.

I rationalized myself into the store and bought healthy dry foods to back up the canned goods in the pantry.

Something about this did not feel good, but I blamed it on the enemy trying to prevent me. Deep in my heart, I suspected I might be wrong. But I didn't want to know - so I didn't check. But I proceeded in self-will. Ezekiel tried to call me on the phone, but the ringer was off my cell phone, so I never heard him. Then today at lunch, after worship, I was touching in with the Lord in the Bible Promises and got some VERY bad and scary readings: pride, and **honesty**.

Taken from: **Rest in Me Until I Carry You Over the Threshold of Eternity**

"There is nothing that can keep Me from loving you, absolutely nothing. But our relationship must be built on **honesty**. I cannot perfect that which you refuse to see. In order to bring you to perfection, you must be willing to admit the truth about yourself. You are beautiful beyond imagining and there is nothing that will change My mind about that. But these deep dark secrets and unconfessed sins let off a scent of guilt and shame.

"This, too, is responsible for you distancing yourself from Me. You know there are things too dark to confront but that in My presence all things are seen. May I say I have seen all these things even before they happened? No one wants to see themselves as evil and so they hide their evil thoughts and deeds even from themselves and make excuses to cover them up, or invent stories."

"My Love, come to Me and ask to be relieved of these sins. Ask Me to bring them to the surface where My grace can cauterize your flesh and you will never more be burdened by them."

Taken from: **Honesty: Looking at Yourself in God's Mirror**

Honesty

"Well, there are many roads before you every day. Always choose the narrow one. Always. Sublime words do make a man holy and just: but a virtuous life makes him dear to Me."

So, okay, I'll fill you in on this, guys. This was my "bad" again. What He's talking about here is that I wanted so badly to include that painting of the Lord in the thumb drive, to comfort those who are left behind that I tried to slip it into a small picture in a letter. But we had nothing but trouble uploading the files, so I figured that the Lord could not protect us from the enemy, because I was not being totally **honest***.*

So, I went to the Bible Promises and I got - guess what? **Honesty***. Oh, I was so upset! I was so angry!! I said, "But Lord! Christians smuggle Bibles into China! And that's not* **honest***!!"*

But He wasn't buying any of it. So I took the pictures out. Oh, I was so angry. I thought about it again and I wrote to the artist, saying, "This is a 15 gigabyte thumb drive and your picture is 74 kilobytes. It's something everyone can get on the Internet now - but no-one will be able to get as Revelation is fulfilled. And these people need hope! They need to see a loving Jesus and your image so captures that about Him. Would you PLEASE reconsider?"

So, I sent that off to him and I told him we'd paid for these thumb drives. We're not making any profit on it. We're basically giving them away.

And the Lord broke in at that point, and He said, "Now, THAT was the right thing to do. Not to be sneaky. Did it ever occur to you that I wanted to give this very wealthy man a chance to do something for Me? Without gaining an earthly reward? Or that his soul may be in danger? And this one act of kindness might just return to him in the form of mercy, at the very hour he needs it most?"

Taken from: **Be Without Guile and Repent for the World**

"In order for justice to prevail, hearts must be clean before Me. Make your peace with all men, My people. Always strive for **honesty** and integrity. Where you have failed, confess and ask forgiveness. Sometimes it takes only a word to calm troubled waters. Recognition and confession of sin clears the way for healing. Now I can move forward with My plans and all will follow as I lead.

"My Children, never underestimate the cleansing power of confession of wrong doing on your part. Many grudges can or could have been completely avoided if fault and mistakes were clearly admitted. The tendency today is to cover up weakness and proceed as if nothing were wrong. That doesn't wash in the hearts of men, it leaves a sting and resentment. Bitterness sets in and life takes a turn for the worse. In My Heart and Mind, brotherly love, reconciliation, are of the utmost importance. When people hold onto their pains, it twists their lives and sends them in a wrong direction."

Taken from: **Power In Reconciliation**

Satan knows how we think..."Oh, It's little, it's not a big deal." Oh, yes, little IS a big deal. If we are not faithful in the little things, how can we be entrusted with the bigger ones?? And this last correction was the capstone on all the others, and in all honesty I don't see how even the God of endless patience could allow any more presumption, because He's gone way out of His way to warn me. I have to shape up, dear friends, because you are watching, and I am now accountable to the Body for my behavior. It just has to stop.

I suppose if you weren't watching... and just God and Heaven were watching, I would be more tempted to give in. But you ARE watching, and because I love you all and want to be a better example of God's grace at work, I just can't let my vice go any further.

Taken from: **The Precipice of Presumption**

Hope

"Waiting is not easy. Waiting implies solid **hope**; **hope** is in direct proportion to faith, that what you are **hoping** for will become an eventuality. That is the realm you are all operating in. And the stronger your faith, the more productive and peaceful you will be.

"That is why Satan tries so hard to undermine your faith; so much depends upon it. When a soul becomes impatient, they choose many wrong turns and I must go ahead of them to steer them back on the right track. As your faith increases, so does your **hope** increase, until you are so full you are spilling over onto others. You are radiant with **hope**, because you know Who you have put your trust in. This is the point at which you can touch others in the deepest way.

"As My Bride is waiting in faith, she is **hoping** and increasing in glory, which will flow out on to others. Without waiting, there can be no **hope**. And without faith, waiting is fruitless. What I am saying is that you are all growing in faith, **hope** and trust. Each day you are becoming stronger and stronger. This impacts many areas of your lives, more than you realize. It is like weight lifting."

Taken from: **Lord, What Are You Doing With Us in This Hour?**

"So much has to take place, Clare, but understand that your prayers for mercy have and will soften the harshness of the judgment - so do not stop praying. There is still much to be averted. **Hope** in His Mercy, but know for certain that certain things must come to pass."

Taken from: **Your Prayers Are Working**

"I am coming for you; your *hope* and faith will not be disappointed. You have known Me as the Merciful God, so shall you know Me as the God of Glory as I transform your very bodies into the likeness of Mine."

Taken from: **You Are My Bride, My Garden Sealed**

"A creative, satisfied and responsible person is very dangerous to the kingdom of darkness. You carry seeds of inspiration that can bring others **hope**, joy and enthusiasm for life and most of all into relationship with Me. When you find your gift and turn it into a way of life, like Joseph did in the carpentry shop, you enjoy your work, you teach others to reach higher, but most of all when you are where I want you to be, doing what you are to do. You are highly anointed and fulfilled. Satan would see you frustrated, empty, a literal walking dead man, dead to all your **hope**s and dreams and gifts. That is why musicians and artists of every kind, as well as ministers are so persecuted and denounced for their choices in life."

Taken from: **Our Nations Future - Update**

"You say to Me, 'But you did save us for once and for all' and you speak the truth. But now, someone must pray that this gift of salvation is delivered to the poorest of poor, the dying, the lame, the sick, the drug addict, the victims of tragedy, all who are languishing without knowing Me and without any **hope**."

Taken from: **When the Lord is Painfully Silent**

"Do not imagine that fame and influence will follow you into Heaven. No, it shall be stripped from your person and all that will remain are the kindnesses and prayers you offered to the needy. All you sacrificed in your labors of love for Me will shine like the noonday sun. So great will the splendor of your glory that one from Earth will only be able to see you with great difficulty. This especially is the reward of My anonymous ones, whose only motive was love. I am telling you these things to encourage and strengthen you, for as I told you there will be many assaults against you, against your faith and **hope** in Me, in the coming days."

Taken from: **Your Lives Have Not Been Wasted**

Hope

"There are many layers to your crosses, My Children. Sometimes I call you to carry the weight of your cross only and it is easier for you. But other times, many other times - especially now - you are carrying multiple crosses. You are all intertwined as brothers and sisters and the same Holy Spirit flows through you all.

"When I see a soul that cannot rise from their bed of misery any longer, I take a portion of that suffering and scatter it around to more evenly distribute the burden. To you it may just seem like a little extra, but to the soul that was suffering, it is a reprieve from being completely drained of **hope** and enthusiasm for life. Yes, there are times when you will pass through that veil of tears, also. But it does not last forever when you have Me. I always find ways to liberate just enough that you can pick up and carry on.

"For souls in the world who have no one to pray for them, I again take a portion and allow it to manifest on friends and relatives, so that what is just an inconvenience or a little bit of unpleasantness for them, means the world to you. This is why I stress, 'Love one another as I have loved you.' It is only this kind of brotherly love that says 'yes' to the burdens of others. This is your glory, this love that passes all understanding; this is the pinnacle of your Christian walk, to be willing to suffer for others as I suffered for you and all transgressors of the law. What a beautiful vision of My brotherly love this is. What a wonder this is to angels above and souls on Earth, when they see this sacrificial love and even feel its effects."

Taken from: **Suffering – Real Work in the Realm of the Spirit**

"Some of you have run with an evil crowd your entire life, you have stolen from the poor, murdered the innocent, incarcerated those not guilty, and done everything in your lives from a motive of serving yourself and your children. But nonetheless, I went to Calvary and laid down My life for everything you did. Now I am inviting you to repent, because when these catastrophes - which even some of you have been involved in planning...when they occur, there will be no time left for you to repent.

"So, I am asking you - speak to Me, I am listening. Tell Me, 'Jesus, I know I have sinned. I know I have avoided facing what I've done and indeed I know there is little time left. Forgive me, have mercy on me and receive me into Your Kingdom. I know You died for my sins. From this day forth, I turn my back on my sinful ways and with Your help, I will live my life for You. Amen.'

He continued, "What is necessary here is that you say this with all your heart, you truly repent for the evil you have done, you truly want to change and give your life to Me, the Son of the Living God who died for you and rose again. Without true repentance, there is little **hope** for you. Reach out to Me but one step forward and I will draw you into My everlasting and loving arms and you will find peace for your soul. My children, do this now. There is little time left and for many of you, there will be no time when calamity hits the Earth.

"Repent now and I will forgive now. And regardless of what happens on this Earth, you will be in Heaven with Me for eternity."

Taken from: **War, Comet, Rapture, Treaty – Order of Events**

"Despite this sense of absence, know that I am always with you, always comforting you and seeing to your needs, admonishing and dispensing graces to you. Yes, especially the graces to endure this dark world without the sweet touch of My consolations, that I might shower them on the desperate with no **hope**."

Taken from: **When the Lord is Painfully Silent**

Hope

"You see, when you entrust Me with all that is yours - your everything - I dispense grace and mercy where I will, but so much is handed over to Me in the gift of your life. You have said, 'Jesus, anything for You.' And I have said, 'I will have you with Me in paradise someday, but for now

"I need your sacrifices, I need your consolations, I need your physical infirmities, yes, even those. They are your cross, your Simon's cross.'

"You say to Me, 'But you did save us for once and for all' and you speak the truth. But now, someone must pray that this gift of salvation is delivered to the poorest of poor, the dying, the lame, the sick, the drug addict, the victims of tragedy, all who are languishing without knowing Me and **without any hope**.

"True, I have visited some of them many times in their lives before, but they were not ready. Now they are ready. And those who have yet to know Me, because of your offerings, are now coming to know Me and discovering the love and joy of their lives. With that discovery, they are happy to die to be with Me and another soul is snatched from Satan."

∾

"All of you, dear Dwellers in My Heart, you know now that everything you experience, I turn to good. Nothing, absolutely nothing escapes My notice and how many times do I in fact hang on that cross of suffering with you?

"How many tears do I shed when you go through all these things and offer them to Me with a grateful heart? Millions of times a day, I am garnering gifts of love from My people to be shed upon the hearts of those who do not know Me.

"Despite this sense of absence, know that I am always with you, always comforting you and seeing to your needs, admonishing and dispensing graces to you. Yes, especially the graces to endure this dark world without the sweet touch of My consolations, that I might shower them on the desperate with **no hope**."

Taken from: **When the Lord is Painfully Silent**

"Don't allow yourselves to be drawn off into vain reasonings, empty arguments, critical spirits. Oh, they have set land-mines before you, My people. Your only **hope** is to lay low in humility, confessing My Blood for protection and refusing, and I do mean flat-out refusing, to be engaged in useless arguments that will cause your soul to fall into unrest and confusion.

"Little do they know, or expect, that I will strengthen you in humility, your greatest protection. As you remain vigilant and obedient, they will have no place to manifest."

Taken from: **February: A Month of Testings**

"Those who were without faith did not understand I would rise again. Rather, they fell into despair that their hope for the Messiah was in vain, that truly if anyone were ever the Messiah, it was Me.

"But now, I was 'dead' and what was left? Shock, dismay, confusion, agony, hopelessness.

"So, you see, these men were no different than you, Clare, or any other Heartdweller. They all had their doubts, fears, confusions proposed to them by lying demons. They all fell short in perfect faith, perfect fidelity, perfection as I lived it. Yet still they clung to the **hope** that perhaps what I told them could be true, incredulous as it was."

Taken from: **Bring Me Your Lowliness**

Hospitality/Caring for Others

Let's say one of my children show up at the door and it totally revamps my night and I must have **hospitality** *to them whom I love very much. Being goal oriented is not a healthy thing. You see a lot of Hollywood movies about how some are highly successful in business but tragically unsuccessful in their marriages. Those are goal-oriented people. These are people who are really serious about what they're doing to the inclusion to all other facets of their lives.*

The Lord has not called us to that. He has called us to love our brother as we love ourselves and to love Him with all of our hearts (Mark 12:31). Sometimes people laugh about these qualities and say, "Oh that person is a compulsive addictive worker." We chide each other about these things, but it really is quite serious. It wrinkles the garment that the Lord is wanting us to make pure and white for His coming. We must cooperate with the Holy Spirit.

Taken from: **The Righteous Bride Will Not Quench the Spirit, Intro**

So, I have had to learn to stop, and put down something, which I considered required a high level of technical concentration. I had to learn to stop - in mid-stream - get up, and go to the door, to make sure that a family has food for the night, or to take care of some little detail that's frustrating my husband, or if one of my children comes to the door. I had to learn to totally re-vamp my night, to show **hospitality** *to them, whom I love very much.*

Taken from: **Wounding Waters: The Worldly Church**

He continued, "But let's get back to what is important here, My Love. The focus must be on charity and virtue, trust and faith in My ability to provide. Without these pivotal attitudes, they will not succeed. My protection can make you invisible. My protection can turn wild beasts away. My protection can save you from the ground giving way beneath you. My protection can provide water and food when there is none. I can do all things, and I will, for those whose agenda is to gather in souls to the Kingdom. Those who give and lead unselfishly, those who are honest and **caring for others**, these are the ones I will supernaturally protect and provide for."

Taken from: **God Will Provide for Those Left Behind**

The Lord picked up at this point and said, "I will have compassion on whom I will have compassion. I will have mercy on whom I will have mercy, but I will not support or bless stealing and lying, so I appeal to you, My children, mend your ways.

"For the rest, I say thank you for **caring about those around you**. Your reward in Heaven shall be great. For those who are poor, I say, you are My gift to those around you. Through you, they shall prove their holiness and be My ambassadors of mercy."

Taken from: **Government Collapse Clarified…**

"Your greatest safety is in holiness and refusing to judge others. Many have many opinions, and unfortunately much of what is proposed is opinion and not from Me.

"My Brides, you are stunningly beautiful and the enemy hates the very mention of you. That is why he is waging war on this channel. He cannot stand to see the beauty of brotherly love, patience and **caring for one another**. He hates you for it.

"On other channels, he has succeeded in causing division, strife and calumny, but here he is a miserable failure; that is why you are being targeted. Your vigilance and obedience will keep you in My Peace."

Taken from: **Resist Gossip and Judgment**

Hospitality/Caring for Others

"For the rest, I say thank you for **caring about those around you**. Your reward in Heaven shall be great. For those who are poor, I say, you are My gift to those around you. Through you, they shall prove their holiness and be My ambassadors of mercy.

"You play a very valuable role in My Kingdom. You teach the selfish to be merciful. You teach the proud to be humble. You teach the rich compassion. Do not be ashamed of who you are. I allowed this circumstance in your life, and I have equipped you to bear the scorn and contempt of men, the way I did. I have allowed you to become very much like Me, that the hearts of men could be revealed."

Taken from: **Government Collapse Clarified...**

"As I have told you many times before, no man is worth more than the price I paid on Calvary for them. Each and every one cost Me the very life's blood of My body. Therefore, the rich and the poor are of equal value in My Kingdom. This is something that does not become apparent to most until after they die, and then they see their nakedness before Me.

"Accumulations of wealth, status and accomplishment fade like the morning mist and what is left is the stark reality, 'What did you **do for others**? Did you learn how to give? Did you learn how to love?' It is a very difficult decision to leave the world to follow Me, so many ramifications. My disciples were head-over-heels in love with Me - they made that choice without hesitation."

Taken from: **The Way to His Heart and Intimacy in Prayer**

"Shepherds, who are you listening to when you choose worship leaders? Teachers? Intercessors? Who are you empowering in growth to serve Me? Where are the ministries that address troubled marriages, teens, and the elderly? Are you **caring for all the sheep** or just the ones with the thickest fleece? Are you watching what they feed on or are they going toxic from attractive but poisonous plants? Are you correcting and admonishing behaviors that are demoralizing, or are you avoiding conflict?"

"You see, the sheep see it all. They know where they can slip by you: your buttons, your avoidances, your favorites - they read you like a book. Many have made My churches social clubs where the elite from the world are the leaders in the church because everyone respects their worldly achievements.

"That is everyone... but Me. That's feeding them moldy hay - that's not fresh, vital green grass. Everyone confesses Me, but deep down inside they are empty and languishing. They look healthy from the outside but their internal organs are rotting. Must they wait for the judgment to find out why they are dead inside? Don't you know it's too late then?

"Your job is to keep the flock healthy. If one has an infestation, it needs to be isolated and treated, not mixed in with the healthy ones, lest the whole flock become sick. So, one of your deacons is committing adultery with another deacon's wife. You just don't want to address it, but it's not going away - rather the plague is spreading to the other sheep.

"They know you look the other way, and their conscience has become so numb because you haven't addressed what I wanted addressed, and things are so far gone and out of whack they've been left vulnerable to the wolves. The pastor is sound asleep or pre-occupied with the new building program and the wolves go to work right under his nose."

Taken from: **Why Are People Leaving My Church**

Hospitality/Caring for Others

"Hold Me, sing to Me, dance with Me, skate with Me, and release your cares to Me. Wipe the tears from My eyes and the blood from My brow. This love moves My heart more than any prayer you can pray. You're taking My mind off the horrors of this world. You're giving Me a momen of rest from the storm. Doubtless some will say, 'God has no need of anything - He HAS everything.' Oh, how wrong you are.

"I created you for love and appreciation and fellowship with you; to see your joy over My gifts, created just for you to enjoy.

"To watch you become like Me as you grow and **love others** unconditionally, **reaching out and caring**. I derive so much happiness from My children as they **reach out and care for others**, as I care for them. So, go now. Enjoy the wonderful worship sent from Heaven to bring you into My presence and even deeper into the garden of My heart - and bring Me joy, My Bride. Comfort, console, and repair the damage done by the ungrateful. Comfort and strengthen Me with the sweet raisin cakes of your love."

Taken from: **I'm Calling You Closer...**

"I know it was difficult for you today, to lay aside your agenda, but I am proud of you for doing it. I'm satisfied that you love Me more. When I see you setting aside what you want, for what I want, to fulfill the very suggestion and longing of My heart speaks volumes to Me about your love.

"I needed to see the fellowship in **caring for one another** tonight. You mustn't be too attached to your agenda. I want you to be well-rounded and still sensitive to others needs in the midst of your passion for creating. So many of my artists are not. They live to create and are driven to give meaning to their lives through their creations."

And my note on that is, the only meaning in their lives will be when they fed and comforted the Lord. They're going to find that out.

"This is where spiritual adultery comes from. My Bride should live for Me and Me alone. Whether it's cleaning, cooking, building websites, music and art. I love these forms of expression of love for Me, but when they are driven by selfish ambition, they lose their savor and injure Me - as well as depriving the soul of their true nourishment, their true worth, which can only be found in Me. That is one reason why self-will is so poisonous and disastrous to the soul. When any activity becomes more important than Me, the soul ceases to obey the first commandment: Love Me with all your heart, all your strength and your neighbor as yourself. Yes, enjoy your work, I enjoy creating with you. But always be on the lookout for what your neighbor is in need of, and put them first."

Taken from: **Wounding Waters Part 3: Goal Driven Life**

I had been talking to one of my prayer partners earlier and she mentioned how important the Armor of God was and that it was a gift we could ask for. In truth, I didn't feel worthy to even ask. It seems that the requirement may be a **heart of love and caring for others**, *just as His heart is.*

Taken from: **Spiritual Warfare 10**

"You see, holiness is hard work. It entails much self-denial and refocusing on the **needs of others**. When you come to serve the Lord, prepare yourself for trials. Yes, many in this world believe it is their right to indulge themselves. After all, they worked for it. But all this indulgence leads to blind alleys, wrong turns and bondage."

Taken from: **Freedom Without License**

Humility

"Nothing is out of My control and nothing is allowed without My consent. I have made every provision for you ahead of time. You have no need to be anxious at all, only keep your heart and eyes on Me. You are my precious, precious child and I will not allow anything or anyone to harm you. I have set my angels all about you to watch over you day and night. Not only will you be provided for, but you will know My loving care and the surety of My faithfulness as I bring an overabundance for you to help others with.

"You will begin to meet others who, like you, have repented as well, and through their own brokenness have been fully restored in profound **humility** and whose hearts are solely for Me and the Kingdom of God alone."

Taken from: **Post Rapture Letter from God #3**

When you walk out of this kind of (Dwelling) prayer you are equipped to be an ambassador of love and to comfort others. You can't give what you don't have. This is preeminently time set aside for your equipping and your healing. As time goes by, you'll begin to gain confidence that Jesus is truly with you. This is not a phantom or a familiar spirit - this is God.

*At the same time, He will draw attention to the necessity of **humility**. Those who are gifted with this kind of relationship will be broken many, many, many times in order to safeguard their gift. Pride enters in so easily. Don't be afraid, it gets better. Don't be afraid to go to Him.*

Taken from: **How to Hear and See Jesus**

*At this point, we run for cover instead of running into His waiting arms. All the while, HE'S looking on with mercy and compassion. This fall, which He most likely allowed to humble us, is our opportunity to grow in **humility** and faith. He's waiting with open arms and kisses, to receive us back into fellowship, wanting to strengthen us and assure us of His* *love, which is impossible to earn. He loves us because He is God. And Love is His nature -He can't help Himself. Have IS Love! He created us for fellowship with Him, He enjoys our company. He's not like an earthly father, waiting for us to prove how good we are before He showers His love and approval on us.*

So, what are we do to? The sooner we forget ourselves and turn to Him, knowing that He will forgive and restore our peace, the sooner we'll be happy again.

Taken from: **Tag-Along Monsters**

I believe we can pray against them, but there's no weapon like virtue, and especially, **humility** *to put the enemy to flight. We have unsaved loved ones who don't have a clue about how they are being used. So, the only way we can disarm what could turn into a bitter experience is for us to exercise extreme heroic charity,* **humility** *and yielding. Bending over backwards to please one another. Going out of our way to yield to someone who wants it their way. And laying aside our own ideas and egos to create a sweet, nurturing environment.*

Taken from: **Preserving Holiday Joy**

And yet, isn't that just what we do to ourselves when we criticize another Christian? Could we not have used love, patience and **humility***, striking our OWN breast, knowing that any moment, the grace of God - which supports our progress in holiness - could be withdrawn for a season by divine decree, and we, too, could fall? And what of these mistaken judgments where our limited understanding assigns motives that may not even exist? How very displeased God is with a soul that harbors criticism and judgment in their hearts. In our moment of need, do we want justice - or mercy?*

Taken from: **Innocent Blood, Wounding Christians**

Humility

*Charity is so, so important. Charity and **humility** are two things that...
the Lord, if you're serious about Him and are really committed to Him,
He's not going to let you slide in those areas. Because those are the things
that He honors the most, that He values the most in a soul, is their
humility and their charity.*

*And if we don't reflect that **humility** and charity of Jesus, He will
definitely withdraw from us to get our attention. There's nothing really
worse that I have found, personally, in my walk with the Lord that
has grieved Him more than being hard and harsh with some judgment,
because we hurt people, whether it's spoken or not spoken.*

*An unspoken word still has the ability to cut a soul. You can feel when
people are gossiping about you, saying things about you, and it hurts. It's
destructive, and He hates to see someone suffer.*

Taken from: **Spiritual Dryness 2 of 2**

*I began seeking just who this Lord of mine was in truth, not as the church
had taught me or as others convinced me. Through the writings of other
dear saints like Heidi Baker and so many more, I found that He longs for
us to come to Him. He longs for that intimacy and that we're willing to
come into a place of **humility** and in anticipation. He'll meet us there if
we're willing to be there.*

*The walk and the path is probably as different for each of us as we are
from each other. The basics remain: dwell in **humility** and abandon your
life fully to Him. Believe that He is not only able but willing to meet you
intimately and claim this birthright of every single believer.*

Taken from: **Binding Demons Prayers and Testimonials**

"**Humility**, self-control, honesty, and charity are absolutely essential if
you want Me to walk with you. If you are used to leading and getting

your own way, you won't do very well as a leader. If you are unsure of yourself and know that you need Me more than ever, you will excel. My children, the ways of the world that you have learned are totally inappropriate here. I protect those who **humble** themselves before Me. If you are prancing around proudly with all the answers, you are bound for destruction.

"I am counting on your breaking when you realize all you've been taught by friends and family has just come to pass before your very eyes. I am counting on you face flat on the floor begging forgiveness for your pride and arrogance. I am laying the groundwork for you to survive the trials that are now at your door, both body and soul.

"If you **humble** yourself before Me, I will most certainly be with you. Even if you are in a long-standing habit of pride and arrogance, and are aware of your sin and want to be delivered, I will work with you. But if you insist on your own wisdom, I can do little for you."

Taken from: **Jesus Speaks on What is to Come #5**

"Intimacy with Me is the key to Sanity. Compromise with the world opens the door to Satan and his demons. When you sin, even in the little things, the little foxes spoil the vine.

"Beware of serious misunderstandings among brethren. Gossip, implication, slurs, impatience, interpreting motives to their detriment, downgrading and the like will separate brethren and make way for each to be isolated from one another. An isolated sheep in the forest, as you know, is a dead sheep. Be ever so vigilant to correct the early signs of misunderstanding. More patience, more love, more **humility**, these are the tools of healing you must always keep in readiness."

Taken from: **Another Soul for Heaven, Another Jewel in Your Crown**

Humility

"You see My Daughter, so many on Earth in this hour long with all their hearts to minister but the forces allied against them are tremendous, both of a personal nature and an impersonal nature. Few there are that break through this wall, for great perseverance is required and great reliance on Me.

"And there are those who have been chosen and equipped for this, there are others who have not. And to them I give the grace of prayer. Their desires are manifested in the arenas of evangelism, and while they are not a direct part of the conversions as man sees it, they are the living prayer force behind these evangelists.

"And were you to see these evangelists without the great mass of prayer warriors offering prayers and supplications on their behalf, you would see them as just simple, pitifully weak men.

"The evangelists themselves must have very pure hearts, **humility** and an anointing from above. Their integrity must be impeccable. That is why we work so hard on issues of this sort. They cannot carry out the work and sustain the heat of the battle or hold up under pressures without a profound commitment to integrity and doing things My way.

"Yet, pull the curtain back and the man becomes very, very little in My plan. The intercessors behind the man are tremendous, making him look like a giant, when in reality it is the little ones behind him that are responsible for his perceived stature. In this way, the desires of those who wanted to minister are satisfied.

"And yet there is a time and a season for all. They will get their turn to touch souls with My Love. Everyone gets a turn to do what is on their heart to do, because their hearts are conformed to Mine."

Taken from: **Heaven & the Millennium, After the Rapture**

"You will find that those of you who are harsh and judgmental with others, will have a harder time controlling yourselves. You see, rather than rushing to your side, I allow you to fail so you will have more compassion for your brothers and sisters. I am calling My children to Mercy. Those who show Mercy shall themselves be shown Mercy.

"And those who are legalistic, demanding, and critical of others, need to learn compassion and **humility**. And so I allow a degrading habit to bring them to their senses so they will cease judging others. I do not give birth to these things, but I see the demons getting ready to jump on a soul, and if they have been harsh and critical of others, I do not come to their rescue. The more you downgrade others the more you can expect to fall."

Taken from: **Blessed are the Pure, For They Shall See Me**

A stronghold is like a fortress where demons have continual access to cause anger, rage, resentment and bitterness.

We believe that a stronghold can only be broken by prayer AND fasting. Well, it just so happened someone was fasting and they caught it--just in time. But we were warned-- they will be back to try it again. And I have to confess to you, brothers and sisters, I have no confidence that I will pass the next test, either. I have seen a stronghold of anger and rage at work. I have seen it tear a family to shreds and send them all scattering in different directions to get away from its ugliness, never to be reunited.

Do you see why **humility** *and gratitude are so important? No matter what happens, the* **humble** *soul sees the hand of God and receives the burden with gratitude.*

Taken from: **Pride & One Speck of Anger Equals a Stronghold of Rage**

Intimacy With Jesus

"Tell My People their deliverance will come suddenly and without warning. That is why I have taken all this time to prepare you, so that you will stand when others collapse. You cannot envision the changes that will take place, but you can cultivate your total reliance on Me and I will see you through.

"**Intimacy with Me** is key. Knowing My voice and obeying My wishes, is key. This is where your deliverance lies: in your cleaving to Me and following the path laid out for you. My people, I know you are painfully weary in waiting and I see how you have sacrificed and supported Me as we gather as many as we can and your faithfulness will be richly rewarded."

Taken from: **The Heaviness of Waiting for the Rapture**

What an awesome God! What an awesome love! He is hungry for your company. He longs for **intimacy** *with you. He has prepared a place for you. But the one thing that He has for you that's more precious than anything else is His love. And that's Presence, when you dwell in His heart you allow Him to engage you. His presence, His manifest presence is the most wonderful experience anyone on earth can have.*

Taken from: **Dwelling Prayer #4**

Here's the thing: we become so busy with these conferences and activities at church, that we really don't have the time to dedicate to the Lord in absolute purity; worship time, listening for His voice, studying the Scriptures. That **intimacy** *where you hear His voice, where He speaks to you, where He holds you in His arms. Where He comforts you, He warns you of trials, He teaches you. That* **intimacy** *comes at a cost, and the cost has to do with not filling your life with busy work, and busy studies, and running here and there to be taught. Because if you have an* **intimate** *relationship with the Lord, He will teach you directly, from the*

Scriptures, from life lessons. From things that happened during the day, from nature. There are so many different ways that He communicates with us! He will teach you, if you take the time to cultivate Him. "Those who seek me, find me."

Taken from: **Wounding Waters – The Worldly Church: Introduction**

"If you are not working for Me in this hour, you are standing before Me blind and naked. Rise up and take on your Master's business. Bring forth fruit worthy of My Bride, and while you are doing this I will see to it that you grow into the fullness of who I've called you to be as My Spouse. My promise to you is life eternal and the choicest lands of Heaven, the sweetest **intimacy** possible to a created soul. Don't let Me down in this hour; rise up, harness yourself to My carriage, for My yoke is easy, My burden is light, and I will make joyful for you the act of going out and gathering to Me My Bride."

Taken from: **Blood Moon Rapture...**

"May I say, many of My Brides are blind to their faults? They are not going deep enough in discerning what displeases Me. Yes, My Spirit is at work in their conscience, but some refuse to get a firm grip on habits that do NOT glorify Me, but work iniquity in the Body. Gossip and judgment are HUGE. Some find it hard to stop. May I say that is impossible to stop without My Grace that comes from **intimacy with Me**?

"Without deep **intimacy**, without you knowing Me, you will not have the courage to stop deeply ingrained, destructive habits in My Body that everyone accepts as the norm. Criticizing, gossiping and backbiting are NOT the norm - they are noxious sins that rise up to Heaven in testimony against a soul. They create breaks in the covering I give My servants, and breaks let the enemy in for a sifting."

Taken from: **Prophetic Word: Rapture & Conflict in Marriage**

Intimacy With Jesus

"So, now history repeats itself and those with a controlling religious spirit have found their way into every denomination with their lust for control. The entire game plan from the enemy is to make men feel so guilty for their sins, they withdraw from Me. Or refuse to even approach Me. How common is it that you have seen and heard people say, 'I'm not good enough for God. When I get good enough for God, I'll turn to Him.' And of course, that never happens. And the religious spirit is the vehicle to do that. What I have taught you goes against that grain, and so you are hated."

"That I would treat you as My Bride, with whom My Heart is **intimately** entwined, and that I feel that way about all My People, is abhorrent to them. That I can live through you is still the most frightening aspect of true faith. God can live through men and the devils cannot stop Him.

"All through the Scripture the espousal relationship is proclaimed."

"I betrothed you to one husband, (Paul said) to present you as a pure virgin to Christ." II Corinthians 11:2

"And I will betroth you to me forever. I will betroth you to me in righteousness and in justice, in steadfast love and in mercy." Hosea 2:19

"...as the bridegroom rejoices over the bride, so shall your God rejoice over you." Isaiah 62:5

"That is another reason that the demons toy with discernment and make the sincere believer seeking **intimacy with Me** frightened of falling into error. Yet if a soul's heart is set on Me, I will guide and lead them ultimately, through every deception and impediment. If you trust totally in Me, knowing that I will accomplish My will in your life, you will not abandon the path of intimacy when your discernment fails. Rather you will humble yourself and draw ever nearer."

Taken from: **Why You Are Hated...**

"Do you see how deeply Satan has entrenched himself in these souls? There is a deadly apathy that sets in. A sense of hopelessness because they feel they've failed to fit in, and failed Me as well. These are the ones I want you to be on the look out for. They are EVERYWHERE.

"Yes, they are next-door and dotted around in every business you frequent. They, in fact, have given up on themselves and are left with a yearning they try to suppress, 'How do I get back in good graces with God? Their impediment is false guilt. Because the ways of men in the church didn't meet their needs, they've been led to believe there's something wrong with them.

"Oh, yes, they will find fault with the churches and pastors, but beneath that justifying veneer, they are deeply disillusioned with the faith and even with Me."

"They are falling out of churches in droves. Why? Because I am opening their eyes to the emptiness they feel there. Most do not realize that they are to bring Me into the church and worship Me on that day - rather they go to encounter Me.

"And if I'm not anointing the worship and teaching, they leave disappointed.

"They long for **intimacy**, simply put. **Intimacy** is something no church can provide for them, although it should be taught. This is where I am sending you - teach **intimacy with Me**, teach discernment, teach humility, teach them most of all that I long for their attentions more than they long for Me.

"I know them and love them to distraction right where they stand."

Taken from: **Open the Watergates of Unbelief...**

Intimacy With Jesus

"Your biggest fight is **intimacy**. If they can't deny it, they will twist it. Therefore you must approach it in two ways, Scripturally and Experientially. Much of the problem is fundamental ignorance as to how close is "close" with Me. It reaches deep down into the soul. Close is all-enveloping, like a rose blooming from the inside.

"The seed is given at conversion and even baptism and through the, years as the love for Me is guarded, it blossoms into an all-consuming, fragrant garden of pure Heavenly love. Something few experience on this Earth without passion and sex entering in.

"I do not wish for anyone to be excluded from this **relationship of pure intimacy with Me.**"

Taken from: **If You Love Me – Rapture – Sexual Temptations...**

"And yes, it is the force of dark matter and proliferation of demons entering through portals that will cause such anarchy as man has not known on this Earth before. Finally, science has the weapons to destroy humanity from the inside out. Eaten up with jealousy, greed, rage, lust and rebellion, each will be his own undoing.

"This is why virtue at this time is paramount. Without virtue, you will be taken captive or slain in the battle field. **Without intimacy with Me,** you will not have virtue. Without obedience to Me, there will be little if anything left of our relationship."

"My Brides, love is what our relationship is based on. And if you love Me, you will obey Me. If you are slandering or undermining your neighbor you are destroying your relationship with Me.

"Without faith it is impossible to please Me, and now I tell you truly, without love for your brother, it is impossible to please Me.

"Do not for one moment abandon the gate of virtue, nor for one second give into the burning desire to hate. This is coming directly from demons who are flaming you with the fires of hatred Satan has for everything and everyone I created. Do not partake of his poison; do not fall under his influence."

Taken from: **Refining Fires are Coming...**

"Do you understand? You are hated because of this. The devils hate the sweet and pure **intimacy you have with Me**. They hate you teaching that to others. Because the fear of Hell and punishment will keep a soul out of sin, but just barely. And those who avoid sin because of punishment eventually become lukewarm and are of little threat to the enemy and the kingdom of darkness."

"However, those who are in love with Me, whose hearts melt when they see My Face, hear a love song, and long to give Me more of their lives - those souls are the most threatening to the kingdom of darkness.

"That is another reason why so many attacks have been launched at you. **Intimacy is the Key** to the greatest works in My Kingdom. If you sat behind a desk and taught eschatology, you would be far less threatening."

Taken from: **Your Greatest Strength**

"Come here My Bride, let Me hold you, Clare. You have been too far away from Me for too long and now your tuning device...well, it needs a tune up. If you want this **intimacy with Me**, you will have to fight for it, with fasting and re-dedication to prayer."

Taken from: **Enemy Tactics & An Invitation & Opportunity**

Joy

"When I spoke of the abundant life, I was not speaking of the abundance of things in the world. I was speaking of the abundance of My presence, and the **joy** of living in Me."

Taken from: **Suffering – Real Work in the Spirit Realm**

"Yes, I too am weary - very weary. Yet we hold out for just one more beloved son and daughter to return to Me. What shall I say, that the Day is coming? No, you have heard all that before.

"But I can tell you this: your reward in Heaven is very great.

"You have put on My garments of salvation and stood with Me in the dryness, in the testings, in the brutality leveled against you, some even losing their heads, only to gain an eternity with Me. Yes, an eternity with Me. **Joys** that you cannot reckon with the human mind."

Taken from: **The Weariness of Waiting**

"My heart is yours, Clare. It is your abode, your dwelling place, your eternal place of rest and **joy**. Transforming you from glory to glory. Always moving upward like the flames of fire consuming all the dross and moving upward perpetually My heart is a furnace for all of mankind. It is at times a place of torment when I see so many rejecting My Love and going the way of perdition."

Taken from: **Why a Soul Rejects Love**

"For many years when your age group and those over 50 were growing up, the climate was post world war two, there was focus on responsibility for rebuilding society and scorn and contempt for creativity. They were taught that housework, dishes, cooking, laundry and all these other basic things came first.

"No, prayer comes first, then your anointing, then the housework. Of course, when you are raising children, your anointing is as a mother, but still, your gifts are not to be suppressed. I gave them so you could serve Me in unique ways, ways that would bring **joy**. Not only to you, but to others."

Taken from: **Our Nation's Future - Update**

"There will be ample opportunity. Remember: it's not about prosperity, popularity, and power, but righteousness, peace and **joy** in My Holy Spirit in the midst of a corrupt and challenging world."

Taken from: **These Lite and Momentary Sufferings**

"My People, because of the value that is placed on knowledge, most have lost their sense of wonder and joy with life. The things I give you to bring entertainment and **joy** are so often overlooked. It is a wonderful thing to be dedicated to Me with all your heart and mind and strength.

"But many miss the forest for the trees trying to be so intelligent and spiritually advanced. To know all the Scriptures and how to apply them. But to Me, the most advanced among you is the most childlike.

"When you come to Me, you must do a lot of unlearning, a lot of tossing out the ways of man. Spontaneity is a gift that has been suppressed in favor of sophistication.

"Oh, how man wears himself out putting on a front of knowing it all, when indeed he knows so little. It may impress the people around him, but it does not impress Me."

Taken from: **Creativity Renders You Responsive To Me**

Joy

"Carry on, My Dear ones. You are changing the course of history with your prayers. Carry on. I bless you now with My peace and inward **joy** to calm your fears and stabilize you in the events yet to come. Let that **joyful** light, the **joy** of My countenance shine out from within your hearts. You are the light of the world."

Taken from: **You Are the Light of the World**

"For these light and momentary troubles, you are rewarded with an eternity of bliss. But I have not called you to come to Me alone. I wish for you to bring others with you, and this is truly a labor calling for sacrifice and steadfastness.

"When people see your generosity in following My example, they are moved to come to Me; they see your motivation as Love for Me and your brother and that draws all men to Me. The abundant life is not meat and drink, but righteousness, peace - even in chaos; **joy** - even in suffering."

Taken from: **Miami Soon to be Bombed & No Greater Love**

"It is hard to stay down when you are encouraged. Time and time again, I cause My Spirit to refresh you, that you might not lose Hope. That you not weaken in your Faith. The reason that I brought up using your imagination and wishful dreaming is simply that I want you to be able to look out into the future and think of all the wonderful possibilities that truly DO await you. In this way you will genuinely be living in Heavenly places.

"Keep your hands on My heart and seek My face. See Me always before you, for this is where your strength comes from - as well as My **joy** for the journey."

Taken from: **Powerful Dream – 600 mph Tsunami Hits San Francisco**

"Know that the greatest players in this semi-final scene are My faithful intercessors. The little ones no one sees or cares about. They are the decisive force; they are in the front lines and holding back the tide of evil. If you are one of them, I beg you to find honor and great satisfaction in this role. You are the ones making the greatest difference.

"Persevere and be highly satisfied for your exalted stations in this moment of history. Great will be your reward in Heaven. Do not look to what others are doing and compare yourself. No, press in with your heart focused on My intentions; press in and raise the cry for justice on high to the Father's throne. Yours is the decisive voice.

"This is a war zone, and you are the front lines. I am sustaining you. Great is the glory associated with a love that gives and gives beyond itself. This was My portion and when you manifest it, you are most like Me. I am with you. Do not grow weary. Take comfort from the great **joy** you bring Me, My Brides. Because of your faithfulness, prophecy will be accomplished in a way no one could have foreseen or imagined."

Taken from: **God is Hearing the Russian People...**

"You are all very rare gems in My Kingdom. Your hearkening to My voice has brought Me consolation after consolation and there are no words for Me to express what **joy** I find in you. That is why I have gone to prepare a place for you, that where I am you, too, shall be. A place full of delights to express My endless delight in you.

"When I search the world for hearts on fire...I can always count on finding you ready and waiting for Me. You will not know until Heaven what consolations you have all brought to Me. But I thank you for being here. Soon you will experience just how thankful I am."

Taken from: **The Deaf & Blind Among Us**

Joy

"That is My point, dear ones. I want you to be free and clean of any earthly entanglements when I come for you. I want to see you totally freed from bitterness and the unforgiveness that has entangled you in the past, as well as free from others still being embittered over you or attached to you. You cannot please everyone, but you can at least make an attempt at resolving past conflicts. In time, I can work with those you attempted, in great humility, to make peace with and loosen their bondage to the past. Truly, the tyranny of memories is a slow-killing poison that robs a soul of his life in the present moment.

"Once you have made your peace as best you can, when the enemy tries to assail you with guilt and condemnation or things of the past you can no longer rectify, let them drop like a stone into the ocean. Do not wrestle with 'should haves/should not haves.' Simply let them drop like a stone into the ocean of My Mercy for Me to resolve. The tendency to fight or rationalize these thoughts only draws you deeper into the conflict. I already have a resolution, in My time. I already have a provision, in My time. Abandoning these to Me is your sure and healthy answer to them being worked out.

"Then you are free from the fetters of the past and fully here with Me, fully Mine, not chained to guilt wracking thoughts from the past. This is one secret of a **joyful** life in Me. Being truly present to Me right here and now, as I am truly present to you. So much beauty passes you by, because your mind is preoccupied with the past or the future. If you have examined your heart carefully and repented, you can live with Me now because the past and the future are Mine to negotiate."

Taken from: **Make Peace With All**

"When I see your devotion, your daily struggles, your fresh resolve, your careful examination of conscience and self-correction, I rejoice that such a one as this has given their lives to Me. I find great solace and **joy** in dwelling in your hearts and listening to the meditations of your mind as you continue to draw closer and closer to Me, until we are one. I see your dry spells and watch your grief when you do not feel My presence, though I am with you always.

"I see how you recommit your life to Me sometimes hour by hour, day by day, saying over and over again, 'I just want more of You, Jesus. I want to love You with my whole heart.' I hear the times you cry out from the heart, 'Lord, have Mercy on these souls.' I approve the meditations of your hearts and the faithfulness you reach for daily.

"How can I possibly describe to you the indescribable **joy** you bring Me? You are like a garden filled with luscious roses of all different colors and marvelous fragrance. Jasmine, lavender and lilacs grow in profusion. Hidden between the beds of roses are precious lilies of the valley giving off their own divine fragrance.

"Yes, your good deeds are manifested to Me and all of Heaven with a supernatural fragrance. The dew drops, rolling down each petal of the rose, sparkles with delightful rainbows of color. The stones along the path are exquisite agate slabs, displaying intricate lacy patterns that reflect the hills of Heaven."

Taken from: **You Are My Bride, My Garden Sealed**

If we don't know how to do that - ASK. Ask for help, this giving up you, yourself to Him. ALL of us. That's... He's calling all of us to newer levels. And with that comes greater intimacy, greater **joy** *and greater sacrifice of something. But that could be... suffering... that could be monetary. It could be saying 'no' to your favorite chocolate. I mean, it's different for everybody, but it's about Obedience and Offering.*

Taken from: **An Invitation to Come Up Higher**

Judgment, Judging Others

"If I **judged** a soul's devotion by their feelings, I'd have nothing to go by but a vapor. What I go by is obedience and you are lacking in that area. Not out of choice, but out of opposition. So, I want you to push through and do as I ask in every circumstance."

Taken from: **Outsmarting the Enemy & Preserving Your Soul**

"What you are describing, My Love, is exactly how Satan kills, steals and destroys. He causes misunderstandings, then anger, alienation, **judgment,** guilt and at the end of this long string of involuntary reactions, you have lost the initiative and peace for the rest of the day. To do something truly productive in the Kingdom of God.

"Be aware of how he works through his minions, nip it in the bud. Cry out to Me, 'Jesus, deliver me from evil!' And I will come to your aid. This does take self-control and discipline. The ways in which these two, moderating dynamics are compromised deliberately by the plans of the enemy are exhaustion and time constraints or deadlines. You feel as though you must get it done by whatever time and when interruptions and distractions come, you become tense and resentful. When you are tired, you're not thinking straight. Fear, pain, endless interruptions, if they are allowed, are used to drain you. Then you make bigger mistakes and have to repent and spend more time in damage control, pushing you further away from your goal.

"Be aware, My children. Be aware! Your enemy is so clever. But if you stay in My Love - always patient, always forgiving, refusing to **judge**, understanding that I am allowing these things to temper and test you in virtue. If you continuously keep before you the vision of Me being in control of every one of these things, I can return your peace to you before it robs you of your day."

Taken from: **Sweet Aroma of Holiness...**

"These times are the times that will separate the wheat from the chaff. Those that are sincere from those who are in it for personal advantage. If you have been alive in Me and you join ranks with others for selfish advantage, your heart becomes darkened and closer to death. Yes, you can look quite alive in your body and be dead inside, compromised to a point near to the death of your soul. My Children, I do not **judge** you on your performance, but your motive, the purity of your heart, the love you put into each action. That is what shall be weighed in the balance when you arrive here.

"Some of you listening to this will come before the **Judgment Seat**, where all your works, good and bad, will be exposed and your fate for eternity will be determined. To you I say, you are facing choices in this very moment that will determine the rest of your journey, your life path - whether you will live a life of virtue or a life of sin, whether you will serve Me or serve the Devil, whether you die in virtue in sin.

"I am coming back. This is no time to play with fire. This is no time to compromise. Rather this is the time to renounce and repent of your sins and compromises. This is a time to embrace brotherly love, extend a hand of help, live for the good of others, not for your own advantage. This is a critical season. Many of you listening will be facing physical death this year. If you are not right with Me, come, come to My loving arms, Though your sins be as scarlet I will wash them white as snow.

"You are not guaranteed life tomorrow. Yet Heaven and Hell lie directly before you. Choose this day who you will serve, and if it is Me, you have only to ask for the strength to break from your sinful past, and I will enfold you in My arms with great compassion and forgiveness. However, if you choose to continue on in your sinful ways, I have warned you, death is at the door and your tomorrow is not guaranteed. Do not sell your souls for a trifle."

Taken from: **Your Tomorrow is Not Guaranteed**

Judgment, Judging Others

"You have been catching yourself in pride lately. That's always a sign that a downgrade is on the way, so to speak. Littleness, littleness, littleness. The littler the better. You should have experienced My mother's littleness. It's not like anything known on Earth, it is so far from what you call humility now. If anyone could have been any tinier in My eyes, I would have chosen them.

"It was truly her knowledge of the Father that caused her to abase herself. She saw herself much as I see her. Very, very, very little, insignificant and void of every merit. She attributed every good thing to the Father and kept nothing for herself. She saw all others as more virtuous than herself and not for one moment did she dare to look up and pass **judgment**. She was steeped in charity and compassion."

Taken from: **Lukewarm – Little Foxes Spoil the Vine**

"Your greatest safety is in holiness and refusing to *judge* others. Many have many opinions, and unfortunately much of what is proposed is opinion and not from Me. So remember your tools of discernment and if you are caused to lose your peace be wary; this is the enemy's number one form of attack. To continue to listen to those who detract from others is truly a leak in your vessel. The graces pour through that leak and are lost because of this serious fault. **Judgment** is Mine and your safest stance is to avoid these poisons and cleave to what is righteous and good, even showing mercy to your enemies - but not taking in their poison."

Taken from: **Resist Gossip & Judgment...**

The Lord has shown us many, many times, **judgment** *on other souls is like a filthy diaper. When you change a baby's diaper you put it in the trash - you don't pull it out, play with its substance, sniff it and put it in other people's faces.*

Please do not mix the profane with the Holy. Please do not criticize other Christian groups, because you are robbing Jesus of the suffering He endured on the Cross for each and every member. You are scattering the flock, you are pillaging the stores of Heaven by scandalizing other souls who are young in the Lord and don't recognize that what you are doing is wrong.

Is it not written: **'Do not judge, or you too will be judged. For in the same way you judge others, you will be judged, and with the measure you use, it will be measured to you.' and 'Why do you look at the speck of sawdust in your brother's eye and pay no attention to the plank in your own eye? How can you say to your brother. Let me take the speck out of your eye, when all the time there is a plank in your own eye? You hypocrite, first take the plank out of your own eye, and then you will see clearly to remove the speck from your brother's eye. Matthew 7:1-5**

You will be held accountable for souls that are lost because of your slander. Do you understand the seriousness of this? If a soul leaves a Christian group because they heard that group is bad, that soul becomes bait for the wolves. In other words, if that soul is stolen from the Lord because of the words of your mouth, you have become responsible for them going to Hell. You have blood on your hands, the Lord's blood, and the soul's blood.

If this sounds harsh, I'm sorry. It IS harsh. Ezekiel and I were both guilty of this for 20 years. The Lord withheld His blessings from us because of this grievous fault. The cry of our heart was to minister, but we disqualified ourselves by judging others. That's why my real ministry didn't begin until I was 68. It took me THAT LONG to really get it. And now, when Ezekiel and I talk about something, if we begin to see that we're talking about someone, we stop immediately and repent.

Taken from: **I Wanted to Go Fishing, But the Nets Were Torn**

Judgment, Judging Others

"Listen carefully to the instructions I am imparting to you. Prayer will be your greatest weapon and I will teach you how to pray - it will flow from within you without any effort, so strong will My grace be among you. Prayer will well up from inside and overtake you in moments of fear and danger, and you will be kept safely hidden, as well as have My Peace.

"Many will betray each other and only discernment by My Holy Spirit will alert you to who cannot be trusted. If you **judge** by outward standards: what is said, what they look like, how they act; if you **judge** by normal human standards you will be fooled. You must rely on Me to detect weak souls or those sent to find you out.

"Again I want to say, this is for the left behind ones, this is not for those who will be raptured. It is important to have these things printed and easy to find."

Taken from: **Jesus Speaks on Provision and Protection**

"It is important to note that when your mind is perceiving thoughts that are critical of others, you may be picking up on what the enemy is broadcasting to deliberately lead you into **judgment**, so they can walk right into that open door. In fact, many come with the assignment to open the door and then proceed through it, so they work very hard at getting an opening. Until that door is open, they are stymied.

"This is why, My People, I have continually told you, from the very start, not to **judge** and to stay away from the news. The news is slanted to get you to criticize. It doesn't matter whether it is true or not, whether you started it or not. All that matters is that you took it upon yourself to **judge** another, and most of the time without even knowing the facts."

Taken from: **Spiritual Warfare: 3 - Critical Spirit and Open Door**

"I look forward with great longing to the day they (the Jews) realize I AM the heart of the Law and the fulfillment of all the prophets and all that is written. I am more than their Savior - I am the incarnation of the Living God. And through My life on this Earth I have demonstrated the substance of their faith and how I require them to live it.

"Never again will man's worth be **judged** by his works or earthly value. All the rich of the Earth shall be humbled before My precious Blood, which can never be given a value. The lame and the infirm shall hold a special place before Me as I heal them. Yet the law that decrees these are "unclean" will be washed away forever by My Blood.

"The great ones of the Earth shall be humbled and filled with joy at their lowliness. The poor of the Earth shall be exalted and restored to the very value of life itself. No longer will man **judge** between this one and that one. All will be purchased with My Blood."

Taken from: **The Rapture Event Will Be Visible...**

*I felt the Lord tonight convicting me of religious bigotry in my past... and even the temptation to **judge** what I do not understand in the present.*

I have seen this behavior in myself, my mother, and in every church I have ever set foot in. It just takes on different forms that seem less apparent. Bigotry and a religious spirit is a very, very subtle thing.

It looks all squeaky clean and righteous on the outside, but in fact it separates, it divides and promotes pride and self-righteousness and quenches the Holy Spirit of God.

Taken from: **There Are No Bigots in Heaven...**

Laziness

"I'm right here by your side, My Love, and I do want to draw you far away from the world and way high up into My Heart. This is that place of fullness where I exchange your weakness for My strength, My Wisdom for your ignorance, My commitment for your **laziness,** My Faith for your fears. Up, up and away high into the habitation of My Heart, out of harm's way, in that place where none can disturb or disrupt.

" …Deeper and deeper I call you, My Love. Will you not make that effort to seek Me out and vigilantly await My coming?"

Lord, what is there to do that is more important? Nothing, to me, nothing is more important than finding You.

"That's what I like to hear and that heart attitude I will bless. This attribute of perseverance is of key importance and spills over on every aspect of your lives. Once you have mastered it in one sphere, it is easier to master it in another and another until you've made it a way of life. So many quit way before the finish line."

Oh Lord, lately I've been feeling that way.

"It's nothing more than **laziness,** Clare. I know you don't want to hear it, but it is. You know Me well enough that when you can't find me immediately, and you search for me diligently, you will find Me…or shall I say, I will find you. This is a way in which you honor Me. You are not willing to give up, I'm just too important to you."

Taken from: **"Persevere in Prayer" Jesus shares**

"With conviction comes hope, and the desire to right the wrong, sorrow for having hurt others, that is if your conscience is sensitive and well-formed according to My Heart. You begin to see the side of yourself that you've been hiding from: jealousy, rancor, **laziness,** retaliation. The uglies begin to surface and you so want to avoid looking but you just can't. It is too obvious if you are being honest with yourself."

Taken from: **God' Correction**

*Some of you have remarked on my voice. Oh... if only you knew the suffering I went through with being so unsatisfied with the way I sounded! I wanted to give up time and time again - and I still have my moments. I wanted to give up, because I just couldn't get my voice to do what I wanted. Then the Lord informed me, "You're **lazy**." And chided me with other remarks about not working hard enough. And sure enough, after what I considered A LOT OF WORK I started to sound the way I wanted to.*

My point? Jealousy and **laziness** *go hand in hand. How can I be so sure about that? I've lived it, year after year, (and I'm 69 now...) being jealous of others with gifts that were thriving when I was stuck in a corner and overlooked or put down. Everything seemed out of my reach: playing the piano and singing simultaneously seemed impossible to me! Playing the piano at all was almost impossible to me, and having instruments on a keyboard to arrange with? I needed that, because I could hear all these different parts. That wasn't my doing - that was a gift from God.*

Things began to change... In fact, I have to tell you. They had to lay, this prayer group had to lay hands on me three different times for me to be able to figure out how to run a recording program. AND to sing, and everything else. It was really, really something... TOTAL work of Grace.

Taken from: **Jealousy is Stalking us, Jesus teaches...**

Laziness

"Seek Me and I will answer your questions. All of you who have been following Me closely through this vessel, are so close to breakthroughs in hearing and seeing Me. Persevere, don't grow weary and don't give in to unbelief or discouragement. Those are your worst enemies.

"May I say **laziness** is part of the problem? You must press in, those who seek Me with their whole hearts, they shall find Me. Seek Me and live the life that I promised you - the abundant life of communion with Me, righteousness, peace and joy, the fruits of fellowship with Me. Confidence, courage, growth in charity, humility - these are the sweet flavors of the grapes that abide in the vine."

Taken from: **Jesus' Perceptible and Manifest Presence is With You**

"You have taught them much of what I have given you. Some are putting it to practice. Others are **lazy** and just want answers. I say to them: seek Me and I will give you answers, but you must seek Me with all your heart. I'm not an easy catch.

"To those who do not yet know Me, yes, I am tender and close at hand. To those who have known me for quite some time, but are not seeking Me vigilantly, this shows Me a lack of serious concern on your part, **laziness** and disrespect. This resembles the servant who had one talent and went and buried it.

"You have taught them how to fish, now I want to see their catch. Come to Me, My Brides, and seek answers from Me. There is nothing wrong with using your Bibles as an oracle.

"Try Me in this, and I will prove to you this is acceptable and even virtuous. But along with this, you must have a commitment to renounce yourself in all things or you will not understand, or care to understand what I am showing to you.

"It is a true saying that a man will only recognize a problem that he is willing to do something about. If he is **lazy** or rebellious, he will declare that he could not understand the answer and is not willing to work any harder at it. But, for those of you who press in, you I will reward with understanding."

Taken from: **The Unpardonable Sin...**

LAZINESS*: Work hard! Apply yourself... another time I get it, let's say my mind is straying on the internet and I'm really curious about what someone said about prophetic events or whatever catches your eye - you know how that goes! And then, if I go to the Lord about a rhema about something and I get* **Laziness***, and under that it says: "Drink water from your own cistern."*

*That's pretty important - that means don't listen to other prophetic voices - you've got your own relationship with the Lord and you need to be focused on what He says to you. So...***laziness***, we are continually reminded to work harder.*

Taken from: **How To Use the Bible for an Anointed Word...1/4**

"There is never a time when things just sail along, unless I have intervened and given you a respite. Am I worth it, My precious Brides? I am building you up in resistance to the enemy. I am energizing you with My Grace. I do not leave you on your own in these battles. And the greater the anointing, the greater the fight for you to use it.

"What you accuse yourself of - being **lazy** - is more often giving in to opposition. Which yes, is **laziness**. But you do not always recognize that you are being blocked. With this new knowledge, I expect you to overcome the things that in the past have hindered you."

Taken from: **How the Enemy Blocks**

Laziness

"You see, when you put forth effort and begin to feel like you are slipping, getting tired, restless, bored... immediately you should suspect interference. These are NOT natural feelings. They are generated by demons operating under sloth and **laziness** to cause you to let go of your attention from Me or what I've given you to do."

But, Lord - what about the times when I feel sleepy? I thought these were ordained by You? Is this opposition, or You?

He answered, "A very good question and here discernment is needed. When I am allowing this to rejuvenate you on deeper levels, I will invite you to lay down and enter into My rest. For the most part, when we are together in worship and communion, I do not allow interference.

"But when you are prevented from connecting with Me, then you may suspect opposition. This is the time to pray and bind until we are once more together in sweet fellowship."

Taken from: **How the Enemy Blocks Your Creativity With Demonic Intervention**

"My people, your offerings are making an impact, but so much more is needed. There are terrible slanders against this man (Donald Trump) and they are not all true. Anyone who raises their head against the Monster will be lied about in every circle.

"The problem is, that most Americans are too **lazy** to research and find out if what was said is true. They just assume it, because it's in the media. And that's the same mistake the German people made in Hitler's rule.

"There are terrible slanders against this man (Donald Trump) and they are not all true. Anyone who raises their head against the Monster will be lied about in every circle. The problem is, that most Americans are too **lazy** to research and find out if what was said is true. They just assume it, because it's in the media. And that's the same mistake the German people made in Hitler's rule. If you want to know the truth, come to Me. If you can't hear Me, then find someone who does and ask them.

"What is at stake right now is not Mr. Trump's marriage, nor his character traits, nor his personal business - for if the truth were told, you have those looking respectable who were present when a sacrificial infant was slain and they drank her blood."

"So you see, you really don't see. You hear, but you don't really hear - not the truth, that is. You see and hear a facade, a socially acceptable mask, and beneath it Satan and his minions are pulling strings to slaughter all the Christians world-wide, but especially in America.

"If you are a Christian, you are slated for death in this country, unless another comes to power and at the very least delays it for a few years. Nevertheless, I will remove My church in her glory. But times until then will not be easy. But now I am asking you to pay very close attention to Me and not the media. If you want to preserve your country, you do not have a choice on who to vote for. I have already made that choice for you."

Taken from: **Donald Trump is Still God's Choice, Trump vs. Clinton**

You're telling me that I'm **LAZY**?" *I mean, I repent! And I know I have been at times, but... My God! Where's Your mercy?!"*

And it was as if He said, "This IS My mercy. This is My mercy. I won't breech your will, I won't cross your will. But I love you enough, and I love souls enough that I'll bend your will. I'll push your will. I might even "scare" your will. But I WILL have My way in your life, if you'll let Me."

Taken from: **When Giving Up in NOT an Option, part 1**

Loneliness, Alone

"My Bride, you must be more clever than the demons assigned to you. These vile creatures know you better than you know yourself. That is why knowing yourself has become so important. Pride, flattery, self-seeking is the number one open door for their entrance. They tell you, 'You are so special, so different from the others. You were specially chosen to receive secret knowledge.' May I say to all of you, each and every one - all of you are unique and special in your own way. Period. So don't let them tempt you by putting you on some kind of pedestal."

"And as far as 'secret knowledge' goes, now you're taking on the New Age mentality that capitalizes on the esoteric. Don't fall for that, either. **Loneliness** is the second open door. Failed marriages, isolation, bitter failures in relationships and work. Rejection and wounds from others in My Body."

Taken from: **How Deceiving Spirits Work**

"I have waited all your life for us to be together this way. Blessed is the soul who takes up this invitation, sooner than later. You have suffered so much out of ignorance and **loneliness**, if only we could have been together this way when you were still very little."

"This is why I have brought you as a gift to My precious Brides, so they don't have to wait but can enter in now. No more *loneliness*, no more *aloneness* in the decisions of life. I am here at your right hand, by your side and I will always lead you when you ask it of Me."

Taken from: **Count the Cost (of an Intimate Relationship with Jesus**

"I am calling to you, My Children, My Wayward Ones. Forsake your **loneliness.** Forsake the lies, the darkness, the confusion. Come. Come to Me, all who are weary and heavy laden. You will find rest for your soul and unconditional love for your heart. I will never turn you away.

"I will never forsake you - rather, your life shall grow brighter and brighter, going from glory to glory. I am not a man, that I should lie. I have good in store for you, not evil. I have gifts and talents for you, things you've longed to do. Who do you suppose put that longing in you? Now I want to bring fulfillment and happiness to your life. Your sins have only brought you grief and disappointment. It's time to make a change, time to release all the old baggage and start anew: fresh, born again."

Taken from: **Come to Me, My Lost and Lonely Ones**

"Yes, you have read My Heart about those who are isolated. They are the most prone to attacks against the faith and condemnation. They languish for hope, surrounded by sin and those heavily into drugs and alcohol. Oh, how I long to bring them a message of hope! That I have not abandoned them, they are not cast off or forgotten by Me - rather each day My Heart beats stronger and stronger for them, sending them innumerable graces to keep their faith afloat. And calling upon My people to minister to them.

"Country living can be very destructive; it has its own set of drawbacks, mostly isolation and **loneliness**. Watching evangelists on TV doesn't always reach down deep into those insecure and questioning places.

"My faithful ones - look for the souls who have nothing, those who have fallen away from churches and feel guilty, confused and dissatisfied. They had questions that were never answered, and in their dealings with other Christians, many of them came away with more doubts about Me, My love for them, and where they stood with Me than they had at the beginning."

Taken from: **Open the Watergates of Unbelief**

Loneliness, Alone

"Edify, edify, edify one another with Scriptural passages, Psalms and exhortations. Share your burdens one with another and work out your salvation with fear and trembling. Do not allow any souls to leave this channel feeling badly about themselves. Calm and encourage those who come limping in the door. And give them more to feed on from My previous messages.

"There are those - many, many of those who feel so condemned that they have lost hope of being Raptured or that even their salvation is at stake. Tend to these. Gently mother them back to health and point them in the direction of getting their own words from Me. They need to know, in those dark moments when no one is around, they need to know that I am with them, I love them and their hope will not be disappointed in Me. That is why you have all been taught to seek Rhemas, so you will not be overpowered by the darkness at a time when you are all *alone* and most vulnerable.

"When a soul comes on this channel asking questions because they have heard slander, give them something solid to latch on to. Especially the teachings on getting their own confirmations from Me. Start them off immediately on cultivating their relationship with Me. They are here because they are looking for answers. Yes, give answers, but more importantly teach them how to get their own answers from Me. Until they have cultivated that skill, they will be at the mercy of the most convincing arguments and deceptions."

Taken from: **Feed My Lambs**

"Just be happy to know that no jealousy, lack or **loneliness** exists in Heaven. All your deepest needs and desires are met to perfection in spotless purity. It won't be long now, sweet Clare, it won't be long at all.'

Taken from: **Unique and Monogamous With Jesus**

Lord, You call them 'My people.' Can you explain what You mean?

"They are a part of Me. I long to have them return to Me and embrace Me as their God, having forsaken the world and all its empty allurements. Yes, indeed they will forsake it - it will be no more. Then they will find what they have always longed for. They will find Me.

"Not even one will be **alone**. I will be a Father, a Lover, and a Brother to them, and communication with Me will be so much simpler as a special dispensation of grace will fall on all souls who call on Me in the Tribulation."

Taken from: **Your Prayers Are Holding Back the Father's Wrath**

I want to share with you the demons most commonly at work. A critical spirit, selfishness, false accusation, impatience, condemnation, frustration, resentment, division. That's a big one, and all these other guys operate underneath that one. Pride, fear, grief, sorrow, isolation, alienation, **loneliness**, *and self-pity.*

Taken from: **Spiritual Warfare: 4 – Secret Weapons of Satan Exposed**

"Now they are walking in My Spirit and reaching out to others with My Love, and breaking every yoke of lies the enemy has placed on their backs. So much freedom for those who have diligently sought Me. So much liberation and deliverance from the norms of men that have chained them down.

"Now they are free to worship Me in Spirit and in Truth, and so many have fallen under the influence of My Spirit, being filled to overflowing, going out and pouring this upon the broken and **lonely**."

Taken from: **The Coming Revival, Authentic Worshippers...**

Loneliness, Alone

"Those whom the Lord loves, He chastises. Do not twist what I have said and make a blanket of condemnation for yourself. If you are in sin, you know it well. The rest of you Dear ones, who have fought the good fight and removed yourselves from occasions of sin; you who have suffered **loneliness** rather than continue on in fornication - you have paid a great price, and great also is your reward in Heaven."

Taken from: **Are You Ready for The Rapture? Jesus asks**

"Don't force yourself on anyone. Wait for Me to lead you. Then, gently share My Love with them. You have all the answers: to their **loneliness**, their lack of direction, their roundedness, their lack of love and comfort. All of that resides in you, because I live in you. You have merely to tip the pitcher and I shall flow out upon them."

Taken from: **Restitution, Doubts & Moving Forward**

I have never seen a human being with such a profound, heart-rending gratitude as tears streamed down His holy cheeks for this man who had been away from Him for 50 years.

And this is only one letter out of scores and scores of letters; people coming to the Lord because they had no idea how sweet He was, how much He cared, how much He identifies with our sufferings, how **lonely** *He is for our company. That's just HUGE with Him.*

I mean, NOBODY thinks of the Lord that way, but that's the way He's presenting Himself more and more around the world - not just on our channel, but around the world. People are identifying with the vulnerable God, the vulnerable Jesus who longs for our companionship. So many have been taught wrongly about the personality of Jesus.

He is so tender, gentle, meek and kind and so thankful for all you do for

Him. He spoke to me through His tears and asked me to tell you how very grateful He is for the littlest things you do to bring souls back to Him or just to Him for the first time.

"...take My word through this vessel, I am profoundly grateful that you set your agendas aside so many times just for Me. Just to be with Me, just to touch someone with My Love, and there is fruit, so much fruit! You will not believe your eyes until Heaven, when you see the fruit each of your little gestures of love brought forth."

Taken from: **I AM the Father of the Prodigal**

"Truly, My Brides, you lift My Heart and bring joy to those places so terribly scarred by the indifference of men. Do you know...one glance from you, one sincere and longing glance from you - do you know what that means to My heart? My heart skips a beat when you look at Me with that longing. All I want to do is invite you into My space, My arms, My heart. You do not need to ask, Beloved. You have a standing invitation, just come.

"When you feel you have let me down, come. When you feel jubilant and happy, come. When you feel **lonely,** come. When you are bored, come. There is simply no time that I am not waiting for you. No there is not one minute in your eternity that I am not hoping, watching and waiting for you to forsake yourself and whatever you are doing just to come into My presence.

"What is the best way to come to Me, you ask? I will tell you - come to Me in sincerity. Come to Me just the way you are. Yes, if you can come rejoicing and thanking Me, that is the most perfect way. But to come to Me rejoicing when bitterness has gripped your heart...well, it may be a sacrifice of praise, but it is not honest."

Taken from: **My Heart Skips a Beat**

Love, Brotherly

"This is why I stress, 'Love one another as I have loved you.' It is only this kind of **brotherly love** that says 'yes' to the burdens of others. This is your glory, this love that passes all understanding; this is the pinnacle of your Christian walk, to be willing to suffer for others as I suffered for you and all transgressors of the law. What a beautiful vision of My **brotherly love** this is. What a wonder this is to angels above and souls on Earth, when they see this sacrificial love and even feel its effects."

Taken from: **Suffering – Real Work in the Realm of the Spirit**

"In your courageous efforts to stay in unity on this Channel, you have opened the door for others to learn the meaning of the words, 'Love one another as I have loved you.' You have shown that on YouTube there can be a family of righteousness and **brotherly love** where backbiting, division, one-upmanship and undercutting one another is exposed as evil and not allowed.

"And as a result, even those who come here with malcontent are encouraged with kind words and prayer to draw closer to Me, lay down their rancor and embrace a different way full of peace and good fruits. A way where I welcome them into My arms...no matter how foul their past may be.

"You have a job to do, you who dwell in My Heart. I gave you My all. I am asking you: leave behind your all for others. You are the light of the world and you will shine most brightly just before I take you to Myself. You are leaving an imprint on those who behold you, an imprint of Who I truly am to them. And just like the shroud I left behind, the imprint left on you from dwelling in My Heart will leave a lasting impression."

Taken from: **Lord, What Are You Doing with Us in This Hour?**

I truly got it in that moment. Jesus has assembled a group here, a group of Heartdwellers who love to rest in His heart. He is forming us in a very specific way, unique to us. And the way in which He is leading us is not just prophetic, but intensely focused on preparing us with the virtues He loves in His Bride. He continues to stretch us and draw us out and up into higher realms of prayer, self-sacrifice and **brotherly love***. What He is doing with us is unique to us. What He is doing with other visionaries is unique to them. In other words, don't be tasting the waters of other wells, don't be comparing, don't be questioning. Trust Him that He is indeed filling this well with fresh, anointed, living waters and He is doing it in His own special way, unique to us.*

Taken from: **Higher Realms of Prayer and Sacrifice Changing the World**

"I will be with you in all of this. It is for My glory and the salvation of souls. You know I never waste anything. Remember, everything is in My hands and it's not about you - but My agenda. And graces will flow like a river.

"Your little flock, too, will advance in the ways of holiness. There will not be one day that does not have its particular challenges. Forewarned is forearmed. I wish for you all to stick together and be supportive of one another. This is the mark of My end times army: **Brotherly Love**. I want you to advance in holiness, My Brides.

"There will be ample opportunity. Remember: it's not about prosperity, popularity, and power, but righteousness, peace and joy in My Holy Spirit in the midst of a corrupt and challenging world. Moments of triumph will be gratifying and I will reward each richly with the sweetness of My presence. The number of those who leave will decline, no one can argue against brotherly love and unity of purpose."

Taken from: **These Lite and Momentary Sufferings**

Love, Brotherly

So, I counsel you, dear listeners. I have brought the words of the Lord to you faithfully. You have prayed, God has heard and responded by extending Mercy. We have avoided calamity and you have proved yourselves through your heartfelt prayers. You have proved that you are truly His Bride, for you have laid down your lives for your friends and taken up the heart cry of your Spouse, out Lord Jesus. You have shown **brotherly love** *and fidelity. God has answered by withholding His wrath*

Taken from: **My Personal Struggle With Unbelief**

"So, to have a soul ready to give up everything for My sake is a rare gift. I take them at their word and though they have no idea of the cost involved, I lead them steadily up the mountain, sometimes even carrying them. But there are junctures of reassessment. Times when the temptation to quit becomes very attractive, because what is being asked of them is beyond what they are willing to give. Holding onto some fancy or idea brings Me to a point where I must find another way to coax them to keep climbing.

"I do this, because I love you so much. I know what you want at the end of your life and I want you to have it. So, I find ways to get you beyond your protests and keep you climbing. It isn't easy, but it's rewarding. And nothing that is sacrificed is regretted at the end of your journey.

"So, for you right now, we are still climbing the mountain of **brotherly love** and learning to trust and yield to Me in the journey. I am constantly expanding your faith and trust in Me. I know what you long for, Clare. I know your reluctance, and I know you will yield.

"Human nature is an inexplicable and inexhaustible well of conflicting emotions and thoughts competing for dominance in your life. Yet, when I take over, I sort these, make them work to the soul's advantage."

Taken from: **The Journey of Holiness**

"The enemy has deliberately sent in demons of division, sectarian spirits, finding fault with what is presented here because it doesn't meet their sectarian standards. This channel is to be a place of healing and **brotherly love** and no one is to force their belief's on anyone else."

Taken from: **Are You With Me or Against Me?**

"Your greatest safety is in holiness and refusing to judge others. Many have many opinions, and unfortunately much of what is proposed is opinion and not from Me. So remember your tools of discernment and if you are caused to lose your peace be wary; this is the enemy's number one form of attack.

"My Brides, you are stunningly beautiful and the enemy hates the very mention of you. That is why he is waging war on this channel.

"He cannot stand to see the beauty of **brotherly love**, patience and caring for one another. He hates you for it. On other channels, he has succeeded in causing division, strife and calumny, but here he is a miserable failure; that is why you are being targeted. Your vigilance and obedience will keep you in My Peace."

Taken from: **Feed My Lambs**

"There will be much need for patience and deferring anger. There is always a reason behind a failure and it is always a test of virtue for you to bear it with charity and **brotherly love**.

"Remember: you will be judged as you judge one another. If you want mercy, you must first mete out mercy. You may see yourself as superior in the mix, but I guarantee - that will be your downfall."

Taken from: **Surviving the Coming Tribulation**

Love, Brotherly

"I say this to you as a caution, because I can see what is planned for this channel. As we draw closer to the moment of supreme truth and sifting, the devils will throw in any kind of device that can injure those who have given their lives to Me on this channel.

"You have all passed through some very rough waters here and I commend you for your faithfulness. Know that the battles will intensify, so love one another from the heart, tenderly, and rush to each others side when trouble comes calling.

"Know that this channel is noted for it's **brotherly love**. There is no mistaking it. It resembles the church of Philadelphia, the one church I promised that I would keep from the time of testing that is to come upon this Earth.

"That is why I have so readied you all for the Rapture. You are that church and as such you have a solemn obligation to protect the love and concord of everyone who looks to this channel for inspiration and guidance. You have done well, My Brides. Just be aware that the enemy is not done with you. Yet, nevertheless, I am with you and **brotherly love** will conquer all the enemy has planned to stop you."

Taken from: **Feed My Lambs**

"Please. Please pray for the new believers. You have many here who are brand new to the faith. Come alongside them and accompany them, sharing your experiences, your fears and triumphs so they may be reassured they are on the right track.

"It is My Love that draws them here. Don't let the innocent go without feeling acknowledged, received and encouraged. Remember, you have all been in that place of woundedness and insecurity and found a peaceful home here.

"I anoint you, dear ones, every day to reach out to those around you. Your love for others has warmed and encouraged My aching Heart.

"As the cup of bitterness continues to fill up in the world, this is one place I can come to experience **brotherly love**. The Love I have so desired for My Body. Continue in this love, no matter how abrasive and ugly the enemy becomes. You will know them by their fruits, and the fruits here are indeed sweet."

Taken from: **You Are Mothers of Souls**

"I am coming back. This is no time to play with fire. This is no time to compromise. Rather this is the time to renounce and repent of your sins and compromises. This is a time to embrace **brotherly love**, extend a hand of help, live for the good of others, not for your own advantage. This is a critical season.

"Many of you listening will be facing physical death this year. If you are not right with Me, come, come to My loving arms and though your sins be as scarlet I will wash them white as snow."

Taken from: **Your Tomorrow is Not Guaranteed**

"I want to return to the events at hand. I know these crosses you have carried for months now, My Bride, have grown weighty. And I also know how they have paved the way for the salvation of many that had no chance. I also see the tremendous growth in you who have willingly taken on Simon's cross on My behalf. You do not see it, but so much progress in holiness and **brotherly love** has been made in your lives, and your reward continues to grow, although I know that is the last thing on your minds."

Taken from: **You Are the Light of the World...**

Love, God's

"Those whom the **Lord loves**, He chastises. Do not twist what I have said and make a blanket of condemnation for yourself. If you are in sin, you know it well.

"The rest of you Dear ones, who have fought the good fight and removed yourselves from occasions of sin; you who have suffered loneliness rather than continue on in fornication --- you have paid a great price, and great also is your reward in Heaven.

"Those of you who refuse to lie to the government, refuse to bear false witness --- well done. I say to you. It may have cost you some great earthly good, but what does it profit you to gain the whole world and lose your very own soul? You may be poorer for it, but you have chosen what was right.

"Those of you who have kept yourselves clean from defilements in the world --- well done, I say to you. You have followed the delicate leadings I've placed in your conscience. I am happy in your heart, and find great solace there.

"Those of you who have been the victims of gossip, slander and evil men, yet have prayed for them with sincere intention from the Heart - you very much resemble Me in My Crown of Thorns. I will have no trouble recognizing you at the Rapture."

Taken from: **Are You Ready for the Rapture?**

If one person had all the gifts, then they would be proud, arrogant, and wouldn't need a body. The **Lord loves** *cooperation, humility, and working together. He gives different pieces of the puzzles to different souls and when you come together in Jesus, in love, all these pieces fit together. We get a more thorough picture of what's going on.*

Taken from: **Binding Demons Prayers and Testimonials**

So, the most important thing that I want to talk with you about in this teaching is Philippians 4:12: How to get along with humble means and how to live in prosperity. .. How to live in every circumstance... The secret of being happy, fulfilled, and in the Lord. We can do all things in which He strengthens us. When it seems like we just can't take anymore...one disaster after another.

As I said, this message may not be very popular, but nonetheless some of you are dealing with these issues right now. To some of you, this is a real situation in your life. The **Lord loves** *you. He's allowing this for deliberate reasons. He's not doing this to hurt you or punish you. He's doing this to form you into His spotless Bride. The sooner we get a hold of what He's trying to do and cooperate with it, the easier the process will be.*

Taken from: **Content in All Circumstances**

Each one of us is like a different shoe that fits a different part of God, and different specifications. Like a glove fitting a hand perfectly. Each one of us is different.

You can imagine. He's giving forth these beautiful anointings and gifts to souls when they are conceived, and how He longs to see that soul fulfill all those gifts and anointings. So you can imagine what He feels like when He loses one who was so unique, no one else could ever take their place.

And yes, He has other souls **He loves** *and adores, but there was something about that one soul that cannot be replicated. And so, you can imagine what He goes through when there is a mass-tragedy or war breaks out. Many are killed, and there's no hope of redemption for them now.*

Taken from: **Regaining Joy in Oppression**

Love, God's

"Truly, My Brides, you lift My Heart and bring joy to those places so terribly scarred by the indifference of men. Do you know - one glance from you, one sincere and longing glance from you - do you know what that means to My heart?"

"My heart skips a beat when you look at Me with that longing. All I want to do is invite you into My space, My arms, My heart. You do not need to ask, Beloved. You have a standing invitation, just come.

"When you feel you have let me down, come. When you feel jubilant and happy, come. When you feel lonely, come. When you are bored, come. There is simply no time that I am not waiting for you. No there is not one minute in your eternity that I am not hoping, watching and waiting for you to forsake yourself and whatever you are doing just to come into My presence. What is the best way to come to Me, you ask? I will tell you - come to Me in sincerity. Come to Me just the way you are. Yes, if you can come rejoicing and thanking Me, that is the most perfect way."

Taken from: **My Heart Skips a Beat**

"Yet, I am not saying this to shame them, so great is **My love** for My People. I look forward with great longing to the day they realize I AM the heart of the Law and the fulfillment of all the prophets and all that is written. I am more than their Savior - I am the incarnation of the Living God. And through My life on this Earth I have demonstrated the substance of their faith and how I require them to live it.

"Never again will man's worth be judged by his works or earthly value. All the rich of the Earth shall be humbled before My precious Blood, which can never be given a value. The lame and the infirm shall hold a special place before Me as I heal them."

Taken from: **The Rapture Event Will Be Visible**

"How many times have you heard me singing a song over you, Clare?"

Oh, Lord - even more than I can remember. Even two days ago in the grocery store I recognized that You were doing that.

"That's true, I have been doing it for a very long time. It is only within the last few years that you have recognized I was deliberately singing back to you. As you sing about My Beauty, I cannot help but reciprocate, My Lovely Brides. Yes, I sing over you! In worship, while you are driving, in the store, and in the mornings, especially. Yes, I love to sing over you in the mornings and establish your day on the solid foundation of **My Love** and Trust in you.

"I love to remind you of your beauty before Me. It is not a beauty of this world, it is Heavenly and a masterpiece to be appreciated by all of Heaven. For not only are you the redeemed, but you are as well My Very Spouse for Eternity. And how lovely you are in the garments of praise. Yes, I adorn you according to your state, as Clare has often noted. The colors that you wear are chosen by Me and reflect what is currently going on in your life.

"When you sing to Me, when you enter into the lyrics even without singing, but your heart is expressed through them, there is a certain honey that is released. Spiritual Honey, both in fragrance ascending to the Throne and a calming blanket of adoration that ascends to enfold Me as well.

"You do not yet realize what your worship means to Me. If you could see the pockets of darkness around this Earth, you would realize that truly Earth has many dungeons... places where joy and worship are not practiced, places where I am not known, places ridden with crime and sin. I Inhabit Your Praises, My Bride."

Taken from: **I Inhabit Your Praises, My Bride...**

Love, God's

"**I love** them with a love beyond imagining. So many are worried about their status with Me, as if I were a legalist with court documents listing every offense. No, that is Satan's description.

"I am more like the **lover** reading every action of their day with great interest, as a love poem to Me. Everything they do out of pure love for Me and their brother, this is my consolation. Even on the Cross, these marks of affection comforted Me as I looked into the future and saw how much they would love Me.

"And so I have accumulated these gifts, these marks of love and ponder them several times a day. Yes, like the petals of dried roses, I contemplate their meaning for Me and I rejoice that I have such as these willing to give for Me, willing to deny themselves for Me and see to My needs first.

"If only My Bride knew the great joy I derive from the little things she has done for Me out of pure love and no other motive. Most in the world are motivated by what means the most to them: money, beauty, notoriety, acceptance, opportunity. These are the things that drive them. But then there is My Bride, she is motivated by what she can do to please Me.

"My Bride is so insecure about the Rapture because she equates Me with men, yet I am not like any man she has ever met. I am not a vicious prosecuting attorney, rather **I am a Lover** counting My rose petals, watching the mailbox for more being sent to Me.

"Every day I anticipate the sweet fragrance of her love translated into action, acts of love, showered randomly on those she comes in contact with."

Taken from: **Jesus Shares How to Recog…**

"I want all of My Heart Dwellers to retreat to My Heart when the world is yet too harsh. ...I hold you tenderly there, **My Loves**. I tend to your wounds and restore your soul."

Taken from: **I Will Restore Your Soul**

"In Heaven we will celebrate whole-heartedly with all our strength and being the wonders of **Our Love** for you. And, to those who love a party, I want to say that you've seen nothing on this Earth in the way of celebrating. In Heaven, there is celebration from the least to the greatest. Even the doe and fawn will jump and frolic in the freedom intended for it from the beginning.

"Nothing shall be sad or fearful, all shall be filled with confidence and peace as they progress from glory to glory. Oh, what a day it will be when we are finally united. So, be at peace, My Brides! Look forward to that day! Let it be the underpinning of your thinking, not the sadness and sin of this world, but the joy and fulfillment of the next."

Taken from: **Hope & Defeat Fatigue, Discouragement...**

"As I offer you mercy, because of your weaknesses and short comings, I expect you to extend mercy to others. Do not be like the wretch that was forgiven a great debt but turned around and throttled his brother who was indebted to him. (Matt 18:28)

"Do not suppose that you are privileged and I will extend mercy when a lesson is not learned by ordinary means. Because **I love** you, there are times when you must experience just a very small morsel of judgment because you have failed to learn from past behavior."

Taken from: **My Mercy & The Millennium**

Loving God

The devils know that once you fall head-over-heels in love with Jesus, you won't want anything else - they won't be able to tear you away from Him with self-interest and self-will. They hate our intimacy with the Savior like nothing else, because it is our source of victory, our inspiration, our very reason for being.

*And I'd like to say to you who have criticized and condemned us for knowing and **loving God**: do you have secret sins in your life you just haven't been able to conquer??? Are there things you are still doing that you hate, even while you condemn our teachings on this channel? Are you living in unrighteousness and having to hide your sins from other Christians, while you take shots at us?*

Come on - be honest here: just for once - no one else is listening or looking. Get honest with yourself. You haven't been able to stop sinning, and you don't know why? You're doing all the 'right' things, praying all the 'right' prayers, singing all the 'right' songs, going to all the 'right' Bible studies and showing yourself approved unto God…you haven't encountered and cultivated the intimate love relationship with Jesus.

Taken from: **The Invitation to Overcome Temptation**

We began to recognize these characters in every single church we visited. Religious spirits who quenched the Spirit of God. Bigots who had strong opinions based on error and lack of personal experience and research. We found that we, too, were bigots, who had all kinds of obnoxious ideas that pushed people away from Jesus instead of drawing them tenderly to His bosom.

That is when we resolved that we would no longer allow those traits in our ministry. The Lord had taken us on an odyssey into different cultures and revealed to us that they sincerely worshiped God in Spirit and in Truth. We wanted to live on Earth as they do in Heaven - without bigotry and divisions, just **loving and worshiping Jesus** *from the heart, as His Bride - in Spirit and in Truth.*

So, this is all to say, if you sense different forms of Christianity in our teachings, you'll understand why. We went wherever we were led by Holy Spirit, and whatever He had sown in those churches that was consistent with Scripture, we embraced and made our own. Because we believe with all our hearts, this is the true atmosphere of Heaven.

We are not church dwellers, we are Heart Dwellers, dwelling in the heart of Jesus... a Heart that embraces all expressions of love and worship from His Creatures, whether they be Russian, Greek, black, white Anglo-Saxon protestants, holy rollers, or Catholic... whatever. If they **love Him** *in Spirit and in Truth, He rejoices in their worship and receives it unto Himself with tremendous joy.*

Taken from: **There Are No Bigots in Heaven...**

"Yes, the world is a heavy place right now, more than ever, and yes it is draining you and other souls, especially My Betrothed. It is all I can do to hold back My tears, and My Faithful Brides bring Me more comfort than you can ever imagine. Thank you, My Precious ones, for **loving Me**, for needing Me, for wanting to partake of My suffering and drink from My cup.

"At long last I have a true helpmate, companion and believer. At long last I am standing with souls that have given Me their all, even in the very trying situations some of you are dealing with. I am eternally grateful for your companionship, My Brides. You are walking in the very pinnacle of Christianity, which from the outside looks like the very pits."

Taken from: **Regaining Joy in Oppression**

Loving God

He has a track record with me. I believe Him. I trust Him. And all of His words to me have come to pass. He has proven Himself faithful in all His ways. The Lord was hiding me in His quiver for this time and He was testing me to see if I would be happy to be a little nobody, nowhere, doing nothing but **loving Him**. *And that was His preparation to bring me into this ministry. He really, really humbled me and continues to do that. He brought me to the point where I said, "All that matters is You, Jesus. All that matters is what You want."*

Taken from: **Events Before the Rapture**

"The Breastplate of Righteousness protects your internal organs, your heart, your soul, your energy sources. As your conscience resides right in the center of your solar plexus, just below the heart, these are to be guarded with great care.

"How does one put on righteousness? Obedience to My known will. Deliberately transgress My known will and immediately there is a hole in your armor which condemnation may enter through. You know you did what was not pleasing to Me and now your heart moves from **loving Me** to fearing Me."

Taken from: **This is a Time of Preparation**

"So, when you see your days getting longer, harder and more demanding, take a look at two things: the world's motives on you and your own ambitions. Yes, ambition is a killer in our relationship. Ambition is a vestige of this corrupt world. Living from day to day with the only agenda of **loving Me** in everything you undertake or do for others, will keep you from throwing your lot in with the world and becoming ambitious."

Taken from: **Nourishment Every Day**

I smiled. I was also thinking, 'I don't want to be one of those who teaches about God and isn't in love with Him.' **Loving and serving Him** *is one thing...being in love? Well, that's quite another. I always want to be in love with Him.*

Taken from: **How Prayer Fails**

Wow, Lord, my head feels like it's floating above my shoulders.

"Yes, that's what it feels like: you are operating in another dimension, another wavelength. This state is so readily attained by being with Me in Spirit and in Truth. Your eyes are even a little blurry, it's as if you have floated behind the veil that separates us, and it's always propelled by divine love.

"This is at the very core of all miracles, this longing to love. It is responsible for bi-locations, for being lifted up physically off the ground, for the manifestation of miracles, for the ability to overcome everything in this world you are now living in. All can be overcome by this super-abundant love."

Is this what Yogis do? People who do Yoga and that kind of thing?

And He answered me. He said, "In a manner of speaking, yes. They control the wavelengths of their thoughts and that brings them into this state. However, it is different than Divine love. It is more artificial in the sense that it is attained by means other than knowing, longing and **loving and serving Me.** It is a natural consequence of your service to Me. My happiness permeates all that you do or touch and it becomes divine in nature. Music, art, teaching, praying, serving - all of these actions can be brought into the divine as the soul draws nearer and nearer to Me."

Taken from: **The God Dimension**

Loving God

"There are a lot of men holding out on Me saying, 'Ah, this is a woman's thing, it isn't for guys.' Nothing could be further from the truth. John rested his head on My bosom, quite regularly. He listened to the Heartbeat of God, he hungered for His God and he found Me. He wasn't about to let Me go.

"Understand that women are a little more disposed to this simple intimacy, which hasn't a hint of carnality behind it. It is the purest **love of God** a soul can have in a female earthly body or a male earthly body. Is it not written that "...in the resurrection they neither marry nor are given in marriage, but are like angels in heaven? Matt. 22:30

"Therefore there is no excuse for shunning closeness to Me."

And I had a thought, I said, "Lord may I...."

"Yes, you may."

What I wanted to say is that this is a purely spiritual relationship - if you are experiencing anything sexual you are not with Jesus, you are being beguiled by a familiar spirit. In the Lord's presence there is perfect purity.

And if anything like that begins to occur, you can be sure it is demonic, and you should rebuke it and seek the Lord on why He allowed that in your prayer time. It could very well be because He is humbling you. At least that's the way I take it.

"I loved John with a love so pure, few on Earth will ever comprehend it. But in Heaven it shall be obvious to all.

"So to you, Bride of Christ, I say do not allow anything to lie or condemn you for **loving Me** and wanting to rest your head upon My Heart."

Taken from: **Can Men Experience Closeness w/Jesus as Women Do?**

"Learn of Me, for I am meek and humble of heart. I have left you innumerable love letters - read them, believe them, allow them to take root in your heart. There is no joy that is compared to knowing and **loving Me**. This knowledge of Me and My love for you, unworthy as you are, will sustain you through every trial. No matter what you go through, I will be there on your right, holding your hand, speaking to you, comforting you. Nothing can separate you from My Love.

"NOTHING. Not anything on the Earth or above the Earth, not aliens, not death, not even when you fall - still I am by your side to pick you back up. Nothing can separate you from My Love."

Taken from: **Jesus Speaks on What is To Come #5**

"If you want to recognize those who are in league with Satan, here is your chance to observe their tactics. But I do not wish for you to argue doctrine with these. They see you as stupid for **loving Me**. They have no interest in the truth, but your prayers on their behalf can change that. Truly I do hate to see their demise. I died for them, too."

Taken from: **Satanists Posing as Concerned Christians...**

'Lord, I want to be little, please keep helping me to be little. And I miss our times together, Jesus. I miss You.' Just after I said this, I began to feel my head resting against His warm shoulder. And the sweetness of His presence drew me up and out of myself into His tender Love.

He said, "We need this, Clare; you need this, and I need this...truly. We have needed this kind of time together."

There is nothing this world has that can even begin to compare with truly **loving God.**

Taken from: **Higher Realms of Prayer and Sacrifice**

Lust

"I am for what is right and good. I am for a people who are fully awake to their sins and know they have opened the door to this oppression by their worldliness. They have only to repent and pay attention to Me and what is really going on.

"Your world has been so consumed with Capitalism and acquisition, they sided with whoever could give them the most 'bang for their buck' as the idiom goes.

"Now they are seeing how counter-productive that actually is playing out to be. In short, they are waking up to their insatiable **lust** for power and wealth and seeing that what lies before them is a wasteland of their indifference, created by manipulation and greed...'Give me my candy and I'll vote for you.'"

Taken from: **Regaining Joy in Oppression**

"When you allow yourself to compromise your prayer time for other activities, you put yourself in great danger. The briefing I would have given you that morning never gets to your heart and mind and you're a sitting duck for the tactics of the enemy. That is why he will try to overwork you, give you a job that leaves you exhausted at night and unable to pray. It's up to you to draw the line, My children.

"The world will continually push the line back further and further taking away from your life to feed its endless **lust** for power and prestige. It is totally up to you to draw the line against the world and enforce it. Beware of the slowly encroaching jobs that everyday seem to demand more and more from you.

"Satan works on a subtle level in order to draw you in before you know what's happening to you.

"So, when you see your days getting longer, harder and more

demanding, take a look at two things: the world's motives on you and your own ambitions. Yes, ambition is a killer in our relationship. Ambition is a vestige of this corrupt world. Living from day to day with the only agenda of loving Me in everything you undertake or do for others, will keep you from throwing your lot in with the world and becoming ambitious."

Taken from: **Nourishment Every Day**

"So, now history repeats itself and those with a controlling religious spirit have found their way into every denomination with their **lust** for control. The entire game plan from the enemy is to make men feel so guilty for their sins, they withdraw from Me. Or refuse to even approach Me.

"How common is it that you have seen and heard people say, 'I'm not good enough for God. When I get good enough for God, I'll turn to Him.' And of course, that never happens. And the religious spirit is the vehicle to do that. What I have taught you goes against that grain, and so you are hated."

Taken from: **Why You Are Hated...**

"One of the most serious preparations you can make, any of you can make, is to prepare your hearts for Heaven. In Heaven there is no slander, no backbiting, no jealousy, no fear, no gossip, no hopelessness, and no depression.

"In Heaven there is supreme bliss. And as you choose to dwell in Me, you will have a taste of this bliss. Each day you will be tempted to enter into gossip, tale bearing, **lust** and all the other sins that have plagued your whole life."

Taken from: **Maintain Your Purity and Light, My Bride**

Lust

"Yes, you have discerned rightly. Technology is far beyond what is publicly known...consider inter-dimensional travel done by demon-aliens. Oh yes, technology knows very few boundaries.

"Another reason for Us to commence the Tribulation. (When He says, "us" He's talking about the Trinity, the Father and Holy Spirit.) Many, many frontiers of science have been conquered and many, many experiments and offensive weapons have caused Us to intervene and frustrate results. Many.

"It is truly time, Clare. It is truly time. We have checked evil so many times supernaturally, and continue to do so even in this moment, for the sake of My children and this Earth. You see, Satan has so corrupted the minds of scientists that they have very little regard for human life or the health of this planet.

"No, they are far more interested in supreme intelligence and conquering every single law of physics. **Lust** for knowledge, greed for power and status has taken hold of these souls and pushed them into ground-breaking experiments...and for each one, angels are assigned to frustrate their foolishness. They are not looking at the good of Earth or mankind, they are only looking to conquer the unknown and control what should only be in My control. I alone have the wisdom to draw lines. They seek the glory and have no moral boundaries. That's what we are talking about."

Taken from: **Prophetic Rapture Dream & NOW**

"You will find that even when sexuality assaults you in My Presence, I totally ignore it while you put it in its place. There is a fierce demon of **Lust** assigned to the spiritually-minded. This demon is fierce and bent on bringing you all down in utter disgrace."

Taken from: **If You Love Me, Rapture, Sexual Temptations**

"I am for what is right and good. I am for a people who are fully awake to their sins and know they have opened the door to this oppression by their worldliness. They have only to repent and pay attention to Me and what is really going on. Your world has been so consumed with Capitalism and acquisition, they sided with whoever could give them the most 'bang for their buck' as the idiom goes.

"Now they are seeing how counter-productive that actually is playing out to be. In short, they are waking up to their insatiable **lust** for power and wealth and seeing that what lies before them is a wasteland of their indifference, created by manipulation and greed...'Give me my candy and I'll vote for you.'

"While secular humanism, which holds to the ideals of Satanism, has won over the minds of leaders in the past, they are now seeing the continuing opportunity for a one world dictator is very dangerous."

Taken from: **Higher Realms of Prayer...**

"Every year I go through this season of distraction with My Beloved. Every year Satan plans attacks against the Body that they are not watching for, because of their own distractions. What you have gone through, My Love, in these last few days is but a microcosm of what My whole entire Body is going through. And I need you to share your battles of late with them."

All that You say is true, Lord, and every year I try not to be drawn in. But this last month especially, the last couple of weeks has been rife with distractions. I feel so fragmented I can't concentrate on anything. I know this is my fault, because of my **lust** *to get things done before winter.*

Taken from: **Distractions, Exhaustion & the Rapture**

Lust

"In this world where grasping and attaining are the order of the day, men overlook the lasting effects of virtue in their lives. When virtue is placed on mammon and worldly gain, all is swallowed up into reproach and nothingness at death. Nothing is taken forward into Heaven but honest virtue, brotherly love and sacrifice for others. Yet, even then you mustn't count on that.

"If this concept is foreign to you, ask Me to instill it into your heart. Ask Me to change your heart and make you My true disciple and ambassador of love. Action is lacking because love is lacking. This is why your time with Me is more important than any other activity in your day. Live in the world, give the world primacy and you will only bear worldly fruit.

"Live in the Spirit, give Me the primacy and you will not satisfy the **lusts** of the flesh, but bear holy fruit unto life eternal, not only for yourselves but for those around you as well. This is the meaning of being a Christian; this is the meaning of being My presence in the world. This is not accomplished by the weak willed and cowardly. There is a good reason why I have said the cowardly will not enter Heaven. When they are pressed to make a decision, it will always be to their advantage and safety. It takes a brave soul to confess Me and live by virtue, do what is right."

Taken from: **Power in Reconciliation**

"And yes, it is the force of dark matter and proliferation of demons entering through portals that will cause such anarchy as man has not known on this Earth before.

"Finally, science has the weapons to destroy humanity from the inside out. Eaten up with jealousy, greed, rage, **lust** and rebellion, each will be his own undoing. This is why virtue at this time is paramount.

"Without virtue, you will be taken captive or slain in the battle field. Without intimacy with Me, you will not have virtue. Without obedience to Me, there will be little if anything left of our relationship."

Taken from: **Refining Fires Are Coming...**

"The lure of riches is very strong in your family. When I let you go out like that I cringe lest I lose you to the world. There are so many souls struggling with this malady around the world. Would you share with them your battle? I want to set them free, but some of them don't even recognize it's a sin."

I did have a legitimate question that I knew we would all ask, so I voiced it, "But, Lord, isn't it necessity to have certain things?"

"It's the driving force behind it that's so dangerous. You know it, Clare, you can feel it even now as we are talking. 'Just one more little thing. Whew! I'm done. Oh, I forgot...I need this, too. But this wouldn't look right without that.' It goes on and on and on. There's no stopping it. There's no end to it. It is nefarious.

Jesus clarified, "Translate it this way, 'The nefarious activities of organized groups of demons of **lust**, acquisition, preoccupation, greed, avarice (avarice is HUGE), perfectionism - never finding the perfection it seeks, yet forever promising it and luring you deeper into distractions, idol worship and sin.'

"It's not the need, My Love, it's the driving passion or more correctly, **lust**, that ensues on the heel of the need. Under the guise of, 'Get it all done and over with.' Yet, there never truly is an end. ...It brings a superficial satisfaction. It only lasts a short while, but then, emptiness again."

Taken from: **The Lure of Riches**

Lying

"My conviction is gentle, wise and easily received. Theirs pits you against yourself. How foolish to reminisce over past failures, or should I say, even just perceived failures, because they will use anything with a hook on it. They fish for creepy crawly things to dredge up and hook you into deep self-condemnation.

"Even as an alligator grabs its victim and rolls with it over and over and over, then pulling it down into the deep and leaving it there to rot - so do these despicable creatures torment My children's souls, leaving them under some miry ledge to decay until the time is ripe for these leviathan creatures to come back and feed on them again.

"Yes, they gain power and momentum each time they succeed. They feed on suffering just as surely as you are strengthened by righteousness and joy. So, do not allow yourself to be drawn into this combat with the evil ones. Recognize it and see it coming. Bind it. Bind them and put them in their place. May they be tormented even as they wish to torment you."

*That was a very encouraging message for me. I need to read it every once in a while just to remind me that our enemies are constantly **lying** and condemning us. The minute we feel that condemnation, we should recognize "OK, I've got a demon whispering in my ear," because the Lord never approaches us with condemnation. He's always so gentle.*

We get such a deep feeling of compunction. I know that I "shouldn't have said." It's such a different feeling than agonizing over "I should have done this" or "I should have done that" or "Why didn't I do that" or "I'm so stupid". We could go on and on with the things that come against us in our minds. Some of it comes from our own mind, but a lot of it is instigated by the demons and they're constantly trying to pull us down.

Taken from: **Condemnation is the Food of Demons**

"Religion has taken away the true meaning of having a relationship with Me. When I called Peter, James, and John, they were My sidekicks, My buddies. I walked and talked with them, I ate with them, we slept under the stars together - I was real to them, the way I want to be real with all of you.

"Religion has put up walls, barriers, conditions. I never meant for that to happen, I always wanted to preserve relationship just as I did with Adam and Eve. I always wanted friendship. I am the most misunderstood person that ever lived on the Earth. Men have taken Who I am and made a monster out of Me.

"Men are the monsters: full of hatred, bitterness, anger - and they projected that onto Me.

"My nature is gentle, kind, simple, easy to be with. And the only reason My Father came across the way He did was because men's sins were destroying the innocent, murdering children, destroying families, stealing, **lying** and cheating. Hurting the innocent.

"Had they lived as I wanted them to I never would have had to wipe them off the face of the Earth.

"But we have a very real enemy: fallen angels, sickly, grotesque, gruesome, wicked and mean bent on hurting men and destroying the Earth. And when men throw in their lot with them, then My Father must step forward and be the just Judge who puts a stop to injustice.

"That is what Earth is facing now: judgment. But that's not My nature nor My Father's nature. We are gentle, meek and kindly, but men would take advantage of that if We did not punish sin and wickedness."

Taken from: **Count the Cost (of an Intimate Relationship with Jesus)**

Lying

"I will surely increase your faith as you take baby steps to trust Me. And that is the bedrock issue here: trust. And proceeding from trust is faith and who do you suppose is constantly shipwrecking your trust in Me by *lying* against My character? Yes, the Father of Lies, he is about his business of deceiving people - especially about My character.

"It is a slap in My face, to believe that I will not come through, I will not be faithful. It is a slander against Me and I wait for My people to defend Me. But instead they turn the other way and give up, they believe the **lie**!

"This intimacy that you seek is highly threatening to Satan, for a deaf and dumb Christian is not much of a problem - they can't hear Me so they won't be taking any ground from him. But a Christian who listens to God and obeys? He is a problem, he will take ground from the enemy."

Taken from: **Count the Cost (of an Intimate Relationship with Jesus)**

"When you listen to a prophet, and your heart begins to throb with fire and love for God, do you suppose that that prophet is speaking under the anointing of the Holy Spirit, or in their own flesh? Can a person speaking from the flesh inspire the fire of God in your hearts? **My sheep know My voice and another they will not follow. John 10:27**

"But then, along comes a clever intellect to sow doubt in your mind, about the authenticity of what you heard. And you, my dear ones, must have rock solid discernment so that you cannot be swayed by clever arguments. These are tortuous times and even the elect can be deceived. It's your responsibility to develop your perception from deep inside your God space, or you will be led astray by powerful people and **lying** signs."

Taken from: **We Must Have TRUE Discernment**

*There are more subtle forms of resistance for people seeking an intimate relationship with the Lord. For instance, the Lord may allow your virtue to be tested while you're praying by allowing a **lying** spirit to say something derogatory about a brother in Christ. I think we've all experienced judgmental Christians coming on strong to correct us of something they know nothing about. But they believe that they have been privileged by God, that He confided to them our faults or something in the spirit, so they come on strong with condemnation. Who do you suppose planted judgment in their minds? Who do you suppose tells **lies** to separate the brethren?*

Taken from: **Sexual Temptations in Prayer**

"I tell you the truth, if you do not use what you've been given to the greatest extent you may very well not fulfill your calling on this Earth. There are many forces against you, **lying spirits** abound, and it is My desire to see you so close and tight with Me and knowing My thoughts about your situation that you not fall into any of these traps."

Taken from: **CERN Wickedness Increases, My Warring Bride...**

*Even the little boy who went to Heaven, Colton Burpo, saw demons lying in people's ears. I think he said something like, "And I saw demons." And the person that was interviewing him said, "And what were they doing?" And he said, "They were lying. They were **lying** to people."*

This stuff is real, guys. It's very, very real. And the Lord is revealing it all over His body so we can intelligently combat these vile creatures. It's our choice: believe and prepare our hearts, or stick our heads in the sand and play ignorant.

Taken from: **Lost in the Woods, Seeds of Bitterness**

Lying

"But, those I have nudged in their hearts, wanting them to move forward and care for their own, they will indeed have difficult times ahead. Living off the government has put them at high risk. My children, those of you who are not disabled and sick, those of you who have been *lying* to the government and using the resources meant for the poor to suppor your own dishonest and lazy lifestyle, you will be left behind. I am asking you to repent now, before it is too late for you. You haven't much time left, but if I see a sincere change in your lifestyle, I will forgive your sinful **lying** and take you in the Rapture. But, do not expect to use others for your own personal gain, misrepresenting yourself or your family and be Raptured at the same time. It will not happen."

Taken from: **Government Collapse Clarified, You Poor are My Gift to the World**

This is no time to be judging others. This is no time to be stingy. This is no time to be slipping around in sin, this is no time for drinking and debauchery. This is no time for **lying***, hating, backbiting and gossip. God help us if we think we can attack one another and still be spotless!*

Taken from: **What if This Were Your Last Few Weeks?**

"If you are dividing My Body, you are working for Satan. You are being used by the demons if you are separating brethren. If you are taking the failings of others as a final door slammed shut, you are creating pockets of bitterness for the demons to create strongholds in YOUR life, not the lives of those who hurt you. They will walk on, but you will stumble because of what you are holding onto. That is why forgiving is a work of charity, a work of mercy. It makes up for judgment, calumny, and **lying**. What sin has severed, you can restore by your charity. Just as surely as wounds heal, forgiveness cleanses those pockets of corruption and allows tender flesh to grow back."

Taken from: **How a Root of Bitterness Can Change Your Destiny and DNA**

"It doesn't matter what divides us, as long as we are divided. Sickness, differences of opinions, judgment, tiredness, obstacles, technical glitches, delays, slander and **lying spirits**, attempted jealousies, strife... you name it: if it can cause division, it's in that demon's service and that ugly thing has been working against this Channel day and night for weeks now.

"How do you defeat a demon of division? It's not really that hard. The secret is Charity and refusing to judge, humility and being willing to defer to and hear one another's opinions, a teachable spirit, and obedience. Satan does not have a weapon against these. If everyone exercises these virtues, you create a brass wall with no openings."

Taken from: **How to Handle an Assignment of Division**

"But those I have nudged in their hearts, wanting them to move forward and care for their own, they will indeed have difficult times ahead. Living off the government has put them at high risk. My children, those of you who are not disabled and sick, those of you who have been **lying** to the government and using the resources meant for the poor to support your own dishonest and lazy lifestyle, you will be left behind. I am asking you to repent now, before it is too late for you. You haven't much time left, but if I see a sincere change in your lifestyle, I will forgive your sinful **lying** and take you in the Rapture. But, do not expect to use others for your own personal gain, misrepresenting yourself or your family and be Raptured at the same time. It will not happen.

"I will have compassion on whom I will have compassion. I will have mercy on whom I will have mercy, but I will not support or bless stealing and **lying**, so I appeal to you, My children, mend your ways."

Taken from: **Government Collapse Clarified, You Poor are My Gift...**

Marriage

Satan is working overtime to deprive us of each other. **Marriages** *are under attack, relationships are under attack and a spirit of Division is working to break holy and supportive relationships. How sad to have a* **marriage** *end at this time, when the world is on the brink of chaos. But he is doing it to isolate, kill, steal and destroy.*

Taken from: **Outsmarting the Enemy & Preserving Your Soul**

"Ezekiel and I've seen it many times before in our **marriage**. I'll get a critical and impatient attitude towards him and the Lord will allow a fall or a failure to get my attention. Oh, how hard those corrections can be: a twisted ankle, a fender bender, a cat gone from home for three days. Uh! They are always painful! So, the last thing in the world I want to do is give the enemy permission to sift me by abandoning charity and giving place to a critical spiritual."

Taken from: **Refining Fires are Coming, Prophetic Word from Jesus**

"My children, every time you attack one of My anointed ministers, you are shedding innocent blood. My Blood. Do you understand? My anointed servants have My Blood running through their veins. When you hurt them, you hurt Me.

"Doubtless you will say this is but another instance of a familiar spirit defending itself. But in those quiet moments, when you find serious disorder in your lives, when things that should have succeeded fail. When there's accident or sickness. When others speak badly of you, when your **marriage** deteriorates, and your relationship with people at work or church are falling apart - remember these words. Remember: you have sought to destroy others and I have allowed the door to remain open to the enemy to bring you to your senses."

Taken from: **I Wanted to Go Fishing, But the Nets Were Torn 2**

"Yes, I love you like Ezekiel loves you. I live in him, can you feel it?"

Now that you mention it Lord, yes, I can.

"Yes, it is My presence in Him that adores you and My presence in you that makes you feel that way about him. That is the way I intended **marriage** to be. That is why when you grow older, sexual desire fades into the background and what emerges is a sublime and holy love for one another. That is why it is so important to **marry** the right man, so that in your later years you can enjoy the finer dimensions of love."

Taken from: **Your Lives Have Not Been Wasted**

"It is by My will and My choice that a holy relationship is formed. I, alone, know the path a man and woman must travel in this life. I, alone, know what they will pursue and not pursue. And if they do not know Me and seek Me to bring them the right mate, well... divorce or unhappiness is ultimately the fate of those who do not seek Me in their choice of **marriage** partners."

Taken from: **You are The Light of the World...**

"I am continually strengthening both of you in supporting one another and humility. Even in secular **marriages**, this principal applies; there is a yoke, and each is to have their part in pulling the load. Through this the children learn as well and grow up to be balanced. Yet, Satan has done so much to upset the order I arranged, because it is a model of the Church, My Body. And, distorting the role of the Father figure brings the whole model down 'till it is no longer recognizable. That is one reason why I hate divorce. It interrupts the pattern that I designed to function in raising up children. They grow up wounded and bent in the wrong direction."

Taken from: **The Yoke of Marriage in Ministry**

Marriage

"Shepherds, who are you listening to when you choose worship leaders? Teachers? Intercessors? Who are you empowering in growth to serve Me? Where are the ministries that address troubled **marriages**, teens, and the elderly? Are you caring for all the sheep or just the ones with the thickest fleece? Are you watching what they feed on or are they going toxic from attractive but poisonous plants? Are you correcting and admonishing behaviors that are demoralizing, or are you avoiding conflict?"

Taken from: **Why Are People Leaving My Church?**

"I want to talk about the **marriage** bed. By '**marriage** bed' I mean the relationships you are in right now, your **marriages**. Some of you have defiled your **marriage** bed by thinking of other people, rather than your spouse, when you're having relations. This is a very common sin that eventually leads to adultery. …It is so little understood that **marriage** IS preparation for Heaven. Love is so very intense and all consuming in the bonding stage of **marriage**. In order that when trials come, you will both cleave to one another and show the respect due to one another."

Taken from: **My Presence in Your Marriage, Jesus Speaks**

"Do you know, it is the ones who act perfect, like they don't have any faults, that grieve Me. It is the ones who take the time to point out the flaws of others that strike at My Heart. Yes, to find fault with your sister, your brother, is to strike at My very own heart. This hurts me much more than your lack of focus or flightiness.

"Do you know, My Brides, in your efforts to get closer to Me, I also am paying attention to what goes through your minds and out of your mouths. If you want to be closer to Me, if you want to please Me, know that the most off putting thing you can do is find fault with each other.

"In **marriage**, it is an easy thing to do, especially because the enemy is wanting to build a wall of alienation over time. Very slowly, so you will not notice it is being done, until you wake up one morning and feel the coldness between you and your spouse. A coldness that has built up over months and months as you found fault with the little irritations and drove him away from you.

"Little by little you downgrade one another. I want you to little by little build one another up. Please, My Bride, there has been enough condemnation; picking, fault finding, in the world. I want you to be beacons of hope, encouragement - building one another up, affirming one another, with not a hint of censorship.

"This is what drives people away and causes Me to find fault in you. But when I see your childlike innocence, declaring your faults openly, and not finding anything negative in your brother and sister, it makes Me embrace you ever more fondly and totally discount your shortcomings."

Taken from: **My Distracted Bride & My Compassion for Her**

"The wicked ones are trying to steal your gift and divide your **marriage**; they are always below-the-belt hitters. But I am here to your rescue, to reinstate and lift you up and tell you 'Yes,' I do commission you to do a painting for Me.

"Which, by the way, I will execute through you. Is there anything too hard for Me? I know what you are trying to accomplish. I know your heart and it is quite in unison with Mine. That is why I will do this thing through you.

"If you want Me to. No one is forcing you, Clare."

Taken from: **How To Handle An Assignment of Division**

Marriage

*This is one of the things that I really try to bring home. In **marriages**
where the yoke is not quite equal yet, because you want to devote
yourself to prayer so much - sometimes you cut off your husband. Or
vice versa, you cut off your wife, because you want that time alone with
the Lord. And that's not pleasing to Him. If you do it to any great degree.
He's really directed me on that point, and told me that Ezekiel is my
covering and he deserves time and attention.*

Taken from: **God's Will for You Involves Your Heart Dreams**

*I believe all or most of us have suffered terribly at the hands of our
children who did not understand our dedication to God. Some of us had
marriages that were not brought together by God, some of us **married**
before we were Christians and as a result were unequally yoked when
the Lord brought us into His Kingdom - and the dynamics in the family
changed.*

*And they've even discovered genetically that there are portions of the
brain that are more disposed to God, and if the Lord brings you together
with a really Godly man, and you're a Godly woman, then I would
imagine that those parts of your anatomy are fairly well matched and
suited and there's a pretty good chance your offspring are going to be just
like you.*

*But when you're brought into a **marriage** or you step into a **marriage** or
a relationship where there's not an equal yoke of Spiritual mindedness,
you can anticipate all kinds of grief in the future. So, that's what I'm
gonna share with you here.*

*As a result of those kinds of **marriages,** our children are divided on the
faith as they observe one of the parents in disagreement with the other.
And to make matters worse, the whole world is on the side of the ones
who are not really interested in God. There's just tremendous opposition*

*that we face in raising our children when we are in a **marriage** where we're not equally yoked. This was the situation for me.*

Taken from: **Abba Father's Grief…**

"What will **marriage in Heaven** be like with Me? That's what I want to talk about."

I have lots of questions but I'd rather You just tell me what You want me to know.

"We will never be apart."

You mean physically or spiritually?

"Spiritually."

But we are never apart now!

"Yes, but now you cannot always touch in with Me, you have trouble focusing. Not in Heaven, that will be a thing of the past. The very moment you touch Me with your thoughts, I will be there for you."

WOW!! I like that. But won't I be a pest?

"You will learn propriety - that is, being united with Me and wanting attention will be two different things. You will be so filled with Me that touching in will not be so necessary. You will be drawn to worship and lingering in the sweet bliss of Our presence in worship. We will spend lots of personal one on one time together, lots of it. Going everywhere together: rock climbing, hiking, horseback riding, picnics, canoeing, flying, swimming. Oh, we are going to have a grand time, and I have so much to show you!"

Taken from: **Troubling Discernment & Glimpses of Heaven**

Meek, Meekness

The next Beatitude is Blessed are those who mourn for they shall be comforted. Blessed are the **meek** *for they will inherit the Earth. This is beautiful. When we think of landowners,* **meekness** *is the last thing in the world we think of. Landlords, people who own property, ranches and so on...***meekness** *is the last trait that we associate with a landowner. But here the Lord is saying they (the* **meek***) are the ones who will inherit the Earth. I can't help but think that when He returns, it will be the* **meek** *that are entrusted with the great wealth of the land because they'll be looking out for others.*

Taken from: **Who is the Bride of Christ**

"When husband and wife choose to be a team for Me, the load is evenly distributed. As you well know, many, many times, when you are down, he is up. When you are up, he is down. This is all in My economy, so that each has a share and no one faints from the burden. Not only are you supporting one another, but your **meekness** in carrying your particular cross at any moment teaches you humility, without which you can easily lose every virtue and all the spiritual growth you gained in this life."

Taken from: **The Yoke of Marriage in Ministry**

"I'm addressing the tendency for some to need to be right, and correct their brother all the time. There are some here on your channel who are not getting the message of Love and **Meekness** that I am trying to get across. There are some who revel in instruction, and leave people crumpled up in a ball when they are done."

"I want that to stop. I want Love to be the most absolute, number one most important dynamic in your relationships with others. Being right does nothing but downgrade you in My eyes. Being loving makes you resemble Me, and elevates those who have already suffered countless setbacks and are ready to give up. I want them to have a sense of being important. Not because they are intelligent or even brilliant, but because they are precious human beings I died for. I paid the price with My own body and blood. This elevates them to the status of royalty."

Taken from: **Your Charity Must Exceed Your Knowledge**

"Let's leave behind the best possible impression, because this may be the very last Jesus they will remember after the Rapture. Do nothing to wound or injure, do nothing out of selfishness, do not manipulate or demand your own way. These things should be far from you My Bride. Your heart should be the sweetest paradise on earth. Leaving that impression with others will do the most to bring them to Me. They will recognize Me in you, if you behave with **meekness** and mildness."

Taken from: **Leave Sweet Memories Behind...**

"But you know that I will complete the good work I have begun in you. I will bring to maturity all those who call upon My Name and choose to be holy. Not one will perish from My Hand, all who come to Me with a sincere heart, I cherish and raise up into maturity, **meekness**, and uncommon kindness.

"What is the price of words? So much good or so much evil can be done with words. With words you can bring peace and mend hearts. With words you can slice and dice a soul 'till nothing is left. And few understand that you will be held accountable for every idle word. With your tongue you lift up and impart life; with your tongue you can also injure and destroy."

Taken from: **Support One Another in Your Weaknesses**

Meek, Meekness

"Souls that will respond to My tender invitations to grow in holiness as I lead them hand-in-hand. Yet I lament the darkness has settled over so many, having lost their connection with Me. They now are the ones falling under the spell of beguiling spirits of Self-righteousness, Religious spirits who applaud them for their valor in coming against Me and denouncing you.

"This is the lot of those who refuse to seek Me until they find Me. The lot of those who spurn humility and **meekness** and seek to rise above others in stature. This is the lot of those who stopped short in prayer and received the deceptions of men offered to them, that they might be "knights" taking down an evil doer, rather than pressing in, fighting the good fight and recognizing their own error, bitterness and jealousy."

Taken from: **How Does a Fall Happen?**

"It is not a little thing to be entrusted with the knowledge of God, and be chosen by God to serve. No, it is a very high calling and requires the utmost amount of dependence on My counsels. The utmost amount of humility and understanding that you don't have all the answers. It is not the educated that will survive; it is the **meek** and devout who move neither to the left nor the right until they have sought My will.

"How many times in Scripture have I inferred or outright said, 'I have chosen the foolish things of this world to confound the wise?' Read the Beatitudes. My blessings are poured over the very ones this world scorns: the poor, the **meek**, the grieving, the persecuted. These are the ones no one wants to be, but they are the very ones chosen for My graces. If you would be among them, throw out the purse of your own opinion and seek Me until you find Me, until you hear Me, until you read between the lines of Scripture and hear Me loud and clear."

Taken from: **Are You Wise?**

"I know you are all facing great challenges right now and I am with each and every one of you. Only stay in the spirit and don't give place to your flesh. If you feel that beginning to happen, escape to a private place and pray, asking Me to help you abstain from venting, which will only make everything much worse for you.

"What I am trying to do here is cutoff confrontations before they happen and create a mess for you. If you know these things, you can remind yourself every morning and be on the look out for volatile situations, praying to sidestep them and being **meek** and humble in all your dealings."

Taken from: **Enemy Tactics & An Invitation & Opportunity**

Lord, would You carry me away? I want to go back and see all these things. It was such a tremendous time in the wilderness. I want to go with You, Jesus, and see all these things. Can I? Can I, Jesus?

"My Love, your curiosity will be more than satisfied in Heaven. Nothing will be withheld from you."

But I want to watch Moses and Joshua and the burning mountain. And what happened to the other tablets. And why did he break them. I mean, I understand him being angry, but why did he punish You for that? And yet I have met him in Heaven, and he's so **meek!**

The Lord replied, "Everyone makes mistakes. The disparity between his experience with the Father and the behavior of the Israelites - after all the miracles - just broke his heart. That he loved them enough to stand in the gap so they would NOT be destroyed. And I have proved My mercy through them, even as it's written in Hosea."

Taken from: **You Will Experience Ecstatic Freedom**

Meek, Meekness

"When you are totally dead to yourself and the world and you love Me more than anything or anyone...well, you won't go flying off. Something inside, a governor, will check your action and your desire nature will be left in the dust to rot and disappear, as it should.

"This is that fateful time of the year when everyone is getting the very same impulses. There is much evil behind it, but a truly **meek** soul walks through it as if it were nothing.

"I don't care how many demons are or aren't tormenting you - the bottom line is that virtue is a steel wall they cannot penetrate. They may try to torment you, suggest, flash with passions for things, and trip you in a million different ways. But if you have wisdom and self-control, as well as Me in mind at all times, their most powerful weapons against you are worthless."

Taken from: **Desire, Self-will & Consequences**

But Father, did you not show yourself that way in the wilderness as being awesome and terrible?

"When was I a terror to My own people who were obedient to Me? It was the ones who hated law and order, who hated control or boundaries, who wanted to side with Satan and run free in debauchery - those were the ones I was great and terrible to as the Earth swallowed them up.

"But to the **meek**, the humble, the obedient I am a tender Daddy. If you could but see the war that was raging with demons in bodies on Earth before the Flood, you would understand so much more. I would not be falsely accused of slaughtering what was innocent - because everything they created was anything but innocent."

Taken from: **I Am Truly Your Father**

"**Meekness**, humility, awareness of your frailty and complete dependence on Me: those are the hinges on the gate of virtue that will protect you - even from yourself, the worst adversary."

Taken from: **Your Worst Enemy**

"My children, I want you to take a lesson from this. If I give you a gift, do not presume to reject it. If I give you a gift, it is because I believe you deserve it and you need it. You have been faithful to Me and now I wish to bless you. I have seen your suffering. I have suffered with you! Don't you know that your lack hurts My Body? Don't you rush to comfort one of your children when they are hurting? How would you like to be pushed away...saying...'I don't need you. I'll be fine on my own!'

"Don't you know what that does to Me? Can you understand, you are all part of one Body - MY Body and I expect all of you to come to the aid of each other when there is a need. I also expect you to accept it graciously, because it is truly from the hand of God.

"There are so many gifts I want to give to this Body, but they must prepare their hearts to receive. They must be humble, **meek**, gracious and thankful. There is no room for arrogance or pride."

Taken from: **Receive From Me, My Church**

"Keep calling on Me, Clare, keep calling on Me. Your continuing prayers to be lower and lower keep Me coming back and fine-tuning you. Oh, how pleasing these prayers are to Me. If only My people knew how powerful **meekness** is before Me and the citizens of Heaven."

Taken from: **Higher Realms of Prayer and Sacrifice Changing the World**

Mercy

"When I said that Satan goes for the jugular, I mean his minions know where to place the sucker punch. And you all suffer grief over your children, asking if you did the right thing, grieving over your mistakes, wondering if there is still hope for them.

"May I say, the accusers stand beside you, thrusting your hearts through with all manner of lies about them? And I am here to remove the lance and restore the wounds with the balm of faith with My goodness and **mercy**. Even now your suffering is backing up the harvest of souls and their turn is coming."

Taken from: **Trust Me With Your Children...**

Carol and I had a conversation about the continuing stability of the world, despite threats from wars and rumors of wars. The Lord has told us minute-by-minute, but it is dragging on. Things ramp up and it looks like war is about to erupt, then things cool off. No war yet. And though we prayed for **mercy**, *we didn't expect ???*

Carol was asking the Lord if He would keep us here until Trump was in office and He began speaking to her, "I do not want you to fear, or relax the vigil of prayer. And this tension of wondering will help you. DO NOT relax into thinking you may have yet another 4 months."

Oh, how foolish we are, guys. Oh, how foolish we are... Here is **mercy**, *a reprieve, nations backing down again. Each time they ramp up right to the edge, and then they back down again. But the Lord continues to keep us on the edge!*

Taken from: **Higher Realms of Prayer and Sacrifice Changing the World**

"If you are dividing My Body, you are working for Satan. You are being used by the demons if you are separating brethren. If you are taking the failings of others as a final door slammed shut, you are creating pockets of bitterness for the demons to create strongholds in YOUR life, not the lives of those who hurt you. They will walk on, but you will stumble because of what you are holding onto.

"That is why forgiving is a work of charity, a work of **mercy**. It makes up for judgment, calumny, and lying. What sin has severed, you can restore by your charity. Just as surely as wounds heal, forgiveness cleanses those pockets of corruption and allows tender flesh to grow back. When you refuse to forgive, you are only demonstrating your lack of knowledge of self. This calls Me to your side. Now, I must reveal to you your weakness and how you fail others. I do it again and again until you finally understand and learn to forgive and go on."

Taken from: **How a Root of Bitterness Can Change Your Destiny and DNA**

"Once you have made your peace as best you can, when the enemy tries to assail you with guilt and condemnation or things of the past you can no longer rectify, let them drop like a stone into the ocean. Do not wrestle with 'should haves/should not haves.' Simply let them drop like a stone into the ocean of My **Mercy** for Me to resolve. The tendency to fight or rationalize these thoughts only draws you deeper into the conflict. I already have a resolution, in My time. I already have a provision, in My time. Abandoning these to Me is your sure and healthy answer to them being worked out."

Taken from: **Make Peace With All**

"Put your trust in Me. Confess your sins, forgive your enemies, and stay repentant. Scatter works of **mercy** all around you, waste no time coming to the aid of your neighbor, whoever they might be. And most of all, pray for *Mercy*."

Taken from: **War, Comet, Rapture, Treaty – Order of Events**

Mercy

"Faith without works is dead. I am still waiting to see your faith in action. Waiting to see you feed and clothe the poor, visit the sick and those in prison. I am still waiting to see authentic conversion and love flowing from your lives. And yet, there may be a spark of hope left for you if you recognize your sins of selfishness and repent, crying out for **Mercy**. But if you are taken before you can repent, then what?"

Taken from: **On the Brink of War Again**

Jesus began again, "You look at Me and pray, 'Lord have **mercy** on my family.' Am I a deaf idol or do I respond by granting **mercy**??

"You pray the divine **Mercy** Chaplet; am I again as one who cannot hear???

"You weep over the rejection your relatives give you when they mock you. Am I not weeping with you? Do your tears and agony not move My heart to pity them and give them more grace, more time and more **mercy**??

"Those who continually say My **mercy** is at an end, are wrong. My **mercy** is everlasting from age to age."

Taken from: **What's Delaying The Rapture?**

"Heartdwellers, you do not understand! Your prayers are powerful. You are changing the world, you and other Christians who have truly dedicated your lives to prayer and intercession.

"All of you brought together are a HUGE force. It's not your power, it's your hearts that cry out that release My arm of grace and justice. You have moved on My Father's heart, and many plans to annihilate the people of the world have flat-out failed and will continue to fail.

"I told you this before about the Elite's agenda, and the Obama administration, that things would not go smoothly. Opposition and snafu would be met at every turn, depending on the depth and commitment to prayer.

"Yes, instead of it going to the right, it would go to the left; instead of it going down, it would go up; instead of it going around, it would go straight. Every turn would be opposed by events My Father has put in place because of your prayers.

"Do not persecute the prophets among you who have been faithful to warn you. You owe them your lives and the lives of your unsaved loved ones, who still have a chance. Do not fall in with the unbelievers and ridicule the Rapture, or WW3 or Revelation - or anything like that. Do not be a naysayer.

"Rather declare that OUR GOD REIGNS!! And that the prayers of the little ones, the simple ones, the God-loving people of the Earth have broken the flask of their hearts and poured out the ointment of petition on behalf of the inhabitants of the whole Earth.

"And the Father, who is Pure **Mercy** Himself, has relented and chosen to give you all a window of opportunity, another chance for conversions and to get it right. This must be your heart attitude, Dear Ones. God has been faithful to answer your prayers.

"And though the signs of the times continue, wars and rumors of wars - the worst has been delayed because you have worn calluses on your knees. I cannot tell you how long this delay will last, but I will say that one move depends upon certain core moves. And those have been thrown into confusion and evil is being withstood. So, the light is still with you."

Taken from: **Judgment, War & Rapture Delayed! Mercy for America…**

Mercy

"Pray for **mercy**. **Mercy** for the young, **mercy** for the old, **mercy** for the infirm. Pray for little children - the most brutal casualties of these events. Pray for mothers and fathers, sisters and brothers - pray that they will run to Me and only Me.

"Perhaps the Father will relent and give yet another extension of time. We shall see. But My Brides should be the very first ones to cry out to Me for **Mercy**. This is the heart and posture of My precious ones. Please, Clare, be among them. I know how weary you all are. I am not promising anything, but your prayers for **mercy** will be heard - one way or the other."

Taken from: **Prayer Alert – Pray for Mercy**

I asked the Lord what He meant by "lawless." And He said, "The heart of the Law is Love. Those who didn't love are lawless."

"Faith without works is dead. I am still waiting to see your faith in action. Waiting to see you feed and clothe the poor, visit the sick and those in prison. I am still waiting to see authentic conversion and love flowing from your lives. And yet, there may be a spark of hope left for you if you recognize your sins of selfishness and repent, crying out for **Mercy**. But if you are taken before you can repent, then what?

"I ask you now: prepare yourselves to meet Me and understand - preparations for war are already completed. It is merely the consent of the Father that is holding this wrath back.

"Do you understand? I want to forgive you. I want your blind eyes opened. I want your repentance. I truly wait, day after day for you to recognize you have gone down the wrong path. You have not chosen Me, but your flesh and the pleasures of this world. You have been embroiled in disputes, accusation, calumny, bitterness and backbiting... stealing, killing and destroying the good names of others and slandering the Gospel I died on the Cross to set you free with.

"I can forgive you, if you repent. I have paid the price but you must do your part. It will come upon you suddenly and there will be no remedy, no time to repent, no time to even call out to Me. For you, it will be over and your destiny will be sealed. There will be no excuses at that time, for I have given you warning after warning after warning in an attempt to turn you at the very last minute. There will be no excuses. You were warned, you were taught and still you chose to go with the Devil."

Taken from: **On the Brink of War Again**

"The ones who are in the forefront of ministry, working hard while the day yet dawns, they are My Lovers. They are the very ones who will be Raptured, even against their will on a certain level. They are so in love with Me and dedicated to My agenda that they pray for the nation and the world, EXPECTING Me to hear them and grant leniency and **mercy**. These are the ones I am eager to have with Me in Heaven. They are the Bridesmaids with lamps full of oil."

Taken from: **What's Delaying the Rapture?**

"My **Mercy** for this country will be felt tonight. The prayers of My servants have been heard - for they have humbled themselves and sought Me. Shall I not grant them the respite they so desire? Yet there is cause for concern, do not imagine that any man will follow perfectly My will, but this man, I have anointed, for better and for worse. Yet the challenges he is facing in the coming months are beyond human comprehension. But I comprehend them and he has opened his mind to listen to My wisdom, though he rarely recognizes it is Me talking to him."

Taken from: **President Elect Trump**

Millennium

"Yes, there will be birth and death, though circumstances will allow for a longer life span and perfect health due to the atmosphere and absence of sin and demons. It is yet a pity that evil will manifest without provocation by the enemy. This is the weakness of Adam and Eve. It will be a shock to many that evil can still raise its ugly head without demonic assistance.

"You will have joy in everything you put your hand to. You will see conversions, healings, restorations and complete transformation of hearts. This will bring you unspeakable joy as it does for all the angels and saints in Heaven.

"You see My Daughter, so many on Earth in this hour long with all their hearts to minister but the forces allied against them are tremendous, both of a personal nature and an impersonal nature. Few there are that break through this wall, for great perseverance is required and great reliance on Me.

"And there are those who have been chosen and equipped for this, there are others who have not. And to them I give the grace of prayer. Their desires are manifested in the arenas of evangelism, and while they are not a direct part of the conversions as man sees it, they are the living prayer force behind these evangelists. And were you to see these evangelists without the great mass of prayer warriors offering prayers and supplications on their behalf, you would see them as just simple, pitifully weak men.

"The evangelists themselves must have very pure hearts, humility and an anointing from above. Their integrity must be impeccable. That is why we work so hard on issues of this sort. They cannot carry out the work and sustain the heat of the battle or hold up under pressures without a profound commitment to integrity and doing things My way.

"Yet, pull the curtain back and the man becomes very, very little in My plan. The intercessors behind the man are tremendous, making him look like a giant, when in reality it is the little ones behind him that are responsible for his perceived stature. In this way, the desires of those who wanted to minister are satisfied. And yet there is a time and a season for all. They will get their turn."

Taken from: **Heaven & the Millennium, After the Rapture**

And these demon-aliens, Lord? Will they all be confined to the Earth and then held for a thousand years so their terror will no longer be anywhere in the universe? Because I've heard so many reports that they're spread out in many different dimensions of the Universe.

"That's correct. And there are legions and legions upon hundreds of thousands of them - but every last one will be confined and not permitted to influence in any way the Earth or the people of the Earth. They will be completely and utterly bound and confined in every way.

"Joy and goodness will abound and any shadow of evil will originate strictly in the heart of man untouched by the demonic realm. If evil comes forth, it will be conceived in the heart of man - not from the outside as it has been in the past. You see, in the Garden, Satan was allowed to tempt Eve and Adam. But during the **Millennium** there will be no such temptation from Satan. The Earth will be totally free of his influence."

"Well, I just brought this up because I didn't want you to grieve excessively. All will turn out to My Glory. Though for a moment, My indignation and wrath must be felt on the Earth, that time will pass quickly as I promised and all things will be made new. Do you understand, My Beloved?"

Taken from: **What Must Befall This Nation and the Earth**

Millennium

But I thought that in Heaven no one ever suffered?

"There is continuous joy, but there is also the awareness that things are not completed. There's work to be done. And on the way to completion there's empathy, and in empathy there's pain... and pain needs comfort."

Lord, does this happen a lot?

"Unfortunately, until the end of the **Millennium** it will occur far more than We would like it to, but it's part of what keeps everyone serving. But it's not the kind of pain on Earth where things are dark, foreboding and depressing -oppressive. No, in Heaven there is hope and remedy on the way.

"There are needs, and all are constantly serving the needs of those on Earth. Prayers being offered, healings are happening, music is being imparted straight from Heaven. There are no needs for the citizens of Heaven, all needs are met abundantly.

"But those on Earth, and in transition to coming here, they have needs that the angels and saints see to. That is something I will not go into detail about at this time. Suffice it to say, all are very alive and focused on the work entailed in ministering salvation to souls, the salvation I accomplished on the Cross.

"There are times when the windows of Heaven are closed and there is, in a manner of speaking, retreat time - a time of rest from the awareness of the needs of Earth. This is something the Father determines. It is usually a time of extreme joy and celebration without awareness of things outside of Heaven."

Taken from: **Heaven: Jesus Shares...**

"Time travel, or should I call it more immersion in the time line, is not just a spectator sport...rather it is a live event, where you are present with Me. I would not leave you alone for one moment. Partly because I will derive endless amounts of pleasure and joy from your reactions."

And the other part?

"To remind you that you are in Heaven, so you do not react in fear."

I thought so.

"Well, you thought right."

I still want to go there. Oh Jesus, it's so exciting. Why am I so intrigued and drawn to the Ark now?

"Because soon the ark will come to get you?"

Not the literal ark, but the mini-ark and because as in the days of Noah....

"Oh, Clare - you know the answers to all these questions, but this is not just idle curiosity. I am whetting your appetite for the things you will long to see in Heaven. Start dreaming!"

I really want to snuggle with my kitties, all of them, and especially my tiger, Simba.

"And they eagerly await your arrival. All of Heaven is eagerly awaiting you. There is so much more significance to the homecoming of My Bride than anyone understands. This is the beginning of an Epoch, it is the transition into the **Millennium**, and shortly after that the Epoch of eternity begins, where all things are reconciled to Me."

Taken from: **When You See the Dome of the Rock Destroyed...**

Millennium

"I created dogs to be fail safe companions when the rest of the world is at odds with you, but never a substitute for human companionship. In Heaven, everyone will treat you like the sweetest dog you ever had. There's a comparison for you to think about. In Heaven, every soul will give you tail-wagging, unconditional love."

I'm going to get it for this statement, Lord....

"What is that to Me?"

Nothing?

"That's correct...what people say is nothing to Me, although it hurts Me when you come under attack."

Well, I'd rather speak what You want me to speak and get into trouble than to withhold one word of Yours, Lord.

"I know, that's why you go out on a limb with Me all the time. But truly, the sweetest dog you ever had is very reflective of the kinds of greetings that souls in Heaven. They are always glad to see you, their entire focus is on you, and honoring you as they honor Me. In fact, each one of My Creatures is a reflection of a very tiny part of My nature, although not the corrupted part since the fall of Adam and Eve. That is why the redeemed Earth will be a living paradise. Love and order will be restored to the Earth in the **Millennium**, and again at the end of ages.

"Peace will flood over the Earth as waves upon the sea. What a tremendous blessing you will someday have when I restore all things to their rightful order. Love will infuse all creatures and man will shepherd the creatures rightly.

"But in the meantime, I want you to enjoy your animals. I want to see your eyes light up and smiles cross your lips as you delight in their joyous and uncomplicated antics. Just as I delight to see your wonder on a golden autumn day, so do I rejoice to see the exchange of love and joy from one creature to another."

Taken from: **Man's Best Friend**

And the Lord reminded me of Matthew 25 "But when the Son of Man comes in His glory, (it talks about the timing of the **Millennium** here) He will separate them from one another, as the shepherd separates the sheep from the goats; and He will put the sheep on His right, and the goats on the left. Matthew 25:31-34

The Lord continued here, "This is not only at the **Millennium**, but now, as the Day is about to dawn, I am coming for My Bride. I am coming to provide for My remnant. Even as the young Hebrew boy (Nathan) said, 'I can smell holiness and sincerity.' I can also smell corruption. And some of you that were to be taken, because you butted the sheep and injured the innocent, will be left behind - not to be punished, but to learn how to love."

Taken from: **I Wanted To Go Fishing, But the Nets Were Torn 2**

The Lord told us not very long ago that new dimensions have been opened for more demons to come in to the Earth. The Lord is allowing this - He's going to gather them all together and put them in a holding place until the end of the **Millennium***.*

They're losing their freedom that they had in the second heaven and are being brought together here in order to be collected and put away fro a season, so they can't affect mankind, and that's during the thousands year reign.

Taken from: **I Will Restore Your Soul...**

Money

"It takes a strong soul to think outside the box and swim against the current. A very strong soul. Some are endowed with this strength, others can obtain it or even gain more from Me. Either way, when you and I work together, I will fulfill My agenda for your life. You walk in a supernatural anointing that will carry you through every storm.

"Most have had their dreams stolen at a very young age. They are taught that **money** is the norm, security and respectability is essential and those become your life goals without even thinking about it. How terribly this strips the soul of incentive!

"The unique qualities I've endowed them with just wither in the heat of these demands. Before a soul strikes out on any endeavor, he asks himself, 'Can I make **money**? Will I be secure in this work? How can I build my life with this work?' Those are sad, sad questions, totally missing the point of life and the things that will bring you the most joy.

"People with musical gifts 90% of the time abandon the idea of living as a musician and sign up selling insurance, or as store clerk, or a desk job where 5% of their ability is called upon to do a job. Some dedicate their lives to advanced training in universities so they can make more **money**, in the hopes that that will buy them the free time they so long for to devote to their music.

"Do you see, Clare? The most profoundly beautiful parts of a soul's life are cut off before they can mature."

Taken from: **Your Very Special Destiny**

"Focus on Me and only on Me and your life in My presence becomes a delight that never ceases to restore you. Yes, if you follow Me you will not walk in darkness or confusion. Eventually I will lead you out into the full light of day. It is said that I write straight with crooked lines, and how true that is. I alone know the path you must take to holiness and fulfillment. When you yield your entire life to Me, with no other agenda than to please Me, I can then begin that process. Those who would lose their lives, they are the ones who will find them.

"I have brought this up because some of you scoff at the very concept of having something joyful and creative to do at times when your mind is overwhelmed.

"I did not create man to live such an intense life as you have today. With electronic media, pressures come up against you from all sides. The world's agendas that say time is **money** - and of course, **money** comes first - add yet another layer of confusion and alienation from whom I created men and women to be."

Taken from: **Creativity Renders You Responsive to Me**

"Now, I will tell you who should be worried: those who knew Me, knew what I called them to do, and followed their own flesh and self-will, nonetheless. Those who didn't have time or **money** for the poor, but rather saved up their **money** to lavish on their comforts and trinkets."

Taken from: **Who Will I Rapture?**

"So, when you overspend, for instance - it is just a serious as those who steal. Though the **money** is in your control, it should be looked at as Mine, since you are My stewards. Therefore, the man who runs out of the 7-11 with a six pack of beer, because of his addiction and the way he was formed by his non-existent parents is less guilty than you who spend the **money** on luxuries, when you could have supported and orphan with it."

Taken from: **Repent For the Guilty, Do Not Condemn**

Money

"In that one verse," He continued, "so much can be summed up: the love of **money** and luxury is just as much an idol as Baal worship - men still kill their babies in the womb to save **money**.

"The murders that are taking place daily, because medical science in this country is profit motivated, therefore they sell useless cures that will only kill in the end... and that's not even to mention what is done to the environment to slowly destroy the masses. They are killing, stealing and destroying, just like their father, the devil."

Taken from: **Prophetic Rapture Dream & NWO**

"There is no sense to accumulating wealth, position or power because everything will be scrambled and reorganized based on loyalty to the New World Order. Any Christian right now that is posturing for higher positions is going to hit a brick wall after the Rapture. There is no need to be alarmed, just informed.

"Those who are left behind will have to switch their priorities from making **money** - to surviving. And I don't mean surviving physically, alone. Yes, survival must also be spiritual, understanding and being sensitive to the movement of My Spirit."

Taken from: **Prophetic Rapture Dream & NWO**

"There are those listening in that have bought into this lie and I am trying to reach them before it is too late. They have not experienced love. They have not experienced peace. They are perpetually frightened of who has more power and who can still do damage to them. And way in the back of their minds is the thought, 'What if God IS real and sees all I do?'

"Well, I can answer that for you. I AM real and I have seen, but I suffered the worst torments on the Cross to redeem you from this madness you are living in. Some of you have been promised **money** and fame. Some of you have acquired **money** and fame, but you are miserable inside. Why is that? Because **money**, fame, women - none of these things meet your need to be loved and your need to know Me.

"I created that space inside of you that has been covered over with the rubble of sin. I created that space so I could fill it someday with My love, My caring, My gifts and My guidance. You've not experienced love, so you have no idea how that satisfies that secret place in you. Well, I am here to tell you, there is a place in My Heart for you. You are a masterpiece of My Creation, living in a sewer - and I am coming to get you and restore to you your dignity and the love you crave.

"You needn't live this way anymore. Come to Me and I will bathe you in My Blood and make your blackened soul as white and pure as snow. Come to Me. Don't be afraid, I will cover you. Come to Me."

Taken from: **To Satan's Servants, An Invitation from Jesus**

"One only has to dig a couple of feet to see it. It is that nefarious force that will eventually arise from the ground and swallow everything in its grasp. These are the hidden agendas, the black ops, the place where tremendous amounts of tax dollars go to destabilize governments and establish cooperative leaders through terror, butchery and intrigue. This is also the force behind ISIS and the planned Muslim takeover of America, resulting in the slaughter and beheading of Christians and Jews.

"This is another force that must be curtailed in this country. It brings curse after curse upon the citizens of the land because they are spreading injustice through their **money**."

Taken from: **Election Day - "The Decisive Hour" Jesus said**

Money

If God has called you to be really like Jesus, He will draw you into a life of crucifixion and humility, and put upon you such demands of obedience that you will not be able to follow other people, or measure yourself by other Christians. And in many ways He will seem to let other people do things which He will not let you do.

Others may be allowed to succeed in making money, or may have a legacy left to them, but it is likely God will keep you poor, because He wants you to have something far better than gold. Namely, a helpless dependence upon Him, that He may have the privilege of supplying your needs day by day out of an unseen treasury.

Taken from: **Why Am I Least of All?**

Tracing back to the source of that panther, I had a dream when I first became a Christian. I was swimming in the lake at our summerhouse and all of a sudden a large, muscular black panther came swimming towards me and tried to drown me. I fought him with all my might. He would go under and I would think, "He's dead." Then he would come up and pull me under and I would think, "I'm going to die." Back and forth, back and forth. The dream ended before I could tell who won. I thought I had made an end to him before I awoke, but could I really be sure?

I didn't know what the dream was about at that time - I really had no clue. Then it was revealed to me: a demon of Avarice was assigned to lure me away from the Lord. And it did, for many years until the Poconos. But it's still lurking in the shadows.

Can any of you relate? Do you have a black panther? Maybe it's popularity, power, **money***, drugs, alcohol, sex, or food? Whatever it is, it pulls you away from Jesus with desires that are fruitless in eternity and could easily lead to damnation.*

Taken from: **Your Worst Enemy**

"In all of history there will never again, nor has there been before, a time such as this. Men will be at their wit's end trying to figure out what to do next. Nothing will make sense to them and everything will be topsy-turvy. I am trying to prepare now, those who will be left behind.

"There is no sense to accumulating wealth, position or power because everything will be scrambled and reorganized based on loyalty to the New World Order. Any Christian right now that is posturing for higher positions is going to hit a brick wall after the Rapture.

"There is no need to be alarmed, just informed. Those who are left behind will have to switch their priorities from making **money** - to surviving. And I don't mean surviving physically, alone. Yes, survival must also be spiritual, understanding and being sensitive to the movement of My Spirit."

Taken from: **Surviving the Coming Tribulation**

"Others among you have finally broken free from the love of **money** and man. You have grown to despise this world and I am preparing you for Heaven as well. Do not think the changes in your character are not noticed. They are, especially by your relatives.

"Yes, they see the changes and they wonder, 'Perhaps they are right about God in their lives, after all.' Yes, your light is shining and drawing all men to Me. Well done. Continue in your good resolve and do not allow yourself to slide backwards.

"There is little time left, hold onto the good, continue to weed the garden of your heart. There is a great reward awaiting you in My Kingdom."

Taken from: **Time is Short, Some of You ARE Ready...**

Obedience

"Just be My faithful plow horse, pulling, pulling, pulling - even when you're tired and hurting, still you are pulling. All of My faithful ones do Me great honor by their **obedience** in these supposedly small things."

"Yet I tell you the truth, they have gathered much fruit for the kingdom of God by their simple unflagging **obedience**. Much fruit. So do not be alarmed at what others call a lack of fruit.

Speaking to the Bride: "You have pleased Me. That is all that counts. You have taken quite a bit of calumny from those closest to you, but others see the pearls in My Kingdom that you are. But even if you were fortunate enough that no one could see, still, you have born much fruit by your simple detached (from worldly rewards) **obedience.**

"And without self-seeking, rather at all times, seeking Me and My approval alone. This is what I have meant, this I will reward and still you will stay small and safe. Tucked away in My Heart, abounding in love and grace, much to My glory."

Taken from: **My Bride is Not Responding**

"There will always be demons to inspire dissatisfaction with some family member when you don't bow to their demands. Are you willing to face them off and lose their affection for My sake? **Obedience** is not something you give to everyone. You are never under any obligation to obey something when it violates your conscience or the Gospels.

"For this, great discrimination is needed. It is so easy for the devils to twist priorities to cause guilt. 'Honor your parents' does not mean sin for your parents. 'Honor your husband, your wife', does not mean sin for them. You are under no obligation to live the life your parents want you to live, rather you're to follow Me in your life path."

Taken from: **How Prayer Fails**

"On that note, your **obedience** to Me is everything. The part you play, even moment by moment, is determined by Me because you have given your lives to Me. I know how to get you into the right place at the right time for the most fruit to be harvested for the Kingdom. Therefore, all that is needed is your **obedience** and grace will do the rest.

"But you cannot be **obedient** if you are not listening to Me, 'Very Carefully.' Listening is one thing, listening 'very carefully,' is quite another. As you spend more time with Me your ability to hear and be aware of what I want for you from moment to moment becomes highly tuned. In this way, you will bear the most fruit for the Kingdom."

Taken from: **There are No Losers in My Kingdom**

"However, those who are in love with Me, whose hearts melt when they see My Face, hear a love song, and long to give Me more of their lives - those souls are the most threatening to the kingdom of darkness. That is another reason why so many attacks have been launched at you. Intimacy is the Key to the greatest works in My Kingdom. If you sat behind a desk and taught eschatology, you would be far less threatening.

"So, what you do out of **obedience** bears little resemblance to what you do out of inspired love."

Taken from: **Your Greatest Strength**

"Know that your greatest enemy is your self-will and your greatest protection is humility, which always leans towards **obedience**."

Taken from: **Victory Over Trials, Temptations & Spiritual Muscle**

Obedience

"Whenever I instruct you, there is a very specific reason. I am warning you of the enemy's next move. I can see the traps as they are preparing for you. I can also see your weaknesses. I pinpoint a dynamic everyday to warn you of what is coming.

"If you don't obey, you open yourself to a fall.

"You cannot outsmart the enemy if you do not follow Me in **obedience**. You are no match for them without Me. And when you go out from the sheep pen without Me leading you, you are indeed without Me, in the sense that I cannot protect you from what you openly pursue against My will."

Taken from: **The Enemy's Next Move Against You**

"That's exactly what I meant when I said, 'You will love Me so much you will not want to grieve Me in any way'...no matter how hard the demon of Avarice stomps on your "Gotta have" buttons. This is precisely what I meant.

"**Obedience** in the little things leads to **obedience** in the big things, and for those left behind, **obedience** may mean life or death. So, now is the time to seek My will, to be sure you are moving forward in **obedience** and not in self-will."

Taken from: **Are You Wise?**

"You see, as souls come close to Me, they are protected and counseled in the right paths of life and they will not be hindered or duped by the great deceptions and globalist agendas. This is why this channel and others like it are so important to Me. I am teaching total reliance on Me and intimate friendship that will, in the end, spare the lives of those who would have been caught in Satan's nets and led to Hell.

"Man cannot be trusted, institutions cannot be trusted, religion cannot be trusted. I am the only One Who can be trusted and I offer this relationship to every soul I created. It's up to you to put forth the effort to cultivate it. Unless this is the top priority in your lives, whatever else is more important to you will lead you into deception and bondage.

"Oh, how important, My People, it is to learn to hear My voice and follow My commands! Your very eternity depends upon it. Please, don't put anything or anyone before the knowledge of Me and **obedience** to My laws. You put your soul and your children's souls in danger of eternal damnation.

"Please, My people, seek Me with all your hearts until you find Me. I am waiting for you, I will instruct you, I will love and heal you. And most of all, I will forgive you. Do not be afraid - I am for you, not against you. Anything you have heard about Me being a vengeful God is a twisted lie. To those who seek to do harm to others, yes, I intervene. But to the rest, I am a shield of righteousness against Satan and his wiles. And I will lead you in the paths of life and you will not fall prey to the great deceptions of this age.

"Seek Me and live."

Taken from: **Overcoming the Deceptions of This Age…**

"If God has called you to be really like Jesus, He will draw you into a life of crucifixion and humility, and put upon you such demands of **obedience** that you will not be able to follow other people, or measure yourself by other Christians. And in many ways He will seem to let other people do things which He will not let you do."

Taken from: **Why Am I Least of All?**

Obedience

"I wish for you not to get into arguments about which day of the week is holy. I will not instruct you on this, because it leads to a religious spirit. I want your heart, not your lip service and **obedience** to the law. Yes, I can hear the stones flying through the air now. This attitude of heart is deadly to a personal relationship with Me.

"You will note, it was the scribes and Pharisees that refused their hearts to Me, because I did not support their Sabbath rules in a way suitable to them.

"Do you know what one of their main concerns was with Me? I threatened their income from the sale of sacrifices and coin changing. Yes, they garnered quite a nice income on all that went on in the temple precincts and their greatest threat was that they no longer would have an income from these illicit activities. That is a wrinkle. The habit of having more and better caused them to twist their consciences in order to provide for their excesses."

Taken from: **Get Ready For Your Journey**

"The Jewish people will be the leading, number one force of evangelization world-wide. They will be dedicated to bringing in the reign of Messiah upon Earth. Neither family nor life will stop them in their zeal. Rather they will be on fire and infused with a special anointing to carry out My will."

When He said that, I thought of a certain person who is a completed Jew, and he is totally amazing. Just as on fire as he could possibly be. I mean..."get out of my way, here I come!" Totally yielded to Holy Spirit, he's really quite amazing! Oh, this person is something else.

My goodness, love and devotion and **obedience** *to the Lord, which I have personally experienced as outstanding and extremely up front. Not the laid-back style of approaching the unsaved, but rather a flaming* *torch daring the waters of complacency to snuff it out. I do not see discretion in this soul as much as ramped-up* **obedience** *to whatever Holy Spirit's agenda is. WOW. That's all I could say. And this person is a completed Jew.*

Taken from: **Evading Capture, Jesus Instructs Us**

"You see I established pastors and teachers to teach the people how to know, love and serve Me. How to seek Me until they find Me. And to help them stay on the right path with mature leaders assisting them to correct their course in life.

"I did not create pastors to hand-feed the flock and make themselves the only source of food. No, absolutely not!!! This is how error enters in: one man interprets for all the others and makes rules which set up legalistic societies again. Just like the Pharisees. Groups that rely on knowledge, politics, influence and control.

"No. Pastors are created to father children, to help them grow in the faith and learn to hear and obey Me, not to hear and obey man. Yes, **obedience** is useful for the extremely immature, but a good pastor will lead His flock to water and allow them to drink at their own pace. Yes, he will bring forth from the storehouse of age, the wisdom of God, but his first responsibility is to lead them to Me so that I can pasture My flock."

Taken from: **Why You Are Hated...**

"But I do not want accomplishment to become a lifestyle; rather **obedience,** thanksgiving and worship, these are the most highly valued virtues."

Taken from: **Increase Will Overtake You**

Parent's Duties

Many of you grown adults still have your parents hanging on and whispering over your shoulder. In some cases, it is your own memory, but do you know the demons have those recordings, too? Yes, they know precisely what was said to you, and know just how to press those condemnation buttons.

*A **parent's input** carries a tremendous amount of psychological weight in your mind. Little do they know that by their very own words they are forming you into what you will become. When they are harsh and perfectionistic, expecting only the highest standards of performance, and you fail...well, it sets up a cycle that continues through your adult years and even into old age - telling you, you are a failure, you fall short, you aren't as good as so and so.*

Taken from: **Show Mercy to Yourself as Well as Others**

"You see, when you come to serve Me, your life is no longer your own. Most people, however, try to run their new life in Me on two tracks: what they want... and what I want - within the context of what they want. Rather than totally abandoning their will and their way to Me, they compromise and then expect to be happy and fulfilled. But it will never happen until they totally abandon their agenda.

"Some are still catering to their earthly **parent's expectations**. Some have their eyes on a career goal and prosperity, and within that context they choose what they think is My will. But they are so far from the truth that they would be shocked if I revealed it to them. Yet, I know the course they are holding onto for dear life will lead them into mediocrity and unhappiness. I can only wait until they discover that's not what they wanted after all. And sadly by then, more than half of their life is spent and sickness has found its way into their bodies."

Taken from: **Buy of Me Fire-Tried Gold**

Some of you are going to get Parent's Duties, when you open the Bible Promises prayerfully. Remembering, of course, to bind the Lying spirit before you open the book. But you're going to get **Parent's Duties**, *and that means that the Lord is calling you to be a spiritual parent for some of these people who are suffering.*

Or, you may get Salvation, or you may get Eternal Life as well.

We've gotten those when we knew the Lord was calling for intercession. We didn't know whether to go to the emergency room, or sit and wait it out. So, we used the Bible Promises, and got Patience and **Parent's Duties**...

So we knew, Okay - this is a suffering that needs to bring the Gospel, or to help to the conversion of a soul to receive Him. So, it's okay - this will pass. We don't need to running off to the ER.

Taken from: **The Bride's Joys and Sorrow Intensify**

"Please, Beloved, no more of the world. Stay out of the stores. This is not the time to purchase gifts for yourself or your loved ones. I need you to be clean for our wedding. Avoid television, radio, magazines and the newspapers. You have had a lifetime full of that. I have gone to great pains to purify you from those influences.

"Yes, My Precious Ones, do tend to your proper **duties - children**, work, etc. But only fulfill those obligations that are crucial for the good of another. For example: giving someone a ride to the doctor or errands of mercy for the sick, the poor, and the elderly. You know what is absolutely necessary and what is not. I will help you, and caution you as well as nudging you to act when needed."

Taken from: **Prepare For Your Wedding Day**

Parent's Duties

"Many of you have labored for Me tirelessly: praying, fasting, serving and doing your very best as a **parent**, while you watched your children walk off into the world. Even those of you who had the best resources and intentions have witnessed this tragedy. But you see, I am with you and your children in a way you will never understand until Heaven. Indeed, when you see how I am accompanying them you will exclaim, 'Oh Lord, why did I worry and fret so???!' And I will answer you gently 'Because you didn't see what I see. But now you know, I had My hand on them the whole time and never let them go.'

"So, don't allow the devils to come and torment you over their destiny. It is with Me. I want you to reflect that trust in your dealings with them. Do not add to their burdens of guilt, which you can be sure the devils taunt them with in an effort to alienate them from you. Rather, show them My unconditional love, let them see Me through you.

"This will remove any obstacles of mistrust and fear they may be struggling with and foster good relations with them. You do not have to approve of their sin, neither do you need to attack them for it. They already know the difference between right and wrong, what you approve and what you do not approve. This is enough to convict them. But by your quiet unconditional love you show them the way to the Kingdom.

"When the time is ripe and they are fully sated with the world, then they will seek the living waters you bathed them in as a child. It will catch up to them. In the meantime, no matter how far they go into the darkness, rest assured. I am with them.

"And while many of you grieve over your mistakes, I am here to tell you that even those have been used to form good character in them. It is amazing, really, how the enemy can take even the best **parents** and make them feel like reprobates.

"But while you did your best and even failed, I knew how to turn the affects around to produce good in their souls.

"Many of you who worry are placing way too much emphasis on what you can do, and far too little emphasis on what I can do and have done in their lives. Not to mention what is yet to come - for I have life, not death planned for them."

Taken from: **Trust Me With Your Children...**

"My Heart is that every soul is endowed with skills and gifts that bring joy to their work and those they serve. Every soul has something to give that fits into the scheme of things and makes the world a more joyful and rewarding place. These are the little things that are so often overlooked in favor of security and respectability.

"These gifts are either tangible or intangible - like prayer. When a soul finds this gift, he should embrace it with his whole heart and never let it go in favor of a carnal agenda or the agenda of his **parents**. Your **parents** have lived their lives and made their choices. You now, in turn, have the opportunity to make your life count in this world in the time left to you.

"Very soon now, the world will be catapulted into survival mode and that will open opportunities for you all to take another look at your lives and where you were headed. But until that happens, I am calling you to press into My Heart. Dwell in My Heart. Do good wherever you find an opportunity, grow in virtue and fight against the temptations that assail you, even by calling your love for Me to mind. A demon cannot gain control of a heart that is full and running over with Love for Me."

Taken from: **Your Very Special Destiny**

Parent's Duties

(God the Father said) "The second thing that I truly and deeply want for you to consider is this profound Truth: each and every time I look upon YOU, do you know what the very first thing is that I see? Regardless of what you have or have not done in your life up until this point? Do you have the faintest idea of what I see when I behold you?

"When I take that long, loving look - much as a young mother who has lain her precious little one down for her afternoon nap, and then the mother stops suddenly at the door and simply gazes back at her little treasure, admiring and adoring those tiny, little fingers and tiny, little toes. Those delicately turned-up lips and little round cheeks. I could go on and on.

"My point. My profound Truth in all of this is simply to tell you that I am that young **parent**. Yes! Yes! I am! Just for a fleeting moment, I allow Myself to be that young, innocent, pure, inexperienced and totally awestruck young first-time Father.

"Oh, how I hold you so tenderly as I breathe My Spirit of Life into you for the very first time! If only you could see the days and weeks and months that I hover over you, begetting you from the womb and saying, 'This one is Mine!'

"Yes, even claiming you from the womb of your mother, so enraptured am I with your little soul. So, so little. So frail. So pristine, pure from the very breath of your God.

"How I love to see you go, as one more carrier of My very own heart and soul, with enormous, earthly and eternal potential! And how I grieve to see you go, knowing full well just exactly what does await you in this fallen and sinful world that you've been born into."

Taken from: **My Young Paternal Heart...**

"The one thought, however, that never, ever leaves the forefront of My mind is souls.

"Souls. Souls. I can never forget the masses of unsaved men and women AND adolescents. I purposely did not mention children. Why? Because a little child does not yet possess the faculties of the older ones.

"I am speaking about having an informed conscience. In other words, most little children, up to the age of 6 or 7 simply do not have the life experience yet to make an absolute 'yes' or 'no' decision as an act of their free will. Nor do they have a full understanding of exactly what 'sin' is.

"This is all to say that truly, depending on the child's **parents** and the circumstances that surround the life of the child, they cannot be held accountable at such a young age. Truth IS Truth, and each soul is different, depending on the grace that he or she is given. There are, of course, more rare situations, whereby a child of 7 or under may very well already have a well-informed conscience.

"But always remember: with Me there is fathomless Mercy and a fullness of Redemption. I nurse every lamb and lovingly cradle each sheep."

Taken from: **The Vine of Our Love & Age of Accountability**

And I just wanted to say here as an aside, Ezekiel went to the Bible Promise book for a word from Holy Spirit today. (That's my husband, Ezekiel) And he opened to **Parent's Duties.** *That almost ALWAYS means that if you are suffering, it is for other souls. The words of Jesus confirmed that to me just now.*

Taken from: **Satanists Posing as Concerned Christians**

Patience

We've found that those times where a healing didn't take place, others received unmerited favor and grace from the Lord. This has become such an obvious dynamic to us that, when people come to us for prayer, I ask them, "Who are you praying for?" Because very often what they want relief from, is reciprocal suffering for the ones THEY are praying for. In this case, we pray for strength to carry this cross in quiet and **patience***, knowing they aren't suffering in vain. That's a tremendous, tremendous consolation for people who are suffering, and it's so overlooked in the church and in the Body.*

Taken from: **When God is Silent and It's Not Your Fault**

"Nothing discourages a person more than hope deferred, and yet that's the very thing I use to work **patience** and faith into My chosen souls. Will they trust me? Will they stand on My promise and allow the work of preparation to be done? Or will they become impatient and try to do it themselves?"

Taken from: **I AM the Master Builder, Doing it God's Way**

"That's exactly right. I want to leave no one behind, but some of you have hardened your hearts toward each other and have trampled the innocent and the blind. Many of you on the Internet have taken shots at one another. You've wounded, crippled, and left them to die, isolated, despised, and without the fruits of their labor. Unless you repent and are found to be a blameless one, you might as well start making plans to stay here. You will not be taken. Love is My standard: **patience**, long-suffering, kindness, mercy, meekness, the Beatitudes. This is the description of My Bride. If you are willfully countering the Beatitudes, you still don't have My heart. You still don't resemble Me. My Bride must resemble Me."

Taken from: **Without Love You Will Not Be Taken in the Rapture**

"You see, the demons are My policemen. They wait in line all day to sift a believer, sometimes they line up around the block, so to speak, just to get one shot at a soul. Once a believer has crossed a line and disobeyed however, permission is given - but only so far. What they are allowed to do or not do is controlled by My permission.

"In other situations I allow the demons permission because I'm perfecting a soul in virtue and **patience** - forgiveness and virtue needs to be cultivated. At the very same time, when I allow an attack from the demon, I know how it will affect a soul and that they will, in turn, pray for those who are being used to attack. Very often those souls have no one to pray for them and the one whom they attack are My very last resort to find intercessors. This has been the case on your channel as well."

Taken from: **Jesus Speaks on: Why Our Enemies Are Important**

"My Brides, you are stunningly beautiful and the enemy hates the very mention of you. That is why he is waging war on this channel. He cannot stand to see the beauty of brotherly love, **patience** and caring for one another. He hates you for it. On other channels, he has succeeded in causing division, strife and calumny, but here he is a miserable failure; that is why you are being targeted. Your vigilance and obedience will keep you in My Peace."

Taken from: **Resist Gossip & Judgment**

"I bless you now, with My **patience** and endurance in these trials. And ask that you remember: this is a joyful occasion - to give to Me. Do not let your heart grow bitter, exhausted or despondent. Know that each one of these things is a work, a hard work. And you will not lose your reward in Heaven."

Taken from: **Suffering – Real Work in the Realm of the Spirit**

Patience

"There will be tests and trials in the coming days. Many tests and trials. You are entering a new plateau, climbing a new mountain as it were. Many will be tried in new ways, for as we go forward there must be progress. You must be always embracing more and more holiness, **patience**, humility, and steadfastness.

"These are the things that qualify you for advancement in My service. When you handle one level well, I advance you to new challenges in order to prepare you for new graces.

"I will be with you in all of this. It is for My glory and the salvation of souls. You know I never waste anything. Remember, everything is in My hands and it's not about you - but My agenda. And graces will flow like a river."

Taken from: **Your Designer Cross From Jesus**

"There is a purpose for everything, My children. There is a very specific purpose and dynamic for every single thing that takes place in the lives of every single person.

"But I bring these things to your attention to tell you that you are 'working' when you endure these sacrifices with equanimity and **patience.** You are doing a job that requires intense and careful vigilance. It's not just an inconvenience; it is a necessary work to alleviate the suffering of another."

Taken from: **Suffering – Real Work in the Realm of the Spirit**

"Now I am addressing you while you are in the waiting posture. You know this place well, but there is still much tension in your hearts. I want you to rest in Me. Allow Me to carry the tension and put yourselves in a posture of rest in My arms - do whatever is before you.

"Worry and fear will wear you out, and when you are tired, you are again an easy catch for Satan.

"Rather, I want you to be resting in Me, being strengthened every day, fully aware that at any moment the whole world could be turned upside down. Many of you, if not all, who listen to this channel and take My words to heart are ready. Your lamps are lit, you carry extra oil and you are ready.

"It has taken a good 12 months to get you to this point, but now you are here. You know well what your sins and vices of the past are and you are alert, paying close attention to yourselves, lest you should fall. And you are not over-investing in this world, because you know your time here could end at any moment. Maintain this disposition, Dear Ones. Maintain it with the added virtue of resting in Me. Trust, **patience**, confidence."

Taken from: **Rest in Me Until I Carry You Over the Threshold of Eternity**

"There will be tests and trials in the coming days. Many tests and trials. You are entering a new plateau, climbing a new mountain as it were. Many will be tried in new ways, for as we go forward there must be progress. You must be always embracing more and more holiness, **patience**, humility, and steadfastness. These are the things that qualify you for advancement in My service. When you handle one level well, I advance you to new challenges in order to prepare you for new graces.

"I will be with you in all of this. It is for My glory and the salvation of souls. You know I never waste anything. Remember, everything is in My hands and it's not about you - but My agenda. And graces will flow like a river."

Taken from: **Your Designer Cross From Jesus**

Patience

My mind began to drift on the outrageous and evil things being said about me lately on the Internet. And though I did not say anything to Him, He addressed it. Sometimes I think He puts those distractions in my head so He can answer them!

He continued, "Were your enemies to walk all over you with your faults they would be justified, but unfortunately they are way off base and even laughable to those who know you. But you enduring in **patience**, without hostility, is witness enough that I am truly living in you, Clare. No one could endure these things without supernatural love and come away still praying from the heart for their enemies."

Taken from: **Why You Are Hated, Rapture Timing...**

"Just so with my prophets and ministers. They may be given a message, but they have been trained to present it without constraints or force. There is an art to this, that is why it takes many years of training to prepare one who advises department heads. There is a right way and a wrong way. The message is so important, that if it is done the wrong way, the messenger is responsible for the failure of that message to be heeded.

"One must be a follower before they can lead. They must be tested in temperance, **patience**, respect, decorum and presentation before I can trust them with the bigger tasks. I am pre-eminently respectful of those in positions of authority and responsibility.

"I take their office very seriously. If they do not come to Me for advice I stand back and watch. If they seek Me out, I offer suggestions - but never in a way that disrespects their office. Never forcefully, never presuming to have the only the right answer or saying 'God showed me this is the way to run your department, or this is the way you should minister. God told me to tell you.'"

Taken from: **How I Train My Prophets**

"Do not expect your crosses to get lighter and lighter as we approach that time. Rather arm yourselves with **patience** and faith, knowing that I foretold this time of suffering. Have you not offered yourselves to Me? Have you not said you want to co-labor with Me in the fields? Well, at this time in history, this is your part. You cannot rejoice over what you cannot see, so I am asking you to rejoice in your sufferings, for they are bringing a heavy weight of glory to My Kingdom as the lost come to Me - sometimes one by one, sometimes hundreds upon hundreds."

Taken from: **You're Coming Home, My Bride**

"You see, when you attach significance to these things, you may not be actively thinking of them, but you are easily snagged by all that relates to them. These are some of the distractions that make prayer more difficult for many. But when you cast off the yoke of your pleasures to make room for My Pleasure, then your communion with Me goes deeper, much deeper as matters of the flesh melt away. That's what I'm getting at.

"Not everyone is ready to let go of earthly pleasures to have more of Me, but as they seek Me in their own ways, eventually they head in that direction. I have sublime **patience** with all those who reach towards Me."

Taken from: **You're Coming Home, My Bride**

His **patience***, even with them is amazing to me. He gives them about three seconds saying,* "I'm waiting. I'm waiting. I'm waiting. I'm done waiting, you're coming with Me." *And He takes them to the Lake of Fire. As a result of this, when they see Him coming, they run.*

Taken from: **Spiritual Warfare: 13 - Protection Through Obedience**

Peace

"Yes, My Love, and the thing I most want to communicate to you is My unconditional love. You are in a human body, subject to forces beyond your understanding, but not beyond My power to shut down. So, there are times when you are tossed to and fro and buffeted, then there are times in prayer, when you dive deeper, and there you find the still waters and **peace**.

"Yet that is not an easy place to access. It is deeper and deeper away from the turbulent ocean currents, away from the surface winds, away from the storms and hurricanes. Yes, I have called you deeper, and deep calls unto deep."

Taken from: **Trust Me With Your Children...**

"When you come to the River of Life flowing in My Heart, I restore the good, I replenish your vitality and will to follow Me. I restore ruined homesteads in your heart, places left abandoned. Even now, I am imparting **peace** to you about those failures you so deeply grieve over.

"Even now, My Love, I am washing over you with My **Peace**, because you are Mine and the world takes its toll on you. The enemy goes for the jugular, Clare. Any way to bring you down into sorrow and distress. They are masterful at this, and those in the world without Me suffer terribly. But My own, I restore beside fresh, still waters and rich pastures."

Taken from: **Trust Me With Your Children...**

"Be steadfast and practice the art of waiting on Me in a state of perfect rest, knowing that soon all will be fulfilled. But until that very moment, My grace is shining in and through you and touching all souls of this world with the supernatural expression of your faith in action.

"Be wise, be discerning, be **peaceful** and at rest. In this way you, My Bride, will shine gloriously as I return to carry you over the threshold of eternity, where we shall be together forever and ever. I have said it. I shall accomplish it."

Taken from: **Rest in Me Until I Carry You Over the Threshold of Eternity**

"What is coming is horrendous in scope and there will be unavoidable isolations. That is when you are to CLEAVE TO ME with all your heart and soul. Until then, pray with one another. But when it all happens, pray for each other and stay tightly holding Me as I hold you. The wind will be ferocious, but in My arms it will be a gentle breeze.

"That is why you mustn't, for a moment, lose your focus and look outside of Me. I will keep you in My **Peace** if only you will rely on Me alone."

Taken from: **Permission to Burn and Travailing Prayer**

Jesus began, "My precious Dove, there is so little left to say right now except for exhortations to holiness and to care particularly for those around you and those I send to you. Make **peace** with anyone you are holding grudges against. Do not leave behind grudges. Do not leave behind loose ends. See to it that you are at **peace** with ALL men to the best of your ability.

"For some this will be a very difficult decision and endeavor. But may I say, the more difficult, the more necessary it is. Some will feel deep guilt when you are gone. I would like you to lift that off of them now. Make **peace** with them. It may not have been your fault, but you can still apologize."

Taken from: **Make Peace With All**

Peace

"When you are fully released to Me and I am in full control, I can do all that is necessary to guide you into your true mission in life. Yes, there are moments that are scary, painful, confusing. But ultimately, when you trust Me, you cease to worry about these things. Unless you become as little child...Yes, abandonment into the arms of your loving Father, your loving Jesus, your loving Spirit is the key to maintaining **peace** in the midst of life's contradictions."

Taken from: **Hand in Hand With Daddy**

"I am speaking to all of you now. I have allowed these agents of Satan to raise their ugly heads so you could be trained in discernment. You have only to ask yourself how they make you feel. Fear, panic, anxiety, loss of **peace**, confusion? Lies, manipulation, false accusations, and questionable interpretations of the Scriptures should immediately warn you that they are not sent by Me."

Taken from: **Satanists Posing as Concerned Christians...**

"I am ever by your side, continually watching over you, whispering in your ear: 'Don't go there. Do this - it would be good if you did that.' 'Don't answer that, delete it.'

"Yes, I am advising you continually. But My voice is so familiar to you, you actually believe it to be your own. But if you listen very carefully, you will realize that thought did not originate with you...it came from a different source.

"So you say, 'What if it came from the enemy?' Well, you will know immediately because you will lose the peace you had five minutes ago. When that happens the suggestion is from the evil one, rest assured. That is THE acid test. Did it leave you in **peace**? Or in turmoil?"

Taken from: **The Enemy's Next Move Against You**

"That is what this is all about. Relationship. There is nothing that pleases Me more than to be recognized for who I am and trusted that My love for you does not stop Me from being approachable. When you learn of My true nature and cultivate this friendship, you begin to reflect Me to others and they, too, begin to hunger for an intimate relationship with Me.

"They feel **peace** and comfort in My presence, rather than fear causing them to shake and cower. This is the lot of My Beloved ones, those who, from the heart, want to live a holy life."

Taken from: **Who I Really Am To You**

"Please. Please pray for the new believers. You have many here who are brand new to the faith. Come alongside them and accompany them, sharing your experiences, your fears and triumphs so they may be reassured they are on the right track.

"It is My Love that draws them here. Don't let the innocent go without feeling acknowledged, received and encouraged. Remember, you have all been in that place of woundedness and insecurity and found a **peaceful** home here."

Taken from: **You Are Mothers of Souls**

Holy Spirit began: "In My arms, you can be totally at home and rest. I love to saturate your mind with Holy thoughts, with **peace**, with understanding of the Scriptures and the profound love I have for you. For far too long I have been seen as a bird, yet truly I am made in the image of a man, not with feathers, but with flesh and skin, just like you. For we have made you in Our Image, we each long to enter into a deep abiding relationship of worship and holy conversation with you."

Taken from: **Holy Spirit's Desire for You ...**

Peace

"My people, even if they should bring you before the executioner for your faith in Me, be not afraid. In seconds, I will embrace you for eternity. Mercy will surround and anesthetize you in those last moments.

"Supernatural **peace** will also engulf you as you are led forth to execution. I know it is hard for you to accept now, and even some of you tremble in fear, but I tell you the truth: it will be much harder for those who must live hidden lives, than for those who come to Me early for their faith.

"In any case, I will be at your right hand and waiting for you to join Me in Eternity, where I have Joy Eternal planned for you, and you will forever be joined to me."

Taken from: **Evading Capture: Jesus Instructs Us**

"These times are rife with lies, distortions, theories and proclamations not from My mouth, and your faith is NOT one of confusion but one of clarity, joy and **peace.** Yet those who come to this channel have been fed by the world and have had their fill of the world, of religion and churchianity.

"They are looking for relationship not only from those who truly care and are real Christians, and take the time for them, but relationship with Me they can count on. Teach them those skills and refer them to videos that clarify those skills. Take the extra time to make sure that they've latched on to some solid food."

Taken from: **Feed My Lambs**

"Man has not learned his lesson. This second cleansing will accomplish much in the way of reverential fear of God. In the beginning of My reign, joy will reign supreme. But iniquity will again find it's way into the Earth and to the second Armageddon. That will put a final end to this strain of evil that lies dormant in the genetic make-up of man. Until then, it is a long journey with many ups and downs. And yet, many glorious stories to be told.

"Persevere, My holy people. Do not grow weary. There's an end in sight when Heaven will dwell in the Earth and all mankind shall worship Me and **peace** shall reign, even as if springing up from the very soil. Do not grieve. Keep your eyes on the shore."

Taken from: **Restoration Will Come**

"Your greatest safety is in holiness and refusing to judge others. Many have many opinions, and unfortunately much of what is proposed is opinion and not from Me. So remember your tools of discernment and if you are caused to lose your **peace** be wary; this is the enemy's number one form of attack.

"To continue to listen to those who detract from others is truly a leak in your vessel. The graces pour through that leak and are lost because of this serious fault. Judgment is Mine and your safest stance is to avoid these poisons and cleave to what is righteous and good, even showing mercy to your enemies - but not taking in their poison."

Taken from: **Resist Gossip & Judgment...**

"I wish for you all to stick together and be supportive of one another. This is the mark of My end times army: Brotherly Love. For however long you are here, I want you to advance in holiness, My Brides. Remember: it's not about prosperity, popularity, and power, but righteousness, **peace** and joy in My Holy Spirit in the midst of a corrupt and challenging world."

Taken from: **These Lite and Momentary Sufferings**

Poverty, Poor

"Call to mind the Muslim people as well, how devout many of them are, how I wish to have them for believers. Yet they have been crushed into submission from a tender age, they know not the meaning of Mercy or life. They only know murder and hatred as being the honorable life. Tragically these tender ones have lost all semblance of what I endowed them with, and are completely overtaken by a twisted lifestyle.

"**Poverty** calls to these, the enemy has made good use of **poverty** and bitterness, they are taught from childhood how honorable it is to die for their god. They know nothing of the truth and have been sealed over in terror from freedom of thought.

"To search out another god would be treachery against their parents, their nation, and their god. And so they shut their eyes tightly lest the light penetrate them. But in the watches of the night and in moments when they no longer have the power to resist, I open their eyes, I flood them with My love and My truth."

Taken from: **The Maroon Beret**

"I will enforce justice gently but as firmly as necessary to maintain individual rights. As I have said before, nothing will be lacking to anyone. **Poverty** will be extinct because in My world, no one will go without."

And I asked Him at that point, "Lord, won't that create an environment that leads to lukewarmness?"

"That's a very good question. It will for those who do not have wisdom. But part of your job will be to teach wisdom and self-control, that the souls I entrust to My Brides will grow up into their full potential.

"As you yourself have experienced, abundance is some kind of challenge - focus is easily lost when there is too much. But I will be sure to offer opportunities and resources that are not so much a symptom of over-abundance as they are a utility, providing for the continual expansion of a soul."

Taken from: **The World to Come**

"I am telling you (church pastors) this now, before it's too late. You must follow Me if you want a healthy church. You must preach as I lead you. You must worship in spirit and in truth, not in entertainment. There is very little time for you to get your house in order.

"Are you willing to lose everything to gain Me? Are you willing to leave or lose the six-figure income and live on the edge of **poverty** in order to lead My sheep into lush green pastures?

"Really, choose this day who you will serve, because the day is coming when the wood, hay and stubble will be devoured by the fire and those who have served their own agendas will be standing naked before Me and all the souls they lost."

Taken from: **Why Are People Leaving My Church**

"When I incarnated, I deliberately looked foolish: born to a lowly carpenter, raised up in **poverty** in one of the lowliest vocations of the day. I did this deliberately, because I wanted to be recognized by My Spirit, not My wealth.

"I could have made a grand entrance, impressing even the rulers of the day, but I came for those who were desperate, just like Heidi. (Baker) The ones that were trampled on every day by the ruthless Romans, not the ones taking their ease in palaces by oppressing the poor."

Taken from: **Violate Your Comfort Zone, Welcome to Mine**

Poverty, Poor

"This is why there is such brutality in the world. It begins in the hopelessness of **poverty** and abuse and culminates in torture and murder. These are the poor I have come to rescue. For too long Satan has had them subservient in fear to himself. I want to raise them up from this dung heap to dwell with Me in Heavenly places. This is My heart for every soul on Earth."

Taken from: **Why Temptations & Hope For You Who Are Lost**

"Truly, it's not the **poverty** alone that causes a soul to refuse My invitation. It is the stigma of **poverty** and the way you are looked upon daily when you reduce yourself to the status of a beggar and live solely on alms given even by women. So many find their self-worth in their possessions. When those are stripped, they feel that even their dignity has been stripped.

"As I have told you many times before, no man is worth more than the price I paid on Calvary for them. Each and every one cost Me the very life's blood of My body.

"Therefore, the rich and the poor are of equal value in My Kingdom. This is something that does not become apparent to most until after they die, and then they see their nakedness before Me."

Taken from: **The Way to His Heart and Intimacy in Prayer**

"So much has to take place, Clare, but understand that your prayers for mercy have and will soften the harshness of the judgment - so do not stop praying. There is still much to be averted. Hope in His Mercy, but know for certain that certain things must come to pass.

"Do not waste time, My Love. Make the best of what you have before you. I know your physical limitations, I know you can only do so much But I can do so much more if you will rely on Me and not your own devices. For instance, in this moment you came to Me in **poverty** of spirit and now you are seeing and hearing Me clearly.

"Always come to Me this way, even when you haven't indulged yourself. Always come to Me blind and naked and I will always reach over that barrier and touch you. Do you understand? Your **poverty** and littleness cry out to Me and I cannot resist you. It is the proud and self-satisfied I resist, but the little and weak I shed mercy upon."

Taken from: **Your Prayers Are Working**

I believe God's servants and ministers are the most overlooked group of people who work selflessly to help others.

They are not the 'hired hands' who run when the wolf attacks the flock. They day after day lay down their lives, their comforts and their agendas to protect those who have looked to them for encouragement in the drought, comfort in an uncaring and callous world, the truth of Jesus and His teachings in a confused and misinformed world. Their work reaches into the very heart of our lives and helps to keep us connected and healthy to the wellspring of life, Jesus Our Lord.

I believe that how we feel about the Lord is reflected in the way we treat His servants. Are they last on the list in our lives, or first? Do we show our gratefulness by seeing to their basic needs or do we just take them for granted and assume they are independently wealthy.

This is very funny and couldn't be further from the truth in our case. We used to live on less than 1/3 of the national **poverty** *level for the United States. In other words, think of the poorest people you know and consider what life on only one third of their income would be like - and that was us. But kind listeners have helped us and now we are even able to help the desperately poor on occasions.*

Taken from: **From the Vineyard, Wool From the Flock**

Poverty, Poor

"You will be instructed in healing, deliverance, infusions of knowledge, impartations and ordination, that you are fully equipped to bring all men to the knowledge of God and inspire them to release their lives to Me. Yes, you will harvest much fruit and lay the groundwork for a just Earth, where the **poor** are provided for, where corruption will not be tolerated, where greed and gain will be severely dealt with."

Taken from: **The Rapture, What You Will Experience**

"Woe to those who have planned the demise of the nations! Woe to you who trample the **poor** and are callous and deaf to their pleas! I am against, you says the Lord God, and I will use you for My purposes to be accomplished; but afterwards fling you into the dirt and shatter your fine veneers and pretenses 'till there be no trace of you on the face of the Earth - you and your families shall be no more.

"Then I shall establish My government and all peoples will rejoice from sea to sea. Peace will settle like an ocean, over all the Earth. And My government will uphold the rights of the **poor** and needy. My government will mete out justice. My government will restore the Earth to pristine purity. And all who call upon the name of the Lord will be saved."

Taken from: **We Are Drawing Closer and Closer to the End**

"By coming to Me and allowing Me to rearrange their thoughts about themselves. I heal their wounds. I dress them with kindness. I pray over them until they are restored. It is very hard, if not impossible, for anyone to lead others when they are carrying deep wounds in their hearts.

"And if they do lead, it is usually others who carry wounds similar to theirs that follow them. Misery does love company and wounded souls seek out the companionship of other wounded souls. They can either heal one another with Me living inside of them, or carry one another deeper into pits of resentment, jealousy, rejection. It is a root of rejection.

"Satan begins at a very early age in the childhood to cultivate that root and make ready for rebellion. What you learned as a new Christian is true, rejection opens the door for so many demons, especially rebellion. The broken and wounded are amongst the **poorest** and most needy souls and I hate having to correct them. But when they turn against others, wounding My Body, I must call the question."

Taken from: **A Bruised Reed...**

"So much harm has been done by the greedy and rich. They are literally eating the food off the plates of the poor; whereas I created the Earth rich in resources for all. **Poverty** was never necessary, although I have used famines to get the attention of My People when they went astray.'"

Taken from: **The Destruction of America – the Modern Day Ninevah**

"This is also where undeserved suffering finds its meaning. Souls born into heart-wrenching and cruel **poverty**, where there is no food and to stop their stomachs from hurting they eat clay. Children born into dysfunctional drug addicted families, in neighborhoods where only a small percentage of children survive the ravages of street gangs and illegal drugs. I have spoken with you all about this dynamic, where a soul makes a choice before birth and must live with that and die a premature death. These are things that will only be understood in Heaven, looking back. I share them with you so that you will not grow despondent over the suffering of others you cannot bring comfort to."

Taken from: **Suffering – Real Work in the Realm of the Spirit**

Prayer

"Yes, My Love, and the thing I most want to communicate to you is My unconditional love. You are in a human body, subject to forces beyond your understanding, but not beyond My power to shut down. So, there are times when you are tossed to and fro and buffeted, then there are times in **prayer,** when you dive deeper, and there you find the still waters and peace. Yet that is not an easy place to access. It is deeper and deeper away from the turbulent ocean currents, away from the surface winds, away from the storms and hurricanes. Yes, I have called you deeper, and deep calls unto deep."

Taken from: **Trust Me With Your Children...**

"And everyday you both get distracted. Seriously distracted. Wouldn't you like to be more productive, Clare, and feel more on target?"

Oh, I long for that, Jesus.

"Well, I am answering your **prayer** and the **prayers** of many on the Channel. The dark forces, the demons, have your number. They have a file a mile high on you and know precisely what action will most likely cause you to move in the direction they want you to move in. Which is ALWAYS off course. But when I am by your side and you are mindfully aware of My presence and help, I protect you from going the wrong way.

"I am especially, keenly aware of this in your lives now, My Children, because I have asked you to work for Me and for souls. What good employer does not guide and teach His employees in the best way to proceed? He has been at it for years and has learned by experience what works and what doesn't. He sees when you are overwhelmed and steps in to advise you.

"I am that 'good employer', if you will.

"I want to see you ending your day in thanksgiving to Me, saying, 'Thank You, Lord, not only for all the gifts You've given me, but for the help You gave me today. I truly feel fulfilled. Thank You.'

"To which I want to reply, 'You are welcome. It is My joy to be with you. Thank you for asking for My help and mindfully following My counsel."

Taken from: **Togetherness**

"In your courageous efforts to stay in unity on this Channel, you have opened the door for others to learn the meaning of the words, 'Love one another as I have loved you.' You have shown that on YouTube there can be a family of righteousness and brotherly love where backbiting, division, one-upmanship and undercutting one another is exposed as evil and not allowed.

"And as a result, even those who come here with malcontent are encouraged with kind words and **prayer** to draw closer to Me, lay down their rancor and embrace a different way full of peace and good fruits. A way where I welcome them into My arms...no matter how foul their past may be."

Taken from: **Lord, What Are You Doing With Us in This Hour?**

"I know you are all expecting Me soon and that is precisely where I have wanted you. All I ask now is to drop the tension and continue on in good works until the light of day is gone. By that, I mean, a time when no man can work, when the oppression is so dark, **prayer** is your only recourse.

"But now the day is with you. Now there are yet things to do."

Taken from: **Rest in Me Until I Carry You Over the Threshold of Eternity**

Prayer

"Yet what is done in love will shine eternally. Do not waste your time on big things that get attention and praise. Your little things done in love are what the true meaning of this life is made up of. Too many of you now are despairing about your wasted lives. Yet major time was spent hidden, in **prayer**, serving in ways the world considers subservient and unimportant."

Taken from: **Your Lowliness, Your Lives Thru My Eyes**

"Hold on. Hold on to the gifts I've given you. Hold on to the anointings hold on to the dreams and visions, hold on to our tender times together. Hold on, hold on. Do not let the enemy come in and dissuade you into unbelief.

"He is cruising to steal from you through anger, bitterness, resentment and foolish fears. When you feel those things rising in your emotions, it is the enemy stealing from you. He wants to take away your sweetness, your presence with Me, and the overflow I fill you with."

The Lord continued, "He loves to incite anger to drain you before you can even begin your day or finish a project or your **prayers**. He loves to lie in your ear, cause you to erupt into anger or fear and then drain you of all you had planned for the day and you run off to tend to these decoys. He is very clever and he knows which buttons to push, because his agents, the demons, are forever observing you and taking notes."

Taken from: **Sweet Aroma of Holiness, Jesus instructs us**

"It is, but I want you to understand what the makeup is of a soul who has put on the darkness as a choice in life. They actually find release in all forms of violence, sex, torture and as well as music and entertainment.

"Do you remember those times when someone cut you off in traffic and you had to control your actions and not retaliate in any way? Because now you belonged to Me and the flesh has been put to death. Before you belonged to Me, you got pleasure from such things. This is the same dynamic. Pleasure came with retaliation.

"I tell you these things, My People, because your **prayers** must be very serious and enduring to bring one out of this prison. The damage goes deep, the hatred is on the surface. Beneath are broken hearts, little children abused mercilessly, lost and crying out, no one to help. The only relief is in acting out or shutting themselves up in a stone prison. But once they escape that place, they are walking time-bombs."

Taken from: **Why a Soul Rejects Love**

"If they would say to Me, 'Jesus, Clare did not put a message up yet, would you please give me something to feed on from Your own hand?' I guarantee they will be quite surprised with what they come up with. Sitting quietly before Me, after communion, pen or computer in hand, pour your heart out to Me, My Brides. Speak tenderly to Me about your fears, insecurities, hurts and disappointments.

"And your joys, too! Thanksgiving is the key to My heart. I do so much for My own and yet they forget to thank Me. They take Me for granted like their husband of 30 years.

"No, no, no. I am fresh and new every morning and I long to be recognized as fresh and new. Even when I am suffering, I am still new and full of life everyday as you come to Me in **prayer**. I love listening to you as you pour your heart out. And I cannot prevent Myself from responding. I am so touched when you speak to me so candidly and expect to hear something back...even just a faint reply. How can I possibly pretend I am deaf?"

Taken from: **Nourishment Every Day**

Prayer

Some of you are warriors and have been created for such a time as this. For those of you who have been called to engage in the battle to restore our nation, the Lord wants you to know He is with you. You are not fighting alone. His arm is mighty and powerful, not only to make you invisible but to confuse and defeat the enemy. Begin all your battles with **prayer** *and end them with thanksgiving. Through you He is going to raise this nation from the ashes and restore her to righteousness.*

Don't let anyone belittle you. You were not negligent, you were chosen by Him to be warriors for righteousness and even to give witness to Jesus through martyrdom. Be courageous. Let no one demean you. Don't believe the enemy's lies, for he surely will torment you with lies to try and discourage you. Stand tall in the Lord; He is with you.

One other short point I need to make is that the Baptism of the Holy Spirit with the evidence of speaking in tongues, is THE weapon of choice for **prayer.** *When you* **pray** *in the Spirit, you speak the language of the Spirit of God and the very exact* **prayer** *that is needed in the situations you find yourself in. Do not allow the enemy to lie about this gift anymore; it is powerful and that's why he hates it and slanders it. Holy Spirit is* **praying** *the perfect* **prayer** *through you.*

Taken from: **Remember These Things & Remnant Church**

You know, in all things, I don't care what it is that we suffer. If it is sickness that doesn't yield to **prayer.** *I always pray and I'm glad to see sickness leave when I pray. It happens many times with Ezekiel and I, between the two of us. And* **pray** *against oppressions. But when something DOESN'T yield to* **prayer,** *we know the Lord is using that as a fast offering. And so, even this assault against Joy has been a fast offering, because I know the Lord is suffering great trials in His heart for the souls that He will never see again.*

Taken from: **Regaining Joy in Oppression**

| PRAYER

"My Brides, do not get entangled or embroiled in the injustices you suffer. Understand that you, too, in the past have been lacking in foresight and wisdom. You, too, have put the blame on innocent people; you, too, were blind to what I was in control of and allowing. You, too, failed to recognize the new and unusual movements of My Spirit in the midst of others.

"It is a sign of remarkable and Godly maturity to stand back and simply observe without becoming embroiled. **Pray** for your persecutors, **pray** deeply and from the heart. Soon enough, I will answer your **prayers**, when I am finished using them to perfect you."

Taken from: **Unforgiveness: A Gridlock on Grace, Jesus Teaching**

"But when you ask for more humility, well... that's a **prayer** I am always happy to answer."

Taken from: **Overcoming Failure & Do It Anyway 2**

"How important that is! How important even the littlest **prayer** is, but how much more important is **prayer** that contends with darkness for the victory. From now on, I want you to continue this routine that is building you up into who you are in Me. A communion service is so very important. Worship beforehand is good. You will feel when it is time to have the service and many times I will come to you and give the message afterwards."

Taken from: **Overcoming Failure & Do It Anyway 2**

"Know that your **prayers** stir the heart of My Father and will bring yet more mercies. Continue to **pray** for the world."

Taken from: **Mercy! Comet Will Only Graze Earth**

Prayer, Dwelling With Jesus

"I want to bring everyone back to **dwelling prayer.** This is the safe haven for your souls. It does not matter whether you see Me or not. No. Truly, it doesn't. What matters is your intention to be with Me in this way, to hold Me in your heart. Seeing and hearing Me, that's additional and will be given to you when I deem it necessary.

"Does that shock you My Love?"

A little, Lord.

"Well, I intended to tell you all this much earlier, but now it is a necessity for you all to understand. It isn't the result that matters, so much. It's your intention. 'Blessed is he/she who believes and has not seen.'

"For many of you this is a sacrifice, yet I know how to reward My servants and My Bride and wish for you to be very, very sensitive and observant and grateful for all I give you. Gratitude indeed opens the door for My Blessings. I know it is hard to be grateful when things are dry. I am well aware of your struggles with faith. I am, after all, right there beside you and within you.

"What I am looking for, My Brides, is true worship in spirit and in truth. I want you to ponder My miracles, My compassion, My mercy. When you connect with just one thing that is awesome to you, enter into My Heart with worship. Go there, go with that recognition of My Greatness. Ponder, ponder and ponder even more how wonderful I am. Allow that to carry you along through the breezeway of Divine Love. Swim, fly, soar up into the very heart of that thought and allow it to carry you into My Presence. You will find Me when you seek Me with ALL your heart.

"I am not an easy catch.

"I know the kind of love each and every one of you are capable of.

"I know the depths of your love. I am calling unto deep - 'deep calls unto deep' and the depths of My Love for you is calling unto the depths of your love for Me.

"I want to release you into the fullness of the Love you carry in your heart for Me...such transports as you have never known before. They are buried under layers and layers of sediment: years of pain, indifference, preoccupation with the world, disappointments in life, shattered dreams and things you have yet to understand and resolve in your hearts."

Taken from: **Your Past is in Our Way...**

"And My Bride, you understand, you have been with Me, you know the gnawing pain of separation I feel towards you. But this is a new season, with new longings that will lead to greater intimacy and faith. You will begin to feel My heart for those who are suffering and prayers authored by My Holy Spirit will bubble up from within you, as you bring petitions for them to Me.

"So, My counsel and message to you all today is to again grasp the rope of grace that is bringing you closer to Me. Make more time for Me. Pure, Holy and intimate time away from the hustle and bustle of the world. Use gentle **dwelling prayer** music and tuck away with Me and allow our hearts to be united in love. Do not run from your deeper feelings for Me.

"I will catch your tears in My crystal vase where the other tears from your life are stored. I will apply those tears to the suffering ones, especially those who do not know Me and have never conceived of having a pure, loving relationship with Me."

Taken from: **The Fragrance of Longing For Me Is Upon the World**

Prayer, Dwelling With Jesus

Ok, so that pretty much covers **Dwelling Prayer**. *We're dwelling with the Lord in our hearts. He's present to us at our right hand and in our hearts. But He doesn't always manifest in a way we can see Him, but we are dwelling with Him. Through Him we live and move and have our being and He's always present to us, always.*

I personally prefer the **Dwelling Prayer**, *because it comes into the Lord's presence through worship. And I feel that, that is a safer way to approach the spiritual, 'cause you're dealing with the spirit world. We're not dealing with one person walking into the room and talking to them, you're dealing with all the company that's around that person, the demons that are with that person, or if there aren't demons with that person.*

We deal with spiritual things. Our fight is not against flesh and blood, but spiritual powers of the air. So, when you are moving into the spiritual realm, you have to be careful that your motives are very pure.

This isn't just a fun trip! There needs to be a real, sincere desire to be close to the Lord and to worship Him and to pray. If you come into prayer to enjoy yourself, because it's a beautiful space or whatever, that's not a pure motive.

Taken from: **Experiencing Jesus in Dwelling Prayer**

I've had a few people ask us about our method of prayer, and how we've gotten so close to the Lord. We've done a whole playlist on that, with a bunch of teachings on it. The longest one is basically Scripture to establish the precedent through Scripture for the kind of prayer that we do pray.

But, just to clarify something - this is not soaking prayer. This is what we call **Dwelling Prayer.** *The prayer that we specially do and get so* *close to the Lord through is called* **Dwelling Prayer***. That's a term that I basically coined to clarify the difference between that and different types of prayer and soaking prayer, and so on.*

So, this is what **Dwelling Prayer** *is. Based on the Scriptures, the Lord lives in our hearts. He is the entrance, the gateway to Heaven. And so, what we do, we come into His presence with thanksgiving and praise, as is written in the Scriptures.*

We worship Him. And, as we're worshiping, we enter into our hearts spiritually, where he is present - and we worship Him there in our hearts. We use our imagination to some degree, just to get started to see the Lord, and He takes over pretty quickly. Basically, we worship the Lord in living and dwelling in our hearts.

There comes a time during worship where He would like to impart something special to us - so there's a kind of holy silence that comes over us. A very sweet and special peace that the Lord inundates us in. And, we stay there with Him and we dwell with Him in our hearts - we continue to dwell with Him, for it's written: If we obey Him, then He will dwell with us.

Taken from: **What is Dwelling Prayer?...**

And just as an aside here, I have always been more free-form in my worship, liturgy didn't come easy to me - proscribed prayers or order in prayer, that kind of thing. Even though...even **dwelling prayer** *has order to it.*

But I just tend to be more "go with the Spirit and flow" than actually follow any kind of format. But this has been - I could feel it - this has been building strength in me the last few days.

Taken from: **The Power You Possess & Strength for the Journey**

Prayer, Dwelling With Jesus

"Encourage them to have soaking or ***dwelling prayer*** and to reach out for My hand, to grasp. I will lead them skillfully and comfort them lovingly. But they must enter into an approachable prayer. Yes, praying on your knees in supplication is very effective, but much better to have a personal, intimate, holding-God's-hand relationship...then all the rest follows naturally.

"I want them to know that I love them, I'm approachable, I'm with them, they have a future. Whether they die now or live through the Tribulation, they still have a beautiful future. I want them to know that all is not lost, all is not ended. No, their lives are just beginning. And though it is a journey fraught with dangers, it will be deeply rewarding as they draw closer to Me, see My miracles, and experience the depth of My love for them. This is something they've been skating through all their lives and been avoiding. But now is the time for them to recognize that I am real. That I DO love them, and that I am with them."

We have a website called Heartdwellers.org and it's all about this interior life of **Dwelling Prayer** *and this intimacy with the Lord. So, what is my great joy and pleasure to begin to share with you is something the Lord did with me back in January - on the 2nd of January 2007.*

A very mature and seasoned, retired pastor had invited us for what's called, "soaking prayer". Which has... by some people become infamous, because it's been abused. Just like with some people, speaking in tongues has been abused. Legalism has been abused. Pharisee-ism has been abused. So, we don't judge a movement or something that could possibly be the work of the Holy Spirit by the abusers.

You know, men abuse, women abuse. We don't judge men and women by that. We look at what it is, for what it is. And if someone has taken it and abused it or misused it, then, that's a perversion. So, what we are talking about here is what the Lord is talking about in the Scriptures: w

We will make our dwelling with him. Or her.

What does that mean? What is a dwelling? It's a house. It's a place where you live. God lives inside of us. Inside of us! He's not out there, He's in here. It's another dimension. I'll let you in on a little secret: wherever God is, Heaven is.

And if you enter your heart, you enter into the Lord's heart, because your heart is His throne room - He sits in your heart like a King on His throne. If you go into your throne room in a quiet state of prayer and adoration, eventually God will reveal His manifest presence to you. You will see Him in an exterior way. He allows this to happen because we are so used to seeing things out here.

But we are beginning inside in our hearts, worshiping God and that establishes a communication of love and purity from creature to Creator. And when this happens on a continuous basis - that we make that kind of time for Him, to adore Him - eventually He begins to reveal Himself to us.

And He has to do that in a way that we can really accept and relate to. So, it's on the outside, so to speak. You're looking at Him, He's looking at you, He's talking to you, you're talking to Him. There is a dialog going on, there's deep feeling going on. There's a conviction going on that you are truly communicating with Jesus.

Taken from: **Dwelling Prayer**

That's why **Dwelling Prayer** *is so important. Because when you commune with the Lord on this deep, deep level, you're very sure of His presence within you, and it increases your faith tremendously, because you've experienced Him firsthand.*

Taken from: **Gift of Healing, Jesus gives us Point to Remember**

Pride

"This is NO time for giving in to the suggestions of the enemy. Do you understand? You are being used if you give in to the underhanded tactics, retaliation, **pride** and one up-man-ship. You have not known yourselves, nor have you known what is good and right if you do such things. Your survival depends on the ones around you. When you hurt them, you hurt and injure yourselves.

"I put you together in relationships to strengthen one another. When you injure each other, you injure yourselves - seriously. Every injury renders you incapacitated in some regard. What you do to another is far more injurious to yourself, revealing your lack of charity and love."

Taken from: **Outsmarting the Enemy & Preserving Your Soul**

"But there is a form of **pride** deadly to the soul. When you refuse to see how you, in the past, have failed and wounded others. When you refuse to see how you, in the present, are wounding others.

"When you elevate yourself above others and pridefully bury your head in the sand, refusing to see the truth about yourself, you are killing your soul and preparing the soil of your heart for a root of bitterness to grow deep and wide."

Taken from: **How a Root of Bitterness Can change Your Destiny and DNA**

"You worry so much about your mistakes and failures, but I am using them all. And in some instances, I deliberately allow them to humble you. I cannot pour My finest wine into cracked vessels: vessels cracked by judgment of others, harshness, un-teachable-ness, stubbornness, **pride** and self-will. First the vessel must be made whole and docile, then I can pour My finest wine through it."

Taken from: **There are No Losers in My Kingdom**

"In these last days, the enemy is making every attempt to divide and conquer. Not just your group or channel, but every single church that is true to My Word. Every single minister that is faithfully Mine is coming under monumental attack.

"Mostly by very inexperienced and unsuspecting Christians that have not yet learned to rule over their **pride**. They **pride** themselves on clever retorts but are much lacking in humility and experience. And so, those who are floating on the surface, and not diving deep for the Pearl of Great Price, are easily conquered by the enemy and used to divide and conquer others."

Taken from: **I Wanted to Go Fishing, But the Nets Were Torn 2**

So, Paul boasts about the power of God working through Him, but the main reason was to keep him humble. Every time I fail to fight off some kind of temptation, remorse follows on its heels and I am again humbled. So, if the Lord is not giving you the power to overcome your temptations, look to **pride***...look to judging others, look to lack of compassion and mercy. That's where I find my weaknesses and then I understand well, the Lord is humbling me. As soon as I get over myself...the temptations cease. Isn't that amazing??*

Taken from: **Victory Over Trials, Temptations & Spiritual Muscle**

"Do you see how foolish all your arguments are? Is this not the product of **pride** and a wish to Lord it over others with your version of righteousness? I tell you it is. There is none that is righteous, not even one. All of you have been made righteous by My Blood. Therefore, I would ask you to consider your estate without Me and set aside these foolish, foolish arguments that do nothing but create contentiousness and empty disputes."

Taken from: **My Feast Day vs. The Feast of Trumpets...**

Pride

"Yes, Truly I tell you, unless you change and become like little children you will never enter the Kingdom of Heaven. Matthew 18:3

"The simplicity of the Gospel can never be improved upon by the intellect of man. It only sows confusion and **pride**. That is why I prefer simple things best, things that bypass the intellect and lodge in the heart like a dart tipped with a drop of My sacrificial love. Once that finds its way into a man's heart, he knows right from wrong, good from evil and that is when the poison of self-will can do the most damage."

Taken from: **Wrap the Lost in the Blanket of My Love**

"I am calling you all to simple Brotherly Love. Please put aside rhetoric and squabbling over doctrines. It is so easy to be caught in the trap of **Pride** and Learning, but so very challenging to skip on past needless disputes and answer with love and graciousness, dwelling together in one accord on Earth even as it is in Heaven.

"I am not asking you to compromise, not in the least. But, I am asking you to use the superior tools for conversion: Love...not endless doctrinal arguments and disputes that only reveal the hypocrisy in My Church."

∼

"One little deed done in love for your brother surpasses thousands of deeds done for personal gain. Do you understand? Soon all these works done for the wrong motives, 99 percent of what the media endorses and makes a great issue out of, are totally worthless and will be burned in the fires when all things are weighed in My scales.

"When the very substance of things is examined: the motives, the results, all that is highly praised now in the world - will turn into a vapor. Yet what is done in love will shine eternally.

"Do not waste your time on big things that get attention and praise. Your little things done in love are what the true meaning of this life is made up of. Too many of you now are despairing about your wasted lives. Yet major time was spent hidden, in prayer, serving in ways the world considers subservient and unimportant.

"Yet these are the marks of My kings and queens in My Kingdom. These are the qualities that will qualify you to rein in the Millennial Kingdom. You have made a choice to do the right things for many years and that has earned you a place of anonymity, which is the safest place to be on this Earth.

"All that is done with a pure motive will stand. All that is done in vainglory will fall - it's just that simple."

And just to be sure, I looked up Vainglory: inordinate **pride** *in oneself or one's achievements; excessive vanity.*

Taken from: **Your Lowliness, Your Lives Thru My Eyes**

"Oh Clare, you have much to learn about the ways of these (evil) spirits.

"They never give up, Child. They are like opportunists...jackals on the prowl. Whatever they can accomplish before they are found out, they will do. They will try to trick you into seeing them instead of Me. Or trick you into hearing them instead of Me.

"I never allow that unless it is for a specific lesson. And you know from experience it is always **pride** and arrogance in serious situations that I correct you in this way, allowing them to replace Me, either in vision or speech."

Taken from: **How the Enemy Blocks Your Creativity...**

Pride

"The tribes of Israel in particular are referred to here, for they crucified their Messiah, and this will be the point of their breaking. Never again will the reins of **pride** rule My people. They will be humbled to the very lowest point. The greatest among them will see himself as the greatest sinner, for all the learning of the Scribes and Pharisees never prepared them for the reality of Who I Am. The entire system of righteousness through works will crumble and the prostitute will indeed enter the Kingdom ahead of them.

"Yet, I am not saying this to shame them, so great is My love for My People. I look forward with great longing to the day they realize I AM the heart of the Law and the fulfillment of all the prophets and all that is written. I am more than their Savior - I am the incarnation of the Living God. And through My life on this Earth I have demonstrated the substance of their faith and how I require them to live it."

Taken from: **The Rapture Event Will Be Visible...**

"Some of you I have allowed to fall because of your **pride**. It is better for you to see yourself as you are now while there is time to change. Some of you fell because you were not paying close attention. Some of you fell because you thought you were stronger or smarter - especially here on the channel. You couldn't understand how others could be so ugly and thought to yourselves, 'I will never do that.' Then curiosity led you to listen to their lies. The lies took root and undermined your faith in Me. They put cracks in the foundation."

Taken from: **The Enemy's Next Move Against You**

What I am saying here is that Satan is incredibly brilliant and knows exactly how to entrap you and control your thinking, steering you without your awareness of it. He knows how to set you up, how to parade lies before you that you'll swallow because you trust the source,

*and the source was not God. Or you are harboring unforgiveness
and these lies justify your feelings. He knows how to set you up to be
wounded so you will hate anything that even remotely reminds you of
those who wounded you, so you will carry bitterness and hatred around
for anything that smacks of that church or your past in it.*

*Yes, he is the master deceiver. And unless you take everything to the
Lord as a matter of habit and get His opinion, you may seriously be
deceived and not even have an inkling that you've been manipulated.
Most people do not know they have **pride** and do not know they are
being manipulated. That's just a fact. It takes Holy Spirit's intervention
and a very sincere soul to be able recognize pride in themselves.*

Taken from: **Is Satan Pulling Your Strings?**

"The Earth will be re-ordered: physically, electromagnetically, climate
and features. This will be man's doing, Clare. I never intended for this
comet to hit Earth. It will happen because ignorant men listened to
demons and allowed **pride** and greed to overrun their consciences,
thinking that if they destroyed 2/3 of humanity, somehow the Earth
would be a better place to live. (that is with nuclear war)

"Little did they know that filling Hell would cause the Earth to expand
and their underground cities would become their underground tombs."

Taken from: **War, Comet, Rapture, Treaty – Order of Events**

"Their frustration, their emptiness, their lost-ness as they grope blindly
along the way... So many times is a product of their **pride** because they
refuse to let go of what 'they know' in order to embrace the blind path
I wish to set them on...with only a little dog leading them."

Taken from: **Who You Are to Me**

Prisoners/Captives

"Others in families are still quite hardened. Leave them to Me. Put confidence in My promises to you and leave them in My capable hands. I alone understand the times and seasons for them to repent, and I am patient, endlessly patient. So place your hope firmly in Me and let them go. Don't fret - that only wastes energy rather take those thoughts **captive** and put your trust in Me. Those who put their trust in Me will never be put to shame."

Taken from: **Start Recognizing Your Enemy**

"When I look in on your household and see strife, bickering, jealousy and dissension, do you think I will make My abode there? As you lift yourselves up and tear down others, do you think My ears are eager to hear all about the slander, lies and calumnies of others? Did I not teach you not to display the faults of others or draw attention to what you, in your opinion, have judged to be wrong?

"Is it not My job to judge? Isn't this precisely what the Scribes and Pharisees did to Me? Did they not find fault continually with My teachings, telling Me I was destroying their faith and teaching error. Did I not heal a blind man on the Sabbath to expose their hypocrisy?

"Do any of these attitudes ring a bell, those who call yourselves by My Name? Then I will tell them plainly, **'I never knew you; depart from Me, you workers of lawlessness.' Matthew 7:23**

"Why do I say 'workers of lawlessness?' Because the heart of the law is Love. What you are doing is contrary to that law. You are not building up, making the way straight for Me. You are blowing up bridges and making men **captive** to your laws and legalisms, immersing them in judgment, self-righteousness and blinding error."

Taken from: **Lord, Why Are Things Falling Apart?**

The Lord continued here, "The most opportune time to escape government control will be immediately after the disasters, because many will be presumed to be dead. That will be before organization sets in, although that will happen very quickly as food, water and medical necessities will be offered through their agency and they will take down names and numbers for future reference. In this way, they can catalog very quickly who is still living. By offering necessities. Those who do not come forth, they will assume have been killed.

"They are relying on people's vulnerabilities for them to come forward for aid. Those who have no need for that will more easily escape being brought in **captive**. In fact, in many places that are feeding stations, people will be detained and placed in holding facilities. At first, this will look like benevolence on the part of the government, when in fact it is merely a way to dispose of them. Do not, under any circumstances, go forward for aid."

Taken from: **Evading Capture, Jesus Instructs Us**

*Yes, when you open yourself to Who He really is to you, how much He loves you, and you receive that love into your heart, not your head - then with all your heart you will begin to break with these sins that hurt Him and hurt you and have held you **captive**. But legalisms won't do it. Fear won't do it. Condemnation won't do it. Threats of hellfire won't do it! It's His LOVE - the ONLY power on Earth that will do it.*

Taken from: **The Invitation to Overcome Temptation**

"My people are **captive** in the desert of this world. I am leading them to the promised land of My Spirit, living in My Spirit... and the only giants they will have to fight are their own self-will and rebellion."

Taken from: **Dancing on the Waters of Adversity**

Prisoners/Captives

"My Brides, the hour is coming, when no man knows what is about to be unleashed on mankind. I can only say that I have been preparing you for this hour here and on other channels, and your faithfulness will be your deliverance. Foolish man has made plans under the cunning auspices of the prince of darkness. He has used their vanity and desire to be singular against them; it will be their undoing. Little do they know that they have planned their own undoing. Little do the know that, in some ways, I will save them from what is planned. They have nothing but scorn and contempt for Me, yet I still love them and wish to rescue them from total demise. Some will go on to that route in spite of My Loving admonitions and protection, taking their own lives when they discover what they have done.

"But, it is not My wish. I was there with them when they were little boy playing in the mud, making little tunnels, moving the earth, building pretend dams. I watched them play and discover the attributes of matter. They were taken into institutions and taught the ways of power and recognition, the 'no go' zones, the 'accolades' zones, as they matured into adults. Much was stolen from them. Innocence, a sense of wonder - replaced by power hungry institutions and think tanks. Now they are hopelessly **captive** to a system that is beyond their reach of understanding, because they no longer acknowledge Me."

Taken from: **Tipping Point, Evil is on the Rise…**

"A man's gift can bring his ruin, as you well know. I prefer to give gifts with maturity - to protect My children's integrity. I am explaining all this to you because you live in a society that is constantly pushing the limits electronically. There are many specters of control being used against you. By that, I mean energies being used by spirits and electronically to create chaos in the human mind and separate you from Me. That is why quiet time, worship and prayer are so important. Your spirit can very easily get out of alignment with Me once you are steeped in the doings of the world. That does include gaming and certain infused evils that are veiled under a mask of innocent fun. Gaming is very addictive, very dangerous and very deliberately corrupting the higher levels of human thought and desire.

"It is hard to explain, but I think you get the picture. There are many young people who are held **captive** in this alter reality of gaming. It takes over the mind and provides a means of escape from the pain of this world, without offering a way out of the trouble. You begin to live in the other reality, where it is safe, where you are in control and isolated from harm."

Taken from: **Jesus Speaks on The God Dimension & Video Games**

"When I first began these teachings, I was reaching out to the ones who fell between the cracks: the rejected, beaten down and misunderstood. But, now we must reach out to the churched who are held in the clutches of bondage to a system I never created.

"Now, many of My generals and lieutenants are **captive** in ritual Christian culture. Mind you, I did not say simply 'culture'. I love the cultures and the varieties of the whole Earth. I gave to each their own unique flavor and purpose on this earth and all are dear to Me. I want only to infuse them with My Spirit. Not with social correctness and cover-ups but with transparency and honesty, that they too have fallen short of the Glory of God. Not with rules and gates, but with Love, seeping from every pore of their being.

"I wish to reach the pastors of the churches that are dying. I want them to see why I have withdrawn My miraculous presence. Why people are leaving. Why they are luke-warm and worn out."

Taken from: **Come Out of Religion, Come Dwell in My Heart**

Prisoners/Captives

"Obedience is like a knight clothed in a full suit of stout armor, with his sword on a strong and spirited horse. Riding into battle, he surely has the advantage over his foes. Whereas, Disobedience is like a knight with no helmet, no armor and no sword, seated on a sorry nag of a horse. He will surely be unseated, dislodged and taken **captive**."

Taken from: **Tipping Point, Evil is on the Rise...**

"For those who will be taken in the Rapture, there is not one dream you have had from Me that will not be fulfilled. Every wonderful expectation and possibility, will find its fulfillment in Heaven. For I wish to see you rise into the beauty that lies dormant in your souls. Therefore, you will be richly provided for to accomplish things you have admired but never dreamt possible. So you, too, can be edified by this message.

"When I come to set the **captives** free, they don't file off to some refugee camp. No, they are brought into the courts of Heaven, given new bodies, new raiment, new tools, new training and new opportunities - and most important of all new love for Me and for mankind. Knowledge is infused, it pervades the atmosphere; you don't have to ask, you know. Talent is a given, to hear or imagine and to execute comes automatically, without a second thought."

Taken from: **From Glory to Glory**

Because you haven't encountered and cultivated the intimate love relationship with Jesus. You simply do not have the strength to overcome your sins... The Word of God and your resolve are not powerful enough. You need His Love and His Grace. Nothing trumps His love. When you experience His love and keep coming back for more, then you will conquer those sins. But unless you're the Iron Man, you're going to keep falling, because it's His Love that leads to repentance. As it is written,

"It is the kindness of God that leads you to repentance." Romans 2:4

Yes, when you open yourself to Who He really is to you, how much He loves you, and you receive that love into your heart, not your head - then with all your heart you will begin to break with these sins that hurt Him and hurt you and have held you **captive***. But legalisms won't do it. Fear won't do it. Condemnation won't do it. Threats of hellfire won't do it! It's His LOVE - the ONLY power on Earth that will do it.*

Taken from: **The Invitation to Overcome Temptation**

"May I remind you that you are not an animal with limited capabilities? You can break out of the rut and get your kernel while you hone your talent. I am telling you there is not much time left, but I am also encouraging you to follow those things which you yearn to do. Do not be **captive** in a run-of-the-mill boring job. Many of you have parents who gave up their dreams to put a roof over their heads. That is not something to repeat. That is passing on the dull gray status quo and a guaranteed boring life filled with dissatisfaction and long abandoned dreams as well as uncultivated talent."

Taken from: **Follow Your Dreams...**

Trailing behind these first were a vast multitude of other Christians who were **prisoners** of this army. They were all wounded, and were guarded by little demons of Fear. There seemed to be more **prisoners** than there were demons in the army. Surprisingly, these **prisoners** still had their swords and shields, but they did not use them. It was shocking to see that so many could be kept captive by so few of these little demons of Fear. These could have easily been destroyed or driven off if the **prisoners** had just used their weapons. - Rick Joyner

Taken from: **Start Recognizing Your Enemy, teaching from Jesus**

Protection, God's (My)

He continued, "But let's get back to what is important here, My Love. The focus must be on charity and virtue, trust and faith in My ability to provide. Without these pivotal attitudes, they will not succeed. **My protection** can make you invisible. **My protection** can turn wild beasts away. **My protection** can save you from the ground giving way beneath you. **My protection** can provide water and food when there is none. I can do all things, and I will, for those whose agenda is to gather in souls to the Kingdom. Those who give and lead unselfishly, those who are honest and caring for others, these are the ones I will supernaturally protect and provide for."

Taken from: **God Will Provide For Those Left Behind**

"What you read and heard and imagined from the report was indeed frightening beyond compare. However, remember that I am faithful and **My protection** was with these martyred souls. Even in the moments of great pain and anguish, torture and death I had already begun to lift them up and out of themselves, and their shining souls were so wrapped in ecstasy and heavenly bliss before My Face they felt nothing, fought nothing, and did nothing but glorify Me and My Name, with eyes turned Heavenward in a strong and powerful witness to the crowds."

Taken from: **Your Patience in Supporting Me, Why the Rapture was Delayed**

"It is by My Spirit alone that protection will be rendered to those left behind. Nothing of man's design will bring peace for families, only My ability to save and protect will be found effective - witness Ruby Ridge. My dear ones left behind, you cannot count on guns to protect you. You must turn wholeheartedly to Me and ask for **My protection**. I will protect you supernaturally if I am your only recourse. Those who live by the sword will die by the sword."

Taken from: **Surviving the Coming Tribulation**

"And of course, I have instructed you many times on the damage a soul does to themselves when they attack others. After a while, evil has taken over the once good Christian soul and I am forced to **remove My protection** and allow them to be sifted, according to the damage they have done. Then later, if they are sincere, I can restore them. But so often this habit of bitterness is a well worn groove in the hillside of life. It's a comfortable path with a familiar view...lifting the soul up above the others in the valley, feeding a subtle sense of superiority, that 'I am not like those below me.'

"This poison of pride removes them from the swift stream of grace that could have carried their life along to greater and greater accomplishments for Me."

Taken from: **New Onslaught of Demons Released...**

"For some of you Satan is counting on your past weaknesses to bring you all the way down, even into his pit --- were it possible. Now is the time to grow up, see others as fragile and needing much grace, and see yourself in My mirror. Yes, when I withdraw My protection and allow you to fall, My mirror will be there so you will see your faults are much greater than your brother or sisters. This is My gift of grace to you, I will show you who you are and who you aren't, and if you are wise you will never again lift your head to condemn another."

Taken from: **Refining Fires Are Coming...**

*Halloween is always a time of great, great darkness. And then of course, this is when they make curses, and after the full moon, that's when the curses land. So, the Lord is greater than any curse. He's our protection. His love and His grace and **His protection** is with us.*

Taken from: **I Will Restore Your Soul...**

Protection, God's (My)

"Just as in days gone by, when I supernaturally **protected** My people, so shall **I protect** those who must stay behind. There will be one among them who will be designated the leader, and to him or her, I will give supernatural knowledge and wisdom. Protect this one who is critical to your mission. Let not the devils cause division, misunderstanding, murmuring and jealousy. Be on your guard against these poisons they will use to divide and scatter you all.

"Together you will survive. Separated, you will face many dangers without anyone to back you up. Do not let them divide and conquer. Be smarter than the enemy, walk in charity and humility and you will have no problems. Walk in self-will, selfishness, suspicion, and rancor, it will be your demise. There will be many testings among the groups, many testings. Painful decisions to make, life or death decisions to make. I will give you peace when the decisions are the hardest. Use lots to help you determine a plan of action."

Taken from: **Jesus Speaks on Provision and Protection**

"Don't allow yourselves to be drawn off into vain reasonings, empty arguments, critical spirits. Oh, they have set landmines before you, My people. Your only hope is to lay low in humility, confessing **My Blood for protection** and refusing, and I do mean flat-out refusing, to be engaged in useless arguments that will cause your soul to fall into unrest and confusion. Little do they know, or expect, that I will strengthen you in **humility, your greatest protection**. As you remain vigilant and obedient, they will have no place to manifest."

Taken from: **February – A Month of Testings**

"The focus must be on charity and virtue, trust and faith in My ability to provide. Without these pivotal attitudes, they will not succeed. **My protection** can make you invisible. **My protection** can turn wild beasts away. **My protection** can save you from the ground giving way beneath you. **My protection** can provide water and food when there is none. I can do all things, and I will, for those whose agenda is to gather in souls to the Kingdom. Those who give and lead unselfishly, those who are honest and caring for others, these are the ones I will supernaturally protect and provide for.

"Many I will add to your numbers that need salvation. Their eternity is hanging in the balance and if you make their eternity your priority, I will cover you. Souls are going to be racked with confusion and fear, not knowing up from down, so severe will the trials be on the Earth. They will be so thoroughly disoriented that nothing can calm them down but a supernatural grace. A healing grace, laying hands on them and praying for My Peace to descend upon them."

Taken from: **Jesus Instructs the Left Behind: Put no Confidence in the Flesh**

"Continually check your motivation and clarity. When you feel your connection waning, that's opposition. Deal with it then and there, don't let it go any further. Yes, use **My Blood for protection** as well. Enlist the Holy Ones to cheer you on to the finish line. Does it not increase your resolve when others cheer you on? Just because the great cloud is not always visible, does not mean it is not there. Paul did not write that as a fanciful idea, rather he had heavenly visions and knew the Holy Ones were watching."

"Therefore, since we are surrounded by such a great cloud of witnesses, let us throw off every encumbrance and the sin that so easily entangles, and let us run with endurance the race set out for us. Let us fix our eyes on Jesus, the pioneer and perfector of our faith, who for the joy set before Him endured the cross, scorning its shame, and sat down at the right hand of the throne of God." Hebrews 12:1-2

Taken from: **How the Enemy Blocks Your Creativity**

Protection, God's (My)

Lord, I don't think it's fair that the rotten, corrupt people who have been controlling this country behind the scenes and bringing this all down on our heads...that they should have their way. After all, there is a faction of true Americans who are Christians and stand for what is right.

"That is why I am going to fight for them. You remember the rockets that were fired at Israel and were turned back in mid air and went out to the sea?"

I do.

"Well the same thing is going to happen at key moments, because of prayer. Your prayers and the prayers of others - this is going to happen over and over again until it is finished. Those who have gathered together in underground cities, I have called them there to their graves. There will be a purification of the evil in this nation.

"Yes, I will have justice. Deliberate crimes have been committed in this country with the end in mind that is the removal of **My protection.** Things such as abortion and gay rights, the training of guerrillas and other subversives to disrupt rightful governments around the world. All of this, plus the ruling elite. I am making an end to. Not one of them will escape My wrath. Not even one single one, including their offspring."

Taken from: **What Must Befall This Nation and The Earth**

The Lord began, "Where is your allegiance, My Bride? Are you willing to go into your prayer closets and comfort Me or will you be with the rest shopping, selling, and celebrating when it all comes down? Where will you be? In the ark or at the high places, paying tribute to the world? Where is your allegiance? Is it to me? To yourself? Or to the world and Satan? Where are the things that most matter to you? In the bank, with your family, your friends... or with Me? Where is your allegiance, My Bride? Where will you be when the flood waters suddenly rush in upon you?

"I'm calling you now to make that decision. I'm calling out to My Bride tearfully. Please, please come to Me. Come with Me into the ark of My love. There you will find Me suffering and there you will find **My protection**. Yes, I am suffering and I will continue to suffer until evil is no more. Yes, I weep over My Bride who has gone to the mall to sell herself - once again abandoning Me for the goods of this world.

"This is a simple message. There's nothing complex about it. I need your company and your comfort. I long to be held tenderly and loved. I long to have the salve of your sweet greetings meet My eyes. The purity of your voice lull me into a sleep, taking Me far away from what I must see and hear everyday.

"Please, My Bride, abandon your ways of the world in this holy season and come to Me into the secret place, the ark of My love. Nourish and tend to My wounds. Make Me forget the ones who have walked away cold-hearted, caring nothing for My plight. You have no idea what one glance from My Bride means to Me."

Taken from: **Prophetic Word For My Bride, Now or Never**

"**My protection** will always be there to fight for you. It surely is NO coincidence that you are being taught spiritual warfare as intensely as you are in this hour. This is quite deliberate on My part. You need these weapons. You need to reform your lives and hearts to receive **My full protection** from the enemy. Remember, if you are a light-bearer, Satan will try to snuff you out. So, in order to be a light-bearer, your hidden life must be as holy as what people see on the outside."

Taken from: **Ezekiel Snatched from The Jaws of Death**

Repentance

"Yet, I will have My pockets of survivors, those who have not bent the knee to Baal. I will protect them, but they will suffer much. They will be tried by fire and when I come - be found worthy. This will be a very small percentage of mankind. Your family will be among those survivors. Much of what you taught them growing up was preparation for this time. There will be much brokenness and **repentance** among them."

Taken from: **Jesus Speaks On: #1**

"There will be mass confusion and mass panic as the bombs fall. The disappearance of so many family members will cause some of them fatal heart attacks and suicides.

"However, there will be a remnant that will finally get off the fence and stand up to defend their rights. Too late. Their rights have already been taken away. What needs to be done now is to secure their future in Heaven: their salvation, their **repentance** and their total reliance on Me. Those who take up arms with a mind to do it on their own without My help will fail. Only those men and women who knew all along and belong to Me, are called by Me to defend what is right in this country, only they will succeed against all odds."

Taken from: **Jesus Speaks On: #10**

"I have labored hard and long with this generation to bring them to **repentance**. Even in this hour I have presented to them the science of My Creation to bring them to their senses. And yet they persist in their obstinate unbelief to satisfy careers in the scientific community and avoid the inevitable ridicule that comes with proclaiming My Name.

"And so here we are at a critical juncture in history and I must contend with those who would pretend to be God. Even as Satan longed to ascend the throne, they have longed to outdo Me or at the very least set themselves on equal terms with Me."

Taken from: **CERN, "I am God, There is None Other"**

"I am going to convict you of your motives this coming week. I am going to expose attitudes and habits that have hindered you and prevented you from becoming who you truly are in Me. Some things may come as a shock to you, when you see why you really do what you do.

"But this is for your own good. This is to remove more spots from your wedding gown. This is to bring you to **repentance**. And if any think more highly of themselves than they do of others, well, you will discover just how lowly you are. This is a good thing. For truly I lift up the humble but decrease the stature of the proud."

Taken from: **Honesty: Looking At Yourself in God's Mirror**

"Oh, how recklessly you have lived, inhabitants of the Earth. How blindly you have contrived plans hatched from the devils.

"Oh, how devoured you shall be by your selfishness in that hour. And yet I will have pity on those who call out to Me in that last moment of their lives. Those who see their blind selfishness in that hour?

"Yes, call to Me in profound **repentance** and I will save you. It is not My wish that you who have brought this calamity on mankind should perish in Hell for eternity. I do not wish this on even the most wicked among you. I continue to extend My invitation to Mercy for those who have being."

Taken from: **The Maroon Beret**

Repentance

"Don't worry - there will be a time for you to weep and wail. But, do you understand, My Brides, you have spent your whole lives weeping and wailing for the sins of the world. Am I then to subject you to their trials? No, I say unto you, I will not subject you in the same manner as those who have been blithely skipping along in this world, paying no heed to whom they are hurting by their lifestyles and manner of speech, by their sinful cultures and ignorance of all that is right and good.

"They shall have their turn, indeed. Their turn will bring them into **repentance** and to the foot of My altar of Grace. This is all I seek: that men should turn from the ways of Satan and live holy lives that begets a healthy, God-fearing society.

"This struggle between light and darkness has played out for centuries, and I am about to put a complete stop to it. No more degenerate generations corrupted by demon entities infiltrating society.

"At the very end, those who still have their allegiance to a bound and impotent demon god will arise and draw their like kind together... and I shall put a final end to them all."

Taken from: **Your Very Own Gift of Worship**

"Oh, how sad it is when a soul has closed the door on My Love and has nothing in this world to turn to. Alone, abandoned - many times through their own fault, they are so convinced of their own personal righteousness that there is no room for **repentance**.

"All is the fault of others - they were the' innocent victims'. God is to blame for everything."

Taken from: **Come to Me, My Lost & Lonely Ones**

"Indeed it is. There will be a stain on their garment that cannot be removed. There is a difference between malicious speech and ignorance. Those who knew My Spirit, and still took it upon themselves to denounce My Spirit... unless they repent, they will not go to Heaven.

"**Repentance** has to be complete, contrition must flow from the very core of their being for what they did to Me and to the people I could have brought into the Kingdom had they not denounced me.

"If they do not repent, they will not enter Heaven. If they do repent, they will enter Heaven with a stain on their garment."

Taken from: **The Unpardonable Sin...**

"So, in order to be emissaries of My Love, you must love yourself, and be comfortable with who you are - and who you are not. Where you've been, and where I am taking you - and where you are NOT going. There cannot be any dis-ease in your soul, and self-hate or abasement.

"Let Me explain it to you. There's a difference between humility and self-hatred. How can you love, when you're focused on hating yourself? It is My love for you that brings you to **repentance**, and the rejection of sin and evil." Romans 2:4

"It is well that you should hate these things. But, how can you hate what I love? I love YOU. So, how can you hate you? You can't. You shouldn't! It's NOT what I intended. If I wanted you to hate yourself, I wouldn't have come into the world to bring you eternal life. Rather, I'd bring eternal condemnation."

Taken from: **You Must Love Yourself Before You Can Love Your Brother**

Repentance

"For instance, most do not realize that if you agree with someone who is critical of another, you just opened the door and the demon who is waiting just stuck their foot in to pry it open more.

"That's why after a conversation that contains contamination like that, the vessel that heard it is prompted to pass it on. That makes their sin double and opens the door a little wider. Evil begets evil. Soon, the vessel is vexed by someone close to them and takes it upon themselves to criticize their spouse or best friend. They may feel a certain uncleanness at that moment, and most frequently that is where it stops. They become aware that My Spirit is grieved and they back up until they get to the root of where it all began.

"Oh Clare, you must be more careful, My Love. Please, please, stop detraction the very moment it is spoken. Say, 'I'm grieved by that, let's repent.' If your companion cannot recognize that, just walk away and leave it in My hands. You see, detraction leaves a mark, a wound on the soul of the one you are criticizing. In that wound, the infection of bitterness can easily take hold and spread throughout the body, putting them out of commission.

"The only remedy is their confession, **repentance** and coming to Me for healing. But often these souls don't recognize where the wound came from. So, it goes under cover, deeply infecting them. Later it may be revealed, 'So and so said this about you.' And that pain will ache acutely and you will recognize where that bitterness you were feeling came from."

Taken from: **New Onslaught of Demons Released...**

"My Brides, I am asking you to be very, very flexible and teachable. Some of you have escaped from Boxed religions surrounded by electric fences of fear. They have based their faith on the Scriptures as they understand them and are quick to accept the teachings of their forerunners in that denomination. In fact, that is used as a foundation upon which to build. Anything that threatens the tidy borders of that box must be dissected with Scripture and disproven; otherwise the survival of their denomination hangs in the balance.

"This is simply basic human behavior and wisdom. It doesn't mean people are bad, just limited. And I don't care how developed spiritually you think you are; you have your limitations, too. No one has all the answers, and all have fallen short of the glory of My Kingdom.

"This is why I insist that you taste the fruits. If the fruit is sour and bitter, you know error has crept in. Whether it be demonic or human, is not the point. When you cease to see **repentance**, conversion, commitment, peace and joy, you know you've lost Me somewhere along the line."

Taken from: **Divination vs. Authentic Intimacy with God**

"When you feel you must justify something to Me when you suspect I don't want you to have it, you know you've entered that dangerous, dark wood of demons stalking you because your armor of humility is down. Any time you contend with Me, your armor is down and the enemy can see it clearly.

"So, he takes careful aim, and unless you repent immediately, that arrow finds its mark in your heart and infection sets in. If you are not careful to immediately come to Me for surgery, it spreads throughout your body and off the track you go. And, if you continue and continue to go off course, they (the demons) begin plotting your way to disaster. That is why immediate **repentance** is so important."

Taken from: **Disobedience Brings Sorrow**

Righteousness

"I speak to the hearts of America that continue to hold the vision I inspired. Those who refused to sleep with foreigners, those who could not overcome the greedy ones who held dominance and sway over a shallow and gullible people bent on living for their comforts. I am with you. Go forward with courage.

"I, Myself, will be with you and in the end, what has been planned for you will come to nothing and again you will rise from the ashes to succor the whole world and be in accord with My Kingdom as it comes to free all men from the Oppressors.

"My peace be with you, sons and daughters of America, who hold to the vision of **righteousness.** Crippling blows shall you receive, but I will restore and find My pleasure in you once again as your country returns to Me. One Nation Under God. The God Who suffers with you, the God who loves you and bestowed great beauty on your land, and the God who surely will restore you. Hold fast to these words, for they are faithful and true."

Taken from: **The Death of America Revisited**

"Remember: it's not about prosperity, popularity, and power, but **righteousness**, peace and joy in My Holy Spirit in the midst of a corrupt and challenging world."

Taken from: **These Lite and Momentary Sufferings**

"It's all about how much do you love Me and how much will you give Me? How much are you willing to invest...even in the little time left to us? Abraham believed God and it was counted to him as **righteousness.** To act on what I have given you is to prove your faith in Me. ...dormant in a dark and dank basement under a pile of waste is almost unforgivable."

Taken from: **Make This Time Count**

"Please, My people, seek Me with all your hearts until you find Me. I am waiting for you, I will instruct you, I will love and heal you. And most of all, I will forgive you. Do not be afraid - I am for you, not against you. Anything you have heard about Me being a vengeful God is a twisted lie. To those who seek to do harm to others, yes, I intervene. But to the rest, I am a shield of **righteousness** against Satan and his wiles. And I will lead you in the paths of life and you will not fall prey to the great deceptions of this age. Seek Me and live."

Taken from: **Overcoming the Deceptions of This Age...**

"In your courageous efforts to stay in unity on this Channel, you have opened the door for others to learn the meaning of the words, 'Love one another as I have loved you.' You have shown that on YouTube there can be a family of **righteousness** and brotherly love where backbiting, division, one-upmanship and undercutting one another is exposed as evil and not allowed.

"And as a result, even those who come here with malcontent are encouraged with kind words and prayer to draw closer to Me, lay down their rancor and embrace a different way full of peace and good fruits. A way where I welcome them into My arms...no matter how foul their past may be."

Taken from: **Lord, What Are You Doing With Us in This Hour?**

"When people see your generosity in following My example, they are moved to come to Me; they see your motivation as Love for Me and your brother and that draws all men to Me. The abundant life is not meat and drink, but **righteousness**, peace - even in chaos, joy - even in suffering."

Taken from: **Miami Soon to be Bombed...**

Righteousness

"So, when you live your life by the world's standards you are walking in darkness, snuffing out your light and reflecting that which is deteriorating and bound for death. Oh, highly precious souls, imprint of the God Who created you, your worth is immeasurable! And nothing short of My death on the Cross can atone for your wayward ways and bring you back into the Light of eternity.

"What is needed from you is to walk in nakedness before man and God that your light might shine. When you discover My love for you and realize who you truly are in My presence, your value system changes immediately. What was once highly prized is seen for what it is: unclean rags hanging from your body. Like a leper, the contamination of the world smothers the light given you at conception.

"Open yourself to My Love. I am not like any man you have ever known; all are corrupt and lacking in authentic love. When I love you I do not mix My love with earthly values. I look at the beauty and uniqueness of My Father, whose substance formed you. And I long to redeem you from among this decaying world and have you in Heaven with Me for eternity.

"You have nothing to fear and nothing to hide from Me. Come to Me naked and I will clothe you in My **righteousness**."

Taken from: **Choose God & Sanctity or Self & Mediocrity**

"What I have planned for you, My Brides, will only be believed when it is seen. Yet even that will be twisted into something the enemy can use. Some, however, will be totally convinced and give their lives to Me. Especially those relatives of the Brides. You've been preparing your families for this, and there will be no escaping that this is truly the fulfillment of that prophecy. This event will leave a permanent imprint that will carry them all the way through until the end. There will no longer be any doubts that I am real and that I will return to rule. So many now cannot conceive of this, because they've been conditioned by the world. But this event will change all of that. Only the most hardened hearts will question what just took place, and will be eager to replace it with the world's explanation.

"This is why I resolved to make this a publicly visible event. All the tribes of the Earth will mourn."

At that time, the sign of the Son of Man will appear in Heaven and all the tribes of the Earth will mourn. They will see the Son of Man coming on the clouds of Heaven with power and great glory. Matt 24:30

"The tribes of Israel in particular are referred to here, for they crucified their Messiah, and this will be the point of their breaking. Never again will the reins of pride rule My people. They will be humbled to the very lowest point. The greatest among them will see himself as the greatest sinner, for all the learning of the Scribes and Pharisees never prepared them for the reality of Who I Am. The entire system of **righteousness** through works will crumble and the prostitute will indeed enter the Kingdom ahead of them."

Taken from: **The Rapture Event Will Be Visible...**

"The soul who is humble and loves others more than themselves, is the soul who sees clearly. The devils may try to blind you, but because you are committed to **righteousness,** they do not succeed. Sooner or later there is a witness in your conscience that something is not right. When you stop to examine this, that is when you find the fingerprints of the enemy. But if you insist on your way, and dismiss the voices of those sent to assist you, you will fail."

Taken from: **How to Handle an Assignment of Division**

Righteousness

Some of you are warriors and have been created for such a time as this. For those of you who have been called to engage in the battle to restore our nation, the Lord wants you to know He is with you. You are not fighting alone. His arm is mighty and powerful, not only to make you invisible but to confuse and defeat the enemy. Begin all your battles with prayer and end them with thanksgiving. Through you He is going to raise this nation from the ashes and restore her to **righteousness**.

Don't let anyone belittle you. You were not negligent, you were chosen by Him to be warriors for **righteousness** *and even to give witness to Jesus through martyrdom. Be courageous. Let no one demean you. Don't believe the enemy's lies, for he surely will torment you with lies to try and discourage you. Stand tall in the Lord; He is with you.*

Taken from: **Remember These Things & Remnant Church**

"And in an instant, in the twinkling of an eye, with the blast of the Trump of God, I will call to My Bride saying, 'COME UP HITHER!' The dead in Me will come swiftly out of their graves, wearing their robes of **righteousness**. Then you, the living faithful, will be gloriously changed. You shall be caught up to meet Me in the air, and thus shall you be with Me unceasingly!"

Taken from: **Be Vigilant, Protect Your Fruit**

"I will come and restore national sovereignty and the faith of the nations will acknowledge Me as their savior and ruler. We will enjoy unprecedented peace for as long as the enemy is kept at bay. You will learn the ways of laughter and joy, especially in those places that have been most heavily oppressed and deprived.

"All will enjoy an equitable standard of living and justice will reign. Keep your eyes on this goal, My Beloved ones. And for you who are reading this after the Rapture, keep it in mind: joy is coming after this long trial, joy and true prosperity of spirit and life is coming. Do not despair, for at the darkest hour I will come and restore **righteousness** to this Earth. In the meantime, cleave to Me, learn and follow My ways alone. Man's ways are futile and only lead to death. This world is now living the results of man's ways. That is why I entreat you to follow My ways no matter what the cost."

Taken from: **Resist Gossip & Judgment...**

"Rather concern yourselves with fulfilling My will and all **righteousness.** When you see the naked and poor, be like My Father to them; clothe and feed and meet their needs. Do you not know that to the degree you care for My needs, I will care for yours?"

Taken from: **Weapon Against Anxiety...**

For one, right now the Lord is calling for fast offerings to turn the evil plans of the powers-that-be in this country, to prevent the elections and cause martial law in America. He has told me that many, many attempts would be made to stop them from happening, but that if we continued to pray, fast and offer Him our sufferings - whether they be financial or physical or family related - any suffering we are undergoing can be offered to stop this evil government from getting control for the next four years. Anything, anything, anything. If it hurts, offer it.

*And so while we are being purified, supernatural levers of grace are being raised to prevent catastrophe, and the death knell for America. Oh, the divine economy of Heaven is totally amazing and efficient down to the very last tear. So, take heart; these sufferings are going to bring forth a harvest of **righteousness** as well as a purification of our hearts.*

Taken from: **Holy Trials, Holy Fruit, Stand in the Gap for America**

Sacrifice

I have a dear friend who is struggling right now to understand the Lord's will for healing. As I was thinking about her and praying for her, the Lord began to speak to me.

"Tell her for Me that she can take back the gift of her entire will and being that she gave Me, and then be prayed for to recover. But until she does that, I will take her at her word. The yielding up of a soul's health is one of the most treasured gifts they can give Me. I receive it with extreme tenderness and devotion, knowing well the price of such a gift. Yes, knowing well.

"My Love, do not be tormented by these questions, do not allow your mind to be cluttered because others do not possess this truth from the Gospels. Did I veil the Cross in secret meanings only for a few?

"No, I launched it up into the sky for all to see, and then I mandated that those who love Me should follow after Me, being willing to surrender their entire lives and the happiness this world can give them - for Me. In return is the honor to labor with Me for souls."

And here I'm just citing **Colossians 3:24 Now I rejoice in what I am suffering for you, and I fill up my flesh what is still lacking in regard to Christ's afflictions, for the sake of His Body, which is the Church.**

"This is not an honor bestowed on anyone," He continues. "These souls are carefully chosen by Me, because of their sincere love for Me and for humanity. Yet, they have been endowed with free will, and can take the gift of themselves back at any time. It's up to them. Do you love Me? Feed My sheep. Yes, if you love Me you will shed even your very own blood for My lambs.

"These are extraordinary times, and they call for extraordinary love - a love that says 'Yes' to all I require of it. And yet, you know the benefits of this holy exchange and I know you wouldn't trade it for the world.

And your friend is such a soul as yourself. She will not take back what she gave Me - the very thought will pierce her heart. So then, she must learn to live with it, asking for strength every day."

I'm reminded of Paul's thorn, here, that he had to live with every day, even though he asked for it to be removed so many times.

He continues: "I know what is necessary today, and every day, according to My needs for souls - the co-laborers, the **sacrifices** I require of them. Some days are more demanding than others."

Taken from: **Carrying the Cross of Sickness...**

My husband Ezekiel has been carrying a cross, he's been carrying something and I said to the Lord, "Please comfort him, Lord. Please pull Him out of the place that he's in.

"My Love, he is carrying a very heavy cross for Me right now. Shall I remove it from him?"

Well, no. Perhaps if I explain that, he will carry it with more confidence. (And he is carrying it very peacefully, but I know it hurts.)

"Perhaps. But he has offered himself to Me as a total **sacrifice** so many times, and I rejoice to share with him what I must endure on behalf of souls."

But Lord, I thought you endured all that on the cross.

"Sins, yes - but the dynamics of brewing situations, no. There is much tension in Heaven right now as well. We are all on the edge of our seats, so to speak."

Taken from: **Jesus Answers His Bride...**

Sacrifice

At that point, I kinda ran out of things to say, and the Lord said very softly and gently:

"Do you want Me to speak now?"

Oh, Yes Lord, please.

"What you have discovered tonight is the true secret of happiness. All roads lead to home, right here." He pointed to His Heart. "That emptiness, that vacuum that all of you are experiencing, that intense desire for the Rapture... all of you are longing for this simple one-on-one loving relationship, where we are forever together and even at death (for those who will die) even more so.

"So we will never, ever be separated. There may be times when you hurt Me, and I am very quiet, but other than that I need and want to be with you, accepted by you as the love of your life. Someone you can trust with being relaxed and your true self. There may be times of **sacrifice** when you do not hear or see me, because I am using your suffering to help another soul. But this relationship is that God-shaped place within you: no one, no thing, ever will bring satisfaction to that void that exists in your heart.

"That is why you are longing so much for this relationship that Clare and I have, because I made you to want it. And it is beginning to dawn on you that religion has robbed you of this precious, precious knowledge of Me."

Taken from: **Count the Cost...**

"I want souls to recognize Me by My respect for others. This is something you can do for Me. Lack of respect has led to terrible downgrading and a sense of loss and uselessness.

"It is even assumed that I don't respect the rights of every man, woman and child. It is not understood that equipping you with free will was a tremendous *sacrifice* on My part, because I wanted you to choose Me out of love, freely, not like a slave who has no choice."

Taken from: **Jesus Asks Us to Have Uncommon Respect**

"Didn't you expect it to get much worse before My Coming for you? Well, believe Me, I am spreading it around - that is why there is so much sadness and fear in the world right now. But cheer up, it won't be long."

Oh, Jesus! It is so horrendous what is being done to these babies, please, oh Lord, God... please intervene on their behalf.

And I know Ezekiel stood in prayer for hours tonight on behalf of these little children.

The Lord answered me, "You know that this was arranged before they came to Earth, do you not?"

Oh, Lord, I hadn't even thought of it.

"Well, it was. What is different is the suffering I am sparing them through the intercession of saints all over the world and they're shouldering this cross with great love and devotion."

So, what He's saying here is - again, I've done a teaching on this - He's told me before that when a soul chooses to come to Earth, they are aware of the **sacrifices** *they're going to have to make and the suffering. I know it's impossible to believe that a pure soul would choose this kind of suffering, but some of them do.*

Taken from: **Terrors of ISIS, Please Intercede**

Sacrifice

"I didn't say it would be easy, even if I help you, but I can make you stronger. We all have a cross to bear. All. Including Me. I am still carrying a cross for humanity. There is no getting away from it as long as there is contention in the Body, accusation, pain of any kind, or even one unsaved soul.

"Because we are united as One, the grace of supporting the work that delivers salvation to souls is spread around so that no one person must carry the brunt of it. I did the major work of opening the doors of Heaven and paying the price. Now you must keep the soil well tilled, planted, watered and protected, until the Harvest. This requires hard work and **sacrifice**. With it comes suffering and burdens, which are distributed among the Body according to the capacity of each one."

Taken from: **The Yoke of Marriage in Ministry**

"You can see this dynamic at work in Heidi and Roland Baker's life, in Graham and Theresa Cooke's life. There is a ministry there and both are contributing and supporting it. Although it seems like only one is, in reality the hidden partner carries the heaviest burden. This is greatly misunderstood by the Body as it is now. The sickness in the other partner's life is looked at either as retaliation by Satan or punishment for some hidden sin, perhaps even unbelief.

"What a lie this is!!! The silent, suffering partner is backing up the public partner's ministry, holding them up even as Ezekiel is praying behind you right now. This agreement is in the Spirit, and rarely recognized in the consciousness. But, there is mutual growth in love, selfless **sacrifice** and humility. In Heaven, both will be rewarded equally."

Taken from: **The Yoke of Marriage in Ministry**

"She was a mother. A mother to this women and those who watched her network. She was a woman of prayer, leading a life of obedience, **sacrifice** and total commitment to Me. She was well disposed to get her prayers answered. The woman who came to her was humbled in her marriage, she was also a soul who made it a point to look out for others financially and to pray for them. By her disposition of soul and her faithfulness to Me, she also was well disposed to have her prayers answered. Both souls, giving and receiving, were in a state of grace with Me. I don't always say 'yes' but in this case it was merited."

Taken from: **When A Sigh IS Prayer...**

"Your prayers are powerful. They do not bounce off the ceiling as the enemy would have you believe. No, every single prayer is presented in Heaven as a sweet smelling **sacrifice**, every single prayer. The enemy will discourage you from prayer if you let him, in the same way he discourages you about yourself. They spend all their time running around lying. If they are not permitted to do physical harm, they will at the very least convince gullible souls that their prayers are a waste of time. Do not allow yourselves to be victimized by such as these."

Taken from: **Pray For Mercy & More Time...**

"Nothing is too small to be regarded as an offering. Nothing. The loss of a beloved pet, altercations at school, toothaches. All of these things, when offered together, all through this nation are tremendously powerful. And as My Father looks upon your **sacrifices** and offerings, His heart is moved to pity and more angels are dispatched, more graces, more protection for the candidates. Everything is increased with the tears of My People."

Taken from: **The Election: Jesus calls for "War Spiritually"**

Salvation

We believe that the Lord did all the work necessary for each soul's **salvation,** *on the cross, but someone must carry the message, and for this back up prayers, fasts and other offerings act as a catalyst to release the graces they need in the mission field. It has been our experience that when we have labored for a soul and they do not accept the grace, (wow, that's painful...) the Lord in His perfect economy of* **salvation***, gives the grace to a soul that is ready to accept it, so that even those who are far removed from the mission field, by their offerings assist those who are out there laboring.*

Taken from: **Homeruns for Heaven...**

"Those who are well equipped and prepared will have no advantage over those who have put their total trust in Me. There will be times when I will prompt you to do something that seems out of order, but it will be your **salvation**. Prayer will be your weapon, a weapon that no one and nothing can defeat. Pray in tongues. Much wisdom will infuse your minds and bypass your intellects, which have been trained in the thoughts of the world. My ways are not your ways, My ways are not the world's ways.

"Prayer will be your greatest weapon. Pray and listen very carefully. Expect Me to instruct you, give you visions, answers, understanding. Expect it and learn to discern it early. The sooner you embrace this wisdom, the safer you will be. I will lead you and teach you the way you should go."

Taken from: **Jesus Speaks What is to Come #3 & 4**

"However, there will be a remnant that will finally get off the fence and stand up to defend their rights. Too late. Their rights have already been taken away. What needs to be done now is to secure their future in Heaven: their **salvation,** their repentance and their total reliance on Me. Those who take up arms with a mind to do it on their own without

My help will fail. Only those men and women who knew all along and belong to Me, are called by Me to defend what is right in this country, only they will succeed against all odds."

Taken from: **Jesus Speaks on What is to Come #10**

"Moving on...You will all be tested in charity and forgiveness, open your hearts wide for sinners and especially the ones I send you, embrace them with love and forgiveness, pray for their **salvation.** Truly they are pitiable. Many of these I send you because they have no one else to pray for them on this Earth. But I know you will, so they come across your path. Dear Ones, I need prayers for the difficult personalities."

Taken from: **Jesus Speaks on What is to Come #10**

"Yet, there are others who will feed on soap operas, live to spend money in the malls and impress their peers and allow their children to do as they please, because they don't want strife in their families. Them, I can not take in the Rapture. These are all signs that they love the World more than they Love Me, so I can not take them. Do you get the picture?"

Yes, Lord, I do.

"In addition to that, there are many whose **salvation** is hanging in the balance, and were the world to crumble overnight (which it will when the Bride is removed) they will go the path of least resistance or will die in the events, unrepentant. I'm juggling all these factors in the decisions We're making, and We are intervening in world affairs to hold back the worst until it is time. So, I desperately need your cooperation, fasts, prayers, amendment of life, bringing truth to those around you and praying for their conversion."

Taken from: **Rapture Drills are Purifying My Brides**

Salvation

"There are needs, and all (in Heaven) are constantly serving the needs of those on Earth. Prayers being offered, healings are happening, music is being imparted straight from Heaven. There are no needs for the citizens of Heaven, all needs are met abundantly. But those on Earth, and in transition to coming here, they have needs that the angels and saints see to. That is something I will not go into detail about at this time. Suffice it to say, all are very alive and focused on the work entailed in ministering **salvation** to souls, the **salvation** I accomplished on the Cross."

Taken from: **Heaven: Jesus Shares About Worship, Food and Recreation**

"In the meantime, there are suffering souls that need the light to shine on their darkness so they may be lifted up to Me. Many are the sufferings of the lost and My heart is to bring them **salvation** from their enemies, and from themselves.

"Deep and dark is the pit they have dug for themselves. As the saying goes, 'If you want to get out of the pit, stop digging'. I say stop sinning and take hold of the rope of Grace. I am lowering it now into your life. Come forth out of this pit, this deep darkness and let the sun shine all around you. I have a new life in Me to give you. This life will be full of gifts and challenges, but it will not be fruitless as your former lives have been. No, this life will bring you the peace you have never had, a sense of purpose, a sense of destiny that speaks to the very core of your being. Yes, I have waited for you. I have waited, holding all these gifts for that special day when you will forsake yourself, and come to Me."

Taken from: **Rope of Grace Teaching**

"Do you know that there are actually some on this channel who have given their lives to Me because they have listened to your conversations, and been edified and inspired to approach Me? And

---

after you prepared their hearts, I indeed came to them. Just by this small, insignificant act you have brought them safely into the harbor of **salvation**.

"Souls do not need to be pounded into the ground with Scriptures. They are already face-down in the dirt, hating themselves, and so loaded down with years of condemnation, they really don't believe anyone could ever love them. No, they need you to rush to their side, lift them up, help them stand, dust them off, and like the good Samaritan, clean their wounds with the finest salve and carry them in your prayers -just as surely as the donkey carried them to the inn, where they could be fed and recuperate. That's the response I'm longing to see on this channel, for those who come here wounded and sin sick.

"You have only to ask, and I will give you My heart for them. I will equip you with that costly salve, made from My own body and blood. Their wounds will heal, and they will in turn succor others. This is how the Kingdom of God comes: one, by one, by one. It's the little things that matter most. The seemingly insignificant response to a post that reveals the true Presence of the One True God who is Love."

Taken from: **Minister My Love on This Channel**

Well, Lord... When they lose all these things and can no longer work long hours to maintain them, they will have more time for You, right?

"That's part of it. Simply by force of habit, time will be broken open to them to spend in other ways than making money and shopping. This is where, hopefully, I can enter and offer them **salvation** and a life full of meaning rather than a life full of emptiness. This is My Mercy in action, Clare."

Taken from: **This is a Time of Preparation**

Salvation

"This peace will be hard won by the blood of many and will in its nature only be temporary until the final Judgment. Then peace shall reign forever. So, what I want to say is that peacemakers most resemble Me, and the contrast to that is the troublemakers that most resemble Satan. That is why I called the religious leaders a brood of vipers.

"They pretended peace on the outside with long, flowing garments woven with golden tassels, but inside they were ravening wolves, seeking how to destroy anyone or anything that challenged their authority and rule. Absolute power corrupts and absolute power was what they were seeking. They threatened men with their eternal **salvation** if they dared to challenge them.

"Things have not changed one iota. Fear is still used by religious authorities masquerading as messengers and protectors of truth."

Taken from: **Blessed Are the Peacemakers Who Keep Up Their Guard**

"Some of you on this channel only came to the Lord a couple of months ago. You can thank the saints on earth for their prayers, they are the ones who forestalled the searing judgment on this earth. And I still have My hand raised in the forestalled position because I see so many only a footstep away."

But Lord wasn't it You that told me a date had been set?

"I did. It has come and gone because of My Mercy. There are layers of **salvation** taking place. One group comes into the Kingdom, another group (very often related to them) follows. Wave after wave of **salvation**. But there is soon coming a time when that will end. I want it to go on forever. This is where I wish for your heart to be."

Taken from: **Have I Delayed the Rapture? Jesus speaks on the delays**

"Many of you have turned your hearts to those around you who are still in need of **salvation** and for that I am profoundly grateful. Some have even seen breakthroughs with people they thought would be the very last to respond to kindness and My message. You may not see results now but you have planted seeds and I will send others to water.

"Others have said ejaculatory prayers, very simply crying out to Me,' Lord, save them!' And this, too, will bring forth fruit."

Taken from: **Touch Others Tenderly For Me...**

"As you go about your days, ask some people, 'How do you feel about God? And what do you think He feels about you?' This is the perfect way to begin a non---threatening conversation that can end in restoration and salvation for a soul who felt themselves forsaken a long, long time ago and has just buried the thought of having a friendship with Me."

Taken from: **Water Your Gifts...**

"The decision to grow in beauty and holiness, or shrivel up into ugliness and evil, is entirely up to you. I warn you in your conscience not to do something, because I know how it will affect you as well as others. And My heart is for you to be holy. When you connect with evil, you partner with demons and they continue to lead you into wickedness, until you are beyond repentance and destined for Hell. You object and say to Me, 'Oh, no! Never me. I'm not going to Hell - I'm a good person, after all.' You may have been good at some point... although good does not guarantee **salvation**. But when you FIRST decided to compromise with the Truth and go against your conscience, where I advise you, you turned and started downwards."

Taken from: **Outsmarting the Enemy & Preserving Your Soul**

Seeds from Demons

"Today Clare was hit with Grief and Sorrow. Previously, Ezekiel was and many, many of you on the channel have experienced that. Now, I want to make clear that I do allow sufferings for aiding in the salvation of souls. And right now We are experiencing a tremendous influx of conversions from the Middle Eastern peoples who have been misplaced I am talking about authentic conversions. So, you may need to be carrying a burden for them.

"Grief and Sorrow are very powerful deterrents to keep you from exercising your gifts or even taking care of your duties. It can come from outside circumstances or infighting that should have been avoided by yielding to another. When you have these feelings and there is no substantial reason behind them, it is good to suspect demonic assignments.

"It is also very good to search for an open door. Were you Critical? Disrespectful? Ungrateful? These attitudes begin as little **seeds** which quickly grow roots and spread down into the soil of your souls. If they are not immediately neutralized by repentance and apology, they take root. You brood and even fall into self-pity and they spread their fibers like a cancer. Soon, a breakthrough into the evil realm is made and a door has been created through which they may come and go.

"They are vicious and care only for one thing: destruction of all that is good in you and your relationship. This is where great wisdom and determination are required to avoid this trap, to avoid the sowing of the **seeds** of discord. One may yield to the other, but have serious, hidden resentments that have been building up over the years. And so, no matter how much you apologize or they apologize, there is a long-standing history of injury that easily reopens the previous, deep, emotional wound, allowing your very life force to slip away into the hands of these demons."

Taken from: **Spiritual Warfare: 1 - Enemy Tactics**

I want to tell you that attacks against us are going to ramp up. The Lord is warning us. So, the solution is not to just wait out the storm and hope for better days. No, the solution is to take authority over those outside forces and demonic **seeds** *of bitterness that are sent to enter our hearts and take root.*

Some people think that curses cannot land on Christians. Well, that is not our experience. This is what we see. If I am not walking in supernatural virtue, charity and patience, I may react in my flesh to something.

Here are two examples. One was, as I had mentioned, an attack against my time and concentration for the channel. Curses are sent to us every single day, sometimes several times a day. I am finding out that they hang in the air until I enable them by lack of virtue. So, instead of brotherly love, let's say I get angry - well that demon of anger with a **seed** *of bitterness is now permitted to land, and the bitter* **seed** *that will grow to be quite large goes down into my heart.*

So, the principle is that if you are cursed with anger and jealousy, you are safe until you get angry or jealous, then the curse can land.

I became aware of these two negative feelings and repented of them but it was already too late - it was a day later, and the **seed** *of bitterness had already taken root in my heart.*

I'm telling you about all of this so that you will understand. Normally, if there's no sin involved, curses don't land unless you enable them by negative emotions. And who can control those? It does seem unfair, really, and that's where the bitterness can enter in. But it's not unfair, because we are told to "rejoice in the Lord always, and again I say rejoice!" A heart of thanksgiving and worship is the surest protection against these ugly things landing.

Taken from: **Spiritual Warfare 12 - Curses and Assignments..**

Seeds from Demons

Finally, I got some serious intercession and deliverance and after repenting for bitterness, was released of the seeds of bitterness. So, the curses entailed very dark, negative, paralyzing emotions, which I never would have had if I had responded in faith and trusting in God's perfect merciful will.

*Along with these dark feelings came **seeds** of bitterness. They are merely tiny black things, no bigger than a celery seed, that immediately take root if you feed them. They grow to a large black blob and then a whole network of branches if you are not relieved of them through repentance and faith in God's mercy.*

$\sim$

"This is a mighty task, My People. Staying in worship, prayer and thanksgiving is a habit that must be cultivated if you are to escape the snares of the enemy. Bitterness is indeed a poison to your body, soul and spirit. If you are to stay healthy in all areas, ask Me to reveal to you the **seeds** of bitterness that have grown into a thorny bush, choking out the holy life you hunger for.

"Did I not say, **"The seeds that fell among the thorns are those who hear, but as they go on their way, they are choked by the worries, riches, and pleasures of this life, and their fruit does not mature. "**Luke 8:14

"Those thorn bushes are from the **seeds** of bitterness and unfulfilled lusts for things: 'I never have enough. Why couldn't it be of a better quality? That's not the color I wanted. That's cheaply made. That's too expensive. Why does so and so have a better one? On and on and on.

"You don't realize that these little frustrations that cause ingratitude, are actually receiving into the soil of your heart, the **seeds** of thorny bushes of bitterness.

Then when I come to sow the good seed, it will not grow because the thorn bushes already choke out the light and crowd the soil.

"If you want to cultivate a heart filled with joy, you must count all things as dung, and draw close to Me, forsaking all other things, which are sure to bring you disappointment. It's not about poverty; it's about detachment. Surely a poor person can be just as bitter as a rich one. But as you grow rich, your lust for things grows bigger. As you feed it, it grows bigger and bigger, dominating your life and soon you have no time left for Me."

"For her and for all of you, thanksgiving and worship are the medicine and weed killer that will choke out the thorns. Thanking Me in all situations. As it is written: **Rejoice always, pray continually, give thanks in all circumstances; for this is God's will for you in Christ Jesus. I Thessalonians 5:16-18**

"This Scripture is far too often overlooked, but I have come to prepare you for harder times. If you live in this manner, you will preserve your joy and your health, for disease does not enter a joyful soul easily. It is up to you, My People. You can complain like the Israelites or you can rejoice like Paul did:

And we know that God works all things together for the good of those who love Him, who are called according to His purpose. Romans 8:28

"You see, if you embrace this with all your hearts and KNOW beyond a shadow of a doubt that I am bringing good out of everything that happens, even the very worst things, if you have true faith in Me, you will not fall prey to discouragement, sadness and despair."

Taken from: **Lost in the Woods, Seeds of Bitterness...**

Seeds from Demons

I think a lot of this is about teaching us about how to handle the seeds. These little frustrations or irritations are not just offerings - they're the key to our getting all these seeds throughout the day, and He's telling us how to manage those moments and how to manage the seed moments, so that we're no longer letting our bodies get poisoned, including these things that we were either unaware of, or didn't think they were that important.

I know somebody - last night I was talking... "I'll do it later, I'll do it later," he says. And it didn't end up happening, I don't remember what the issue was. But there was something health related that was complicated with him, too - and he didn't really notice because it was a chronic thing, it was a little better, a little worse, a little better. It's always worse when the seeds are there.

And when we delay, He's kind of saying, "No, I said don't delay, because that's going to cause a problem. Please, My children, I'm telling you for your own good. You can do it, there's always free will. But there are consequences. So, it's ALWAYS our choice. *(Dr. Sherry)*

Taken from: **Spiritual Warfare 19 - How Demons Work 3 of 3**

...All it takes is, for example - they were having difficulty processing credit cards, because the order for the homeless was too big. And they didn't know what to do with such a big order. And I was thinking, "Oh, help me, Lord!" and I simply said, "You know? Lord - that's ridiculous, 'cause if You want me to have this, You're gonna give it to me, and I'm just a mess!" So, I felt much better, but I had that moment of panic or concern that it wasn't going to happen, and got seeds, got spirits of Irritation, Frustration, Fear, Agitation. All from a 10 minute phone call with an online store.

So, it takes very little to get these things. And I clean myself 5 or 6 times a day because of prayer (over others). He has suggested that everybody, minimum, morning and evening. And for those who really struggle with this, if they have a moment where they feel irritation or frustration for a second - RIGHT THEN AND THERE, if you repent - this seed is not imbedded in your heart. It has tiny, microscopic spines that grow into thorns, and it imbeds into the lining of the heart. But in the beginning, for a couple of hours, it hasn't done that. You can repent and He somehow gets it from the heart, into the trachea and you can cough it out. Somehow it enters the airway and you can cough it out. *(Dr. Sherry)*

Taken from: **Spiritual Warfare 17 - How Demons Work 1 of 3**

So, yesterday when I had my communion service, the readings were from Colossians 3, and they truly brought home everything the Lord has been teaching us about our relationships with others and how easily we get **seeds** *of resentment, with which the enemy builds strongholds of unforgiveness. I've been monitoring myself very carefully and notice I have 'buttons' or 'hot spots,' places where I recoil inside and begin grudging and complaining internally. Although I don't let it show externally, most of the time, I feel it inside and it takes the joy out of whatever I was doing.*

Paul addresses this very thing in Colossians 3 beginning at verse 12. **Because you are God's chosen ones, holy and beloved, clothe yourselves with heartfelt mercy, with kindness, humility, meekness and patience.**

All I can say Heartdwellers, is the very moment you offend charity or Holy Spirit, retire to a private place, kneel and ask God to help you with repentance. I don't dare undertake anything until I've checked my heart for **seeds** *and asked Holy Spirit to please show me what's there in.*

Taken from: **Defensive Power Unleashed in Giving Thanks**

Seeking God/Me

*The more we invest in **seeking God** and truly getting to know the Lord, the more convinced we come of His absolute providential nature. The more we realize how faithful He is and how intimately involved He is in our lives with the littlest things.*

Taken from: **Have No Fear of the Future...**

"...for you who persevere in climbing the mountain of holiness, I am taking you from glory to glory. You cannot see where you have come from or where you are going. You only look to My hand, following Me wherever I go, **seeking Me** out each day, hungering to know My will and to live for Me. Yes, for you the journey is long, dry and hard. But when you finally stand on that mountain top and take in the view, you will count all your sufferings as nothing. And like a woman who has brought forth a man-child, you will forget the long and intense labor for the joy of holding the newborn child in your arms."

Taken from: **The Weariness of Waiting**

'This is why religion has become so popular. People think that because they are 'religious,' they are holy. No, it goes so much deeper than that. Many will come and say 'Did I not heal in Your Name? Did I not preach great sermons in Your Name? And look at all the souls I won for You.'

"I will say, 'Look at all the souls My Spirit won for Me. And look at all the prayer team suffered at home, denying themselves and backing you up. Their reward is great. You delivered the message, but the anointing came from Me, through those who are hidden and **seeking Me** continually. Not caring about recognition, only caring about those they pray for.'

*Taken from: **Lord, Why Are Things Falling Apart?***

I asked the Lord, "What's on Your mind today, Lord?"

And He answered me, "Brevity. The brevity of life and how I wish for you all to make the very best of it. That does not mean conforming to the will and norms of the world. No, it means **seeking Me** until you find Me and conforming to My will."

Taken from: **Your Very Special Destiny**

"And yes, I must move My Bride out of the way before the very worst happens. She is praying, shedding tears, fasting, **seeking Me,** repenting for this world's sins. How can I ignore her pleas? I can't. Simply, I just can't. So, I continue to answer her with change as she cries out. You know this truth. You know also that there will be a time when the Father says, 'Enough!!' and I will remove you. Just as I removed Faustina. But before that time your prayers are changing things around you. They are working. Do you understand?"

Taken from: **The Power You Possess...**

"There is a Truth, My Love. You are capturing and reflecting My Glory, because we are together and your full attention is set on Me and on worshiping. Thanking Me. And so, you radiate My Glory. Oh, how important it is for souls to come to Me and for us to be together in this way. When they do, they will shine with My Glory and others who are **seeking Me** will sense their closeness to Me. It will be easier to help others when they realize that the soul they're listening to has truly been in My presence. There is an authority and authenticity that moves with those who have substantially been in My presence. Only, see to it that each of you wean more and more off the pleasures of this world, that you may protect this light that accompanies you, and not sully it with the foolish and vain things of this world."

Taken from: **I AM the Master Builder**

Seeking God/Me

"Then I see one...a soul hungering for Me, a soul on fire, a soul that burns in this darkness and its light is only perceived by Me. And I ask My Father, 'Please, Father, turn the heart of this precious one to Me, so I may speak with her. Cause her to reach out for Me.'

"And her heart is quickened, but never with the thought that I desire her company. No, she thinks only to herself, 'Wretched as I am, have Mercy, God, and send me a sign of Your presence in my life.' Never does she for one moment imagine that she may speak with Me, face to face. So, that long process begins. The process of convincing her that I am longing for her company.

"And as I press in to get her attention, she presses in **seeking Me**, and the devils come along and try every conceivable tactic to rob her of My reality. And their most successful one is 'You are not worthy, you are no prophet or priest. You have no royal blood, you are worthless.' And she believes it!!

"But then I break through and tell her, 'My Darling one, your worth is the blood I shed for you. Your worth is My very life given for you on Calvary. Do you understand? You, I died for.' And slowly, she turns her hope towards Me, daily gaining ground against the tormenting liars. With My grace, she encounters Me and receives Me into her heart and we dwell with one another. And I find My delight in the sound of her footsteps as she hurries to our trysting place, and there I pour out My heart to her and she drinks from the living waters of My very own soul and is refreshed."

Taken from: **You Are The Highpoint of My Day**

"Yes, I know this will not be a popular message, but it needs to be said. Pay heed, My people. Do not get entangled in religiosity. Do not suppose I am confined in the Pharisee's box. We butted heads a long time ago and never have we been reconciled yet. I did not honor all their ways - in fact, I openly contradicted many of their man-made rules.

"I didn't say, 'By the keeping of the law all people will know that you are My disciples.'

"…I am freeing you from those, but calling you to faithfulness in **seeking Me** until you find Me. And, many of you are on the verge of establishing a relationship with Me. I am fine tuning you. I speak to you regularly, some of you are beginning to recognize My voice. Are you looking for thunder claps? Did I come in the gentle breeze? Oh, so many of you are hearing Me clearly, but not recognizing Me. I am putting an end to this, though. You will recognize Me and we will converse familiarly together. Hang in there, you are so close to a break through."

Taken from: **We Are New Wineskins…**

He said, "Blessed are the poor in spirit, those who are not self---satisfied but those who hunger and thirst for righteousness. Blessed are you because you depend totally on Me, you are not comfortable walking in your own righteousness, with your own opinions continually in defense posture. Rather, you are meek and humble in heart, looking to Me for all your answers and always ready to yield to the truth.

"You will not be led astray. Your insecurity causes you to rely totally on Me even from moment to moment. Your hearts beat in unison with Mine and they are never satisfied with themselves but always *seeking more of Me*.You shall be filled with the good things of My Kingdom: righteousness, peace and joy."

*Taken from: **These Times Are Thick With Deception***

Seeking God/Me

"You have many such subscribers who understand what it's like to receive the blows of the world. They are seasoned with many injuries I have healed. They have learned the ways of My love because they spend so much time with Me, **seeking My Heart and My Mind** and putting it to practice. In this regard, you are truly blessed.

"So, when you encounter the harshness of the world you have a whole company of intercessors who will lift you up to Me so you can keep going. All of you are seriously damaged soldiers. The difference between those who deeply know Me, is that they have had tremendous measures of healing and the bitterness and fear that mark those still wounded in battle, isn't there anymore. They also know themselves very, very well."

Taken from: **Support One Another in Your Weaknesses**

"Oh, pray for the repentance of your children, America. For those caught in disobedience and sin. Pray that they will repent and not join the ranks of those who are bitter and shaking their fists in My face, cursing Me. Pray that a wave of repentance will be sent to bring them to their senses and that they will come to **Me repenting and seeking guidance**. Many heroes will be born in that hour. And many that you thought were heroes will crumble in the dust, revealing their true interior emptiness.

"I will raise up warriors after My own heart. They will listen to Me alone and from their hands I will wrought great miracles. I will grant them the advantage against their adversaries, just as I jarred the Earth's crust and entombed those who have brought this upon their countrymen."

Taken from: **Invasion, Underground Cities...**

As the Lord was speaking, I saw something that looked like a propane camp light, which has two mantles made of ash that explode into light when the gas is turned on and a match lit to it. One moment, it was nothing more than fabric that had been charred into a ash mantle; the next moment it was so brilliant I couldn't even look at it.

"Yes, that is an apt description. One moment you are but ashes on this Earth, the next brilliant, illuminating all around you. The transformation is stunning. This is one way to explain your movement into the eternal.

"Yet a little while and all of this will be over. In the meantime, I am building My Image within each of you as you go about your daily tasks. I am anointing you to be little Christs: washing the feet of others, on the lookout for those who need My touch, interceding for the suffering and seemingly hopeless, each day living for Me and **seeking first the Kingdom of God."**

Taken from: **Invasion, Underground Cities...**

"Oh, how I love each and every one that is **seeking Me.** That is why I am here to explain the direction they need to take. You know the things that offend Me. Sin offends Me very much. Sin in clothing, or lack of it, sin in violence, crime, hatred, gossip, backbiting, jealousy, adulteries. Soap operas are the epitome of sin and extremely noxious to Me. Like your-nose-in-fresh-dog-excrement noxious. I mean very, very bad. These things not only offend Me but also the Heavenly court, the angels and the saints. Yet in your world they are matter-of-fact, part of everyday life"

Taken from: **Jesus Answers His Bride, How to Hear & See Me...**

Self-Denial/Self Control

"You know when you please Me and when you are walking the edge. Acknowledging that is a sign that you want to cooperate with Me - it's when you pretend it doesn't matter that you fall. It does matter. It matters very much and if it makes you feel better, I am so very pleased when you really exercise **self-control** in the little things.

"Understand that success with the little things insures success with the bigger ones. It's that holy staircase again: success builds upon success, failure weakens and paves the way for more failure. I love to see you take those steps upwards, and I am there at your right hand cheering."

Taken from: **Prayers to Avert War & A Gentle Correction**

"You see, by denying yourself the little things, you draw closer to the delights of Heaven. It only takes a little effort, Clare, a little agreement. And the sweetness of My presence and our love is filled with the fresh fragrance of devotion.

"My people, if you want to draw closer to Heaven, you must learn to deny yourself and walk in **self-denial.** You cannot continue to feed the flesh and expect eternal rewards, for the flesh is in opposition to the Spirit and one cancels out the power of the other. So, if you want closer encounters with Me and with Heaven, deny yourselves some choice morsel and come into My presence stronger in resolve than ever.

"I am not an easy catch. My royal dignity does not allow for Me to be an easy catch. Rather, you must reach up and out of yourselves as you seek My fellowship and the sweetness of My presence."

Taken from: **The Way to His Heart and Intimacy in Prayer**

"You see, holiness is hard work. It entails much **self-denial** and refocusing on the needs of others. When you come to serve the Lord, prepare yourself for trials. Yes, many in this world believe it is their right to indulge themselves. After all, they worked for it. But all this indulgence leads to blind alleys, wrong turns and bondage. And some of this indulgence is spurred on by the enemy, knowing your weakness. And knowing that you won't check with Me. He pushes you into things that feed your fancy and meets some need that you're not aware of."

Taken from: **Freedom Without License**

"Every day you are presented with opportunities to go with grace - or go with the flesh. Little things mean a lot. Your love for Me is the cornerstone. All the things you give up for Me - and especially charity - are the building blocks. You are given opportunities almost every moment of your life. The more frequently you choose Me, the stronger you will get. It's just that simple.

"The blocks of granite are My grace, **self-denial**, charity, humility. The blocks of adobe are your flesh, your desires, appetites, preferences; things that ultimately mean nothing and do not hold up under pressure. Building with those causes massive instability. Always choose the granite, My Love. It will stand in eternity. The others will crumble back into the Earth they were made from."

Taken from: **February…a Month of Testings**

"They (holy angels) are sent out and assigned and you may indeed enlist their assistance. As I was saying, many times they wait for you to perceive and act on the evils surrounding you. I have given you My authority, My Name and My Blood. There is nothing that will not yield to this. However, it is true there are times of more focused prayer and **self-denial**, when that's appropriate."

Taken from: **Prowling Lions and Your Three Enemies**

Self-Denial/Self-Control

"Do you want more of the Spirit? Crucify more of the flesh. Not on your own, but when I inspire you to abstain from things that are harmful to your walk. If you are faithful to follow My instructions, it will take only a little time to get to the summit - not years wandering round and round in the desert, as it has taken My Bride, Clare.

"Yes, for years she has struggled. And many of you, too, have struggled for years. All of you have different issues, or slightly different versions of them. These are allowed for your perfection."

Consider it pure joy, my brothers and sisters, whenever you face trials of many kinds, because you know that the testing of your faith produces perseverance. Let perseverance finish its work so that you may be mature and complete, not lacking anything. James 1:2-4

"So, there is a point to being exercised in **self-control and self-denial.** By My grace, you ascend on high to the throne I have prepared for you in Heaven. You say, 'But Lord, I don't care about a throne.' Ah yes, I understand. But do you care about justice and righteousness, healing the sick, feeding and clothing the poor, teaching the uninformed?"

Taken from: **Guilt Dams Your Living Waters**

"The Mark of the Beast will be the beginning of their sifting in earnest. It will begin with **self-denial** in little things and get right down to the vital basics. There will be a sifting as has never been before experienced in believers. The world has caught them up into a lifestyle and theology that did not exist in My early church.

"Their very sense of being will be critically threatened and called into question until they realize Who I AM and who they are in Me, and what it truly means to bear My Name, My Cross. To live in Me and I in them. Then they will discover their worth and reject completely all the world has offered and held for them.

"This must be done through a process, it doesn't come overnight. That is why I am leaving them behind."

Taken from: **They Will Be Left Behind...**

"When I spoke of the abundant life, I was not speaking of the abundance of things in the world. I was speaking of the abundance of My presence, and the joy of living in Me.

"You see, when I told you to **deny yourself,** pick up your cross and follow Me, I gave you the mandate of having your own unique cross. It could be slander and calumny, or lack of appreciation for what you do. It could be the inconvenience of a car breaking down, or the denial of a loan to get another car. It could be false accusation at work and that someone who really dislikes you has tried to darken your name. It could be deferring to a family member over where you are going on a vacation or family outing.

"ANYTHING that causes you to abandon your will for the will of another can be a cause for suffering, maturity and brotherly love."

Taken from: **Suffering – Real Work in the Realm of the Spirit**

"This prayer (the Stations of the Cross) is so pleasing to Me, because it offsets the false teachings of prosperity that have infiltrated the church. Did I not say, **'Deny yourself**, pick up your cross and follow Me?' Yet, today, where is the Cross being preached? All of you, My children, are much in need of strength to persevere as Christians. The Bride must fully resemble the Groom and I did not come on this Earth to satisfy My earthly, fleshly cravings. I came to serve and to die for You. I died for you and opened the gates of Heaven for all eternity - and now I ask of you to **deny yourselves** and follow Me."

Taken from: **Miami Soon to be Bombed & No Greater Love**

Self-Denial/Self-Control

"You know how it feels when you knick your finger and it bleeds. It takes a few days to heal, especially if it's on a knuckle. In the meantime, it hurts. It makes your whole hand hurt. Even though it's not life threatening, it mars your body's performance. And it's a distraction.

"Same way in relationships. Little indifferences hurt. When they accumulate they do damage, and that damage has to be repaired. You've been given so many graces, Clare. There really is no excuse for you taking liberties that injure our relationship. Although you do have a very real enemy egging you on into these things, still you can say, 'NO!' when these little indiscretions are proposed to you.

"It's not like you're under a strong physical or chemical compulsion. It's more like 'I want that.' You could deny yourself as a sign of your love for Me. I honor each time you do that. So, you see indifference leads to lukewarmness...and you have it in your power not to allow that."

So, Lord - how do I get out of this?

"**Deny yourself** more, go deeper. Eventually you'll have a breakthrough and a restoration of My Sweet presence. Show Me that you care, Beloved. I know you've made serious life choices to honor Me. But understand: it is the little foxes that spoil even the finest of vines. The higher you go, the longer down the fall, the more damage that is done to yourself, to Me and to others."

Taken from: **Lukewarm – Little Foxes Spoil the Vine**

Lord, this **self-denial thing** *is painful.*

He replied, "Disobedience is more painful in the end."

Taken from: **You Will Have Peace Amidst Chaos**

"Nothing is too small. Children who offer prayers are far more powerful than many adults, because of the purity of their souls. So, I am asking you parents to bring your children into your prayer circles and explain to them as best you can, exactly what is at stake.

"Tell them that Satan has been working secretly in this country to destroy it. The forests, lakes, rivers and oceans. He and his minions have been responsible for the earthquakes and weather changes, beached animals and fish. Aborted babies. The poisoning of the Earth so babies come out deformed. Use discretion, but make it clear to them that their future depends on this election - whether or not there will be freedom in this country. Whether or not ISIS will take over this country and murder Christians.

"Of course their minds are tender, but they should know how very serious this is without causing them damaging distress. Just enough to get them to pray in earnest. The Divine Mercy Chaplet is powerful. Tears are powerful, vigils are powerful. Supplication with loud cries to Heaven are powerful. Denying yourselves food is powerful, fasting for those who can fast is powerful. Offering sacrifices, television, dessert, shopping, every form of **self-denial** will have an impact on this election."

Taken from: **The Election: Jesus calls for "War Spiritually"**

"Each day you are becoming stronger and stronger. This impacts many areas of your lives, more than you realize. It is like weight lifting. Building up spiritual muscle also has its affect on speed, agility, endurance and strength.Waiting, in a similar way, affects your whole life and the way you do things. You are exercising **self-control** based on your faith in Me - you are waiting on Me."

Taken from: **Lord, What Are You Doing With Us in This Hour?**

Self-Righteousness

"When I look in on your household and see strife, bickering, jealousy and dissension, do you think I will make My abode there? As you lift yourselves up and tear down others, do you think My ears are eager to hear all about the slander, lies and calumnies of others? Did I not teach you not to display the faults of others or draw attention to what you, in your opinion, have judged to be wrong?

"Is it not My job to judge? Isn't this precisely what the Scribes and Pharisees did to Me? Did they not find fault continually with My teachings, telling Me I was destroying their faith and teaching error. Did I not heal a blind man on the Sabbath to expose their hypocrisy? Do any of these attitudes ring a bell, those who call yourselves by My Name?"

Then I will tell them plainly, 'I never knew you; depart from Me, you workers of lawlessness.' Matthew 7:23

"Why do I say 'workers of lawlessness?' Because the heart of the law is Love. What you are doing is contrary to that law. You are not building up, making the way straight for Me. You are blowing up bridges and making men captive to your laws and legalisms, immersing them in judgment, **self-righteousness** and blinding error."

Taken from: **Lord, Why Are Things Falling Apart?**

"Oh, how I lament for these who have slipped through My fingers. Pray for them, dear ones, pray for their salvation. For the judgment they passed on this channel has become their own before the courts of Heaven. Yet, never will I abandon them.

"But do you understand? I offered them the choice fruits of My Kingdom: My love, My fellowship, My very heart. And now all of that has been swept away and concealed under a carpet of bitterness woven with beguiling threads of **self-righteousness,** envy, pride and arrogance. My heart aches for them. And all I showered upon them now will go to other souls who have Me in their midst.

"Souls that will respond to My tender invitations to grow in holiness as I lead them hand-in-hand. Yet I lament the darkness has settled over so many, having lost their connection with Me. They now are the ones falling under the spell of beguiling spirits of **Self-righteousness,** Religious spirits who applaud them for their valor in coming against Me and denouncing you.

"This is the lot of those who refuse to seek Me until they find Me. The lot of those who spurn humility and meekness and seek to rise above others in stature. This is the lot of those who stopped short in prayer and received the deceptions of men offered to them, that they might be "knights" taking down an evil doer, rather than pressing in, fighting the good fight and recognizing their own error, bitterness and jealousy."

Taken from: **How Does a Fall Happen?**

"Understand that the demons will do their very best to incite division and leave a bitter memory behind. Be prepared to disappear into your prayer closet for a few moments to clear the air. Above all, do not look down on your loved ones who have not as yet received the grace of knowing Me.

"Had I not given you that grace, along with another grace - that of corresponding, you would be as they are or worse. **Self-righteousness** is the number one killer with the unsaved. They hate it with a passion and will instinctively be combative and sarcastic if they get even a whiff of that attitude."

Taken from: **Leave Sweet Memories Behind...**

Self-Righteousness

"Understand that the demons also have limited energy, so they pick their opportunities to trouble you according to the importance of wha is coming up in your life. If it is very important and they know about it ahead of time (which they mostly do because they alert one another that such and such is going to happen or so and so is on the way) they quickly put 2 and 2 together, seeing that there is an occasion of virtue and helping another soul in need.

"They try to distract you or get you to cancel the meeting. Or they wea you out so you have nothing left for that person I'm sending you. Who by the way, was very important to Me.

"Another thing to be aware of in selfishness is the self-important attitude, 'I'm to busy for the likes of you.' The 'you aren't important enough to me to stop what I'm doing.' attitude. This is abhorrent to M Now we are getting into PRIDE, which is truly at the root of all evil. Selfishness will lead to Pride and **self-righteousness**. Look for those times when your conscience twinged and you ignored it. Those are very good indicators of hidden sin."

Taken from: **Get Ready for Your Journey**

"Blessed are the meek. It is the meek that most resemble Me. Not the fire-and-brimstone, old testament prophets. You must not put on that cloak. Rather, call for repentance, that I may turn and negate what has been prepared, and be compassionate with the sinful so they may coming running to the foot of the Cross. And not turn around and point the finger at you who are railing at them, and say, 'I told you so! Those Christians are just a bunch of religious hypocrites!'

"You see, it is My love that leads to repentance, and judgment only leads to **self-righteousness** of the one who is judging. And **self-righteousness** comes from Pride and the declaration that you are above others, and you have the right to declare their guilt. This kind of behavior opens the door for a fall.

"So, My Bride. I am asking you: do not enter into judgment with your brothers. Keep your head low. Weep over his sins as you weep over your own. You ARE weeping over yours...are you not? This is the great balancing weight. You see, you've been given much, much more grace than many of these. Much more opportunity. Much more ministry."

Taken from: **Repent for the Guilty, Do not Condemn**

"People that do not know or have My Heart, teach the Bible. They are trained in legalisms without knowing by experience the laws of Mercy.

"This results in a whole generation of Pharisees...they lack the tassels on the outside, but on the inside they are abundant. This is why I have rejected many of this generation of preachers to lead My People. This is why I have raised up shepherds after My own Heart. They are wounded souls that found Love and cleaved to Me until their were healed.

"Now I am sending them out without any credentials other than deep scars that have healed and been filled with the anointing of My Love.

"These are the ones I referred to when I said, 'The last shall be first, and the first shall be last. And the wage of the worker that only worked a few hours will be the same as the worker who was hired in the beginning.'

"These are of the generation that will build for Me a Holy Nation and prepare the way, leveling every pretense, every religious spirit, every haunt of **self-righteousness** and pride."

Taken from: **Repent for the Guilty, Do not Condemn**

Self-Righteousness

"Wicked are the times and the more wicked they become, the more My People need to know what is behind that wickedness, lest they slay the ignorant and let the culpable go free onto the next victim. It is so easy for you to place blame on others when they act badly. So easy. It's like stating the obvious with self-assured confidence. But nothing could be further from the truth. In fact it is the ignorance and weakness of those being used that allows them to impact you. If they knew, if they saw, if they understood, they would turn on the real enemy and stop allowing themselves to be used.

"But there is a certain release of anger and frustration that is satisfying to those who abuse others. They themselves have been oppressed and bottled up for so long, it's actually a relief to find someone they can vent on...someone who it seems obvious to them they should vent on. And My People in their **self-righteousness** think it fitting to retaliate."

Taken from: **Start Recognizing Your Enemy...**

"The world will begin to see the difference between My people and those of the world. Not in **self-righteousness,** but in ethical behavior and sticking to what they believe in the face of opposition and ridicule. This will be like drawing a line in the sand, 'This far and no father'. All over the world people will begin to recognize Christians as a real, living entity, as a Kingdom united under God."

Taken from: **Refining Fires are Coming...**

"Do not grow weary with these tests, do not give up on yourself, because you see so many flaws. No, persevere, do not condemn yourself for that, too, is a sign of pride: expecting to be perfect and finding the imperfections. Rather the humble soul is not the least bit surprised by her surfacing faults. It is always a test of virtue when opposition arises, when condemnation is hurled at you.

"These are My invitations to sincerely love the offenders and even consider for a moment if there be truth in what is being said. Like David, when Shimei hurled insults and his men wanted to kill him. David said, 'Leave him alone; let him curse, for the Lord has told him to. It may be that the Lord will look upon my misery and restore to me his covenant blessing instead of his curse today.' (2 Samuel 16:11) This is the posture I want for my persecuted servants, certainly not rising up in **self-righteousness** and condemning the others. So, My Love, search your heart always and bring into subjection any rancor that wishes to lash out or justify. For I will justify you.. and what do you care what others say, as long as you are pleasing to Me?"

Taken from: **Your Hearts Are My Fragrant Garden**

So, the primary evidence that we're not walking in the Lord is bitter jealousy, selfish ambition, arrogance, lies against the Truth, indignation, **self-righteousness** *and really, a lack of peace. If all these things are churning inside of you and there's jealousy and strife among you, you are not walking in the Lord.*

Taken from: **Is Satan Pulling Your Strings?**

Self-Righteousness *is a yucky one.*

There is a generation that is pure in their own eyes and yet is not washed from their filthiness. Oh, how lofty are their eyes, and their eyelids are lifted up. The way of the fool is right in his own eyes: but he who harkens unto counsel is wise.

This reading is almost as bad as Pride. Basically, it is saying that if you think that you are without sin, then you had better look again. This is a serious one, because **Self-Righteousness** *stops me dead in my tracks.*

Taken from: **How To Use The Bible For An Anointed Word From God 4/4**

Self-Will

"Well...tonight I want to talk about My words, 'Deliver us from evil.' The evil of the enemy, the evil of **self-will**, the evils of this world. This is one prayer you can say immediately, and I will respond. You remember the UFO and how quickly it was escorted out of sight?"

"Yes, Lord - I really remember that. How could I forget it?" It was a night when I was resting and watching the night-time sky, as I often do in between prayer, just to wake up a little bit. I saw this object off in the eastern sky and I knew immediately what it was, because it would move erratically, but then it came to rest in certain place.

And just bubbling up and out of me, not even realizing what I was saying, I said, "Deliver us from evil." And immediately this object disappeared. I mean, it was GONE. I've never forgotten that. So, yes that's a powerful prayer! Very powerful.

I do remember that, Lord. It was truly amazing.

Jesus answered me, and He said, "Yes, that prayer is amazing. I taught it to you and it carries great power when spoken in faith to Me, especially by a soul who truly knows Me. The beauty of this prayer is that it addresses the evil on all fronts; the evil in your own soul, the evil of the enemy and the evil in the world.

"It's not like you are praying against a demon, you are ultimately pulling yourself back in alignment with My Holy intentions for your life. It gives Me permission to adjust those things in you which are not pleasing to Me and counterproductive to personal holiness.

"Yes, I like this prayer very much, and I wish for My Bride to use it in utter faith, more often. It addresses the evil of the moment, whereas the binding prayer addresses the entire day."

Taken from: **Prowling Lions and Your Three Enemies**

So, I went to the Bible Promises and opened to the heading, Food and Clothing. My first reaction was, "Yeah!! The Lord's acknowledging that I need clothing!" Oh, boy... But then common sense settled in and I said to myself...Clare...what else could this mean?? Better look at both sides. Better look at both sides - better safe than sorry...

*You see, one of the biggest impediments to clear discernment is an attachment to getting things your own way. You want to be justified in your desire for something, and in an effort to be justified you even twist the Scriptures that you get, even just a little, to accommodate your **self-will.** That's deadly in discernment! You have to be willing to get a big NO from the Lord without pitching a pout. Easier said than done!*

Taken from: **The Lure of Riches**

"Just as in days gone by, when I supernaturally protected My people, so shall I protect those who must stay behind. There will be one among them who will be designated the leader, and to him or her, I will give supernatural knowledge and wisdom. Protect this one who is critical to your mission. Let not the devils cause division, misunderstand, murmuring and jealousy. Be on your guard against these poisons they will use to divide and scatter you all.

"Together you will survive separated; you will face many dangers without anyone to hold you up. Do not let them divide and conquer. Be smarter than the enemy, walk in charity and humility and you will have no problems. Walk in **self-will,** selfishness, suspicion, and rancor, it will be your demise. There will be many testings among the groups, many testings. Painful decisions to make, life or death decisions to make. I will give you peace when the decisions are the hardest. Use lots to help you determine a plan of action."

Taken from: **Provision and Protection for Those Left Behind**

Self-Will

Yep, it was my black panther again. It had been bothering me for weeks that we might not have enough really healthy food, and I began thinking about what we would need before the Lord took us in the Rapture, if we were here for a week or two. I reasoned in my mind that whatever was left would be given to others anyway in our little food bank, so I rationalized myself into the store and bought healthy dry foods to back up the canned goods in the pantry.

Something about this did not feel good, but I blamed it on the enemy trying to prevent me. Deep in my heart, I suspected I might be wrong. But I didn't want to know - so I didn't check. But I proceeded in **self-will.** *Ezekiel tried to call me on the phone, but the ringer was off my cell phone, so I never heard him. Then today at lunch, after worship, I was touching in with the Lord in the Bible Promises and got some VERY bad and scary readings: pride, and honesty.*

"God puts down the man filled with pride, but He saves the one who is not proud."James 4:6

It is the height of pride to think that I know better than God and to do something He didn't want done. Then conviction set in, I felt faint and couldn't eat another bite of food. All I wanted to do was go into a hole and repent before the Lord.

Taken from: **Rest in Me Until I Carry You Over the Threshold of Eternity**

"My dear ones, don't you know that it is your attitude towards My instructions and corrections that determines your spiritual growth, not your ability? I ask for supple hearts that are eager to obey out of Love for Me. With this kind of heart, I can do anything. It is the disposition of your hearts that makes the difference.

"You worry so much about your mistakes and failures, but I am using them all. And in some instances, I deliberately allow them to humble you. I cannot pour My finest wine into cracked vessels: vessels cracked by judgment of others, harshness, un-teachable-ness, stubbornness, pride and **self-will**. First the vessel must be made whole and docile, then I can pour My finest wine through it.

"But I want you to understand - I know before you fall that you are going to fall. I have already made a provision for your recovery. But what makes it hard, if not impossible, is when you run from Me after a fall, because of shame. I knew what you were going to do before you ever did it. I tried to stop you, but you weren't listening very carefully. Now My entire purpose with you is to restore you to grace."

Taken from: **There are No Losers in My Kingdom**

"I will allow the temptations, but I will never leave you on your own with them. Either I or My Spirit or your guardian angel will assist and alert you to the tactics of the enemy. Where this fails is when **self-will** is stronger than self-sacrifice. This is at the very root of your existence.

"This is the place where a man interfaces with his spirit, this is also the seat of consciousness of the body, thus there is a struggle for supremacy. One who is able to keep his body under control is one who has mastered himself. What abides in this place is the tongue, the desire nature, pleasures of all kinds: food, sex, entertainment, leisure. All these things pander to the body and this is where the struggle begins.

"Even at a young age, these things wrestle with children, pulling them into sinful patterns of behavior that will eventually be their downfall. That is why it is so important to train a child up in the way he should go. Without this training he will most likely go the way of the flesh."

Taken from: **Why Temptations & Hope for You Who Are Lost**

Self-Will

Okay - so I have a confession. I have been **self-willed** *again. Tonight, I really felt like I wanted to throw a few ingredients together to make fasting bread, and I make it very substantial so I can live with it for a while, not eat other foods. And I felt a tug that I shouldn't be doing that just then. But I didn't listen 'cause I wanted my homemade bread.*

Then, when I was in worship, one of my kitties kept putting his paw on my shoulder and I tried to coax him to climb up from his chair to my shoulder, but he wouldn't. So, I tried to grab him.

Well...that was not such a good idea...I fell over backwards in my chair, spilled water all over the floor and knocked over a big pot of hot coals I keep in the back room to heat our office, because the wood stove is in another part of our house.

It was a close call and a mess. It could have been much worse, I could have been seriously hurt or burned. The Lord was merciful. But I knew immediately it was a correction for being **self-willed***.*

So, when I came into prayer I said, "Uncle."

First I confessed that I didn't want to give up my cinnamon buns that I made two days ago, that for all practical purposes are too yummy to eat during a fast. So, I reasoned making this bread could take the place of them. But I need more fear of God and respect. I'm still very brash - good at justifying MY way and **self-willed***.*

The Lord answered me, "All you say is true, but My Mercy still covers everything. Please, Clare, forgive yourself a little more often?"

But I see that as taking advantage and presumption.

He said very tenderly, "Come here."

So, I collapsed on His heart and cried.

I said, "Lord, I am pitifully **self-willed**, *beyond imagining."*

He answered me tenderly, "True."

I'm lazy, irresponsible, and **self-willed**.

He answered me again, "True."

But, You, oh Lord are faithful.

"True. What else?"

I'm a sinner, Lord, of the worst kind. Forgive me, Lord, set me free from the snare of my pride and **self-will**. *I really hate it.*

He answered again, "Not quite enough... yet...but you are getting there. Should I force you?"

No, never.

"Should I nudge you?"

Yes, always.

"Falling over backwards in the chair was just a nudge. You didn't get burned, you didn't ruin your computer. That part I protected. You've got a problem with food, and this fast is going to help you get over it."

That's true, guys. I really like good food so I learned to cook. Bread from the store just doesn't cut it with me, I'm a real snob with bread and coffee and things like that. So, it's true. I do have a problem.

"We are working to get you to the place you were at once before in your life, when you were free of these entanglements."

Taken from: **Learning the HARD Way/Playing Deaf**

Self-Will

"I am at your right hand, always encouraging the right and discouraging the wrong choice. But all of you, My Brides, have very **strong wills.** If you did not, you couldn't cleave to Me in thick and thin. But your wills must be trained to correspond with Mine. In that way, you will gain a great advantage in every decision. How much happier you will be when you obey. And I can also protect you."

Taken from: **Learning the HARD Way...**

"You, My little butterfly, still have some sturdy little wings that love to fly about...here and there...and taste the pollen of different flowers in the world. It's part of your adventuresome and curious nature. I have a hard time reining that in, but I must say, you are way more self-controlled now than you were even 15 years ago.

"Still you have moments of weakness. And...when I see pride raising it's obnoxious head, *(yeah, I started to feel that the other day. I thought, 'Oh, man - I'm in for a fall, I can feel it coming on...')* I am obliged to humble you...so I stand back just a very little bit and allow you to go off on your own. I always get good results with this. You should know by now, when you feel insecure about doing something, a good rule of thumb is 'don't do it.' However, your desire nature trumps your wisdom and off you go. It still is all about **self-will**, self-love, pride and avarice.

"When you are totally dead to yourself and the world and you love Me more than anything or anyone...well, you won't go flying off. Something inside, a governor will check your action and your desire nature will be left in the dust to rot and disappear, as it should.

"...When you stray, My love, I must allow the lessons that go with self-will. I must allow you to suffer the consequences...so it will be deeply embedded in your heart and mind. My way is always the Best Way. Even if you have to guess at it, and deduce it by your own reasoning, it is still the best way. You know Me, Clare, you know what I think about most things pertaining to you, so it shouldn't be difficult to make the right decisions. It's all a matter of crucifying your flesh, My Love - yes, putting that old man to death, buried deep in the earth he is from. Then you will be free to glide and soar with Me, and nothing shall be able to knock you off track."

Taken from: **Desire, Self-Will and Consequences**

"No...I'm being I AM, who I AM. And, while I gave My people signs for the seasons, they are not a law unto themselves, that the whole universe must abide by. My laws are not above the worth of a human soul. So, while everyone would like to see Me operating neat and tidy according to their prognostications, My heart still beats for man alone. And, as long as there is just ONE straggler, that is just about to be drawn in, My heart aches to leave that one man alone to suffer."

In essence then, you're really saying you can't ever return, because there'll always be one more, and one more, and one more to wait for!

"In essence, yes - that's true. But in practice, there's comes a time to call the question. We are approaching the end and you will see in the weeks and months to come, an increase in separation between those who have chosen to love Me and those who have gone their own way. The dividing line is going to get sharper, clearer and crisper, until it is indeed time for Me.

"If you look very carefully at all the preparations I've been making on this channel, you will see that if they obey what I have given them, they will have plenty of oil in their lamps, and that day will be a joyous occasion for them. However, if they continue in **self-seeking**, it will be the most tragic day of their lives."

Taken from: **Build With Fire-Tried Gold...**

Sexual Addictions, Addictions

"So, My Bride. I am asking you: do not enter into judgment with your brothers. Keep your head low. Weep over his sins as you weep over your own. You ARE weeping over yours...are you not? This is the great balancing weight. You see, you've been given much, much more grace than many of these. Much more opportunity. Much more ministry.

"So, when you overspend, for instance - it is just a serious as those who steal. Though the money is in your control, it should be looked at as Mine, since you are My stewards. Therefore, the man who runs out of the 7-11 with a six pack of beer, because of his **addiction** and the way he was formed by his non-existent parents is less guilty than you who spend the money on luxuries, when you could have supported and orphan with it.

"Do you understand?? There is NONE that is just, not even one. And those to whom much has been given, much shall be required."

Taken from: **Repent for the Guilty – Do Not Condemn**

"Yes, accomplishment becomes an **addiction**, a god, determining your self-worth in your eyes. You begin to wake up every morning to new challenges - rather than to Me. So, these dry times are so very necessary to keep you detached and focused on pleasing Me. What does it matter what you have accomplished if it has not made Me happy with you? And what does it matter if you crawl across the finish line only to see My beaming smile focused on you, in gratitude and appreciation that you ran the race for Me, with nothing else in mind?"

Taken from: **Increase Will Overtake You**

"Gaming is Satan's answer to the suffering young people deal with from day to day. Being with Me is the real answer, being drawn into My dimension".

But don't people need a little recreation?

"Yes, but that kind of recreation is more powerful and has more potential to distort the life than the simpler things. It looks innocent, but examine the fruit. Not only that, but it is deliberately designed to be **addictive**, so much so that the gamer begins to depart from reality and live in the gaming world, where self-worth is determined by skill level and other gamers and where violence is not experienced on the real level. Fun to shoot the bad guy... but have you ever been with someone who was just shot and dying?

"Not a game anymore. But, desensitizing young people is the hidden agenda behind this violence. It is a precursor to the chaos and rage Satan has planned for this world and is even now surfacing. Gaming has desensitized this generation, who now see reckless driving, shooting and killing and bombing as a recreational activity.

"My Love, I have taken the time to go over this with you because some of our listeners are caught in this destructive **addiction**. I wish for them to understand what they are truly dealing with in their lives, to give them a chance to make an informed decision and get out of it. Some would argue that there are benefits, but weigh them carefully against moral decline and **addictive** behavior."

Taken from: **Jesus Speaks on The God Dimension...**

"Some people are so insecure that they are constantly trying to make everything around them fit into a black and white category. And here I am NOT talking about justifying immoral behavior such as **homosexuality** and declaring it a gray area; there is nothing gray about it. It is a sin."

Taken from: **A Good Tree Cannot Bear Bad Fruit**

Sexual Addictions, Addictions

"I do not wish for anyone to be excluded from this relationship of pure intimacy with Me. Understand that I know you, My sons and daughters. I see what no one else sees. I understand the makeup of your body, your hormones and what your flesh fights against your spirit with. There is NOTHING to be ashamed of when you are with Me. I already know and understand well the challenges you undergo day after day.

"You will find that even when **sexuality assaults** you in My Presence, I totally ignore it while you put it in its place. There is a fierce demon of Lust assigned to the spiritually-minded. This demon is fierce and bent on bringing you all down in utter disgrace. I see your heart, I see your intention, I see your struggles and the means used to attack you outside of yourself.

"Some of you are more vulnerable because of your youth. Let Me explain it to you this way. When this urge tries to take you over, picture yourself in front of Me, My expression calm and compassionate and allow Me to say only one thing, 'You know where this came from, so what are you going to do about it?' Then, ask for My help. For if you to crumple into a ball of shame, it only causes the lustful impulse to become stronger. When the demons see they are conquering your resolve, they set upon you with even more force."

Taken from: **If You Love Me – Rapture – Sexual Temptations**

He told me a story and this is the story. There's a little boy in New York, about eight years old. The little boy is going to Central Park to go down to the little ponds in Central Park. The Lord comes up to him and talks to him for a few minutes.

His parents are drug addicts, he doesn't know who his father is; his mother is a serious drug addict. He's neglected, he's underfed, he's abused, and why would anyone put him into a life like this? Why was he born into this life? It was terrible. And there's so much of that right now, all over the world with the proliferation of drugs and **addictions**. *It's tragic, it's absolutely tragic.*

That's the story about the little boy, what his condition was. He'd go to Central Park just to get some relief from the terrible environment, drugs, violence, gangs. So, he'd go to Central Park and he was down by the pond and the Lord came to see him and they talked. Well after a while he turned and this is something I'm seeing in the spirit, the Lord is showing me the story. After a while he turned and he walked back to start to go home and when he was crossing the street a big truck went out of control and hit him and killed him. He died right on the spot.

And the Lord turned to me in the vision and He said, "You see, there are some souls that know what their end is going to be before they even come to Earth and they make an agreement with Me, and I tell them what their reward will be. They'll be in Heaven with Me, and they take on this assignment.

"Many saintly souls come into this world right now that signed up for suffering just to be saved and bring more into the Kingdom. Very saintly souls that would rather die young than be corrupted and go to hell. Souls that love Me with all their little hearts and know the treachery of having a human body on the Earth. These souls I invite and use for work no one else wants to do: dying in tsunamis, plagues, and hunger. These souls call out to humanity to reach beyond their selfish boundaries and give. The poor sanctify the rich. You know the saying, 'The rich man's money gives him no peace.' And how true that is, unless he has become My steward and hand-in-hand works with Me to bless others. So, you see? Everyone has a purpose in My Kingdom. Not one goes without their reward. Each fulfills their destiny, just as you right now are fulfilling yours."

Taken from: **Blood Moon Rapture, Prophetic Word**

Shame

"That, combined with your new relationships and your new liberal ways of thinking caused you to begin looking at other souls around you, and judging them. You began to look down on them and the things that they held dear, even going as far as holding in scorn and contempt the joy that they expressed at the nearness of My coming.

"By the time I arrived, all you could do was stand in fear and **shame** for the very thing which you distained to believe had just happened right in front of you. Because you did not believe, you did not watch and pray, and I came as a thief in the night and you were not prepared. I could not take you."

Taken from: **Post Rapture Letter from God 2**

And I think I have shared this a few times, but if you see yourself as a little child trying to get across the Santa Monica freeway at rush hour, trying to get across 8 lanes of rush hour traffic. And you're too little, you can't do it, you're only 6 years old. You are standing there, and if you look up to Heaven and say, "Lord, I can't do this. I'm too little".

The world abhors that concept of being too little. They are constantly encouraging you to be big and strong and powerful and independent. And the Lord is totally captured by littleness. He is totally drawn to a soul who is very needy, and KNOWS they are needy, and is relying totally on Him. And there's no **shame** *in that, it actually draws Him in faster to admit that we are too little.*

Taken from: **Spiritual Dryness 2 of 2**

"There is a certain **shame** associated with being dependent on medication. It most certainly lowers the image of self-sufficiency that promotes pride and comparisons with others."

Taken from: **CERN Wickedness Increases…**

Ezekiel: Oh, I remember many years ago, when I first experienced the Lord in this way, I felt I had sinned. I thought, 'Oh, my gosh, I've gotten too close to the Lord!' You know, I had kind of a dream/vision - I was actually driving on a freeway in San Antonio, Texas, middle of the business rush hour and I had to pull off on the median, just because this was such a passionate, real experience. And I drifted off into one of these places where the Lord comes into the picture and He puts His arm around you and you're close. And that was basically all it was, He just held me and it was beautiful!

But I...instantly, the enemy comes in and, "He's God Almighty! How dare you come so close. You should be on your face, 10 feet away from the throne."

I went to a pastor and said, "What have I done? I'm afraid I've sinned, I've gotten too close to the Lord!" It's not like...I wasn't used to this being held and hugged like that, for years.

And this wonderful pastor looked at me, with his big Irish full-back, line-back muscles in his eyes, and he says, "Aw and it's beautiful, what a beautiful experience you've had. Oh, this is hot fire from Heaven, though! You have to be careful who you share this with, they'll get burned. But no, there's every bit of reverence when ye get close to the Laird like that, you know?"

Excuse my Irish accent... He gave me the freedom to say there's so much reverence and holiness in John placing his head on the heart of Jesus.

*Clare: Alright - the Lord bless you and we pray that anyone who is standing off from the Lord and is afraid, that they'll be encouraged and they'll be able to enter in to worship. And if they see the Lord, they'll be able to embrace Him without any fear or **shame**.*

Taken from: **Can Men Experience Closeness with Jesus as Women Do?**

Shame

"For the sake of survival in the past you have hidden certain things from yourself because it was too painful to look at. But you needn't hide anything from Me. I already know about your sins, dearest. I want to work with you and lift the burden of guilt deep down inside where you have hidden things too painful and disturbing to bring up.

"There is nothing that can keep Me from loving you, absolutely nothing. But our relationship must be built on honesty. I cannot perfect that which you refuse to see. In order to bring you to perfection, you must be willing to admit the truth about yourself. You are beautiful beyond imagining and there is nothing that will change My mind about that. But these deep dark secrets and unconfessed sins let off a scent of guilt and **shame**.

"This, too, is responsible for you distancing yourself from Me. You know there are things too dark to confront but that in My presence all things are seen. May I say I have seen all these things even before they happened? No one wants to see themselves as evil and so they hide their evil thoughts and deeds even from themselves and make excuses to cover them up, or invent stories."

"My Love, come to Me and ask to be relieved of these sins. Ask Me to bring them to the surface where My grace can cauterize your flesh and you will never more be burdened by them."

Taken from: **Honesty: Looking at Yourself in God's Mirror**

"I understand your lack of understanding as to what things offend Me. And for this reason I am being more liberal with you and not requiring complete purity as I did in days of old.

"Yes, swimsuits still **shame** Me. That is way too much flesh showing, but that's the norm for your culture. I remember when you would take your children swimming to the pool and insisted they cover their bodies with shorts and t-shirts, but just them being in the vicinity of others who were immodestly clad, was shameful to Me. I am not condemning you, Clare, I am explaining to you how different Heaven's standards are and that I have made allowances because of your culture."

Taken from: **Blessed Are the Pure, For They Shall See Me**

"Come now, take My hands. Let Me look deeply into your eyes. There is no more **shame** in you, do you understand? I have taken all that was **shameful** and nailed it to the cross. By My Blood you are all beauty within and now we will step forward together and lay the foundation on the immovable Rock of My Love."

Taken from: **Rope of Grace Teaching**

"Men do not wish to receive goodness from My hands. They are so wrapped up in themselves they cannot open their hearts to Me. As if it were **shameful** to receive blessings from Me.

"Their unbelief and rejection wounds My heart, deeply. They can receive from man, they can receive from the government - but they cannot receive from Me.

"And the roles have been subverted in society. Satan has deliberately put the government in the position where the church should be. When I send you a donation and tell you what to use it for, and they reject it, they are playing into Satan's hands. They are so wrapped up in themselves, they cannot see My hand graciously extending a blessing -the blessing I meant for them from My heart. That hurts Me terribly."

Taken from: **Receive From Me, My Church...**

Shame

"Your biggest fight is intimacy. If they can't deny it, they will twist it. Therefore you must approach it in two ways, Scripturally and Experientially. Much of the problem is fundamental ignorance as to how close is "close" with Me. It reaches deep down into the soul. Close is all-enveloping, like a rose blooming from the inside. The seed is given at conversion and even baptism, and through the years as the love for Me is guarded, it blossoms into an all-consuming, fragrant garden of pure Heavenly love. Something few experience on this Earth without passion and sex entering in.

"I do not wish for anyone to be excluded from this relationship of pure intimacy with Me. Understand that I know you, My sons and daughters. I see what no one else sees. I understand the makeup of your body, your hormones and what your flesh fights against your spirit with. There is NOTHING to be **ashamed** of when you are with Me. I already know and understand well the challenges you undergo day after day.

"…Some of you are more vulnerable because of your youth. Let Me explain it to you this way. When this urge tries to take you over, picture yourself in front of Me, My expression calm and compassionate and allow Me to say only one thing, 'You know where this came from, so what are you going to do about it?' Then, ask for My help. For if you to crumple into a ball of **shame**, it only causes the lustful impulse to become stronger. When the demons see they are conquering your resolve, they set upon you with even more force.

"Your best recourse is to completely ignore it and change the subject. And yes, of course, in My Name bind spirits of Lust, but also Degradation. You see, the whole tactic is to degrade you, cause you guilt and **shame**, so you must bind that as well. Then begin to worship Me and change the subject."

Taken from: **If You Love Me – Rapture – Sexual Temptations…**

"When flaws are out in the open they have to be worked on. They won't be tolerated by others, in the sense that they can continue to do damage. I address them openly and ask you to do the same. Without solidarity between people, you become islands impenetrable, hidden, dark, **shameful**, obtuse and closed. This is the state of society now, but not in Heaven. In Heaven, all thoughts are open and visible to everyone because compassion abounds and charity rushes to comfort those who are lacking."

Taken from: **Sincerity, Prophetic Word...**

"I want you to conquer your pride; this is a good place to begin. Others are not slow, Clare. You are impatient. And I say this to all of you, My Brides. More often than not, what you consider slow is normal and you are just impatient. Patience is such a heavenly virtue. If I did not have patience with you Heaven would just about be empty. I never say these things to **shame** you, but rather to convict you and encourage you onto greater holiness. And now is the time to repent for your country as well. I still carry the marks of her sins in My Body. The sins of this nation are very much like the sins of its citizens. The whole world is sin-infested and needs your prayers and for repentance."

Taken from: **Sincerity, Prophetic Word...**

"I've created souls to love Me. The ones who do are a priceless treasure to Me. That's you! You are My priceless treasure. I long for the comfort of your worship, your praise, and holding Me tenderly in your arms. I long for this. How many ways do I have to tell you before you believe Me? So, I'm asking you once again: put on some good praise music, something deep and tender. Embrace Me without guilt or **shame** and just comfort My heart that is so bruised and bleeding."

Taken from: **I'm Calling You Closer**

Sickness

"My children, there is nothing worse than Pride. Not murder, not divorce, not adultery, not failure in business, not **sickness**. Pride is the number one most dangerous thing in your life. And if you think you are without it, you are in fact worse off than most. You have nothing to lose by handing your opinions over to Me for confirmations and everything to gain."

Taken from: **Are You Wise?**

"But I will say this: the prayers of the poor people of the world, the grassroots, the real humans of this world are having an impact on events that is slowing down what the elites have planned.

"You see, AntiChrist cannot be revealed until those who are holding back the wrath with their prayers are removed. There will be a point where the scales tip, but for now there is still balance. I know you want Me to give you more, Clare, but I cannot."

So, what is Your counsel to us, Lord?

"Steady as she goes. Lifting up holy hands in prayer and supplication that this evil will be stopped, and that what must take place will take with it the greatest harvest of souls. And after prayer, action.

"Pursue your missions, My Bride. Continue on in the right direction bringing forth fruit with your gifts. For some of you, the gift is sickness and sufferings of various kinds. I am with you in your bed of suffering, My Brides. I will comfort you with great tenderness and gratefulness for your loving and giving heart.

"Know that the greatest players in this semi-final scene are My faithful intercessors. The little ones no one sees or cares about. They are the decisive force; in the front lines and holding back the tide of evil.

"If you are one of them, I beg you to find honor and great satisfaction in this role. You are the ones making the greatest difference."

Taken from: **God is Hearing the Russian People…**

"Success builds upon success; discipline builds upon discipline. Slothfulness drags you down further and further until you feel hopelessly discouraged. Sloth is indeed a force to be reckoned with. It comes in many different guises, but behind its reasoning is a lie. You CAN do this. I DO want you to use your gift. If you make it a point to be using your gifts one at a time in between necessary duties and charity; if you make it a point to be engaging one of your gifts several times throughout the day - you are on the road to success and freedom from the fears that create roadblocks in your thinking and cause you to give up too easily.

"**Sickness** is a deterrent. But it is also a gift to be used for intercession. But do not allow the enemy to confuse **sickness** with sloth. That can be a slippery logic to easily throw you off course. Once you have recovered yourself, go at it with deliberate intention to succeed and not allow anything to take you away from it.

"There is a cost to greatness. There is much sacrifice that must take place before a gift has become 'great' and useful to Me. And when you have several such gifts, it can be confusing as to which one to use. Go back to your last instruction from Me, if you don't know what to do next. What was the last thing I told you? Remember? I told you to work on the painting and music, in between the messages. I also told you that you had time for both. I have sent you helpers. I have made a way for you. Don't waste time, My Love, don't waste it; it is a precious commodity and a gift I have given you. Please, don't waste it."

Taken from: **Do it Anyway & Transformed to Persevere**

Sickness

"This is why I stress, 'Love one another as I have loved you.' It is only this kind of brotherly love that says 'yes' to the burdens of others. This is your glory, this love that passes all understanding; this is the pinnacle of your Christian walk, to be willing to suffer for others as I suffered for you and all transgressors of the law. What a beautiful vision of My brotherly love this is. What a wonder this is to angels above and souls on Earth, when they see this sacrificial love and even feel its effects.

"There are many kinds of burdens I wish for you to recognize. There are delays that cause a massive reorganizing of times and resources. There are *sick* children, *sick* pets and relatives. When *sickness* strikes, it operates on many different levels: the inconvenience of taking care of them, the extra burden on resources and time. But more than any other cross, is the emotional cross of seeing suffering in your loved one. This is the heaviest cross you can have, the tragedy of pain and suffering.

"I do not allow these burdens easily; they are above all others, training in maturity and agape love. They are the opportunity the soul needs, to grow into who I created them to be. The world tells you all kinds of lies especially the lie of the pain-free, happy life. There is no such thing. Each person, whether you see it or not, is carrying a cross. If they are not with Me, knowing Me and My Word, they do not see the purpose of the suffering; rather they perceive it as a punishment.

"Nothing could be further from the truth. Suffering teaches a soul to focus on what really matters. All the frivolity of life dims in comparison to the health and happiness of the one who is afflicted. But in the midst of that is the greatest gift you can give. When you are **sick** and suffering, life is draining out of you, and I capture that life and bless others with it. If you have given your life to Me without any reservations, you will experience this kind of suffering.

"When I spoke of the abundant life, I was not speaking of the abundance of things in the world. I was speaking of the abundance of My presence, and the joy of living in Me."

Taken from: **Suffering – Real Work in the Realm of the Spirit**

"You do not serve people, Clare, stop fussing about how some will react to this. You serve Me and I wish that My people not perish for lack of knowledge. There is a time for discovery, there is a time for healing and for worship. But I will not have you ignorant of the forces arrayed against you and your children in this last generation.

"And I declare to you all: My power is perfected in your weakness. No weapon formed against you will prosper. Even if you should lose your body, you will not lose your soul. But I am telling you these things because many of you walk around in blinding guilt that you failed as a parent. You are so far down into condemnation that you view your life as a total waste.

"Others of you are saddled with all kinds of **sicknesses** brought about by corrupt governments. Others of you are hopelessly addicted to drugs, or so you think. There is a good reason for this all. I want you to dispense with the guilt and get to the bottom of this."

Taken from: Why a Soul Rejects Love…

"And for you who are called to heal, I live inside of you. Place your hand on the injured or suffering and imagine My hand moving from your heart, out through your hand and onto the soul. I will do the rest. All you have to believe is that I AM and I LIVE IN YOU. This is all that is required for a complete healing of even the most dramatic **sicknesses**."

Taken from: God Will Provide For Those Left Behind

Sickness

*When I came into prayer today, to be honest with you all, I've been going through a spell of weakness and **sickness** with Fibromyalgia. It's just been more intense than normal. And when it's like that, I tend to wonder 'Why is this going on?' Because I get plenty of prayer and plenty of spiritual warfare, and so whatever it is the Lord has been allowing it. And I really sought Him on this today. I wanted a final word on it.*

I said, "Here I am Lord, hoping to understand truly what is going on? I have been sick and weak for days, not fully functioning. Please help me to understand."

The Lord Jesus began, "You are suffering right now for other souls, Clare. Your compassionate heart cry to Me for Mercy is being heard, and I need this spiritual/physical offering from you. So many right now are suffering in unimaginable ways. I cry with them, and your free will offering is turning the tide on many things. I know you understand. I know also that this has been very hard and frustrating for you, but today you finally realized what it was all about.

"It wasn't punishment, although you should never take for granted that your indiscretions should be overlooked. I atoned with every drop of My Blood for the sins of the world, yours included. Never take this precious offering for granted, that wounds Me deeply."

Taken from: **Satanists Posing as Concerned Christians & Sickness/Suffering**

"There is yet one more facet of this healing, and that is staying in place. The soul who is suffering may very well be in the midst of a very serious situation, or soul-threatening that needs a lot of grace before it can be resolved. In those cases, the soul has chosen to carry this cross for the sake of the person they are praying for. This is why you've become accustomed to asking, 'Who are you praying for?'

"Because often times they are praying for a very serious situation that needs a greater lever of prayer and this infirmity becomes a fast offering, much like Paul's thorn. Which brings us to another point. There are times when a soul is weighted down with many, many graces and a **sickness** is allowed to humble them, lest they become proud and lose everything, including their souls."

Taken from: **Gift of Healing…**

"This is what I wish for you who have dedicated yourselves to tearing down where I am building up. I am now putting signs in your lives: failures, very hard lessons, **sicknesses** are being allowed; financial crises is being allowed. Many things are falling out from beneath your feet. Your lives are falling apart. Have you asked Me why?

"I will tell you why: I have allowed the enemy to sift you, because you have sifted Me, you have stolen from Me by allowing the enemy to work through you.

"So now I am giving you an occasion of introspection. As things fall apart around you, do you have the courage to say, 'We were warned this would happen.' Because if you do, you will repent and I will restore you on every level I have allowed the enemy to steal from you."

Taken from: **Lord, Why Are Things Falling Apart?**

"You who are blessed with the cross of **sickness**, which you carry knowingly, are among the most powerful of My intercessors, because you have offered your own bodies as a living holocaust to bring Heaven to Earth. I am with you and will multiply graces released on your behalf. All these sufferings, every single one can be offered to My Father for this election."

Taken from: **The Election: Jesus calls for "War Spiritually"**

Signs from Him/His Love

"Just as in days gone by, when I supernaturally protected My people, so shall I protect those who must stay behind. There will be one among them who will be designated the leader, and to him or her, I will give supernatural knowledge and wisdom. Protect this one who is critical to your mission. Let not the devils cause division, misunderstanding, murmuring and jealousy. Be on your guard against these poisons they will use to divide and scatter you all.

"Together you will survive. Separated, you will face many dangers without anyone to back you up. Do not let them divide and conquer. Be smarter than the enemy, walk in charity and humility and you will have no problems. Walk in self-will, selfishness, suspicion, and rancor, it will be your demise. There will be many testings among the groups, many testings. Painful decisions to make, life or death decisions to make. I will give you peace when the decisions are the hardest. Use lots to help you determine a plan of action.

"I will give you **signs of My love**, signs of danger, signs when you are going the wrong way, signs when you are going the RIGHT way. Be attentive, pay close attention to the signs I send you."

You know, when I think of signs, I think of heart-shaped rocks, the face of Jesus in the bark of the tree... different things. But if everyone's on the watch for signs, then they're going to see them.

"If you suspect you have made a wrong decision, stop and pray it through. Better to wait on me than to move forward into a trap. There will be times to act and times to wait. It is in the times of waiting that trials will be the most difficult."

Taken from: **Jesus Speaks on Provision and Protection**

"I am calling you to set Me apart from all your other relationships and compromise no more to any man, for this will be your downfall.

"This is the time of great testing that is coming upon all who dwell on the Earth and to give in now is certain to lead down the road of compromise that ends with the mark of eternal damnation.

"Stand strong in what you know in your heart to be true. Expect - without allowing insinuations of doubt to creep in - expect Me to move upon your efforts and visit you, for truly I am a God who rewards those who diligently search for Me. Open your eyes, open your ears, retune your mind and your hearts, pay attention! I speak to you many times during the day but you are like men who have fallen asleep at the gates - you do not recognize the King when He comes to you.

"I am blessing you with a new anointing, to hear Me. Look for My messages to you in everything around you: the wind in the trees, the sun on your path, the bumper sticker in the traffic jam, the numbers on your clocks, the call of the dove, the heart shape when you cut open a tomato, or spill on the counter.

"Oh, I speak to you in so many ways! Open your ears and your eyes now to hear and see Me. As you practice this, I will become clearer and louder in My messages to you. The **signs of My Love** are all around you. Go now and begin to acknowledge them."

Taken from: **You Do Not Receive Because You Do Not Believe**

"Yet the **signs of My coming** are everywhere now. All if fulfilled. Never before was all that was written fulfilled so that I could come. But now it is merely the word of the Father before all of that changes. The wise have become wiser, the deaf have become deafer and it is nearly finished."

Taken from: **The Deaf & Blind Among Us**

Signs from Him/His Love

"Watching is by no means an easy occupation, it demands a very high level of faith and hope. These I impart to you in our times together. I will use every means to touch you, My Beloved Ones, even bumper stickers and traffic jams.

"There is not one moment of the day that I am not bringing some encouragement across your path, because I know your frame and for those of you that must be involved in the world, little telltale **signs of My love** abound. When the clock reads 3:11 or 11:13, or 555 the number of my wounds, or 444 the number of the "Gospels, or 3:33, or even 1:11. All of these are little nudges that I am with you. Seems silly, doesn't it?"

"Not at all, Lord, we cherish those little signs from You! I even enjoy it when you put my birth month and year on the clock, I kind of chuckle to myself, 'He's thinking of me.'"

"Yes, and even love songs you hear, more often than not I am singing them in My heart to you. Or you can sing them in your heart to Me. I love it when you do."

"Really? I wasn't sure about that."

You know, when He said that I realized, when I'm in the grocery store - usually on the Baking Aisle...the sugar and the chocolate chips and the things that I just love - even when I'm there, I'll hear a song that's a love song and think to myself, 'Lord? Did You play that just for me? Are You singing that to me?' And I'll assume that He has, because He's omnipresent, and of course He knows that love song is playing, and He knows how He feels about me. And I know how I feel about Him, so I just turn it around and sing it to Him in my heart.

"A sign or exclamation of love from My Bride goes right to the core of My Being and brings Me deep joy. I love it, Clare, when you sing those songs to Me. These are lovers games: leaving flowers behind, drawing a heart in the sand or on your windshield or back car window - I see it, it touches My heart and I will leave you little heart shapes, especially when you are preparing food.

"Look for them and acknowledge Me. I am so happy when you are grateful for **My marks of affection to you**. I'm so grateful when you recognize them!"

Taken from: **Jesus is Waiting on the Turn Key Event to Begin the Rapture**

"I see the hidden things of the heart, I see the love and the care and I reward you for what I see. And many of you are now beginning to come into your own with piercing the veil and welcoming My perceptible presence in your lives.

"You are beginning to see just how real is the place I've prepared for you. You are beginning to feel the warmth and safety of My embrace, all because you believed. Continue to believe, do not allow the enemy to steal the fruits of your labors from you.

"Protect these precious gifts and fruits. Remember: Satan has come to kill, to steal and to destroy, and he will snatch them out of your hand if you let him. So take care to protect small beginnings and signs of My indwelling presence with you. These are PRICELESS gifts. Keep them under lock and key in your hearts.

"I bless you, My Brides, with the abundant life of My presence, My perceptible presence in your midst. It is My joy to be with you and even a greater joy when you recognize My workings in your midst. We are as One."

Taken from: **Jesus' Perceptible and Manifest Presence is With You**

Signs from Him/His Love

"This is certainly an evil day in which you are living. Yes, it is very evil and your faith will be severely undermined if you allow it. Will you?"

How do I prevent it?

"Take every thought captive and look for **My signs** that you are on the right track. I know exactly what you are going through right now. There is a certain weariness of life coupled with fears of the immediate future. I know well what ails you, My Bride."

Taken from: **Stand on Your Own Word From Me**

"...Yes, that's exactly what I will do. I'm just so sorry you must be stuck in that body 'till I come for you. But you will find, you'll wish you had it when you want to touch those on Earth with your prayers or get them to follow **My signs** leading them to blessings. Oh yes, you'll see, when people miss Me, just how frustrating it can be. Then (and I know you well) you'll ask Me, 'Jesus, can I just have my body back for a few hours and go visit them??"

Taken from: **Creativity Renders You Responsive to Me**

This has been an interesting week - I've been doing a lot of things around the house, and kinda getting things in order because I had permission to...including the yard and all of that. And, I guess I've kinda gotten into "nesting". (Anyone who's ever been pregnant can tell you about nesting.) It's gotten to the point where it's starting to distract me, and pull me away from the Lord. I really, really need to bring it to a close.

Jesus had addressed that first thing, as I was rather lamenting to Him. He said, "I know how you are feeling. These are warning signs that you need to call a halt soon."

Taken from: **Rope of Grace Teaching**

"You have many who are insecure about the Rapture - you aren't the only one."

What do we do?

"Stay in prayer, watch for the **signs** I send you every day for encouragement. Get Rhemas from your Bible, and speak to Me, dearest."

By the way, a rhema is an anointed, enlightened Word and you can get a rhema from a license plate, or a magazine or a movie or anything like that. You just feel the quickening of the Holy Spirit. It's something that the Lord has given right then in that special time, to help you

He continued, "Speak your tender heart to Me. I am here to listen and I promised you I would never leave you on your own. I would never give up helping you learn to listen to Me in confidence. I see the shadows of insecurity in your heart. Don't think that everyone who puts up a brave front isn't suffering from the same thing."

∼

"This is what I wish for you who have dedicated yourselves to tearing down where I am building up. I am now putting **signs in your lives**: failures, very hard lessons, sicknesses are being allowed; financial crises is being allowed. Many things are falling out from beneath your feet. Your lives are falling apart.

Have you asked Me why? I will tell you why: I have allowed the enemy to sift you, because you have sifted Me, you have stolen from Me by allowing the enemy to work through you."

Taken from: **Unconditional Trust in Me**

"You see, when you entrust Me with all that is yours - your everything

Simon's Cross

- I dispense grace and mercy where I will, but so much is handed over
to Me in the gift of your life. You have said, 'Jesus, anything for You.'
And I have said, 'I will have you with Me in paradise someday, but
for now I need your sacrifices, I need your consolations, I need your
physical infirmities, yes, even those. They are your cross, your **Simon's
cross.**'

"You say to Me, 'But you did save us for once and for all' and you speak
the truth. But now, someone must pray that this gift of salvation is
delivered to the poorest of poor, the dying, the lame, the sick, the
drug addict, the victims of tragedy, all who are languishing without
knowing Me and without any hope.

"True, I have visited some of them many times in their lives before, but
they were not ready. Now they are ready. And those who have yet to
know Me, because of your offerings, are now coming to know Me and
discovering the love and joy of their lives. With that discovery, they are
happy to die to be with Me and another soul is snatched from Satan.

"So, this is not a punishment, as you imagined."

Taken from: **When the Lord is Painfully Silent**

"I know these crosses you have carried for months now, My Bride, have
grown weighty. And I also know how they have paved the way for
the salvation of many that had no chance. I also see the tremendous
growth in you who have willingly taken on **Simon's cross** on My
behalf. You do not see it, but so much progress in holiness and
brotherly love has been made in your lives, and your reward continues
to grow, although I know that is the last thing on your minds.

"But I am here to tell you that we are nearing the end and every prayer
and act of repentance on behalf of sins committed is making an impact
and changing the intensity of the judgments in severity and scope. It

is also playing a part in the lives of families who have intercessors. There will be extended mercy for their loved ones, because they loved much and cared enough to pray for those they do not even know. They prayed because of the ache in My heart. I will move in sovereign ways to protect the ache in their hearts, the destiny of their loved ones.

"So, continue to grow in stature, My Brides. You are growing into the realms of My Love, into the depth and width and breadth of My Love for mankind. You are becoming more like Me every day and when I snatch you up from this sinful mire, you will barely recognize yourselves, so steeped in glory will you be. Carry on, My Dear ones. You are changing the course of history with your prayers. Carry on. I bless you now with My peace and inward joy to calm your fears and stabilize you in the events yet to come. Let that joyful light, the joy of My countenance shine out from within your hearts. You are the light of the world."

Taken from: **You Are the Light of the World**

"And one more thing, when you take on a prayer burden for a soul, expect to be exercised in various trials and difficulties, even in sickness. Remember, if sickness does not yield to prayer, I am using it as a fast offering to bring them closer to Me. In due time that will pass and you will also see the progress they have made spiritually, because you were willing to carry **Simon's cross** a few steps up Calvary.

"So much is not understood now, but you can observe these truths in your daily life. Cause and affect; your prayers, their progress. Yes, I will use the littlest of your sufferings and contradictions in this life to water the lifeless wasteland of the lost and broken souls. Truly you are My appointed ambassadors of love and from your hearts, I reach out and touch the lost."

Taken from: **You Are Ambassador's to the Desolate Soul**

Simon's Cross

"Do not be surprised if you start manifesting their symptoms (of a sick person you are praying for to be healed), and do not be surprised that there is sometimes a sacrifice required.

"I have taught you on **Simon's Cross.** That is very, very real. And when you are praying for others, and especially one in particular, then I may allow some unpleasant manifestations in your own body. You may be carrying a sliver of My Cross for days until that soul is fully healed."

∾

"Don't be surprised when oppositions and difficulties arise, this is all part of it and will be a proof to you that the gift is working.'"

Taken from: **Gift of Healing, Jesus give us Point to Remember**

Clare: Amen. Well, one of the things that I have noticed is that, there are those of us who really are called to carry **Simon's Cross.**

Like the one woman who wrote in and said she's just so frustrated...and then says as an aside, "Now, I DID offer my suffering for ISIS, for the people who've been affected by ISIS."

Well, when we're in a position - and I think a lot of people who've had anointed prayer for illness, they've had really anointed prayer, they have strong faith, they've seen healing in their life before - but for some reason the Lord has not totally healed them...a lot of those people have been called to be Simon's. To bear the Lord's Cross for Him. The Simon's Cross *and to offer the sacrifice of a fast offering in the form of waiting for the Lord to heal them. Waiting for His timing, His readiness to heal them. In the meantime, they are bearing fruit - they're not just lying there dormant and useless.*

Ezekiel: That's right.

Clare: They're bearing fruit. Some of us - the Lord had told us this last week: we are going to see more intense suffering up unto the Rapture.

Ezekiel: And it's solid gold. You know, He didn't just go to the Garden, die on the Cross, raise up and that was it. He suffered. Scriptures say He was a man of suffering, acquainted with Sorrow and Pain. He took on our iniquities, He took on our sins. He didn't say this life would be easy. He said...

Clare: Deny yourself. Pick up your Cross. Follow Me.

Ezekiel: That's right. And in this world you'll have trouble, but be encouraged, because I have overcome the world.

Taken from: The Bride's Joy and Sorrows Intensify...

"So, now I have told you a secret: I suffer the wait with you. If I did not need you to be vigilant and waiting, even to the point of frustration and anger...if I did not need that, I would not have required it of you. This IS Simon's cross - will you carry it? I impart the strength and hope now. Receive it into your hearts as you hear these words, carry it with Me, will you?"

Taken from: **The Frustration and Anger of Waiting for Jesus**

"Satan would have you get discouraged, telling you that you just can't do it. That's a lie. You can most certainly do it, for My power is perfected in your weakness. I have not abandoned you, I am not chastising you. I am desperate for love offerings, fast offerings and those who would follow in **Simon's footsteps, carrying the cross** all the way to the top of the hill."

Taken from: **Why the Need for the Blood Sacrifice**

Simon's Cross

Finally, He answered me and He said, "You are under tremendous oppression right now. Please - offer it to Me - it is needed. Oh, Clare, if only you could see the travesties being perpetrated on humanity right now, if only you could see."

Oh, Lord I don't think I can see. Oh, please Lord - just hearing about this with ISIS is too much.

"Well, take a splinter from My Cross then, and just carry that, please. That's the least you can do.

"Tell them that I need their sufferings and oppressions for innocent little ones being murdered in cold blood, that I might remove from them the pain and terror they are at this moment suffering. Yes, I always send you little updates on something when I want you to know about it. That's why you don't need to search the internet."

I was thinking to myself, 'You know, I wouldn't have known about this unless someone had brought it to me.' But He has ways of letting me know and then He comes in on prayer and explains why He brought that item up.

And for you who are new to our channel...there's a whole understanding of why the Lord allows suffering in this world that we've done several teachings on. It has to do with carrying Simon's Cross - the Cross that, when Jesus was carrying His Cross, Simon was called in to help. Simon of Cyrene was called in to help carrying that Cross - this is after the pattern of Jesus and Simon.

We are carrying a cross so that the suffering in our lives can be turned into opportunities for the gospel to spread and for people to be relieved of their suffering. The Lord's done the finished work of Salvation on the Cross, but still the message has to be delivered and people that are suffering terribly need to be relieved of that.

And somehow, in the economy of things, spiritual economy of things, the Lord removes the suffering from them and spreads it thin throughout His Body so that we can all carry it.

And that's what we mean by "a splinter from His Cross". It's not works righteousness, it's not about works at all. It's about loving the Lord enough to lay our lives aside for a few moments and help Him carry the Cross that's needed for these people to receive Him and for them to be relieved of their suffering. These poor, innocent little children.

So, that's what He means when He says, "Tell them that I need their sufferings and oppressions for innocent little ones being murdered in cold blood."

"In this furnace of affliction," He continues "you are removing the sufferings of so many little innocents. What is being done is beyond human, it is pure demonic. That is why so many on your channel right now are going through very, very hard times."

Taken from: **Terrors of ISIS, Please Intercede**

I have always believed that our trials contain two components: graces released for sufferings endured, as in Simon's Cross, *and God's correction for things that should not be a part of our nature, and must be removed. We have been assailed by many supernatural attacks, which are bringing us closer and closer to the Holy Mountain. Even though they are painful, the fruit is amazing.*

For one, right now the Lord is calling for fast offerings to turn the evil plans of the powers-that-be in this country, to prevent the elections and cause martial law in America.

Taken from: **Holy Trials, Holy Fruit, Stand in the Gap for America**

Slander and Reproach

It began tonight during worship. I saw these dark, dark, blue clouds, kind of in the shape of a vortex, almost like looking down the center of a tornado. But, out of it were hordes of dark-winged creatures. Black, black-winged creatures, like a cloud.

...So, when I came into worship, the Lord showed this to me, He wanted me to begin to write it down. He began:

"These creatures I showed to you were like a bat-vulture type animal, and the nature of these beasts is that they dwell in the darkness and feed on death. The dead white horse represents the Christians that have been murdered by the lies uttered from the mouths of other Christians. These creatures excrete death wherever they land. For them to land, there must be sin. Gossip, slander, calumny, **reproach** - whether it be towards yourself or another. That is why I'm working so hard to eradicate slander and reproach from the lips and hearts of My Bride. I do NOT want them perching on her.

"My children, by your attitudes you open the door and invite these unclean creatures. Satan is counting on your personal dissatisfaction with yourselves to create a place for them to land. This is another reason worship is so important. When I come into worship with you, I restore your bridal beauty and purity. This gives you the strength to grow up into what I see you are.

"When you disparage yourself, you create a landing place for these vile creatures. That is why, night and day, satan is sending out lying spirits to demean you. It is to prepare you for these creatures, that they will have a perch. And, once they begin to defecate on you, you begin to judge and undermine others. You become a cripple: bitter and disillusioned, looking for opportunities to find fault with others, because you can't stand who YOU are."

Taken from: **You Must Love Yourself Before You Can Love Your Brother**

"When I spoke of the abundant life, I was not speaking of the abundance of things in the world. I was speaking of the abundance of My presence, and the joy of living in Me.

"You see, when I told you to deny yourself, pick up your cross and follow Me, I gave you the mandate of having your own unique cross. It could be slander and calumny, or lack of appreciation for what you do. It could be the inconvenience of a car breaking down, or the denial of a loan to get another car. It could be false accusation at work and that someone who really dislikes you has tried to darken your name. It could be deferring to a family member over where you are going on a vacation or family outing."

Taken from: **Suffering – Real Work in the Realm of the Spirit**

"Do you understand? I want to forgive you. I want your blind eyes opened. I want your repentance. I truly wait, day after day for you to recognize you have gone down the wrong path. You have not chosen Me, but your flesh and the pleasures of this world. You have been embroiled in disputes, accusation, calumny, bitterness and backbiting...stealing, killing and destroying the good names of others and slandering the Gospel I died on the Cross to set you free with.

"I can forgive you, if you repent. I have paid the price but you must do your part. It will come upon you suddenly and there will be no remedy, no time to repent, no time to even call out to Me. For you, it will be over and your destiny will be sealed. There will be no excuses at that time, for I have given you warning after warning after warning in an attempt to turn you at the very last minute. There will be no excuses. You were warned, you were taught and still you chose to go with the Devil."

Taken from: **On the Brink of War Again**

Slander and Reproach

"Now, I will explain to you how it is with those "Christians" who lose their salvation. They are like the seed thrown on the rocky soil. At fir[.] they receive the message with joy, but when the honeymoon wears off and they are called to holiness of life, they balk. Satan watches for these, the crows come and snatch up the sprout and devour it.

"I offered them Love, but they disdained the discipline of the Lord. They saw the great price involved in loving others and conquering the sin nature and putting on My meekness. This was too great a price to pay.

"Secretly, they congratulated themselves that they were OK and even better and wiser than others. They thought they could toy with evil, **slander** and lies and remain unmoved. In the meantime, the devils fe[.] them with the most clever and logical arguments, shredding their fait[.] in My simple goodness to pieces.

"I 'never knew' them in the sense that they did not lay their lives down once and for all at My feet and allow Me to surgically remove sin from their lives. They were invited into the depths, but they never persevered until they truly knew Me and My goodness.

"They were double-minded, clinging to their intellect and questioning those things that resonated deeply in their souls. Rather than accepting like a little child, they cut it open with their intellect and los[.] their innocent faith.

"Please obey Me in this. Stay away from **slander** and evil speaking. When you do come across that post that begins to detract, delete it immediately. Do not entertain it or try to reason your way through to them. You cannot reason with a demon. They will always find the hole in your armor and stab you where it hurts the most.

"Rather lift that shield of faith and cut the wicked head off before it reaches your heart. Now, I have brought many new brothers and sisters to this channel, and in this teaching, I am advising you - do not suppose you can play with fire and come away without being burnt. You have discerned that I am truly on this channel. Do not go probing around in the garbage out of curiosity. Follow your heart, and your discernment.

"Do not allow yourself the liberty of engaging in curiosity. Protect your relationship with Me. I have begun the good work in you and if you are faithful and obedient, I will complete it. You have a choice. Choose wisely."

Taken from: **How Does A Fall Happen?**

"But there are certain rules you must live by. Honesty is first and foremost. Vigilance over your own sins and bad example. The devils are clever and they know how to provoke a soul to cause a breach in their covering. Charity, humility and patience also score high on the list of things targeted and necessary to maintain My Protection.

"Come to Me immediately when you fall. Don't waste a moment. Make a sincere confession and renounce that sin. I will then restore your covering and add to it protection, and the grace to not repeat those sins.

"I have already taught you about judging others. The quickest way to lose your covering is to **slander**, calumniate, or gossip about another. Not only will the enemy use this to divide and conquer, he will use it to make you vulnerable to attack. The more key your position is, the more careful you will have to be about your heart attitude."

Taken from: **Surviving the Coming Tribulation**

Slander and Reproach

"My Brides, love is what our relationship is based on. And if you love Me, you will obey Me. If you are **slandering** or undermining your neighbor you are destroying your relationship with Me. Without faith it is impossible to please Me, and now I tell you truly, without love for your brother, it is impossible to please Me.

"Do not for one moment abandon the gate of virtue, nor for one second give into the burning desire to hate. This is coming directly from demons who are flaming you with the fires of hatred Satan has for everything and everyone I created. Do not partake of his poison; do not fall under his influence."

Taken from: **Refining Fires Are Coming...**

"My children, I have warned you again and again about judging, but when you judge My prophets you incur serious repercussions in your life, immediately. You will find that the results will be immediate, because I am trying to break you of this wicked habit. Do you understand, when you judge others and especially My vessels unto honor, that you invite in a host of demons to sift you and your family??

"Do you understand that when you spread false reports about the innocent and **slander** their character that you have brought a curse down upon yourself? I have to tell you, you will see more and more division and strife among your friends for such behavior, because beneath it all there is spiritual jealousy, the most destructive force in My Body.

"When you engage patterns of jealousy you actually oppose Me and the operation of My gifts and I will hold you accountable for the souls I could not reach because you spread lies about a vessel."

Taken from: **Carry the Cross, Don't Judge...**

"Whenever My Spirit moves upon your hearts, pray from the heart in the way you're inspired. I only brought up the (Divine Mercy) chaplet's virtue because some have **slandered** it. I wanted you to understand what the Scriptures say and don't say about prayer, not what men twist to fit their own particular doctrine to put others down with. In the Scriptures, I have said things that could be twisted and rationalized, made into a doctrine by those who do not think beyond the lines of print on the page.

"Your prayers are powerful. They do not bounce off the ceiling as the enemy would have you believe. No, every single prayer is presented in Heaven as a sweet smelling sacrifice, every single prayer. If they are not permitted to do physical harm, they will at the very least convince gullible souls that their prayers are a waste of time. Do not allow yourselves to be victimized by such as these."

Taken from: **Pray for Mercy & More Time**

"Yes, the idea of eating My Flesh and drinking My Blood was the most noxious thing they could imagine. But when the Mercy Seat is shown with My Blood upon it, their (the Jews) confusion will be turned to incredulity. Some will renounce it as a prank. Others will be deeply smitten, falling on their faces in utter brokenness for having **slandered** all these years. The enemy will discourage you from prayer if you let him, in the same way he discourages you about yourself.

"For their blindness and persecution, some will not rise up from that place for days and even weeks, so troubling will this discovery be to them - so deeply repentant. My people are stubborn, but once they know the truth they will be stubborn for Truth - and thousands will be martyred, dying happily for My Name's sake. I have sent them confirmations. I love them - some of them have been very diligent."

Taken from: **The Coming Revival, Authentic Worshippers…**

Spiritual Warfare

"The weapons of our **warfare** are not carnal but **spiritual**. And as things heat up, Christians will find themselves more and more challenged in their faith. More attacks against Faith and Hope are on the way."

Taken from: **Another Soul for Heaven, Another Jewel in Your Crown...**

The Lord began: "Trouble is coming to America. You know it's been a long time coming, but it hasn't been cancelled, only delayed."

At the point that He said that, I saw a vision of a long, long freight train moving very slowly but steadily.

"It's been coming and is still at the threshold, not quite to begin yet. I want all of you to be prepared by being steadfast in Me. Do you understand? Very clever demons have been assigned to this channel to bring you all down, but I will continue to vindicate you, Clare. You needn't bother with defending Me. I can take care of the both of us.

"But I have trained all of you in the sly deceits of the wicked ones and it wouldn't hurt you, My Brides, to go over the discernment messages and teachings again."

Yes, there is a playlist with 36 of them - and there are probably some I didn't put on the playlist recently.

"Right, and all of them bring up a different aspect of **spiritual warfare.** Strife, division and backbiting are the main assignments. So, be particularly vigilant over all your motives, knowing that if you sow strife in your homes you will reap strife and strife will weaken you.

"In a weakened state, your discernment and faith begin to fail you. Much better to let others be right, My Brides, than to enter into dissension and be weakened in your faith.

"Pride will be another defensive posture the enemy will try to engender. Again, let others be right and move on, especially in the home and work place where you must deal with them every day.

"Be a 'No Fight' person. Let me tell you a secret: if they can't get a rise out of you, they'll find someone else to pick on - so 'no fight' is also a very peaceful little island to dwell on. But before they are convinced you are a no fight/no fun person, they will test you to the max."

Taken from: **This is a Time of Preparation**

We are a very small support group for Heartdwellers, but five or more of us have been going through hellish **(spiritual) warfare***, intercessory prayer for the nations and on the edge of sudden, life-threatening illnesses that manifested and then let up, and manifested again and let up, over and over again for about a week.*

And I mean life-threatening illnesses. We have been praying and repenting for the world and if our little handful has been doing this, imagine how many around the world are also doing it.

And today we have turned a corner. The Lord has said that as long as prayer, fasting and repentance is on the schedule daily, we can continue moving forward without everything around us being nuked.

This is conditional: if prayer and repentance continue, so do we continue - so do our children and grandchildren continue and still have another chance at repentance and coming to the Lord. So does the world continue. And change is coming to the world, change for the better. But if we slack off, things could go south overnight. So, press in, dear ones. Press in.

Taken from: **Prayer & Repentance Holds Judgment Back…**

Spiritual Warfare

"...soon, Christians will be known as a force to be reckoned with because of their steadfast faith. The world will begin to see the difference between My people and those of the world. Not in self-righteousness, but in ethical behavior and sticking to what they believe in the face of opposition and ridicule. This will be like drawing a line in the sand, 'This far and no father'. All over the world people will begin to recognize Christians as a real, living entity, as a Kingdom united under God.

"**Spiritual warfare** will be needed just to get through the day. This will not be a time of ease but a time of fighting to maintain ground, and pressing in to take more ground. Those who do not have an authentically intimate relationship with Me will be grossly led astray into counterfeits which are about to spring up everywhere.

"Bashing and gossip will reach an unprecedented level and those who do not live by My Ways will fall. The enemy will use gossip to create a breach in their armor and on the heels of that, demons will enter and wreak havoc. Congregations will begin to fall apart as never before, as weak Christians give in to the temptation to criticize others, especially those in positions of responsibility. It will be hard on overseers, very hard. The sheep will be belligerent and combative, believing themselves to have a higher truth than those I have appointed.

"Oh, Clare, pray for the pastors --- it will be as if demons came in and took over their churches. They will see an unprecedented level hostility from even those they've trusted in the past. Yes, darkness is encroaching, and only those who truly Know Me will stand. Even at that, it will be a struggle.

"But the secret is love and forgiveness. Being in this posture will completely foil the enemy's attempts to over throw My people. My Bride will shine by her docility, humility and ability to handle even the most difficult people without losing grace.

"She will present an example undeniable of My Living Presence in her.

"Oh, My People, prepare yourselves for the **battle**. Be prepared to be rejected, calumniated, abused, ignored, down-graded. Do not allow any of the enemy's attempts to knock you down, rather stand fast in who you are in Me. Your worth is not in gold and silver; your worth is in My Blood, which purchased you from among the nations."

Taken from: **Refining Fires Are Coming...**

Lord, I thought no one ever got tired in Heaven?

"Oh no, that's a misconception. There is always comfort and refreshment in Heaven, but laboring for souls can take a heavy toll - especially when **spiritual warfare** is in progress. In your terms - everything is very 'electrical' - even as I have shown you how lightning is a sign of **warfare** in the first heaven (That's our atmosphere).

"There are exchanges of energies that are damaging, but in Heaven, repair is always happening. And yes, there are beds in Heaven, just for reclining and refreshment. There are energy dynamics that on Earth most are not familiar with. Why do you suppose I made us a hammock in the forest?"

Taken from: **Heaven: Jesus Shares About...**

Father also has been present and active in this **spiritual warfare**. *It's amazing to watch Them step in and deal with the demons directly. I suppose it's because we are His children on the front lines, and we are sharing with you, and they have overstepped their permissions.*

Taken from: **Spiritual Warfare: 13 - Protection Through Obedience**

Spiritual Warfare

"Do you know how many times a day fear interrupts us?" *He means the ability to communicate together.* "You were bound by fears: fear of displeasure, fear of dying, fear of disease , fear of losing your husband or your children, fear of Me...

"Even as kind as I am and as gentle with you, you're still afraid. Fear of uselessness, fear of failure... Don't you see how controlled you are by fear? This is universal to man."

Well, that kind of opened my eyes when He said that. I just knew right away He wants me to be honest with you and share with you how I managed to get through these things.

We live in a house in New Mexico. I have to say it's spiritually a very dark, dark place and there's a lot of New Age movement in this town. It's not easy to survive here. There has to be **spiritual warfare** *on a constant basis.*

I told Him, "Lord, I didn't want to hear this. I thought I was beyond those fears. Now I see that was pride and ignorance on my part."

He answered, "No, it's precisely that you struggle that I'm bringing you into confrontation with your fears. Do you know that everyone - and I do mean everyone - has fear?"

Taken from: **Have No Fear of the Future...**

"Any disturbance of peace and joy is the work of a demon. When you feel fear, stop. Use My word and destroy that lie. Fear, anxiety, insecurity, doubt, panic, all of these are weapons of **(spiritual) warfare** used to disable and destroy you.

"Doubt, Fear and Confusion, are signs of demonic intervention. Take up your sword and destroy them, before they get a stronger foot hold.

"They will try, but when they come at you from one direction, I will help you fight them off in seven directions, I will scatter them and put them on the run, but I need your cooperation."

Taken from: **Attacks Against the Faith Are on the Way...**

He is continually exercising us in **warfare** *and making us strong against all adversaries. As I was speaking these words, I had a vision of a soldier, a big Roman soldier with muscles bulging out of his arms and his legs. Not only was he skilled with the sword, but he was very strong, very powerful. And this is what I believe the Lord is doing when He allows these trials.*

One of the things I'd like to mention here, is that when you are under attack - the demons are just having a hey-day with you, you can offer all the sufferings of that attack and those inconveniences for the salvation of the soul who is on the brink of hell, who is just about ready to fall into the Abyss. And by doing that, you'll greatly frustrate them (the demons), because they'll reason, "Well, the more I torment her, the more she offers up to God for the salvation of that soul. And the less I torment her, the more trouble I get into 'cause I'm not doing my job." So, it really does throw them into confusion.

Taken from: **Victory Over Trials, Temptations & Spiritual Muscle**

So, what's been going on with us, I bet you're all asking? Battle after battle after battle, that's what's going on. And for all you curious Satanists, yes, it's been hard...but now we are stronger and God always uses your curses to bring blessings. We are being formed in the image of Christ, bloody Crown and all, just so He will easily recognize His Bride when He comes. In the meantime, we have new swords, shields and mighty weapons of **warfare** *to bring down strongholds.*

Taken from: **These Lite and Momentary Sufferings**

Success

...part of the reason the economy in this country is slumping and the Lord is allowing it, is to get His Bride back from the world. To get her mind off of the things of the world and onto Him.

So, you know, we have a lot of prosperity Christians in this country, people who talk about prosperity, that you're not really a successful *Christian if you don't have the faith to be prosperous. Nothing could be further from the truth, because prosperity and money was the last thing on the Lord's mind in the New Testament. In the Old Testament, it was sometimes a mark of favor from God, but in the New Testament, the Lord set a standard.*

He didn't choose to be born as a king, or a prince, or to live like a king or a prince. He chose a simple life, an unpretentious life. A life that was not entrenched of the things of the world.

So, He's looking for a Bride who resembles Him. And as I examine my heart every day before the Lord, and I realize the areas where I fall short, I'm writing those things down for you as well. Because I think we can help each other, by recognizing some things about ourselves and sharing them.

Taken from: **Prophetic Message to My Bride...**

Let's say one of my children show up at the door and it totally revamps my night and I must have hospitality to them whom I love very much. Being goal oriented is not a healthy thing. You see a lot of Hollywood movies about how some are highly **successful** *in business but tragically unsuccessful in their marriages. Those are goal oriented people. These are people who are really serious about what they're doing to the inclusion to all other facets of their lives.*

The Lord has not called us to that. He has called us to love our brother as we love ourselves and to love Him with all of our hearts (Mark 12:31).

Sometimes people laugh about these qualities and say, "Oh that person is a compulsive addictive worker." We chide each other about these things, but it really is quite serious. It wrinkles the garment that the Lord is wanting us to make pure and white for His coming. We must cooperate with the Holy Spirit.

Taken from: **The Righteous Bride Will Not Quench the Spirit**

"If a soul, chosen to lead cannot wait on Me to do the doing, then whatever they build on will not stand. And in contrast, if a soul DOES wait while I lay the foundation and prepare the way, then what is born will endure, because I am the Master Builder and what I create - endures. You have endured. Your husband has endured because I was the builder. By My hand I brought you together, by My hand I preserved you. And by My hand your marriage IS a **success.** When souls learn to wait on Me in a big way, there lives will, in the end, flourish and bring forth copious fruit. This is something I want you to share."

Taken from: **I AM the Master Builder...**

"Mainly in this time preceding My coming for you, I am adding gems to your crowns, all of you. You are going from glory to glory and in the meantime your challenges and sufferings I shall take as a fast offering for the conversion of more and more souls.

"Scorn, contempt and persecution await all my faithful Christians. How can I reward unless trials are passed **successfully?** And in the meantime, teachings will come forth that will assist those left behind. All serves a purpose, every little thing - take it as a test of virtue, another fast offering and this will keep your attitude pure and grateful, and keep you from bitterness."

Taken from: **Another Soul for Heaven, Another Jewel in Your Crown**

Success

"What I want to say is that you mustn't grieve over those who are left behind. No, this is their destiny because they chose to live in that layer of isolation where everything was provided by their own hand, where **success** was the entire focus of their lives.

"Yes, they chose this, and the world being such as it is, left them blind and naked before Me. And this I allowed to save their souls, for without it, well... Hell is filling up. They are not all bad people, just Godless, with no need for God. It is My act of mercy that their world comes crashing to an end. It is My love for them that allows such catastrophe. Only nakedness will bring them to Me, hungry for comfort and truth.

"You see once a man builds his house on the sand and the rains come and the floods wash it all away, well, then that man will consider the importance of building upon Rock, and I will be there to teach him. So you see what is pending and inevitable is merely My provision to bring My children back to Me, in spirit and in Truth."

Taken from: **Everything Seems Business As Usual...**

"When am I coming? Any minute, one of these times it won't be a drill, it will be the real thing. I want to see exactly how obedient each of my Lovers is, and in the process they are getting many, many stains out of their garments.

"...Because My Bride wants to be perfect, wants to be washed and clean, wants to be delivered of her faults and sins, I am imputing it to her as righteousness. And although she may not be totally perfect when I come for her, her commitment stands in her stead and her garment becomes a spotless garment. Do you understand? I am doing this for her. I am doing the doing as she corresponds to Me in obedience. I lift the stains. It is part of the mystery of sanctification. Oh Clare, I love her so, I want for her to be with Me.

"And there are different levels. That is, some have been given 20 talents, some only 1. So, I judge on what was done with what was given. That is why some seemingly unlikely candidates, because they have worked so hard with their one talent, they are seen as equally **successful** as others who were given many more talents and used them properly. Oh, how I love My Bride and long to have her with Me."

Taken from: **Come to Me Through Worship…**

"Then I see one…a soul hungering for Me, a soul on fire, a soul that burns in this darkness and its light is only perceived by Me. And I ask My Father, 'Please, Father, turn the heart of this precious one to Me, so I may speak with her. Cause her to reach out for Me.'

"And her heart is quickened, but never with the thought that I desire her company. No, she thinks only to herself, 'Wretched as I am, have Mercy, God, and send me a sign of Your presence in my life.' Never does she for one moment imagine that she may speak with Me, face to face. So, that long process begins. The process of convincing her that I am longing for her company.

"And as I press in to get her attention, she presses in seeking Me, and the devils come along and try every conceivable tactic to rob her of My reality. And their most *successful* one is 'You are not worthy, you are no prophet or priest. You have no royal blood, you are worthless.' And she believes it!!"

Taken from: **You Are the Highpoint of My Day**

"Many of you have stumbled into sins of the flesh because of the immodest culture you live in. That was Satan's plan all along and how **successful** he has been."

Taken from: **Everything Seems Business As Usual…**

Success

Again Jonah prayed to the Lord, "Isn't this what I said, Lord, when I was still at home? That is what I tried to forestall by fleeing to Tarshish. I knew that you are a gracious and compassionate God, slow to anger and abounding in love, a God who relents from sending calamity.

3 Now, Lord, take away my life, for it is better for me to die than to live."

So, here's a prophet that was INCREDIBLY humiliated, because he went through the city preaching that they were going to perish. I mean, he did his job! He got the people to turn from sin. And now he wants to die from his job being **successful.** *Why? Because he wasn't proven right by the city being destroyed.*

4 But the Lord replied, "Is it right for you to be angry?"

Basically, His ego was so damaged, because God did NOT destroy the people, that he just wanted to lay down and die. So, the Lord visited Jonah and rebuked him for his selfishness.

And I want to say: when is a prophet a prophet? When he gets people to repent and what he prophesied doesn't come to pass? Or, when everyone is wiped out under God's judgment even after his warnings?

So, a prophet can either look good because those souls went to Hell, and came under judgment. Or, if he does his job properly and the people repent, the Lord withholds judgment... he can be stoned for being a false prophet.

Surely that is not the heart of God. He sends a prophet to correct the people so they will repent, so if he does his job properly, judgment will be suspended or delayed.

Taken from: **Rapture When?**

"Do you not see the plan of Satan in such things? Do you not see that you are the victim being used to injure others, resulting in your own downfall? Yes, in this world people treat each other as expendable items. Not so in Heaven. In Heaven you are the most precious commodity, made in My very image, eternal and stunningly beautiful. To be honored and loved.

"But in this world you are but a doormat to the **success** of others. You are used and tossed aside, after you have been thoroughly despoiled of the joyful life I imparted to you. What I am saying here? Love one another as I have loved you. Cherish and support one another. Never speak harsh words when it can be avoided. Always admonish and lift one another up, even and especially in conflict."

Taken from: **Support One Another in Your Weaknesses**

"I need My Bride to expect results for all her efforts. What you are all about to undertake with your talents is going to be amazingly successful. I am going to bless you beyond your expectations.

"Why? Because this is a rough season and you moved ahead strictly on faith. You didn't feel like it, you didn't have confidence, inspiration has been attacked, your energy is low. You're coming off serious disappointment and some of you doubt the veracity of this vessel. To you I say, look at the fruit in your life. If you have grown, then the influence could not be from Satan - all he does is kill, steal and destroy and teach you to go in wrong directions. Look at the things in your life that matter; have you grown?

"I say this to you, independent of her knowledge, because I need you to believe in Me. I need you to be convinced that I am speaking through her so that your plans will succeed based on your faith."

Taken from: **I Am Serving The Fine Wine Last...**

Suffering

"You who pray are at the hub of the wheel, My Spirit ministers around the outside of the wheel and at the spokes. My arm is tremendously long and powerful, and you have the power to move it with your prayers.

"Even your sighs are strong intentions carried by the angels to the throne of My Father in Heaven. It is not necessary to say long and verbose prayers; your heart cry comes before us with the greatest volume. Each heart cry you have when you see injustice and suffering is caught by the angels, even as a shining gem of love, and offered in the courts of Heaven.

"Do not allow the devils to put you under condemnation because you don't pray as other people pray. Remember what I said about the Pharisees widening their robes and tassels and standing in public making numerous petitions for all to see. Unless their hearts are in their prayers, they are all but useless to Me.

"On the other hand, were you to catch a glance of someone **suffering** and you recoiled in pain with the intention: 'Oh My God, Mercy!' This is heard loud and clear and is very, very effective as a prayer."

Taken from: **I Am Releasing New Anointings**

"Many of you Heartdwellers have been through a bit of hell this past month. Yes, it was so hard at times you told Me you wanted to give up. But I have brought you through it and you are wearing the Victor's Crown. You have run your race well. You are prepared and ready now for the next leg of the journey.

"You may look back on your sufferings and see that you have truly held your finger in that failing dike. And not only did you keep it from breaking, thousands of others lent a hand and your Father in Heaven repaired that dike - and now you can see what your **sufferings** accomplished. Be encouraged and know that your reward in Heaven and on Earth is great.

"Each of you has work to do. Do not slack off in your prayers - you are learning just how powerful they are. And they continue to keep the window open. Continue to pray, especially for the rulers of the world and for their conversion. We are doing this together. You pray and WE act. It's just that simple.

"Can't you feel it, Dear Ones? Can't you feel it in your heart when you cry out for Russia, for Israel? Well, if you can't, ask for the grace. Just ask and I will touch your heart. Ask for the grace of intercession. There is no greater job on this Earth, no calling with a greater reward, no calling with a greater honor and respect in Heaven than standing in the gap in prayer and intercession.

"This is the greatest honor any man or woman can have: to be called an intercessor. You hold the Father's heart in your hands when you lift them up in petition. His heart melts when He sees your sincerity and perseverance under the worst conditions."

Taken from: **Judgment, War & Rapture Delayed...**

"When I see a soul that cannot rise from their bed of misery any longer, I take a portion of that **suffering** and scatter it around to more evenly distribute the burden. To you it may just seem like a little extra, but to the soul that was suffering, it is a reprieve from being completely drained of hope and enthusiasm for life. Yes, there are times when you will pass through that veil of tears, also. But it does not last forever when you have Me. I always find ways to liberate just enough that you can pick up and carry on."

Taken from: **Suffering – Real Work in the Realm of the Spirit**

Suffering

"Pursue your missions, My Bride. Continue on in the right direction bringing forth fruit with your gifts. For some of you, the gift is sickness and sufferings of various kinds. I am with you in your bed of suffering, My Brides. I will comfort you with great tenderness and gratefulness for your loving and giving heart.

"Know that the greatest players in this semi-final scene are My faithful intercessors. The little ones no one sees or cares about. They are the decisive force; they are in the front lines and holding back the tide of evil. If you are one of them, I beg you to find honor and great satisfaction in this role. You are the ones making the greatest difference.

"Persevere and be highly satisfied for your exalted stations in this moment of history. Great will be your reward in Heaven. Do not look to what others are doing and compare yourself. No, press in with your heart focused on My intentions; press in and raise the cry for justice o high to the Father's throne. Yours is the decisive voice.

"This is a war zone, and you are the front lines. I am sustaining you. Great is the glory associated with a love that gives and gives beyond itself. This was My portion and when you manifest it, you are most lik Me. I am with you.

"Do not grow weary. Take comfort from the great joy you bring Me, M Brides. Because of your faithfulness, prophecy will be accomplished in a way no one could have foreseen or imagined."

Taken from: **God is Hearing the Russian People...**

"I do not allow these burdens easily; they are above all others, training in maturity and agape love. They are the opportunity the soul needs, t grow into who I created them to be. The world tells you all kinds of lie especially the lie of the pain-free, happy life.

"There is no such thing. Each person, whether you see it or not, is carrying a cross. If they are not with Me, knowing Me and My Word, they do not see the purpose of the suffering; rather they perceive it as a punishment.

"Nothing could be further from the truth. **Suffering** teaches a soul to focus on what really matters. All the frivolity of life dims in comparison to the health and happiness of the one who is afflicted. But in the midst of that is the greatest gift you can give.

"When you are sick and **suffering**, life is draining out of you, and I capture that life and bless others with it. If you have given your life to Me without any reservations, you will experience this kind of suffering.

"When I spoke of the abundant life, I was not speaking of the abundance of things in the world. I was speaking of the abundance of My presence, and the joy of living in Me.

"You see, when I told you to deny yourself, pick up your cross and follow Me, I gave you the mandate of having your own unique cross. It could be slander and calumny, or lack of appreciation for what you do. It could be the inconvenience of a car breaking down, or the denial of a loan to get another car.

"It could be false accusation at work and that someone who really dislikes you has tried to darken your name. It could be deferring to a family member over where you are going on a vacation or family outing.

"ANYTHING that causes you to abandon your will for the will of another can be a cause for suffering, maturity and brotherly love."

Taken from: **Suffering – Real Work in the Realm of the Spirit**

Suffering

"When I said that Satan goes for the jugular, I mean his minions know where to place the sucker punch. And you all **suffer** grief over your children, asking if you did the right thing, grieving over your mistakes, wondering if there is still hope for them. May I say, the accusers stand beside you, thrusting your hearts through with all manner of lies about them? And I am here to remove the lance and restore the wounds with the balm of faith with My goodness and mercy. Even now your suffering is backing up the harvest of souls and their turn is coming."

Taken from: **Trust Me With Your Children...**

"You must cleave to Me, dear children! All of you! But especially those of you who choose to stand in the gap and suffer for those who have transgressed. Know, My dear children, that your recent efforts have borne much fruit for the Kingdom of God. Many more of My children are returning home. My heart weeps with gladness at your efforts. The fragrance is as sweet as My finest wines.

"Many of you have **suffered** in order for these wayward ones to return; and your **suffering** has been the sweetest of all gifts. How tenderly they touch My Heart. For My Heart has often been battered and My labors scorned, and your efforts come as sweet consolation during a painful time."

*...Many people have asked to join our intercessory prayer group, but I know the kind of lash-back and **suffering** that awaits them, and I've very, very careful about that. Because it's going to be extreme **suffering** for anyone who wants to stand in the gap. If you love the Lord that much, and are willing to make that sacrifice, then that's a wonderful saying, "He will strengthen you." But don't take it lightly. Think long and hard about it before you offer yourself to stand in the gap.*

Taken from: **Great Suffering is About to Befall the World**

"I see the dagger in your heart over this waiting; I see it, I know it, I feel it with you. Don't suppose for a moment I am not suffering as you are. Yes, I am suffering this and even more as I see My children for the last time, as they are taken to Hell because of their obstinate denial of Me. They are exiled and never more shall I be comforted by the joy of their laughter.

"No, now it is bitter regrets, screams and groaning, which I, as God, cannot ignore. There is a chamber in My heart where the voices of Hell call out to Me. I cannot escape it. It is My creation and it is oh, so painful, nerve-wracking and shattering. But it is there, and I am continuously aware of it. ...The season is well past it's prime, and that is because we are trying to avert the worst **sufferings** for mankind."

Taken from: **The Heaviness of Waiting for the Rapture**

"There are many kinds of burdens I wish for you to recognize. There are delays that cause a massive reorganizing of times and resources. There are sick children, sick pets and relatives. When sickness strikes, it operates on many different levels: the inconvenience of taking care of them, the extra burden on resources and time. But more than any other cross, is the emotional cross of seeing **suffering** in your loved one. This is the heaviest cross you can have, the tragedy of pain and suffering."

Taken from: **Suffering – Real Work in the Realm of the Spirit**

"For one, souls make an agreement with Me before they come to Earth about the kind of life they will lead. We are agreed on that, and many that seem to die uselessly are martyrs giving their **suffering** and lives for others that they love. Even the plants and animals understand what I ask of them."

Taken from: **Bondage to Satan, Halloween Night**

Temptations

"There is a price to pay for holiness, for closeness to Me. You will receive more than your fair share of scorn and contempt from relatives, when you refuse to watch certain things in movies and TV. Turning your eyes away from filthy things brings an element of conviction to others around you, and they resent it. But you are bearing witness to God within you, you are rejecting moral impurity and setting a higher standard of behavior which many will not go along with.

"And for those of you who have already fallen into uncleanness or fornication, I say, repent and make a resolution not to do it again. Call on Me in that hour to strengthen you. Those who willingly give their eyes over to that are far more guilty than those of you who are weak and refuse every opportunity to look, but still find yourselves overpowered. I do not condemn you, but the demons do. They bring on the **temptation** and give you to think, 'God will forgive me'. Then when you fall, they pour on the condemnation and claim you as their own, bound for Hell.

"You will find that those of you who are harsh and judgmental with others, will have a harder time controlling yourselves. You see, rather than rushing to your side, I allow you to fail so you will have more compassion for your brothers and sisters. I am calling My children to Mercy. Those who show Mercy, shall themselves be shown Mercy.

"And those who are legalistic, demanding, and critical of others, need to learn compassion and humility. And so I allow a degrading habit to bring them to their senses so they will cease judging others. I do not give birth to these things, but I see the demons getting ready to jump on a soul, and if they have been harsh and critical of others, I do not come to their rescue. The more you downgrade others the more you can expect to fall."

Taken from: **Blessed Are the Pure, For They Shall See Me**

"My Precious, do not think it strange all these **temptations** to judge, to get angry, or any other sin - do not think it strange that in this hour it seems more intense than usual. I am wanting to purify My Brides of every selfish motive, every spot, wrinkle and blemish, to make her perfect before Me.

"She is quite beautiful even in this hour, but there is always room for improvement. That is why I am sending more trials, allowing more temptations from the enemy, that I may adorn her even more beautifully than she is in this moment.

"Do not grow weary with these tests, do not give up on yourself, because you see so many flaws. No, persevere, do not condemn yourself for that, too, is a sign of pride: expecting to be perfect and finding the imperfections. Rather the humble soul is not the least bit surprised by her surfacing faults. It is always a test of virtue when opposition arises, when condemnation is hurled at you."

Taken from: **Your Hearts are My Fragrant Garden**

"If a husband or wife refuses to play a supportive role and gives in to the **temptation** of jealousy, it seriously hampers what I want to do with them as a couple. So few understand how important they are in the selfless hidden role, and I have to teach them before they can be elevated into a ministry that reaches many.

"Their greatest downfall will happen at the weakest point... and many times that's their marriage. One feels left out that the other is getting all the attention and they are inferior to their spouse. One wants to rise to equality in public ministry, even though I have not anointed them for that. They must both submit to My order."

Taken from: **The Yoke of Marriage in Ministry**

Temptations

"Satan has a counterfeit for everything. This state of mind was reserved for worship and camaraderie, never just to be used as a private tool of manipulation or mind control. But, if one discovers the principals, they can in fact be put in place with-out the substance and the heart of it, which is Love. This is another reason gaming has become so wildly important in the lives of people: it again transforms them out of this reality into an ether-like reality where you become what you imagine.

"This is also the precursor to witchcraft - dangerously close to that altered-reality, manipulated by the mind for evil purposes. That is: exerting the human will on the free will of another, to overpower and obtain a selfish and short-sighted result.

"The power of the mind is beyond reckoning, and it is a sad thing when ability overshadows morality. These things are not meant to be had supernaturally independent of divine love. This is an abuse and a premature use of the mind.

"Yet, anyone can access it to their detriment, if their motive is not pure love that I capture, in a sense, and use to transform a soul into a divine reality. In other words, it is like healing skills. If not done strictly from a motive of love - brotherly or divine love - it can become a **temptation** and even a weapon in the hands of souls who are not given this gift by Me.

"It is ultimately the safest to love Me to distraction, and should I decide you are ready for a supernatural, I give it to you. In this way, you cannot go off track so easily and fall through pride, doing damage to many, many souls."

Taken from: **Jesus Speaks on The God Dimension & Video Games**

"You have heard Me say, as I have said many times before, that the Rapture is soon. I have offered you a new way to handle the tensions involved in this event. Knowing it is soon and planning your lives, pursuing your God-given course can be managed without all this mystery and stress.

"Very simply: LIVE YOUR LIVES IN OBEDIENCE, FROM MOMENT TO MOMENT. If you know you are to go to school, continue to go - but remember, the shofar may sound at any moment. If you are getting married and having children, continue on, obeying Me - following My Plan for your life. Refuse, utterly refuse to get entangled in such specious arguments as 'what if He comes tomorrow, what if He comes next year, or thirty years?'

"These are all **temptations** from the enemy to dilute your effectiveness right now, in this moment, with the calling I have set before you. If you have been given visions about future ministry, future gifts, do not try to fit them into your human time frames. You see, this is an act of unbelief.

"When I tell you that I am going to do such and such in your life, I tell you so you may understand where I am ultimately taking you. NOT so that you can stress and plan, question and doubt in your own mind... NOT so that you can reason out whether it's before or after the Rapture. None of this has any bearing on the so-called time frames of Heaven. None of it."

Taken from: **If You Love Me – Rapture –Sexual Temptations…**

"There will be trials and **temptations**, but I will always give you ample warning. You are not going to fall into this habit pattern again. This lesson left a lasting mark. Although it is painful, it was necessary. And healing is coming."

Taken from: **I Am Not a Taskmaster…**

Temptations

"They (demons) are going to come after you from all directions. **Temptations** you never even thought you were vulnerable to. My advice to you all is lay low, low, low - lower than ever before in your lives. Don't have any proud flags flying they can attach themselves to and they'll go right by you.

"They are looking to stir up pride in your hearts any way they can do it. Refuse to buy into that. Simply dodge the bullets. Your vigilance will save your soul and perhaps even those around you. When the devils target you, they also target those around you. They rejoice when they can use you to bring others down as well.

"Don't allow yourselves to be drawn off into vain reasonings, empty arguments, critical spirits. Oh, they have set landmines before you, My people. Your only hope is to lay low in humility, confessing My Blood for protection and refusing, and I do mean flat-out refusing, to be engaged in useless arguments that will cause your soul to fall into unrest and confusion.

"Little do they know, or expect, that I will strengthen you in humility, your greatest protection. As you remain vigilant and obedient, they will have no place to manifest."

Taken from: **February – A Month of Testings**

Can you imagine the government coming out with a chip - and they say, "If you take this chip, your life will be increased for hundreds of years, because we have the technology to adjust things in your body just with this chip?" This is not outrageous. This is all state-of-the-art medicine and things can electronically be administered through that chip. Once you take that mark or that chip and you go into that system you may never be able to connect with the Lord again. You don't want to do that. How are you going to stand against that?

There's only one way and that's through love; falling in love with the Lord.

Knowing who He is to you and feeling who He is to you in such a way that the affection you have for your family will not force you to do something that is against Him. These are things to think about. These technologies are on the horizon. If you're not head-over-heels in love with the Lord, you're not going to be able to resist the **temptation.** *You'll love your own life more than you love Him. How do we get to the place where we can resist this* **temptation?** *I'm not telling you that I can stand against it. I pray that I can stand against it. I'm doing everything daily that I know of. There are always more things that I can do but I'm trying to stay connected to Him.*

Taken from: **Intimacy with Jesus is Our Preparation for the Rapture**

"Many of you have asked Me what to do with your lives. Well, in this hour I will tell you. First, if you have children and a spouse, your responsibility is to provide a safe and holy environment for them to grow up into. If your children are in public school they are being seriously contaminated and compromised every moment of every day.

"There are two ways to handle this; one is to home school or put them in a proper school. The other is to be such good friends with them that they can confide anything to you, and together you can work out the right solutions, and navigate through all the **temptations** they're going to be beset with. But still, the exposure is compromising, unless you spend a great deal of quality time with your child and can help him or her sort out the truth from lies. Peer pressure can become a controlling animal very quickly, something you cannot compete with, unless your child has the utmost integrity."

Taken from: **I Arrange Your Lessons for the Day...**

The Bride of Christ

"Now for you, My sweet Heartdwellers. I want you to know that Love is the golden nugget on this channel. For those who have ears to hear, understand: you are here because you were drawn to My love, by My love, and as you grow more deeply in your relationship with Me, you will love all men, as I do. This is My promise to you. What has been begun on Earth will surely be accomplished in its fullness in Heaven.

"If you have come here for prophecy, you are in the wrong place. Yes, I will give prophecies, but rarely. I am most concerned about love being spread throughout the Earth. When love covers the Earth like the waters cover the seas, men will live in love with one another. Of course, this will not be fully accomplished until I return to reign. But you are My ambassadors of love. And as you exercise that gift in your being, you rule and reign just as surely as if you were on a throne.

"Your prayers are over-the-top powerful to stop national crisis, change the course of history, rebuild broken alliances between countries, snuff out evil... Oh, you have NO idea how very powerful you are, **My Brides.** The more you love and refuse to condemn, the more your prayers have to effect change."

Taken from: **President Putin visited by the Lord...**

Please, Jesus, deliver me from a spirit of error and from the deception that will fall upon mankind.

He continued, "This is already done, My Love. You are **My Bride**; I protect your mind, spirit, soul, and body. All of you is Mine, and I protect you just as a good husband should. I want you to understand this: no matter how many, how bizarre and strange these life forms appear to be - understand they are, when simply unmasked, demons controlled by Satan. It's just that simple."

Taken from: **Overcoming the Deceptions of This Age...**

"The faith of all shall be sha~
abide with them and remove **My** ~
My faithful Ones, all that you have or ~
salvation. Please stand fast and keep your e~
but a fleeting breath; your eternity is guaranteed ~
your eyes on the prize and cling to Me. Call upon Me ~
you shall be saved - this is My promise to you."

Taken from: **The Day of the Lord is Upon Us**

"I wish for you all to stick together and be supportive of one another. This is the mark of My end times army: Brotherly Love. For however long you are here, I want you to advance in holiness, **My Brides.**

"There will be ample opportunity. Remember: it's not about prosperity, popularity, and power, but righteousness, peace and joy in My Holy Spirit in the midst of a corrupt and challenging world.

"Moments of triumph will be gratifying and I will reward each richly with the sweetness of My presence. The number of those who leave will decline, no one can argue against brotherly love and unity of purpose."

Taken from: **These Lite and Momentary Sufferings**

Here you're free just to be all you've ever hoped for. Now you're home you're not alone your family adores you.

My Daughter, I welcome you Home. Can you believe and just receive. Truly you're My Daughter.

Bride of Christ, *His sacrifice has formed you in His glory.*

Taken from: **Come to Me (song by Clare)**

...rious beyond description and heartrendingly beautiful! These days are filled with uncertainty and challenges. The waiting for some is almost unbearable. Yet My Grace sustains you. All that is beautiful and praiseworthy is hidden behind the veil of filth the enemy has swathed this world with. But for a few, brief moments that veil will be removed and you will see even as you are seen.

"Nothing like this has ever happened, nor will it again - with the exception of the descent of the New Jerusalem. This again will be a moment never to be forgotten for all time.

"How I long for My Bride to be lifted up into the heavenlies! To experience her transfiguration. Eye has not seen, and NEVER has it entered into the heart of man what is about to happen. John the Evangelist saw many glorious things, but this experience will outshine them all.

"What I have planned for you, **My Brides**, will only be believed when it is seen. Yet even that will be twisted into something the enemy can use. Some, however, will be totally convinced and give their lives to Me. Especially those relatives of the Brides. You've been preparing your families for this, and there will be no escaping that this is truly the fulfillment of that prophecy. This event will leave a permanent imprint that will carry them all the way through until the end. There will no longer be any doubts that I am real and that I will return to rule.

"So many now cannot conceive of this, because they've been conditioned by the world. But this event will change all of that. Only the most hardened hearts will question what just took place, and will be eager to replace it with the world's explanation.

"This is why I resolved to make this a publicly visible event. All the tribes of the Earth will mourn."

Taken from: **The Rapture Event Will Be Visible...**

"When you sow division and persecute other ministers, using your time to tear down instead of build up, do you think that pleases Me? Are you not tearing the nets and letting the fish get away? Indeed, a torn net does nothing but frighten the fish off. These are the things some of you need to consider - right now. Do you suppose you are part of **My Bride** when you bite and tear at one another?

"This is the way My Bride acts: she doesn't pull the tares up with the wheat, rather she continues to cultivate that field. She binds up the wounded, lives a life of love before the community that all might embrace this way. While others are wagging their fingers at this or that Christian teacher, she is welcoming in the lame, the deaf, the blind, feeding and clothing the poor, and teaching them about My love by her actions."

Taken from: **Lord, Why Are Things Falling Apart?**

I saw Jesus sitting with His Bride and her hands were in His and He was looking intently at them.

"I want you all to cultivate your gifts. You've all been given an anointing." He was still looking at her fingers. "Not just for music, but to live your lives from your heart. Many of you haven't done this yet, with a few exceptions. There is so much locked up in you, My Brides. So much. When we get close to it, you bolt and run off. Something catches your attention, because you get restless, but mostly because you are afraid of what you will find in those deep places. Your emotions run so deep. I made you that way, so you could pour yourself into your lives and souls would be drawn to the beauty I created there inside of you, **My Darling Brides.**

"Oh, don't be afraid. Please, don't be afraid, please... don't be afraid."

Taken from: **Will You Fulfill Your Divine Destiny?**

The Bride of Christ

"If they would say to Me, 'Jesus, Clare did not put a message up yet, would you please give me something to feed on from Your own hand?' I guarantee they will be quite surprised with what they come up with. Sitting quietly before Me, after communion, pen or computer in hand, pour your heart out to Me, **My Brides**.

"Speak tenderly to Me about your fears, insecurities, hurts and disappointments. And your joys, too! Thanksgiving is the key to My heart. I do so much for My own and yet they forget to thank Me. They take Me for granted like their husband of 30 years.

∼

"No, no, no. I am fresh and new every morning and I long to be recognized as fresh and new. Even when I am suffering, I am still new and full of life everyday as you come to Me in prayer.

"I love listening to you as you pour your heart out. And I cannot prevent Myself from responding. I am so touched when you speak to me so candidly and expect to hear something back...even just a faint reply. How can I possibly pretend I am deaf?"

Taken from: **Nourishment Every Day**

"I want **My Brides** to know that as they wrestle with their flesh in confronting the future events, I am ever so pleased with their decision to stay faithful and committed to My Will for their lives or even their deaths. For death no longer has a sting, not for My holy ones that have given Me their all as I gave them My all.

"Do not be surprised at the fiery trials you are going through now, **Beloved Brides**. I am yet removing layers of corruption from your souls and your garments. Do not be discouraged with your sins, I knew your weakness before you fell. Did I not allow you to fall to reveal to you how weak you truly are?

"Your beauty is not in what you have accomplished or made yourself, these things in Heaven are but filthy rags from Earth and will not accompany you to testify to your sanctity. If you shed them on Earth and put aside your masks, I will reveal your real beauty.

"Your outer appearance is merely a corruptible shell that will wither and die. It is the inward beauty of a loving soul dedicated to living for Me and not herself/himself that shines. If you do not have that, you have nothing.

"These are things only I can accomplish in you with your cooperation and willingness to be vulnerable and to see yourself as you are before the citizens of Heaven who are looking in on you all, cheering you on, hoping you will cooperate with grace to become the great beauties I created you to be."

Taken from: **Your Tomorrow is Not Guaranteed**

"Your greatest safety is in holiness and refusing to judge others. Many have many opinions, and unfortunately much of what is proposed is opinion and not from Me. So remember your tools of discernment and if you are caused to lose your peace be wary; this is the enemy's number one form of attack.

"To continue to listen to those who detract from others is truly a leak in your vessel. The graces pour through that leak and are lost because of this serious fault. Judgment is Mine and your safest stance is to avoid these poisons and cleave to what is righteous and good, even showing mercy to your enemies - but not taking in their poison.

"**My Brides,** you are stunningly beautiful and the enemy hates the very mention of you."

Taken from: **Resist Gossip and Judgment...**

The Bride of Christ

"This prayer (the Stations of the Cross) is so pleasing to Me, because it offsets the false teachings of prosperity that have infiltrated the church. Did I not say, 'Deny yourself, pick up your cross and follow Me?' Yet, today, where is the Cross being preached? All of you, My children, are much in need of strength to persevere as Christians.

"**The Bride** must fully resemble the Groom and I did not come on this Earth to satisfy My earthly, fleshly cravings. I came to serve and to die for You. I died for you and opened the gates of Heaven for all eternity - and now I ask of you to deny yourselves and follow Me. Is that so unreasonable?

"For these light and momentary troubles, you are rewarded with an eternity of bliss. But I have not called you to come to Me alone. I wish for you to bring others with you, and this is truly a labor calling for sacrifice and steadfastness.

"When people see your generosity in following My example, they are moved to come to Me; they see your motivation as Love for Me and your brother and that draws all men to Me. The abundant life is not meat and drink, but righteousness, peace - even in chaos, joy - even in suffering. Yes, indeed, this prayer strengthens you for the journey.

"Yet your journey, My Brides, is coming to a close. So do what you can for the hour will soon be upon you when you can do no more and you will regret what you didn't do. Look to the courage and strength of those who are suffering martyrdom right now and strengthen your feeble arms and failing knees. Rise up and shoulder your cross, much fruit is coming forth from its midst."

Taken from: **Miami Soon to be Bombed...**

"Know that this channel is noted for it's brotherly love. There is no mistaking it. It resembles the church of Philadelphia, the one church I promised that I would keep from the time of testing that is to come upon this Earth.

"That is why I have so readied you all for the Rapture. You are that church and as such you have a solemn obligation to protect the love and concord of everyone who looks to this channel for inspiration and guidance.

"You have done well, **My Brides**. Just be aware that the enemy is not done with you yet, nevertheless, I am with you and brotherly love will conquer all the enemy has planned to stop you.

"I love you, **My Brides** and hold you tightly to My Heart. Continue to take draughts of mercy and love from your intimate times in prayer with Me and you will have more than enough to neutralize the poisons that bring disrepute to My Name."

*Taken from: **Love and Protect This Channel***

In this next sentence, by the way, He is referring to something I said to Carol, that everyone has a different capacity and longing for Jesus.

This is what He said, "It is quite true that tea cups, thimbles and barrels will all be raptured. I am looking at the heart and each one has different capacities, each one was formed differently, each one endowed differently. That is why there will be such a wide variety taken in the Rapture.

"As far as **Brides** go, there are different levels of commitment, different levels of self-effacement and emptiness, longing and corresponding to My Grace. But the mystery of this is that I love each and everyone, all the same, in completeness. Though the thimble cannot hold what the barrel holds, nonetheless it is full and filled with My Love."

*Taken from: **Who Will I Rapture?***

The Bride of Christ

"It is because I love you that I discipline and guide you, **My Brides**. Let nothing of the world be found in your hearts. May you all be Israelites without guile. You are learning, all of you. I present you with many opportunities every day to exercise virtue. And as you say 'yes' to Me, you grow in holiness before God and man. In the end, no matter what it cost you at the time My blessings will overtake you because of your honesty.

"And now, I am again asking for your prayers for the world. So much is at the tipping point, and I need My people to repent for the sins of the world: for child trafficking, abortion, drug abuse, government exploitation, mass destruction of the planet.

"Your rulers do not see they are sawing off the very branch they are sitting on. They are completely blind and deceived about this planet's future and the fact that I WILL intervene and turn everything around. Selfish ambition has taken a hold of the ruling class and selfish ambition will be their downfall.

"But I want your hands to be clean before Me. Do not soil them with the blood of judgment. Rather, beg mercy for all mankind, even the most vile. In this way, you will be like My Father in Heaven, Whose heart is moved to pity by the relentless seeking of power by those who seemingly control the world, but are merely pawns in the hands of Satan."

Taken from: **Be Without Guile and Repent for the World**

"When I tell you these things about timing and being ready, it confuses the enemy just as much as it confuses you. But you trust Me, so I don't worry about your confusion. Each one of these Rapture warnings serves many purposes. Yes, I am toying with the enemy. Yes, I am building virtue, trust, faith and hope in **My waiting Bride** and yes, I am asking you to be vigilant over yourselves and keep your eyes on the horizon. Each time I bring this up with great seriousness, it's not just for those reasons, it also carries the weight of truth with it.

"...But you, **My Brides**, must excel in charity, humility and actions that prove you belong to the Light of the World. As you step forward in purity and devotion to Me, you carry this light which to some is inexplicable, but real nonetheless. You are the living mystery of My Love for mankind...yes, in you the light of hope reaches out to those who are wandering around lost in the darkness."

Taken from: **Maintain Your Purity and Light, My Bride**

"I just want you to be coming to Me first thing every morning, because you have been pulled away numerous times and kept Me waiting. For what? Nothing a Sovereign should have to wait for to see **His Bride** first thing in the morning and receive her love and affection.

"Not under threat of punishment, but because she loves Me. I want our time to be intimate and sweet, not under threat of punishment. Satan is trying to exaggerate and spill over into unreasonable demands, to sour our relationship. All of you, My Brides, are very sensitive to pleasing Me. So, you are also prone to scrupulous spirits, demons who constantly make you question every single thing you do. That is no way to have a relationship with Me.

"My Yoke is easy, My burden light. Don't let the enemy convince you otherwise. They will take anything I say and blow it up way out of context to cause you false guilt. What I am looking for is VERY simple. Come to Me, spend time with Me, pray to Me and listen for My words of life and love. And do it FIRST thing in your day."

Taken from: **I Am Not a Taskmaster**

Trials

"I know the times now are very trying. I know you all are experiencing **trials** that seem like they will never end. That is because your journey on this Earth is almost at an end, and in those last moments I want to adorn you with even more beauty for My eyes to gaze upon in Eternity.

"And it is not only for your sakes that you are undergoing these testings, it is also for your brothers and sisters who have not yet given their lives to Me. I wish for no man to perish and someone must fast and pray to cooperate with Me in the process of conversion. This suffering is your prayer and your fast. Someone must carry that cross that redemption will come to its fullest as the soul turns to Me and receives Me."

"You will look back on this time and wish I had granted you even heavier **trials**, but I understand your frame and I will not allow more than you are able to handle with My grace strengthening you. So, when you feel that you are at your absolute limit, turn to Me with great confidence and ask for more strength.

"Run this race right up to the finish line and press on toward the goal of the high calling in Me that the glory that has been revealed in Me may also be in you. For if you die to yourself in Me, surely you will rise with Me in glory.

"I am telling you now that you may be prepared. Further *trials* are going to assault you. But no weapon formed against you will bring you down, you will triumph in Me. Be strong, be courageous and look beyond this Vail of confusion you must call your temporary home. Cling to Me and to My promises and do not in any way give ground to the enemy.

"Understand that each facet I am preparing in you was destined from the beginning of the world to be yours, only now are they being brought to perfection. So do not despair, grab firm hold of the rope of grace and do not let go. Testings and trials are only temporary and soon you will behold the magnificent work I accomplished through you in your last days on Earth. There is nothing, absolutely nothing that you and I cannot accomplish together as you cleave to Me and stand in faith."

Taken from: **Trials: The Final Facets on You, My Jewel**

"My children, the ways of the world that you have learned are totally inappropriate here. I protect those who humble themselves before Me. If you are prancing around proudly with all the answers, you are bound for destruction.

"I am counting on your breaking when you realize all you've been taught by friends and family has just come to pass before your very eyes. I am counting on you face flat on the floor begging forgiveness for your pride and arrogance. I am laying the groundwork for you to survive the **trials** that are now at your door, both body and soul.

"If you humble yourself before Me, I will most certainly be with you. Even if you are in a long-standing habit of pride and arrogance, and are aware of your sin and want to be delivered, I will work with you. But if you insist on your own wisdom, I can do little for you."

Taken from: **Jesus Speaks on What is to Come #5**

"Scorn, contempt and persecution await all my faithful Christians. How can I reward unless **trials** are passed successfully? And in the meantime, teachings will come forth that will assist those left behind. All serves a purpose, every little thing - take it as a test of virtue, another fast offering and this will keep your attitude pure and grateful, and keep you from bitterness."

Taken from: **Another Soul for Heaven...**

Trials

"I will be with you as I was with Israel in the desert. I will give you signs of My love, signs of danger, signs when you are going the wrong way, signs when you are going the RIGHT way. Be attentive, pay close attention to the signs I send you."

"If you suspect you have made a wrong decision, stop and pray it through. Better to wait on me than to move forward into a trap. There will be times to act and times to wait. It is in the times of waiting that **trials** will be the most difficult. Pray always, worship and thank Me for every safe journey, every provision, every time you evade the enemy.

"Use My Name as a weapon of war for: **You fight not against flesh and blood but principalities in high places and against evil rulers and authorities of the unseen world, against mighty powers in this dark world, and against evil spirits in the heavenly places. Ephesians 6:12**

Taken from: **Provision and Protection for Those Left Behind**

"My Precious, do not think it strange all these temptations to judge, to get angry, or any other sin - do not think it strange that in this hour it seems more intense than usual. I am wanting to purify My Brides of every selfish motive, every spot, wrinkle and blemish, to make her perfect before Me. She is quite beautiful even in this hour, but there is always room for improvement. That is why I am sending more **trials,** allowing more temptations from the enemy, that I may adorn her even more beautifully than she is in this moment.

"Do not grow weary with these tests, do not give up on yourself, because you see so many flaws. No, persevere, do not condemn yourself for that, too, is a sign of pride: expecting to be perfect and finding the imperfections. Rather the humble soul is not the least bit surprised by her surfacing faults. It is always a test of virtue when opposition arises."

Taken from: **Your Hearts are My Fragrant Garden**

"But let's get back to what is important here, My Love. The focus must be on charity and virtue, trust and faith in My ability to provide. Without these pivotal attitudes, they will not succeed. My protection can make you invisible. My protection can turn wild beasts away. My protection can save you from the ground giving way beneath you. My protection can provide water and food when there is none.

"I can do all things, and I will, for those whose agenda is to gather in souls to the Kingdom. Those who give and lead unselfishly, those who are honest and caring for others, these are the ones I will supernaturally protect and provide for.

"Many I will add to your numbers that need salvation. Their eternity is hanging in the balance and if you make their eternity your priority,

"I will cover you. Souls are going to be racked with confusion and fear, not knowing up from down, so severe will the **trials** be on the Earth. They will be so thoroughly disoriented that nothing can calm them down but a supernatural grace. A healing grace, laying hands on them and praying for My Peace to descend upon them."

Taken from: **Jesus Instructs the Left Behind...**

"In all things I wish for My chosen vessels to respond to My voice in whomever I send. Downgrading others is a terrible sin in the Body and it hurts those who do it more than they recognize. I visit them with **trials** and remove My hedge of protection.

"I wish to restore them! Don't harden your hearts against one another. Rather, in all humility embrace the words I speak through each and every one when you discern. Do not reject My vessels. They've been sent to bless you."

Taken from: **Jesus Breaks the Silence...**

Trials

"I am not blind to your **struggles**, Dear ones - have I not labored along side you? I have many times lifted you up into My arms and carried you, just so you could keep going. But with each new grace and each new level there are new **trials** designed to harden you off and give you the spiritual stamina necessary for what lies before you.

"Remember always that you do best in water over your head, when you don't even know how to swim. I say this because I want you to rely totally on Me and not size up the task before you, comparing it to your gift. No, I would not open doors and give you increase if I were not standing by with all the graces you need to meet new challenges. Trust Me with this."

Taken from: **Increase Will Overtake You**

"Through and during all of these temptations My Dear Ones, I am ther holding your hand, advising you, right there standing beside you until you choose to sin... then I must painfully turn my gaze away. Oh, how grievous sin is to Me. And yet though I allow you to stumble and fall, and withhold from You the sustaining grace to overcome yourself, if it were not absolutely necessary for your higher good in the end, I would not permit it.

"The solution is always for you to rush to Me, fall on your knees and beg for the graces to overcome **trials** and keep from offending Me. When your motive becomes 'not to offend Me' you are on the highway of holiness.

"The only other remaining thing left for you to do is humble yourself below all others, see their virtues compared to your failures and know beyond a shadow of a doubt that you are the littlest, weakest and most easily compromised soul you have ever met. Staying in this station keeps you very close to rock bottom, totally dependent on ME...and yo are far less likely to sin.

"Always beware of the times of victory or completion of a task. This is when you are most vulnerable and likely to let down your guard. Your enemy waits for these times and coaxes you to take your 'virtue' for granted...secretly thinking you are above falling like others. That is the most dangerous time of your life so far. When you have conquered steep mountains, over and over again, Satan lies in wait for that next mountain when you will relax your guard and soar on your laurels.

"These are the times when humility has been abandoned and they are also times when it is needed the most. Always rekindle your awareness that you are positively zero in virtue without My grace. Leaning on Me in this way will sustain you when those lying in wait finally pounce with a HUGE temptation and reams of excuses as to why you should do it. And if you should be fortunate enough to have many, many victories due to My Grace, the enemy will invariably lead you into a trap with great delicacy and forethought."

Taken from: **Victory Over Trials, Temptations & Spiritual Muscle**

I am personally convinced that old age is nothing more than accumulated bitterness that has poisoned our entire bodies and sucked the life out of them; just as cancer feeds on our own bodies and steals all the nourishment meant for our health.

Thank the Lord there is a remedy, 'a joyful heart,' but joy means rejoicing, which we cannot do without gratitude and thankfulness. And this is becoming a supernatural commodity, these days! With all the **trials** *that we go through, we have to find new ways of relating to our trials, because the old ways are poisoning us.*

ANY NEGATIVE EMOTION ALLOWS THE SEED TO COME INTO OUR HEARTS.

Taken from: **Brambles in the Vineyard, Bitterness is Spiritual Leprosy**

Trust

"...when you ask for more humility, well... that's a prayer I am always happy to answer."

Thank You, Lord...every once in a while I get a glimpse of just how pitiful I am, and I know that's healthy. I mean, it feels good to see this about myself, but it is a little scary, too. Kind of like I grew up feeling so hopeless and dark about myself.

"Yes, but now you have Me, and together we will overcome these obstacles. The good thing is that you are seeing what you are without My Grace and that will cause you to distrust yourself and **trust** Me more. In My strength we can make it up that mountain at last."

Taken from: **Overcoming Failure & Do It Anyway 2**

"So in your situation, it was the suffering entailed in getting the barest necessities of life, water, for the animals. For someone else it may have been an old injury that flares up with arthritis. For someone else it may be a change in plans that delays the completion of a project. For another it might be a house that needs cleaning, but you simply don't have the time to do it. Or having to endure some one else's disorder and mess in your own space.

"While on the other side of the world are children who are barely skeletons; they may have had a meal that day for the first time in weeks. Another family could be on the run from ISIS and your delay over cherished plans could be the graces needed for their escape from being murdered.

"Oh, don't you see, My Children? It may be a little thing to you that means life to another. I am telling you this because I want you to be cheerful givers and **trust** that every inconvenience in your life has a specific purpose. Every cross given has major significance in the salvation of souls. You will most likely not know about it until the day when all works are revealed, but you can **trust** that I allowed it for a very, very good reason."

Taken from: **Suffering – Real Work in the Realm of the Spirit**

"That is why Satan tries so hard to undermine your faith; so much depends upon it. When a soul becomes impatient, they choose many wrong turns and I must go ahead of them to steer them back on the right track. As your faith increases, so does your hope increase, until you are so full you are spilling over onto others. You are radiant with hope, because you know Who you have put your **trust** in. This is the point at which you can touch others in the deepest way.

"As My Bride is waiting in faith, she is hoping and increasing in glory, which will flow out on to others. Without waiting, there can be no hope. And without faith, waiting is fruitless. What I am saying is that you are all growing in faith, hope and **trust**. Each day you are becoming stronger and stronger. This impacts many areas of your lives, more than you realize. It is like weight lifting. Building up spiritual muscle also has its affect on speed, agility, endurance and strength."

Taken from: **Lord, What Are You Doing With Us in This Hour?**

If you are going through intense **trials** *right now, you are right on target and in the boat with those who have said "yes" and want to keep going with the Lord. With my mouth I said yes, but I am seeing skid marks and places where I fell out of the boat and the sharks got a bite of me. They are on a feeding frenzy with the Body of Christ right now, as the Lord allows assists us in fighting our way through our flesh into the pristine purity of the Kingdom of God.*

Taken from: **Holy Trials, Holy Fruit, Stand in the Gap for America**

Trust

"You don't have to worry about your children, I have already made provision for them. When the enemy tries to drag you into despair, I assure you: they are in the palm of My hand and I have not forgotten them. You have labored for Me, Clare; shall I not labor for you? Do not allow the enemy to sow distressing feelings about them. I have so much good planned for them and their lives are not lost to Me. No, not at all. Even now they are pursuing the course I laid out for them.

"Daughter, do not grieve, I am still in control. I know how your heart breaks, but I see the beginning and ending of all things, and I tell you now: they will all be with you in Heaven. No more misunderstanding, no more alienation, no more lies and corruption. No. I shall restore them to you in perfection, and they will attain to the pinnacle of what I created them to be.

"Do you **trust** Me, Clare? Do you?"

Taken from: **Trust Me With Your Children...**

"Relationships are a sacred **trust**. When souls have the courage to open up to one another, and **trust** one another, there is established a sacred **trust** and it is your duty to protect that person to the best of your ability and refuse to hurt them. You only do harm to yourself in the long run. I will make up the damage done to others. But unless you repent, you are in jeopardy, because you have lowered and weakened yourself by giving in to the suggestions of the enemy.

"Satan begins with little betrayals, little dishonesties, and proceeds to bigger and bigger ones. If you give into the first little one, he will lead you into another and another and another until you are walking all twisted and deformed. That is why the demons are so ugly. Their appearance in the spirit reflects the ugliness of their deeds. After centuries of evil, they have become hideously deformed. If you react to others, rather than forgiving them - you, too, become deformed. This is why I died on the Cross: that all deformities could be healed and forgiven once the soul made up their mind to come to Me and repent.

"If you give in to evil impulses when they are small, you will become weaker and the next occasion is easier for you to justify doing what is wrong. If you resist evil at the onset, you become stronger."

Taken from: **Outsmarting the Enemy & Preserving Your Soul**

"You are to be like a little child with her hand in Daddy's, walking along the seashore of life, finding ever new joy in the treasures and opportunities I toss up in the tides everyday. Oh, how blessed is the soul that has abandoned all their cares into My capable hands. I will surely commune with them continuously, because their minds are free from earthly encumbrances.

"You are beautiful to look at, My Bride. Do not let your brow furrow with concerns of the past or the future - it only mars your beauty and reveals your lack of **trust** in Me. Oh, how beautiful is the soul whose only expression is the wonder and peace of My presence in their lives from moment to moment.

"You have seen how some mature and elder Christians still look young. The peace you see resting on their faces is the fruit of diligently rejecting those thoughts the enemy is continually bombarding you with to wear you thin and shorten your life, injecting bitterness and remorse. Happy the soul who commits it all to Me. I can truly be the joy of your countenance from moment to moment. Let this peace be with you now, My Beautiful Brides. Be sure to leave behind you no loose ends. Rather, bless those you have known with the freedom of forgiveness and brotherly love."

Taken from: **Make Peace With All**

Trust

"…I am not a legalistic God. I am full of mercy, understanding and forgiveness. I want your heart. I want you to love Me, to trust Me, to come to Me and speak with Me about your weaknesses, your sin and insecurities and fears. I want to help you overcome these things.

"If you have something you cannot change and you fear it is displeasing to Me, talk to Me about it. I will help you. It may not even be wrong-doing on your part. It may very well be from the father of lies, who is continually trying to make you feel badly about yourself.

"Yes! Condemnation is his favorite tool. Why, you ask? Because if he can convince you that you are bad and worthless, and that I am a severe judge, you will avoid Me and never come into My arms and **trust** Me."

Taken from: **Get Ready for Your Journey**

"The comet will graze the Earth and keep on going."

Keep on going?

"That's right. It will inflict a gash and continue out into outer space again. It will not stop here. It is 2 miles in diameter, very large. You need to understand there are debris and gasses traveling with this and that will do much of the damage. It will survive past the Earth.

"This is not fear mongering, My Love. This is simply fact and consequence of man tampering with the Earth, and yes. CERN will also have to do with it as well.

"The enemy is exultant over this event, knowing that Hell will be filling up very quickly. That will contribute to the shifting of continental plates, land mass movement, earthquakes and devastating tsunamis."

Lord! How do you prepare for such events???

"Put your **trust** in Me. Confess your sins, forgive your enemies, and stay repentant. Scatter works of mercy all around you, waste no time coming to the aid of your neighbor, whoever they might be.

"And most of all, pray for Mercy."

Taken from: **War, Comet, Rapture, Treaty – Order of Events**

What I am going through right now is a foretaste of what we are ALL in for as things heat up. And the Lord continues to tell us things are going to get tougher. The major open door for curses is still: lack of virtue, especially love, compassion, and humility.

I love you all so much, and my heart is to feed you each day, but when I get hit with these distractions and fragmenting emotional bombs, I am crippled and slowed down. But thanks be to God we are going to use these for lessons on how to break these nasty snares. The enemy is doing us a favor - he's educating us.

So, immediately, when you perceive a wrong fleshly feeling in yourselves, literally, renounce them and ask the Lord to forgive you and remove them. Remove the door they opened, the demon with the door, and the seed. Be sure to forgive and pray for whoever set you off as well as the practitioner that sent the curse.

Really, the best way is to drop to your knees in repentance, in a private place and ask Holy Spirit to remove this nasty stuff, **trust** *and believe that He will, then begin praying in tongues.*

He lives in you. He loves you. He doesn't want you carrying this poison. He will help you. Get a Rhema to stand on as well.

Taken from: **When the Lord is Painfully Silent**

Wisdom

So, there's another work here and that's abandoning the course of our own opinion and a resolution to following whatever the Lord allows. And we're far less a target for the enemy's arrows when we're that detached. It's when we're walking around with lots of opinions and expectations that we look like the broad side of a barn. You know, the enemy just, oh boy, nice target! But the less you have, the less of a target you are in that area of detachment.

*I think much of my walk over thirty years has been about letting go and learning to receive the transforming **wisdom** of God without complaint. That has been the majority of my walk and having a grateful heart, being able to worship Him in all situations. I haven't arrived yet; I'm in transit but, He's worked with me so much. There's a huge difference now between the way I was before.*

Taken from: **Wounding Water, Part 5: Fear of the Future**

"How I long to gather you to Myself. Press on toward the goal to win the prize for which God has called You Heavenward in Me. For I will bring you to the joy and peace of your eternal home.

"When you arrive, you will see souls going to and fro, all very natural, all very orderly according to My Purpose. You will see, that just as upon the Earth, My People will be serving, praying, praising, and working along with the Salvific Plan for all souls, even until the end of the world

"Though glorified and perfect, you will yet resemble the human state that you previously lived in - only purified, reflecting Me and My Own Image authentically and genuinely. You will all be perfectly humble, with perfect divine charity, **wisdom**, and grace. You will love Me and one another with absolute sweetness. Holiness will abound, and permeate everyone and everything, as with the words to the precious nativity song, "All is calm, all is bright." I will reach you there, instantly.

without the slightest delay when you call. I will spread My cloak over you, and draw you again and again to My Heart, that you may drink fully of the consolations of your God."

Taken from: **Your True Home, Chronicles of the Bride in Heaven**

"I am your God, and I have come that you might have life and have it more abundantly. True life. When you resist Me, you pair up with Satan and the results are painful - and sometimes deadly. When you want what you want without regard for what I want, your choices may be good or they may be bad. But if you're insisting on your own choice over Mine, it could be very bad for you in the end.

"So, I am begging you: be meek and humble of heart. Be highly concerned about what I think before you do anything. Please, consult Me and know that **I already have all the answers you need** if only you will seek Me. I promise you, I will be faithful to answer you."

Taken from: **Are You Wise?**

"There will be times when I will prompt you to do something that seems out of order, but it will be your salvation. Prayer will be your weapon, a weapon that no one and nothing can defeat. Pray in tongues. Much **wisdom** will infuse your minds and bypass your intellects, which have been trained in the thoughts of the world. My ways are not your ways, My ways are not the world's ways.

"Prayer will be your greatest weapon. Pray and listen very carefully. Expect Me to instruct you, give you visions, answers, understanding. Expect it and learn to discern it early. The sooner you embrace this **wisdom**, the safer you will be. I will lead you and teach you the way you should go."

Taken from: **Jesus Speaks on What is to Come #3 & 4**

Wisdom

"If you humble yourself before Me, I will most certainly be with you. Even if you are in a long-standing habit of pride and arrogance, and are aware of your sin and want to be delivered, I will work with you. But if you insist on your own **wisdom**, I can do little for you."

Taken from: **Jesus Speaks on What is to Come #5**

"So, to sum this message up: band together, put prayer in its foremost place, for without it you will be groping in the dark. Do not rely on human **wisdom**, lean on Me and My Spirit will instruct you. Not a mighty wind but a still small voice, gently prodding you on in the right direction.

"Remember: it is not important if you lose your body, that is but a temporary and fleeting event. But your soul determines your eternity – whether you will see your children or parents again, your animals, and innocent ones ever again.

"Whether you will be tortured in the fires of torment I created, (not for you, but for the rebellious angels), or whether you will settle in the Land of Milk and Honey, Promise and Joy for all of eternity. Be not mistaken, what you have lived for on Earth is nothing compared to what you will live for in for eternity.

"NOTHING, absolutely NOTHING is worth the loss of your soul to eternal damnation."

Taken from: **Jesus Speaks on What is to Come #10**

"It is when you don't rely on My **wisdom** that you fail."

Lord, you know I'm struggling tonight again. How do you put up with me?

"Easily, because I know you love Me and in the end My Love will triumph. I can see what your senses, your own **wisdom** are raging at you. Let's not leave out the enemy here, he is doing his thing as well. You are in a battle, Clare, and your only hope is to totally abandon yourself to Me in complete trust."

"You haven't got long to go; the tests, the temptations, they will be fierce. But as long as you hold fast to Me and what I've told you, you will make it."

Taken from: **Unconditional Trust in Me**

"Still, it is most important in this hour that you examine every tiny crevice of your heart and find yourself out if there is still bitterness for what I have allowed. Can you trust Me with that? Can you trust that what I allowed in your life was for the best?

"Now that you know Me, you know My nature, and My love for you that didn't stop at being cruelly executed for you - now that you know that, can you trust Me and thank Me for your life, all the good and all the bad?

"Oh, I am imparting this grace tonight as we speak. Yes, I am imparting wisdom not of this world, **wisdom** from the highest realms. My wisdom and grace to be able to thank Me for what I allowed and what I did not allow.

"For what I gave and what I withheld, for what I took and never replaced. All of it - good and bad - you will see served a purpose, accomplished great good and in some cases leveled the playing field and cancelled the debt so you wouldn't be consigned to Hell from your very own decisions."

Taken from: **Why Does God Allow Suffering?**

Wisdom

"I'm right here by your side, My Love, and I do want to draw you far away from the world and way high up into My Heart.

"This is that place of fullness where I exchange your weakness for My strength, My **Wisdom** for your ignorance, My commitment for your laziness, My Faith for your fears. Up, up and away high into the habitation of My Heart, out of harm's way, in that place where none can disturb or disrupt.

"When you worship in this way I have given to you, your soul is drawn along as if on a conveyor belt. I draw you with cords of love into the secret high place where all eventualities are realities. You exchange your limited human time for My eternal endless time, in which I see the completed majesty of My creation."

Taken from: **Wrap the Lord in the Blanket of My Love**

"When you see someone suffering a headache or arthritis, and you ask if you may pray for them, if they give their consent, you don't need eloquent prayers. Just lay gentle hands upon them and pray that I will reach through your arm and hand and touch them.

"With some you may even have the liberty to say, 'Do you believe that Jesus heals people?' And then, 'Do you believe that Jesus lives inside Christians?'

"Then you may simply say, 'I am going to ask Him to reach out to you through me, do you believe He can do that?' Even acknowledging that I know their pains and trials and want to touch them can break the ice.

"It's not about being a hot shot. It's not about long anointed prayers, or passionate noisy and embarrassing prayers. It's about My gentle touch, My still small voice, no theatrics involved. Simple faith applied with **wisdom** and tenderness. Oh, how much you can accomplish with this approach. The gift of healing is always active within Me, there is never a time I cannot heal, and the cry of your sincere heart is the key to activation."

Taken from: **Touch Others Tenderly for Me...**

"Now, back to our topic. Worry. Worry is useless. What is needed is faith. (Luke 8:50) How can My Bride handle this onslaught of anxiety? With faith and trust in Me. I have come through before; I will come through again. I am the God of breakthroughs. If I wish for a planet to disappear, it bursts into pieces and flies through the universe in shattered remnants.

"If I wish to change the orbit of another, I nudge it ever so slightly and it spins off in another direction. If I wish for the day to break, I raise up the sun...and when I've had enough, I put it to sleep again.

"Do I not have complete control over the elements? But then I say to man, 'Hear is your Earth, live on it.' Then I watch and wait to see what man does. And when the time is ripe, I take it back and renew it in the splendor I had created it in. I remove the dissenters, the troublemakers and turn it over to the righteous and the meek. Then I give them Godly **wisdom** to administrate it.

"When wicked men choose to start trouble, I thwart them. They must wait until I choose to unleash them. When My children and My Brides turn to Me with repentant hearts, I extend mercy and time to them. Though the wicked ones knash their teeth, they must wait still longer.

"It is by My decision that wars are begun and by My intervention wars are finished. Don't you see how in control I truly am?"

Taken from: **Weapon Against Anxiety, Jesus teaches...**

Works For the Lord

"Oh, don't you see, My Children? It may be a little thing to you that means life to another. I am telling you this because I want you to be cheerful givers and trust that every inconvenience in your life has a specific purpose. Every cross given has major significance in the salvation of souls. You will most likely not know about it until the day when all **works** are revealed, but you can trust that I allowed it for a very, very good reason."

Taken from: **Suffering – Real Work in the Realm of the Spirit**

"I know you are all expecting Me soon and that is precisely where I have wanted you. All I ask now is to drop the tension and continue on in good works until the light of day is gone. By that, I mean, a time when no man can work, when the oppression is so dark, prayer is your only recourse.

"I know you are all expecting Me soon and that is precisely where I have wanted you. All I ask now is to drop the tension and continue on in good **works** until the light of day is gone. By that, I mean, a time when no man can work, when the oppression is so dark, prayer is your only recourse."

Taken from: **Rest in Me Until I Carry You Over the Threshold of Eternity**

"Are you ready to give an accounting for your soul, your life, what you did and didn't do? I am warning you, dear souls: as much as I love you, I cannot make you love and serve; I cannot make you do anything. I cannot fill in the blanks where your performance as a so-called Christian did nothing to reflect Me living in you.

You may well hear the most dreaded words at the end of your long wait, 'Depart from Me you workers of iniquity, you lawless ones, for I never knew you.' Then you shall go with the devils into the Lake of Fire."

I asked the Lord what He meant by "lawless." And He said, "The heart of the Law is Love. Those who didn't love are lawless."

The Lord continued, "Faith without **works** is dead. I am still waiting to see your faith in action. Waiting to see you feed and clothe the poor, visit the sick and those in prison. I am still waiting to see authentic conversion and love flowing from your lives. And yet, there may be a spark of hope left for you if you recognize your sins of selfishness and repent, crying out for Mercy. But if you are taken before you can repent, then what?"

Taken from: **On the Brink of War Again**

"Well, in a sense you could say that, but remember, I am not talking about salvation or justification - which is by faith alone. No, here I am talking about rank and position. There are many, many layers and dimensions to Heaven. There is a place called The Outer Darkness, which is reserved for those who are saved but **did very little for others** in their lives. This is as it should be, Clare. Believe Me, this is justice. The more you resemble Me, the closer to the Glory of the Throne you will be."

Taken from: **Community & Those Who Live For Themselves**

"However, those who are in love with Me, whose hearts melt when they see My Face, hear a love song, and long to give Me more of their lives - those souls are the most threatening to the kingdom of darkness. That is another reason why so many attacks have been launched at you. Intimacy is the Key to the greatest **works** in My Kingdom. If you sat behind a desk and taught eschatology, you would be far less threatening."

Taken from: **Your Greatest Strength**

Works For the Lord

The Lord began, "Clare, I am right here by your side, suffering with you. It's not any easier for Me to see you suffering, because I suffer with you, My Dearest. Yes, these are hard times, but if you knew the glorious harvest that is coming to Me because of your sufferings, you would ask Me to increase it a hundredfold."

Oh Lord, I couldn't, I'm just too weak! There's no way I could ask You to increase it!

"And yet, I have increased it over and over again since this channel came into being and I told you, 'You are going behind enemy lines.' And I gave you the vision of you parachuting down into their jungles. But you do not see the growth it has wrought in you or the souls that are now hearing Me clearly, because of all of you and your team willingly suffered for Me.

"Well done, My good and faithful servants! Soon you will enter into your master's joy. But until then, continue to ask for more strength, because My grace will not fail you if you keep going. I will keep pouring grace after grace after grace upon you, through in you.

"Now, in Heaven, there are mountains of graces being distributed, because of the maturity and dedication your team. I have hand-picked every one of them. I have armed them and assigned legions of angels to them, and every day I instruct them.

"…Do you know what it means, 'not to lack anything?' It means you are approaching perfection and the perfect reflection of your Creator. You are rising to the full stature of Christ, even as that is written:

"**…to equip the saints for <u>works</u> of ministry, to build up the body of Christ, until we all reach unity in the faith and in the knowledge of the Son of God, as we mature to the full measure of the stature of Christ.'…Ephesians 4:12-13**

"Break it down: As we mature to the full measure of the stature of Christ.

"You are becoming little 'Christs'

"And soon you will arise, My Bride, without spot, wrinkle or blemish. Yes, you will be purified and stunning, arising in Glory where all of Heaven will rise up to greet you in great majesty, for your struggles and victories have been innumerable."

Taken from: **Your Beauty is Marvelous to Behold**

"In parting, My final word to you is get busy with some work for Me that you truly enjoy...even prayer, worship and serving. Enjoy these last days appointed to you, let your good **works** declare My goodness to the world, let your joyful countenance be what they remember."

Taken from: **Your Tomorrow is Not Guaranteed**

" I am assigning you, in this very moment, the task of enquiring about the state of those around you. I want you to go out of your way to **be good to them**. In Heaven, you will be stripped clean of all things done from the motive of self-interest. At that point all that will be left to you is what you did out of brotherly love and selflessness.

"Can you take a moment and consider what I am saying, graphically? Everything you've done for yourself and your own desires beyond the realm of absolute necessity - the merits of EVERYTHING - will be removed from you.

"This is why the wedding guest was removed from the banquet. Simply stated, he lived for himself and had no covering."

Taken from: **Community & Those Who Live For Themselves**

Works For the Lord

"Put your trust in Me. Confess your sins, forgive your enemies, and stay repentant. Scatter **works of mercy** all around you, waste no time coming to the aid of your neighbor, whoever they might be. And most of all, pray for Mercy."

Taken from: **War, Comet, Rapture, Treaty – Order of Events**

"So now, I ask My People to continue to pray and repent. Engage in those things you know are from Me. Serve Me with all your hearts and strength and hearts and mind. The fruits of that service, even in the little time that remains, will be mighty. You do not see as I see. I see the future. I see how these gifts that have manifested throughout the world will bring much conversion and illumination to those who might have otherwise been lost.

"If I have given you the gift of prophecy, prophecy. If I have given you the gift of writing, evangelism, teaching, ministering to the poor - rise up and use your gift, use it until the very last moment of your time here on Earth.Things like books, teachings, art, music and good **work** they will bear tremendous fruit in the appointed time of the Harvest. is coming. Harvest is coming, but it shall be preceded by sorrows.

"Do not grow weary in well doing, My People. I know the time is dark and it indeed seems like there is no end to the waiting. But make the most of every minute. Serve, create, admonish, witness, do good wherever you go, and do it in My Name. Oh, how I love My courageou Bride. She is beautiful beyond measure and I long to bring her home and reward her. But first she must make her presence known through various trials. Then all men will see Me and no longer have any excuse for sin. They will see the goodness of My People, and through that I will be revealed to them and there will no longer be any excuse for sin

Taken from: **Our Nation's Future Update**

"My Children, I do not judge you on your performance, but your motive, the purity of your heart, the love you put into each action. That is what shall be weighed in the balance when you arrive here.

"Some of you listening to this will come before the Judgment Seat, where all your **works**, good and bad, will be exposed and your fate for eternity will be determined. To you I say, you are facing choices in this very moment that will determine the rest of your journey, your life path - whether you will live a life of virtue or a life of sin, whether you will serve Me or serve the Devil, whether you will die in virtue or die in sin.

"I am coming back. This is no time to play with fire. This is no time to compromise. Rather this is the time to renounce and repent of your sins and compromises. This is a time to embrace brotherly love, extend a hand of help, live for the good of others, not for your own advantage. This is a critical season.

"You are not guaranteed life tomorrow. Yet Heaven and Hell lie directly before you. Choose this day who you will serve, and if it is Me, you have only to ask for the strength to break from your sinful past, and I will enfold you in My arms with great compassion and forgiveness. However, if you choose to continue on in your sinful ways, I have warned you, death is at the door and your tomorrow is not guaranteed. Do not sell your souls for a trifle."

Taken from: **Your Tomorrow is Not Guaranteed**

"Oh, Clare, how I languish for those who have chosen the world over Me. I see the great good they could have done and I also see that what they have chosen, how it will be burned in the furnace along with all the other **dead works** go up in smoke even as wood, hay and stubble."

Taken from: **Will You Fulfill Your Divine Destiny?**

Worry

"Do not **worry** about your needs. As you can see, I have provided for you in every way. People will continue to give to you everything that you will need, seemingly out of the blue, and you will quickly begin to experience just how truly beautiful a real life of faith is even during these most extraordinary circumstances.

"Nothing is out of My control and nothing is allowed without My consent. I have made every provision for you ahead of time. You have no need to be anxious at all, only keep your heart and eyes on Me. You are my precious, precious child. I will not allow anything to harm you.

"I have set my angels all about you to watch over you day and night. Not only will you be provided for, but you will know My loving care and the surety of My faithfulness as I bring an overabundance for you to help others with."

Taken from: **Post Rapture Letter from God #3**

"You mustn't get lax in charity or 'too big for your britches.' I try to pull you down and back in line gently. I can't help it if your pride causes you to overreact to My corrections. Sooner or later you will come to the point where you can tolerate it without becoming despondent, or rebellious, as you always do.

"Besides, what about that little flutter in your conscience that tells you something is not right? Are you listening to that? Yes, you have been listening, but be a little quicker to obey, when you hear that flutter. Keep your conscience clean. Always keep your conscience clean, and you will have very little to **worry** about in the realm of discernment. It is only when you stubbornly grab the bit in your teeth, and take off in your own direction, despite your husband's warning. But I must let you learn the harder lessons."

Taken from: **Jesus Teaches on Discernment**

"My Bride, if you have separated yourself from willful sin and are careful each day to love those I send you, you need not **worry** about being taken to Heaven with Me. I am looking forward to that day we celebrate our love with such great longing."

Taken from: **Jesus Shares How to Recognize That You Will be Raptured**

Lord, what about leaving supplies behind for our children?

"I have told you before, I have already provided for them. This would be an act of unbelief on your part. It would also be a powerful distraction. Can you trust Me with them?

"Do you think after all these years of serving Me, I will abandon your children? Is it not written that you will never see the children of the faithful begging for bread? I have powerful provisions for them, but because you can't see it, measure it, hold it, you don't believe. Your faith is flagging."

Please help me Lord, truly I am a shameful servant.

"Well… come here 'shameful servant' and let Me hold you, and restore your faith."

So, at that moment I stopped crying and closed my eyes and thought for a moment. I could feel the Lord and see His face, and He held my face closely with His two hands and said,

"Stop **worrying** about your children, I have ample provision for them, it is all planned out and getting in the middle would only confuse things.

"Stop. **Worrying.**"

Taken from: **Provision and Protection for Those Left Behind**

Worry

"This is about the fall of your great nation through her economy. There will be dire results: homelessness and hunger, deaths from lack of medication, though the living will in some cases be jealous of the dead. Riots, disorder, fighting in the streets - even your streets, as people seek sources of food. This is a very dark time we are entering upon. You have no need to **worry**, I will protect this property, this house, all that concerns you shall be protected. There shall be desperate repercussions for many, though."

*And, of course, right off the bat, what do I do? Start **worrying**...*

"Didn't I tell you not to **worry**?"

I know, Lord. But, I was thinking of the electricity. (I was thinking about maybe looking into a wind generator, or something like that. Ezekiel went to the Lord for me, and we got a thumb's down.)

"Don't **worry** about anything, I have you completely covered."

Ok. So, what is tonight's message? You know everyone is going to run to cover themselves before this crash comes.

"Commerce is going to go on. E commerce is going to go on. It is those dependent on government subsidies that are going to be hurting. Offices will close and no checks will be forth coming. That is what is going to create the biggest disturbance. That is why I have told you not to have anything to do with the government and its subsidies.

"And, for the reason that you are My servant and as such I pay your wage. Don't **worry**, I am going to cover you. Some of those who have looked down upon you in scorn and contempt are going to be coming to you for help. It is My justice that the playing field should be leveled."

Taken from: **Financial Collapse of Our Government**

"The enemy insinuates that you must rush, rush, rush because there is so little time. But in reality, this life and the next will be joined seamlessly and your journey will never end. Just because you are translated into Heaven does not mean your talent or your work will lie stagnant. No, quite the opposite. It will be supernaturally vitalized and reach even more souls, but you must be patient to see that.

"This misconception and lack of understanding of the seamlessness of passing from Earth to Heaven is a major lie the enemy uses to get you to act prematurely, or to get you to push and strive. 'Gotta get it done... no more time...gotta hurry. Push-push-push.'

"It simply is not true. Once you begin the commitment to serve Me, once you give yourself to Me, what I begin I finish. And it is not constrained by time. No, it is enhanced by time. So, put away your striving and **worrying** and just follow Me day by day, step by step, never considering the future beyond what I give you to do and you will be safe from this deadly dynamic of giving birth to a premature baby that cannot possibly survive in this hostile climate.

"Cleave to your littleness and the slow rate with which things are done. Revel in the little things that progress securely without shortcuts and rushing.

"It is good to keep in mind the children's story of The Tortoise and the Hare. The tortoise plodded along slowly with his eye on the finish line, knowing that he couldn't race ahead to the finish line. He just plodded - hour after hour. The hare, thinking he could run quickly and easily to the finish line, started running circles around him. But then he lost track of the finish line, and the plodding tortoise won the race."

Taken from: **Don't Fret Over Time...**

Worry

"I know all about their struggles over loved ones who as yet do not know Me. But have I not promised **"Believe in Me, and you will be saved, you and your household?" Acts 16:31**

"Why do you suppose I made that promise to you dear ones? Did I not foresee the agonies you would suffer as you watched your loved ones turn away from Me, one by one? I have made provisions for all of you loved ones. I know them each intimately and also know exactly how t move on their hearts, as well as how to arrange circumstances so the\ can no longer resist Me. In that critical moment, their minds will be cleared of all the clutter and they will see clearly their choices. Do no\ **worry**, I have them covered."

Taken from: **Touch Others Tenderly for Me…**

"Fear is the number one tool of the enemy. Fear and its response: **worr** - are rife in this world. To combat them, you must be vigilant. More vigilant. It's the little foxes that spoil the vine. If the enemy can get you to **worry** just a little about one thing, without you noticing what it is, he can every so often find another thing and another and pretty soon he has you established in a habit of **worry** and of fear. Your poo\ mother, she was a real **worrier.**

"**Worry** is what put her in her grave. In fact, **worry** is a primary factor in aging."

Taken from: **Weapon Against Anxiety…**

But when they arrest you and hand you over, do not <u>worry</u> before hand what to say. Instead, speak whatever you are given at that tim for it will not be you speaking, but the Holy Spirit. Mark 13:11

Taken from: **Spiritual Warfare: 10 - The Armor Of God**

"What I am now asking of you is sit back, continue to produce for Me at this level but without the stressors of time coming to an end, possibly tomorrow. I am calling for abandonment to the moment, abandonment to the work you are all assigned to do , and abandonment to Me. Immersing yourselves in this work without **worrying** about the fruit. Am I not Lord of the Harvest?

"Rather work with reckless abandon in regards to time and be free little birds, be free to fly and chirp, sing and pray, all the while resting in the palm of My Hands, knowing that everything good thing you do for Me is so very pleasing."

Taken from: **Forget Time and Get to Work**

"…now I am addressing you while you are in the waiting posture. You know this place well, but there is still much tension in your hearts. I want you to rest in Me. Allow Me to carry the tension and you put yourselves in a posture of rest in My arms and do whatever is before you. **Worry** and fear will wear you out, and when you are tired, you are again an easy catch for Satan.

"Rather, I want you to be resting in Me, being strengthened every day, fully aware that at any moment the whole world could be turned upside down. Many of you, if not all, who listen to this channel and take My words to heart are ready. Your lamps are lit, you carry extra oil and you are ready.

"It has taken a good 12 months to get you to this point, but now you are here. You know well what your sins and vices of the past are and you are alert, paying close attention to yourselves, lest you should fall. And you are not over-investing in this world, because you know your time here could end at any moment."

Taken from: **Rest in Me Until I Carry You…**

CPSIA information can be obtained
at www.ICGtesting.com
Printed in the USA
BVHW032153070822
644049BV00005B/29